Latsploitation, Exploitation Cinemas, and Latin America

Routledge Advances in Film Studies

1. Nation and Identity in the New German Cinema
Homeless at Home
Inga Scharf

2. Lesbianism, Cinema, Space
The Sexual Life of Apartments
Lee Wallace

3. Post-War Italian Cinema
Daniela Treveri Gennari

4. Latsploitation, Exploitation Cinemas, and Latin America
Edited by Victoria Ruétalo
and Dolores Tierney

Forthcoming:

South Asian Cinema
Gender, Justice, and Dissent
Alka Kurian

Korea's Occupied Cinemas
Brian Yecies and Ae-Gyung Shim

Zizek through Hitchcock
Everything You Always Wanted to
Know about Slavoj Zizek but Were
Afraid to Ask Alfred Hitchcock
Laurence Simmons

Latsploitation, Exploitation Cinemas, and Latin America

Edited by Victoria Ruétalo
and Dolores Tierney

Routledge
Taylor & Francis Group

NEW YORK AND LONDON

First published 2009
by Routledge
711 Third Avenue, New York, NY 10017

Simultaneously published in the UK
by Routledge
2 Park Square, Milton Park, Abingdon, Oxon OX14 4RN

Routledge is an imprint of the Taylor & Francis Group, an informa business

First issued in paperback 2011

Typeset in Sabon by IBT Global.

Library of Congress Cataloging in Publication Data

Latsploitation, exploitation cinemas, and Latin America / edited by Victoria Ruétalo and Dolores Tierney.
    p. cm.—(Routledge advances in film studies ; 4)
    Includes bibliographical references and index.
    Includes filmography.
    1. Exploitation films—Latin America—History and criticism.   2. Sensationalism in motion pictures.   I. Ruétalo, Victoria, 1971–   II. Tierney, Dolores.
    PN1995.9.S284L38 2009
    791.43'653—dc22
    2008046097

ISBN10: 0-415-99386-5 (hbk)
ISBN10: 0-415-89854-4 (pbk)
ISBN10: 0-203-87892-2 (ebk)

ISBN13: 978-0-415-99386-9 (hbk)
ISBN13: 978-0-415-89854-6 (pbk)
ISBN13: 978-0-203-87892-7 (ebk)

Contents

List of Figures   ix
Foreword   xi
    ERIC SCHAEFER

Acknowledgments   xv
    VICTORIA RUÉTALO AND DOLORES TIERNEY

    Introduction: Reinventing the Frame—Exploitation
    and Latin America   1
    VICTORIA RUÉTALO AND DOLORES TIERNEY

1   Before Exploitation: Three Men of the Cinema in Mexico   13
    ANA M. LÓPEZ

PART I
Latsploitation Beyond Borders

2   "Perversa América Latina": The Reception of Latin American
    Exploitation Cinemas in Spanish Subcultures   37
    ANTONIO LÁZARO-REBOLL

3   Roger Corman Dis/covers Peru: National Cinema and Luis
    Llosa's *Hour of the Assassin/Misión en los Andes*   55
    JEFFREY MIDDENTS

4   "I Wonder Who the Real Cannibals Are": Latin America and
    Colonialism in European Exploitation Cinema   70
    ANDREW SYDER

PART II
Latsploitation Auteurs

5   Emilio Vieyra: Argentina's Transnational Master of Horror   87
     GERARD DAPENA

6   Arty Exploitation, Cool Cult, and the Cinema
     of Alejandro Jodorowsky   102
     JOSETXO CERDÁN AND MIGUEL FERNÁNDEZ LABAYEN

7   José Mojica Marins and the Cultural Politics of Marginality
     in 'Third World' Film Criticism   115
     DOLORES TIERNEY

8   More Than Simply Cowboys, Naked Virgins, Werewolves, and
     Vampires? The Transatlantic Cinema of León Klimovsky   129
     ANDREW WILLIS

PART III
Politicizing Latsploitation

9   Made in South America: Locating *Snuff*   145
     GLENN WARD

10   Based on a True Story: Reality-Based Exploitation
     Cinema in Mexico   158
     DAVID WILT

11   *Con amor, tequila, y gasolina*: Lola, the Truck Driver and
     Screen Resistance in *cine fronterizo*   171
     CATHERINE L. BENAMOU

12   The *Naco* in Mexican Film: *La banda del carro rojo*, Border
     Cinema, and Migrant Audiences   185
     ADÁN AVALOS

PART IV
Sex, Sex, and More Sex

13 Temptations: Isabel Sarli Exposed   201
    VICTORIA RUÉTALO

14 Sharksploitation: René Cardona Jr.'s Submarine Gaze   215
    MISHA MACLAIRD

15 Sex and the Generals: Reading Brazilian *Pornochanchada*
    as Sexploitation   230
    STEPHANIE DENNISON

16 "Tus pinches leyes yo me las paso por los huevos":
    Isela Vega and Mexican Dirty Movies   245
    SERGIO DE LA MORA

Epilogue   259

17 At the Margin of the Margins: Contemporary Ecuadorian
    Exploitation Cinema and the Local Pirate Market   261
    GABRIELA ALEMÁN

Contributors   275
Bibliography   279
Filmography   295
Index   315

Figures

1.1   Clenched fists in *La Llorona*/The Weeping Woman.   19

1.2   A transition from *La Llorona*/The Weeping Woman.   20

1.3   Ghostly effects in *La Llorona*/The Weeping Woman.   20

1.4   La consolidada in Mexico City in *La sangre manda*/Blood Rules.   23

1.5   A mirror shot in *¿Quién mató a Eva?*/ Who Killed Eva?   25

1.6   Clenched hand gesture in *Luponini (El terror de Chicago)*/Luponini, the Terror of Chicago.   29

1.7   Lupo in disguise in *Luponini (El terror de Chicago)*/Luponini, the Terror of Chicago.   30

2.1   Poster for the San Sebastián Horror and Fantasy Film Festival's retrospective on "Cine psicotrónico mexicano."   39

2.2   Cover of *2000 maniacos*.   44

2.3   Cover of *2000 maniacos*.   47

2.4   Poster for the San Sebastián Horror and Fantasy Film Festival's retrospective on "Perversa América Latina."   48

7.1   "Buttocks-as-aliens" in *O despertar da besta*/Awakening of the Beast.   123

8.1   Mexican advertising for *Marihuana*.   131

13.1   Isabel Sarli's first frontal nude scene in *El trueno entre las hojas*/Thunder Among the Leaves.   206

13.2   Isabel Sarli in *Fuego*/Fire.   209

14.1   A couple fondling each other in *Tintorera!/Tiger Shark*.   224

14.2   Underwater shot in *Tintorera!/Tiger Shark*.   225

14.3   Shark attack in *Tintorera!/Tiger Shark*.   226

15.1   The Svengali and the superwoman in
        A superfêmea/Superwoman.   233

15.2   *A superfêmea*/Superwoman.   234

15.3   Jayme Cardoso is surprised to discover the location of
        Teka Lanza's clitoris in *A B . . . profunda/Deep A. . .*   240

16.1   Isela Vega in *Las reglas del juego/The Rules
        of the Game*.   256

Foreword

Eric Schaefer

Call them what you wish: exploitation movies, badfilms, paracinema, trash, psychotronic films, or cult movies. The appellations are as diverse as the films themselves. But they all share certain attributes: low budgets, lurid subject matter, affiliation with the most debased genres, and a subsistence at the margins of industry and culture. Perhaps incongruously, they have come to exert a growing fascination for academics. The ramparts of the Ivory Tower are now beset by flesh-eating zombies, pimps and prostitutes, satanic cults, biker gangs, primitive cannibals, and assorted other goons and thugs who populate exploitation movies. Fifteen years ago it would have been difficult to imagine that a wealth of scholarly literature would develop around the most impoverished segment of cinema. Yet we see histories of the exploitation film in the United States emerging, theories of reception being promoted, and astute critical analyses appearing in the pages of journals and anthologies. A literature on exploitation cinema in Europe and Asia is starting to come forward. And this volume represents the first serious step in cultivating the history and criticism of exploitation movies from, or set in, Latin America. The barrios, jungles, and cities of Central and South America represent the newest frontier of exploitation studies: latsploitation.

The first film I ever saw in a theater could be classified as "latsploitation." I was five or six years old when my parents, knowing of my fascination with monsters and through some misguided sense of parental duty, took me to see K. Gordon Murray's 1965 release of *Little Red Riding Hood and the Monsters/Caperucita y Pulgarcito contra los monstrous* (Roberto Rodríguez, 1962). Murray, known as the King of the Kiddie Matinee, had purchased a number of cheap Mexican fairy-tale films, dubbed them into English, and released them to unsuspecting suburban families in the 1960s. Just as most of the exploitation films that played to adults in grindhouses and drive-ins were both marginal and disposable, so too were these films, banished to another fringe of exhibition, the Saturday matinee. Their patrons were bored parents and their rug rat charges, most less interested in what was happening on the screen than they were in scoring a massive Milk Dud–fueled sugar rush at the candy counter. I wasn't keen on the sweets, or the treacly Red and her sidekick, a child-size skunk named Stinky. But for a young horror aficionado, there was plenty to revel in: Dracula, Frankenstein's monster, an evil queen, a papier-mâché pinhead, monkey children in Mittle-European garb, and various generic goonies, all playing in flea-bitten costumes against a stage-bound, nightmare landscape. Chases, beatings, and torture were thrown in for good measure. Seeing an undubbed gray market DVD of the film recently—for the first time in forty-odd years—the accuracy of my memory of the film surprised me. Down to the framing, I had vividly recalled a scene in which Red gets tripped up in a rib cage jutting from the forest floor as she is threatened by a tin-can robot. The scene has haunted me for decades. And that illustrates the power of exploitation. It is not only Art, the kind with a capital *A*, which can affect one in profound or troubling ways. Even the shabbiest dreck can take hold of the imagination in an elemental manner.

It is that primal attraction of exploitation films—their sensuality and shock, the chaos of their narratives, their ragged, fevered construction—that first exerts a pull on scholars. But once that initial magnetism begins to fade (and it often does), we are left with the true riches these movies hold. This consists of the cults, communities, and reading strategies that accrete around the films and the resistance they often pose to the established order of things. It also includes the world that is revealed when we consider their original production and reception within the context of the times and places where they were made and seen or procured: the hungry filmmakers and bargain-basement studios, the rundown urban theaters, neighborhood midnight shows, and the low shelves at the back of mom-and-pop video stores. And when it comes to the study of exploitation movies, we're not just looking at an esoteric corner of the field of film studies, but a lively junction where cultural, industrial and economic studies, sociology, political science, identity studies, and regional and national difference converge.

As the essays in this collection suggest, exploitation is one of those cinematic practices that transcends national borders, cultural differences, and linguistic variety. Sleaze is global, trash transnational, and bad taste has no boundaries. The Latin American exploitation scene has certainly been influenced to some degree by Anglo-American and European culture and their film industries, which can be seen as part of a revealing legacy of colonialism, economic exploitation, and religious inculcation. But "latsploitation" has drawn on homegrown mythologies and popular culture as well, which were developed within discrete systems of production, and were subject to unique political pressures and censorship restrictions. The films and filmmakers discussed here, whether from Mexico, Argentina, Brazil, Peru, or other countries, will, on one level, be familiar to those who have even a passing acquaintance with exploitation. But they are also distinctive—as anyone who has ever watched *The Brainiac/El barón del terror* (Chano

Urueta, 1962), *lucha libre* films, or a movie made by José Mojica Marins or René Cardona, Jr., can attest.

With *Latspoitation, Exploitation Cinemas, and Latin America*, editors Victoria Ruétalo and Dolores Tierney and their authors help illuminate movies that were often made outside of the mainstream industry in their nations of origin. At times, as is the case with some coproductions, they even lacked a firm footing in any single country, operating as "international" productions adrift in a "global" marketplace. Virtually all of the films in this book have continued to exist outside the critical and academic establishment, especially in those places where the overtly political has been privileged over the covertly political or the politically incorrect. *Latspoitation* brings them into the conversation on exploitation movies at the international level. But more importantly, it draws these movies into our broader understanding of global film history and criticism. Welcome.

Acknowledgments

Victoria Ruétalo and Dolores Tierney

Latsploitation, Exploitation Cinemas, and Latin America is the product of several years of research and the editors' keen feeling that there was a gap in existing scholarship on Latin American cinema. We hope that the pages of this anthology will go some way to filling this lacuna and also to providing fresh avenues of research for young scholars.

There are a number of people whose work has inspired us and whose help has been vital in bringing this project to fruition. We would like to thank Ana López (whose extensive film library in all its varied contents first provided us with hard-to-come-by exploitation movies) for her mentorship and scholarly training. We would also like to thank Eric Schaefer and Andy Medhurst for their encouragement of this project. We wish particularly to thank the contributors to this anthology for their hard work, scholarly discipline, and enthusiasm for the project. We are also indebted to the Social Sciences and Humanities Research Council of Canada, which provided funds for a workshop that brought all our contributors together in Edmonton, Alberta, in June 2007, and the graduate students Argelia Gónzalez, Lilian Perezcruz Pintos, Delma Gil Wilson, and Marco Katz, whose video presentations entertained us during the symposium.

We gratefully acknowledge permissions to reprint shortened versions of "José Mojica Marins and the Cultural Politics of Marginality in 'Third World' Film Criticism" and "Temptations: Isabel Sarli Exposed," which were both published in the *Journal of Latin American Cultural Studies*, vol.13, no.1, March 2004, pp. 63–78, 79–95. We are also thankful to Manuel Valencia, director and editor of *2000 maniacos*, for permissions to print four images from the fanzine.

We are very grateful to the University of Alberta and the University of Sussex for providing research support and institutional assistance on this project and also to our research assistants Colette Duke and Lilian Shandro. We are also grateful to our editor Erica Wetter for all of her assistance. Lastly we would like to thank our families (Tony and Rachel, Eddie and Nancy) for their patience, support, and for allowing us time away from them while we completed the project.

Introduction
Reinventing the Frame: Exploitation and Latin America

Victoria Ruétalo and Dolores Tierney

Latin American exploitation cinema has a rich heritage spanning many decades and many genres. It reaches back to the gangster films Juan Orol made in Mexico in the 1950s (*El sindicato del crimen*/Crime Syndicate, 1954),[1] to the Argentinean 'sexploits' of Armando Bó and Isabel Sarli from the 1950s through the 1970s (*El trueno entre las hojas*/*Thunder Among the Leaves*, 1957, *Fiebre*/*Fever* 1970), and to the Mexican *narcofronteriza* videos of the 1980s and 1990s. And yet this is a cinema that has been starved until recently of critical attention with most major continental and national histories, at worst ignoring and at best offering a few derisory comments on various exploitation cinemas. Initial work in this nascent research area by the editors (2004) and others (Syder and Tierney, 2005; Alemán, 2004) has rehearsed the reasons for such a lack of critical attention suggesting that, for a critical elite (those who historically define the parameters of national culture) anxious to emphasize the prestige of their own national cinema, these often badly made, 'low'-culture genre films (fantasy, horror, wrestling, sexploitation, gore) provide little cultural capital. This work has also suggested that, for the same arbiters of national culture, the hybridity of these films (i.e., genre borrowings from Hollywood and recut, redubbed English-language versions) can seem problematic with respect to postcolonialist discourses (which seek to emphasize the function and viability of a nationalist cinema in the face of the aesthetic, economic, and ideological hegemony of the Hollywood industry) and subsequently threaten national artistic autonomy (Syder and Tierney, 2005: 38–39). And finally, this work has argued that critics eschew exploitation cinema because—with their exaggerated plots and liberal doses of mysticism, fantasy, sex, and gore—these cinemas threaten to frame Latin American cinema through colonialist stereotypes of the weird, the wonderful, and the 'savage.' Hence, most accounts of Latin American cinema, which seek to dignify its production, either omit exploitation cinema altogether or denigrate it as the product of periods of artistic and industrial decline.[2] Stephanie Dennison and Lisa Shaw's recent *Popular Cinema in Brazil* is exceptional as a survey of a Latin American national cinema in that it does devote at least a few pages both to horror auteur José Mojica Marins and to the *pornochancha* films that proliferated in the 1970s and 1980s (2004: 140–43, 149–78).

Latsploitation, Exploitation Cinemas, and Latin America takes its cue from the groundbreaking work of U.S. and UK scholars (Schaefer, 1999; Hawkins, 2000a; Sconce, 1995, 2007; Jancovich et al., 2003) writing on the similarly once marginal but now increasingly critically accepted U.S. and European exploitation, trash, cult, and paracinemas; exploring the histories, texts, and contexts of different exploitation films made both *by* Latin Americans and by foreign film producers *in* Latin America. The anthology argues that this much neglected area makes an important aesthetic and social contribution to the large body of Latin American cinema, and that the critical focus on it also contributes to the field of Latin American film studies itself. By making such an argument, *Latsploitation* wishes to situate itself at the center of existing currents on Latin American film scholarship as well as suggesting new areas of study in the field. One of the central vectors of contemporary Latin American film scholarship, for instance, is a shift in focus *away* from 1960s New Latin American paradigms of cultural dependency (which preached resistance against the imitation or reproduction of Western cultural norms) *towards* a consideration of Latin America's increasingly globalized and transnational mediascapes (Alvaray: 2008). That many exploitation cinemas embodied globalization or what Arjun Appadurai calls "cultural flows" (1996: 27–44) *avant la lettre* (for instance, the Mexican *lucha libre* [wrestling] films of the 1950s, 1960s, and 1970s, which not only reworked Hollywood horror and superhero films but were also subsequently imported [back] into the United States by minimogul K. Gordon Murray) makes the argument that these cinemas can reconfigure the way we think about contemporary practices in Latin American Cinema.

To begin with, however, this introduction wants to outline a few of the difficulties that a project such as this one presents. As such a diverse cinema, or group of cinemas, ranging vastly across eras, genres, styles, levels of technical competency, formats (from 35 mm to straight to video *narcofronteriza* films or pirated Ecuadorian DVDs), viewing circuits (U.S. Hispanic market, New York's 1970s 'midnight movie' phenomena, the Latin American continental circuits, domestic markets and home video consumption) and production categories (amateur video to fully industrial films), we may wonder how it/they can be brought together without homogenizing what are essentially different cinemas and without simplifying their complex cultural politics. The answer, we feel, is to propose the category of *latsploitation* as an umbrella term that embraces a range of different production, generic, and textual strategies under some overarching shared characteristics and considerations.

Firstly, the term latsploitation is intended to underline the *difference* of Latin American exploitation cinema to the already quite elastic concept of exploitation cinema as it is understood (principally) in U.S. terms and to suggest that this difference has to do with the very different industrial organization and history of Latin American cinemas. By separating out the category of latsploitation from the more generic exploitation, we emphasize that the history of Latin American exploitation cinemas is marked, as is the continent, by uneven economic development, neoimperialist penetration (including dominance of Hollywood products in most domestic markets), and the struggle to come to terms with modernity and that this has had particular implications for the establishment and continued viability (or in many cases the impossibility of the establishment and lack of viability) of national filmmaking endeavors across the continent. Despite such a different context, there is still much in the scholarship on (principally) U.S. exploitation of Schaefer (1999), Sconce (1995, 2007), Hawkins (2000a), and others to aid our understanding of exploitation cinema in Latin America (a fact to which the pages of this anthology attest). However, at the same time Latin American exploitation cinema or latsploitation cannot be simply classified according to the same textual attributes (low budget, amateurism, etc.) as U.S. exploitation and its related fields (trash, cult, paracinema). We have to rethink the category and defining features of exploitation—in its different manifestations, because, as Schaefer argues, the term has changed over time from a historically circumscribed and unique genre to a range of youth-oriented and B-movie subgenres—(1999: 4) for Latin America. For example, a major defining feature of exploitation in the United States is a failure to meet basic levels of technical competency, for instance, the films of Edward D. Wood Jr. (*Glen or Glenda*, 1953; *Plan 9 From Outer Space*, 1959). However, in Latin America, such a basic feature would not in and of itself define exploitation. Although Latin America has produced and is capable of producing technically accomplished films (see, for instance, classical Mexican director Emilio Fernández's 1940s masterpieces *Flor silvestre/Wild Flower*, *María Candelaria*, and *Río Escondido/Hidden River*, or the influential works of Argentine director Leopoldo Torre Nilsson's *La mano en la trampa/The Hand in the Trap* [1961] or *La casa del ángel/The House of the Angel* [1957]), levels of technical competency within its various national filmmaking endeavors, and its three major national industries (Brazil, Argentina, and Mexico) have varied over time as a result of a lack of established infrastructure, periodic glitches in funding (due to economic crises or changing cultural imperatives of different national governments), and a lack of institutional support. Therefore, although an industrial melodrama like *Cuando los hijos se van/When the Children Leave* (Julián Soler, 1969)—made during a period of aesthetic and institutional crisis in the Mexican industry—could be described as demonstrating poor production values and a lack of basic filmmaking craftsmanship (Ramírez Berg, 1992: 31) it is by no means an exploitation film or in any way similar to the contemporaneous (and also technically poor) exploitation film *Santo el enmascarado de plata vs. la invasión de los marcianos/Santo vs. the Martians* (Alfredo B. Crevanna, 1967). Another major defining feature of exploitation, according to Schaefer and others, is its 'low' budget. But in

Latin America, where filmmaking operates on a vastly different economics of scale, defining just what constitutes a low budget is much more complex. (Indeed, the relatively low cost of filmmaking on this developing continent is part of what attracted outside filmmakers [Roger Corman, Michael and Roberta Findlay, Joe D'Amato, Ruggero Deodato, and others] to work here [see Andrew Syder's, Glenn Ward's, and Jeffrey Middents's chapters]). If low budget was taken as a marker of exploitation status, then many mainstream industrial productions and indeed many 'new cinema' films of the 1960s and 1970s would be classified as exploitation.

U.S. exploitation also occupies an aesthetic, generic, thematic, and exhibition 'alternative' to the firmly established mainstream industry (Hollywood) (Schaefer, 1999: 2).[3] Whilst Latin American exploitation cinemas are critically segregated from both the popular and canonical Latin American cinemas in continental and national film histories and do represent in many ways an 'alternative' to official ideologies (see Stephanie Dennison's chapter on the *pornochanchada*), there are three main reasons why it is problematic to talk about them as always representing a similarly alternative space 'to a mainstream industry.' More frequently than not, as in the case of Ecuador in the 1960s (Alemán, 2004), no mainstream national industry (nor indeed even a viable art cinema) existed in these countries. Therefore, the exploitation films made in Ecuador (*S.O.S. conspiración bikini*/The Bikini Conspiracy, René Cardona Jr., 1966) and coproduced with Mexico represented the country's only significant filmmaking output of the period. Equally, many exploitation movies were often made within certain national industries themselves (e.g., the Mexican wrestling movies of the 1960s and 1970s) or by jobbing industrial directors (e.g., Argentinean Emilio Vieyra, who mostly worked for the domestic mainstream industry but made some low-budget horror movies for the Hispanic market in the United States; see Gerard Dapena's chapter) or put on general release and distributed by the state-run production and distribution agency (see Dennison's chapter on the *pornochanchada*). What is also different in a Latin American context is the absence of a production category called exploitation (which is why, as Sergio de la Mora points out, the term has never been used by Mexican critics) and how this can be attributed again to industrial differences. Whereas in the United States, exploitation became a separate category in the 1920s largely as a result of the self-regulatory codes and bodies implemented in Hollywood (i.e., the "Do's and Don'ts" of the 1920s and the later Production Code Administration [1934–1968], which effectively excluded exploitation from the mainstream industry [Schaefer, 1999:5]), the requisite industrial infrastructure (for self-regulation) formed much later in those Latin American countries which did develop industries, and as a result subsequent self-regulation on the prescriptive level of the PCA never really existed. Although censorship did exist (but mostly, in the case of Mexico at least, of subject matter that could damage or offend governments and their representative individuals), the lack of a set of defined rules of what subject matters were and were not allowable meant relative freedom (in relation to Hollywood) to depict whatever. Mexican industry genre films of the 1940s/1950s were therefore free to show or allude directly to such PCA-banned subject matter as mixed-race marriages (*Angelitos negros/ Little Black Angels*, Joselito Rodríguez, 1948), nudity (*María Candelaria*), pre- or extramarital sex (*Trotacalles/Street Walker,* Matilde Landeta, 1951), prostitution (*Aventurera/Adventuress,* Alberto Gout, 1949), and infanticide (*Víctimas del pecado/Victims of Sin*, Emilio Fernández, 1950). Although having said that, in keeping with a conservative agenda, many of these films ended with the punishment of the perpetrators of such 'moral' violations (*Aventurera* is a notable exception). It is therefore difficult to talk about latsploitation as a production category or clear-cut alternative separated off from the main industry through censorship.

Secondly, although we acknowledge that the term latsploitation (similar to the U.S. exploitation terms *sexploitation* and *blaxploitation*) may suggest an implied degradation of Latin America (and indeed this anthology recognizes that many of these films do exploit Latin American locales and continental and national stereotypes; see Ruétalo's chapter on Isabel Sarli) and as such could be interpreted as the continent's internalization of the image of itself held by its colonial oppressors (Freire, 1971), at the same time, by coining the term *latsploitation* we seek to recuperate elements within some of these films which emphasize what could be considered positive assertions of national or local self-image. For instance, Gabriela Alemán's chapter suggests that the ultra-low-budget hitmen films and the *Kichwa* melodramas—that only circulate on pirated DVDs and are consumed in mostly domestic contexts—represent a vital manifestation of Ecuadorian attitudes, desires, and pleasures in the face of a national cinematic culture dominated by multiplexes and Hollywood releases, that is inaccessible to the working class. Equally, Adán Avalos argues that the *fronteriza* (border) films reflect back to migrant workers otherwise inaccessible images of their experiences and economic struggles along the U.S./Mexico border. Similarly, we also want to emphasize (along with another main vector of Latin American film scholarship) how Latin American exploitation cinemas (like the new cinemas of the 1960s and 1970s and some U.S. exploitation cinema) *may* represent a form of contestation and resistance not just to dominant (i.e., Hollywood-derived classicism's) stylistic aesthetic and narrative norms, for example, Alejandro Jodorowsky's 'cinema of cruelty' approach in *El topo* (1969) (see Josexto Cerdán and Miguel Fernández Labayen's chapter) but also to the bourgeois art cinema models that many of the New Latin American Cinemas (despite their rhetoric) ultimately aspired to (see Tierney's chapter on José Mojica Marins).

However, we do not wish to argue that we *must* value these films because they (or exploitation) are *all* automatically or uniformly transgressive. We maintain that, although transgression has been a key unifying trope and mobilizing discourse in the study of exploitation and its related fields—

particularly the 'cult film' (Telotte, 1991: 6)—it is problematic to insist on the necessary transgressiveness of exploitation cinema as Xavier Mendik and Graeme Harper (2000: 11) do because it can result in the oversimplification or in some cases the simple disregard for the actual production context and politics of these films (see Andrew Willis's chapter on León Klimovsky's 'Francoist' cinema). Indeed, we take Barry K. Grant's view that exploitation or cult films can sometimes be simultaneously transgressive and "recuperative," that is, "they reclaim the [dominant cultural values] they seem to violate" (2000:19).

We suggest, therefore, that latsploitation is a more fluid category than the generic term *exploitation*, especially when posited against canonical Latin American films or even its industrial mainstream cinema (even though it can exist inside the industry), that encapsulates both (relatively) big budgeted projects (i.e., Roger Corman's Peruvian films) and small, local artisan-like projects (the hitmen from Manabí series). We also suggest that latsploitation is fluid in relation to its geospatial boundaries 'diluting' national borders in the days before globalization was a recognized process (Alvaray, 2008: 57). Latsploitation can refer to the continental and sometimes hemispheric sweep of these films (playing both U.S. and Latin American markets) or to a transnational model of production (coproductions between Mexico and Ecuador, the United States and Peru) or even to transatlantic flows between Latin America and Spain (i.e., the Spanish films of Argentinean Klimovsky).

Finally, because we are championing Latin American exploitation cinemas as marginal, it is important to remember that, unlike U.S. exploitation, the dominant against which we sometimes define these cinemas but which is also a marginal cinema in world cinema terms, Latin American exploitation cinema is *doubly* marginalized, firstly as the product of the developing, or 'Third World' (or 'emerging market' as it is now euphemistically referred to), and secondly as disreputable material. Hence, when it comes to latsploitation we are dealing not just with a peripheral cinema but a cinema that is at the *periphery* of the periphery.

Through an array of approaches the essays in *Latsploitation* raise a range of historical, industrial, political, and aesthetic questions which suggest new avenues of research in Latin American film studies. The greater amount of essays on Mexico (two of which are in fact situated on the Mexico-U.S. border) rather than any other national cinema is a deliberate reflection of regional film history. The Mexican industry has for a number of reasons dominated exploitation production in Latin America ever since the decline of its classical cinema in the late 1950s. At the same time, *Latsploitation* illustrates a clearly marked shift in the production of exploitation in the 1960s to other parts of Latin America. Essays not focused on Mexico cover the most northern (the zombie infested Carribean) and southern (the snuff-producing Southern Cone) parts of the region. *Latsploitation* begins and ends with two framing chapters that frame the book with the chronological past(s) and future(s) of Latin American exploitation cinemas. While the past in this volume commences in 1930s Mexico, before the consolidation of the national film industry, the future is situated paradoxically and quite consciously in twenty-first-century Ecuador, at the "margin of the margins." The rest of the chapters in the volume are divided thematically into four sections ("Latsploitation beyond Borders," "Latsploitation Auteurs," "Politicizing Latsploitation," and "Sex, Sex, and More Sex") to explore key and common critical points in the study of 'lowbrow' genres—although many of the essays are flexible enough to correspond with more than one of these categories.

Ana López's analysis of the early work of Juan Orol, José Bohr, and Ramón Peón provides a fitting entry to this anthology pondering the 'proto-exploitation' practices of these three directors in early 1930s Mexico. López argues that cinema in Latin America would develop "at a different pace and under different kinds of contextual pressures" than its counterpart in the United States and for this reason exploitation cinemas could not even surface until much later, namely, the 1940s and 1950s, when Mexican cinema consolidated its hegemony over the region. Within this context, exploitation practices would emerge both in Mexico and throughout the region as an alternative to the classical style and mode of production of the Mexican Golden Age. By turning to the period immediately following the introduction of sound, López finds in these three filmmakers the experimentation with narrative, themes, style, and genre that would lay the groundwork for both the Mexican national industry to come and future exploitation cinemas throughout the region.

The first section, "Latsploitation beyond Borders," explores the transnational relationships inherent in exploitation cinemas due to their global and commercial appeal. On the one hand, cross-border associations aid in better defining and understanding the nation, its politics, and its cinemas; on the other hand, they provide a mirror from which the nation can see reflected its own desires and fears of foreign Others. As a site for both foreign and local exploitation production, "perverse" Latin America encourages audiences abroad to provide new ways of rethinking its cinema within the history of global exchange.

In "'Perversa América Latina': The Reception of Latin American Exploitation Cinema in Spanish Subcultures," Antonio Lázaro-Reboll examines the circulation and cultural meanings of Latin American exploitation cinemas in contemporary Spanish fan sites of reception, namely, the Semana de cine fantástico y de terror de San Sebastián (Horror and Fantasy Film Festival) and the fanzine *2000 maniacos*. The chapter argues that fans and critics of 'paracinema' share similar reading strategies and tread analogous critical positions, all of which must be considered in the reconfiguration of exploitation studies and particularly as these begin to enter new histories of Spanish and Latin American film studies.

Jeffrey Middents considers two productions (*Hour of the Assassin/Misión en los Andes* and *Crime Zone/Calles peligrosas*) directed by Peruvian Luis Llosa made in conjunction with Roger Corman's Concorde Pictures (like many of Corman's Latin American productions) primarily for the U.S. video market (though these two were subsequently theatrically released in Peru). Challenging national and regional critics, who have argued that there is little to outwardly connect these Llosa/Corman films to Peru, Middents recuperates *Misión en los Andes* as part of Peruvian national cinema, arguing that its specific markers of national identity (easily readable for Peruvian audiences) expand and enrich a narrow definition of Peruvian 'national cinema.'

In "'I Wonder Who the Real Cannibals Are': Latin America and Colonialism in European Exploitation Cinema," Andrew Syder reviews the Italian cannibal and zombie films made between 1977 and 1985 rationalizing the different representations of Latin America within the contemporary imperatives of the Italian film industry. The chapter explores the reason for shifts in the representation of Latin America in Italian cinema from the urban, chic, carnival continent of the 1960s to the green inferno of cannibals of the late 1970s and early 1980s. Syder suggests that what takes place in films like *Cannibal Holocaust* (Ruggero Deodato, 1980) and *Zombi 2* (Lucio Fulci, 1979) is the displaced return (and denial) of Italy's own repressed (and horrific) colonial past in Africa.

The next section, "Latsploitation Auteurs," focuses on case studies of transnational directors working both inside and outside Latin America to provide concrete and contextualized examples of the conception and reception of the auteur's inventive play with generic conventions, taboo-breaking themes, unconventional approach to style, and vexed relationship to standard notions of authorship. While challenging elitist cultural standards implicit in the idea of the auteur, the essays in this section also question the obvious exclusion of these figures from national cinematic histories, arguing that they too, along with others from the same generation of filmmakers, engage directly with contemporary social and political issues, but acknowledging that they do not always provide a 'transgressive' politics in their work.

Gerard Dapena's chapter demonstrates how, in the late 1960s, Argentine director Emilio Vieyra collaborated with producer Orestes Trucco to perfect a filmmaking model ripe for the international market, particularly U.S. audiences at drive-ins and grindhouses. Within a problematic construction of the auteur, Dapena suggests that Vieyra offers a nonpolitical position on the emerging youth culture, what would distance him greatly from the political 1960s national cinemas which regarded youth culture as yet another neocolonial invasion. Dapena reminds us, however, that this obvious inclusion of the emerging youth culture further detached Vieyra from the political repressive milieu in Argentina which rejected the rebellious nature of this subculture.

Josetxo Cerdán and Miguel Fernández Labayen read the work of director Alejandro Jodorowsky as one that straddles several categories ranging from exploitation and underground cinema, at the 'low' end of the cultural hierarchy, to avant-garde and auteur cinema, at the 'high' end. The authors place Jodorowsky's work within both a Mexican and a worldwide context to see how he exploits references of local and global culture and argue that Jodorowsky's ability to adapt to new models of film consumption from the 'midnight movie' circuit to home video rental has allowed him to more easily infiltrate different markets and has thus encouraged reception at such diverse levels, thereby establishing his cult status worldwide.

"José Mojica Marins and the Cultural Politics of Marginality in 'Third World' Film Criticism" explores the place of Brazilian exploitation horror director José Mojica Marins in Brazilian film history. Dolores Tierney challenges assumptions about the opposition made between avant-garde film and trash cinema by suggesting that, like Brazil's avant-garde *cinema novo* movement, Mojica's films also reveal a Brazilian reality of underdevelopment, poverty, hunger, and racial tension and do so using many of the same techniques and aesthetic strategies (shocking bourgeois sensibility, bricolage-like reusing of the cultural detritus of the 'First World'). By questioning the politics behind Latin American film criticism, Tierney complicates the construction of film canons showing the political reasons behind the erasure of certain directors and not others.

Andrew Willis considers the career of Argentine émigré director León Klimovsky in Spain. By placing Klimovsky within the political and social contexts of both Argentina and Spain at the time of his involvement in these industries, Willis questions the assumption that all exploitation cinemas are necessarily 'progressive.' In fact, his nuanced analysis of Klimovsky's films made in Spain proves otherwise. Klimovsky, Willis suggests, displays a consistent reactionary worldview across his exploitation films. Willis makes a much needed and poignant argument for a contextualized look at exploitation cinema given what he suggests is the slippery nature of these genres.

While politics is not exclusive to the chapters found in "Politicizing Latsploitation," surfacing in almost every chapter of the book, this section chiefly takes exploitation as a venue for the exploration of social, political, and 'real' issues. Snuff, reality-based, and border/"naco" films are sites for both exposing social and political issues (colonialism, politics of place, censorship, class, gender, and immigration) and sites for refracting such 'reality.'

Glenn Ward's chapter inspects Roberta and Michael Findlay's 1976 film *Snuff*, to think about contending ideas of 'South America' in the discourses within and surrounding the film. While there have been many studies centered on this film, few have actually placed *Snuff* within the social and political contexts of the countries in which it was filmed/set (Argentina, Uruguay, and Chile). Likewise, Ward is interested in how the film develops what he calls "competing notions" of both place and space to produce a problematic representation of the Other, in this case the Southern Cone, one that is not easily contained within generic stereotypes of the region. He argues that, while one can easily read *Snuff* through a neocolonial gaze, the many gaps that exist within the film for the audience can only suggest a cultural politics of "unintelligibility."

"Based on a True Story: Reality-Based Exploitation Cinema in Mexico" explores Mexico's reality-based exploitation (rbe) movies—films based on actual events or people—which surfaced in the 1970s and 1980s in Mexico. David Wilt's chapter traces the emergence and flourishing of rbe films to the increased popularization of the *nota roja* (crime or 'bloody' news) and the presidency of Luis Echeverría (1970–1976), an open period when social and political topics were more tolerated and less censored. Wilt shows how these "based-on-a-true-story" exploitation films often blur the dividing line between reality and cinema, sometimes reflecting and distorting the "facts." Furthermore, Wilt suggests that through their study one can trace a history of censorship and a reflection of contemporary popular tastes.

Catherine Benamou centers on the public and screen personae of Mexican actress Rosa Gloria Chagoyán and her performance in border films and beyond to interrogate gender and national representations. Benamou asserts that Chagoyán represents a "woman warrior . . . capable of carrying the nation's burden on her shoulders." Through roles played in the trilogy *Lola la Trailera*/Lola the Semi-Truck Driver, other screen performances, and her public appearances, Benamou emphasizes both the aesthetic and sociocultural dimension of her status, as she contextualizes Chagoyán within the debt crisis of the 1970s and 1980s in Mexico, part of a larger transformative process involving sociogeographic displacement, media consumption, and intensified e/migration

Adán Avalos also looks at the historically contested region of the U.S.-Mexico border to explore what he calls "naco" cinema. Produced by the private sector and made quickly, cheaply, and primarily for profit, this "naco" (low-class, rural, and uneducated) cinema is packed with car chases, gun battles, and migrants' aspirational struggles against an oppressive capitalist system. Avalos argues that these films resonate with the experiences and concerns of their primary audiences: working-class migrant families and their attempts to deal with issues of displacement. In tracing the development of naco cinema, Avalos claims that *La banda del carro rojo* (Ruben Galindo, 1978) is a pivotal film that solidified the genre and provides a model for future border cinema in its references to the unique experiences of recent immigrants.

The final section, "Sex, Sex, and More Sex," surveys the various subgenres of Latin American sexploitation. Some of these subgenres are autonomous to Latin America, such as the *pornochanchadas* (sexy comedies) in Brazil and the 'nature' sexploitation found in René Cardona Jr.'s films—with the references to the ocean and its predators—and the Isabel Sarli and Armando Bó productions—with the relationship between star and landscape. While the emphasis is on sexploitation, this section nonetheless includes star and auteur studies.

Victoria Ruétalo scrutinizes director Armando Bó's construction of star Isabel Sarli, his most 'prized' commodity. By rehashing the myths constructed around Sarli's star persona, within and beyond the films, Ruétalo exposes some of the ideological, historical, and aesthetic contradictions found within these myths. Sarli is unable to move beyond the lumpenproletariat and gender roles which initially define her because, as Ruétalo suggests, she reflects the anxieties and needs of a stifling 1960s/1970s Argentina.

Misha MacLaird delves into René Cardona Jr.'s films of the 1960s and 1970s as examples of the exploitation of female sexuality. MacLaird reads Cardona Jr.'s obsession with the ocean, finding a recurring diptych in his films: the seductive female figure and the powerful and menacing image of the shark. Through the framing, positioning, and interaction between female and predator, this diptych exposes the threat of these 'natural' elements to the patriarchal paradigm in what is, MacLaird suggests, a reworking of the vampire and monster tropes associated with the horror genre.

Stephanie Dennison investigates Brazil's highly popular *pornochanchadas* (state-sponsored sexy comedies) that emerged in the context of the late 1960s/early 1970s military dictatorship. Dennison situates the genre of pornochanchadas within the history of international sexploitation. By doing so, the author provides a different perspective from which to approach the genre which distances her reading from the general consensus found in Brazilian film studies. Dennison contends that the pornochanchada was a site for alternative filmmaking strategies expressing topics of interest that did not necessarily coincide with the military government's worldview.

"'Tus pinches leyes yo me las paso por los huevos': Isela Vega and Mexican Dirty Movies" looks at the career of Mexican actress Isela Vega, which has successfully bridged both commercially successful sexploitation and critically acclaimed 'art' films. Acting in the volatile Mexican film industry with its economic ups and downs, Vega has had to be flexible in the roles she plays across genres. Despite this versatility, Sergio de la Mora argues that Vega has consciously constructed her own 'bad-girl' image outside her work, which will influence the roles she plays in films across genres and boundaries of taste.

This volume ends with a look into the future(s) of exploitation cinemas in Latin America, a trajectory that has witnessed shifting modes of production, exhibition, and distribution of exploitation: from film to 'midnight movies' to 'straight to video' to film festivals and fanzines, and finally to pirate copies. In the anthology's final chapter, Gabriela Alemán explores the circumstances and production methods of contemporary Ecuadorian exploitation films, hinting at the future direction of the genre(s). She suggests that with the breakdown of 'traditional' methods of distribution and exhibition (i.e., the closure of the country's 150 cinemas in the 1990s), alternative patterns of distribution, such as piracy, have arisen to fill in the gap. Her chapter focuses in particular on the production of low-budget hit men from Manabí series, the documentary/gore film, and the *Kichwa* melodrama. She argues that the appeal of these video shot, low-budget films lies in the local pleasures they offer to a disenfranchized audience and that as such these films represent an intensely localized subculture which redefines the expression of 'exploitation' cinemas in the twenty-first century. Alemán identifies a need to continually reinvent the frame from which to think and approach new areas in latsploitation.

NOTES

1. Throughout this book titles appear in original language followed by a translation. In the cases when the film is released in English the translation will appear in italics. When there was no such release then the translation appears in Roman script.
2. Jorge Ayala Blanco, an esteemed and institutional critic of Mexican cinema, is characteristically dismissive of most horror films in the Mexican film industry. He credits this rather late flourishing of the horror genre in Mexico to the decadence of the Mexican film industry's mythic "Golden Age" resulting in the increasing hybridization of national genres and climaxing in low-grade horror as an aberrant stopgap in a struggling industry (1993: 157–8).
3. Of course, even the alterity of exploitation in relation to the U.S. mainstream industry is something that shifted over time. Schaefer is very clear in his book (1999) to distinguish the 'classical exploitation' made in the 1920s through the 1950s by small-time producer-distributors (individual exploiteers like Dwain Esper and Samuel Cummins) from the 'teen pics' made by small industrial outfits like AIP from the late 1950s onwards. He also points out how from the mid-1950s onwards it became more and more difficult to make the distinction between exploitation and the mainstream as the studios started to *also* make films about juvenile delinquency, backstreet abortions, and other subject matter previously relegated (because of a strictly enforced Production Code) to the exploitation circuit (1999: 327–29).

1 Before Exploitation
Three Men of the Cinema in Mexico

Ana M. López

"Yo tengo que vivir del público."

Juan Orol

Eric Schaefer (1999) argues that exploitation film emerged as a discernible category in the United States around 1919–20. Chronicling the public controversy over sex hygiene/anti-venereal disease films in this period, he argues that these films crystallized the possibility of an alternative film space at a moment when the mainstream industry had consolidated its industrial base in Hollywood, established a firm mode of production, and developed a stylistic system anchored in narrative and stylistic transparency. In Latin America, however, filmmaking developed at a different pace and under different kinds of contextual pressures. An exploitation cinema akin to that outlined by Schaefer could not even begin to emerge as an alternative filmic practice grounded in spectacle until the late 1940s–1950s, when the Mexican cinema had become established as *the* cinema for the continent (López, 1994). However, what emerged earlier, especially in the effervescent experimental period after the arrival of sound, were multiple alternative cinematic practices that, attempting to find the 'magic' formulas for box-office success and audience satisfaction, laid the groundwork for both the mainstream 'national' cinema and future exploitation practices.

Focusing on Mexico in the period immediately after the coming of sound, this essay looks at the work of three filmmakers who arrived in Mexico and/or to the new medium in 1930–31 and participated eagerly and with almost innocent glee in the rush to define a national cinema and establish an autochthonous mass audience: Juan Orol, José Bohr, and Ramón Peón. Originally from Spain, but in Mexico since young, Orol had been a race-car driver, boxer, actor, bullfighter, policeman, and artistic director for a radio station before taking up filmmaking with *Sagrario*/Sanctuary (1933). Peón had been making films in his native Cuba (including the famous *La virgen de la Caridad*/*Our Lady of Charity*, 1930) and had spent time in Hollywood before resettling in Mexico. He was assistant director for five films before directing his first Mexican feature, *La Llorona*/The Weeping Woman (1934). Bohr had a long international career as a singer/composer and had worked on Spanish-language films in the United States; his first Mexican film was *La sangre manda*/Blood Rules (1934). Eager for box-office success and engaged in the collective exercise of establishing a 'national' industry, all three directors (a few times in collaboration with each other) adopted a freewheeling syncretic style: they adapted and combined generic strands popularized by Hollywood with national themes and folklore and experimented with new formal strategies for storytelling. In the 1930s their work contributed significantly to the general experimentation and ebullience of a film industry attempting to find (and define) its audience.

THE CONTEXT FOR FILMMAKING IN MEXICO

As I have argued elsewhere (López, 2000), the diffusion of the cinema throughout the continent was defined by its status as an import emblematic of modernity and by the technological infrastructure, political stability, industrialization, and economic activities at national and regional levels. By the late 1920s the larger nations of Latin America had developed cinematic vernaculars and fairly solid production infrastructures, albeit with limited resources, and, above all, had captured national and regional audiences despite the constant competition from U.S. and European imports. Latin American silent cinema inscribed the medium in national histories while simultaneously recognizing it as the embodiment of differential dreams of modernity.

In the late 1920s and early 1930s, however, the introduction of sound technology abruptly cut off this trajectory and, especially in Mexico, subtly shifted the terms of the cinema's main representational paradigms. Aggressively marketed, sound films from the United States quickly took over the exhibition and distribution sectors, while national producers scrambled for capital, technology, and know-how. In Mexico, the transition to sound took place at the end of the first decade of postrevolutionary state building, during which the nation engaged in complex negotiations to sustain governance over disparate and needy populations and to secure its place in the post–World War I international order. The end of the decade coincided with the end of Plutarco Elias Calles's official term as president (1928) and the end of the Cristero Rebellion (1926–29). Unwilling to give up power after president-elect Alvaro Obregón was assassinated in 1927, Calles managed to secure his stronghold over national politics as the 'Jefe Máximo' by appointing three interim puppet presidents over the next six years, a period known as the 'Maximato' sexenio (1928–34). This was also the period when Mexican artists and intellectuals, rallied by José Vasconcelos's exaltation of the mestizo as the future "cosmic race," the culmination of human evolution and the embodiment of Mexican cultural identity (Vasconcelos, 1925), were also deeply engaged in the project of building the cultural capital of the newly emerging nation. In the late 1920s and 1930s, cultural nationalism reigned supreme (Vaughan and Lewis, 2006: 14).

It is important to note that the late 1920s to early 1930s also witnessed the blossoming of other mass media that quickly captured the public imagination. Primary among them was radio, marked by the launch of station XEW-AM in Mexico City in September 1930. Owned by Emilio Azcárraga Vidaurreta (also president of the Mexican Music Company, a record and sheet music distributor affiliated with RCA in the United States), XEW launched as "the voice of Latin America from Mexico." It was the first Latin American radio station powerful enough to reach a mass audience and featured an extensive publicity machine and varied programming that easily captured audiences.[1] Above all, music was the centerpiece of programming: in the 1930s, Mexican radio (led by XEW) codified, standardized, and institutionalized an 'official' repertoire of 'Mexican' popular music (mariachis, boleros, rancheras) and created national 'stars,' which became very important for the cinema. Second only to music, serial dramas, later known as *radionovelas*, also quickly grew in popularity. Drawing their talent from literature and theater—the very same pool that nourished the cinema[2]—radio dramas became popular in the 1930s and ubiquitous after 1940 (XEW aired as many as five different ones per day). Above all, as in other parts of Latin America, radio dramas were notorious for their melodramatic and emotional excesses. Sentimental melodramas punctuated by extreme pathos and enveloped in music became a narrative lingua franca for the mass media in general. As poet Salvador Novo described it in the 1950s, it was "spiritual tequila in everybody's throat" (1951: 171).

The arrival of sound to the cinema in this context of national high and popular cultural effervescence energized intellectuals and filmmakers. Even before the screening of the first sonorized film in April 1929 (Frank Capra's *Submarine*), the impact of sound on the medium and national culture was hotly debated in the press. As Luis Reyes de la Maza chronicles, the cultural intelligentsia presented a united front against the possibility that film would become an English-only medium, resisted Hollywood's inept efforts to produce Spanish-language films, clamored for a national cinema, and debated what it should embody (1973). By late 1930, Hollywood's Spanish-language productions had demonstrated their flaws, among them, problems with mixing accents and nationalities and the lack of convincing star power. Critics like Baltasar Fernández Cue argued in the pages of *El Ilustrado* that only Mexico was in a position to take over the Spanish-language market (Reyes de la Maza, 1973: 246).

As if heeding the critics, President Pascual Ortiz Rubio included film in his 1931 *Campaña Nacionalista* (Nationalist Campaign): import duties were increased by almost 1,000 percent in July 1931 and, within three months, the exhibition sector was in crisis, since U.S. distributors refused to pay the additional fees and stopped sending films (De los Reyes, 1987: 118; de Usabel, 1982: 93). This protectionist move was short-lived: Rubio Ortiz rescinded the protectionist tariffs in late October 1931 since, as exhibitors rightly argued, there just weren't enough Mexican films to show in place of the imports.

By this time, the Mexican exhibition sector was well-established. In 1930 there were 830 movie theaters, 136 already outfitted for sound (De los Reyes, 1987: 118). In Mexico City, between three and six major movie theaters were inaugurated yearly between 1930 and 1935. Whereas total capacity in Mexico City was only 32,888 seats in 1922, by 1937 the total number of seats had grown to almost 125,000 (Alfaro Salazar and Ochoa Vega, 1997: 221–24). This growth paralleled the tremendous urbanization of Mexico City.[3] In the early 1920s the city's growth was concentrated in the old center, but in the 1930s its territory and population grew exponentially alongside the services and consumer options available to citizens. The larger and most elegant theaters remained in the *centro*, but after the implementation of the 1933 planning and rezoning law, the widening and lengthening of the city's main arteries led to the complete or partial demolition of many of the older theaters. Most were rebuilt throughout the 1930s and the exhibition sector developed a distinctly elegant and modern visage. The *colonias*, or planned neighborhoods, whether traditional or modern, also acquired their own theaters, often consonant with their own architectural vernaculars. Working-class *barrios* also had a cinematic infrastructure, though still much more precarious and associated with the *carpa* (tent-theater) tradition (Pilcher, 2001: 23–39). All that was needed to have an industry were Mexican films. . . .

FOREIGNERS, ADVENTURERS. AND ENTREPRENEURS

Mexico had always been a haven for foreign and foreign-trained film entrepreneurs and directors, even in the silent period (Ramírez Berg, 1992; Orellana, 2003). But in the early 1930s it was a mecca. Eisenstein's famous 1930–31 sojourn in Mexico set the stage, although it was *sui generis*: unlike others landing in Mexico in the early 1930s, Eisenstein had no desire to join and/or influence an industry and, as has been well chronicled elsewhere, his pursuits were instead intellectual and artistic (Nesbet, 2003), although his visit left a lasting imprint on the cinema the future Mexican industry engendered (De los Reyes, 1987: 96–116).

Many Mexicans had gone to Hollywood in the 1920s to become familiar with the U.S. industry. Indeed, many had achieved success acting (Ramón Novarro, Lupita Tovar, Dolores Del Rio, Lupe Veléz, Gilbert Roland) while others worked as technicians or as extras or learned the trade as assistants (Miguel Contreras Torres, Raphael J. Sevilla, Miguel Zacarías, Emilio Fernández, Chano Urueta). Many of the European and North Americans that landed in Mexico after 1931 also came via Hollywood, for example, directors John Auer, David Kirkland, and Arcady Boytler (even Eisenstein himself) and cinematographers Alex Phillips and Ross Fisher. The three filmmakers considered here stand out from the rest insofar as they were native Spanish speakers and comfortable inhabitants of Spanish/Latin

American culture. But what is most fascinating about this period is the incredible cross-fertilizations and collaborations that occurred across all job titles. Before the establishment of a tightly regimented 'closed' union system in 1945, there were no limits to what anyone could do and/or contribute to the final product: every film was a collaborative experiment to see what would 'take' and filmic authorship is even more problematic than usual to assert.

OROL-BOHR-PEÓN: FIRST FILMS

Orol, Bohr, and Peón made their first films in Mexico in 1933, a year notable for a significant increase in national production: whereas only six films had been released in 1932, there were twenty-one in 1933. Bohr and Peón were recent arrivals to Mexico City; Orol had been in and out of the city for several years. All had spent time in Hollywood, learning about sound filmmaking and, in the case of Bohr, already an accomplished actor/singer, participating in Hollywood's Spanish-language productions. Witnessing its ebullience, they entered the Mexican film business in search of experience and financial success. Although none directed what were considered to be the 'best' films of this period either by contemporary or later critics,[4] their films opened up new directions for the medium in Mexico and were often very well-received by the public. In subsequent decades, the strands they wove in the 1930s led to the latsploitation cinema analyzed in other essays in this volume. Most importantly, there were deep interconnections among them and between them and others in the nascent film business. Particularly in this period (though the same would be true for the 'classical' post-1943 period as well; see Tierney, 2007), film production was a team effort and teams were fluid and collaborative in their endeavors to overcome production obstacles and achieve popular success.

Peón, with more filmmaking experience under his belt, was the first to direct and his *La Llorona* was the new industry's first attempt to establish a Mexican horror genre. A free adaptation of the popular myth of La Llorona—a woman who is rejected by her husband/lover and kills her children and then herself, either by stabbing or drowning—the film begins in the present as a well-off family celebrates the son's (Juanito) fourth birthday with an elaborate party. After the party, the grandfather warns the father, Ricardo, of a curse on the family that has caused the death of all their firstborn sons on their fourth birthday. The curse is explained via two long flashbacks. In the colonial period, an Indian princess was betrayed by a noble and killed herself and the son he wouldn't legitimize. When she falls to the ground, her spirit rises, spectacularly accompanied by a piercing wail that, literally, stops a sword fight cold. In the present, a masked intruder kills the grandfather and threatens Juanito. Through another flashback we learn that the curse goes back to the Conquest, when Cortez took away

Malinche's son. She went mad and in a fit of despair killed herself with a dagger. As her spirit also rises spectacularly with a long wail, her faithful servant vows to avenge her death for the rest of time. Returning to the present, the masked intruder drags Juanito to an Aztec temple–secret room and is ready to stab him when Ricardo and the police rush in, shoot the masked intruder and eventually discover that she is the boy's caretaker: all the family's servants have been in their employ for generations and have carried out the legendary curse. Her spirit also rises with a long wail and the film ends with the nuclear family united and safe, but without dispelling the legend.

Peón's film is simultaneously heavily indebted to the silent cinema, especially in its pacing, as well as marvelously inventive in its mise-en-scène and editing. *La Llorona* begins by asserting its nationness by announcing that it is "a modern version of the popular Mexican legend." The rest of the credits unfold in front of dimly lit close-ups of Aztec-looking stone carvings, masks, and vessels that continue to assert Mexicanness as well as establish an apt mood for horror. The first scene (a prelude to the story proper) opens with a long shot of a city street at night. A well-dressed man walks towards the right and briefly stops to light a cigarette. Midframe, he gasps suddenly and falls to the ground. Cut to a close-up of his face; his eyes are open and the lit cigarette is still in his mouth, but he is clearly dead. Then the camera pans across his body to his hand as it clenches into a rigor mortis fist. A dissolve on the clenched fist leads to a different space, where a sheet is placed over the fist (see Figure 1.1). As the camera pans left, and tilts up, we discover we are in a hospital or morgue, where a handsome doctor in scrubs proclaims to the medical students surrounding him that the dead man is an example of a victim of a "typical" heart attack. This first scene economically establishes the horror scenario (mystery-death-ghosts), a contemporary setting ostensibly ruled by scientific rationality and proclaims a unique style that Peón will sustain throughout the film: an attention to visual detail and a surprising emphasis on complex transitions that constantly call attention to themselves as artifice. Eschewing the parameters of invisible style editing, Peón's transitions catapult the spectator into a strange/estranging narrative universe and (perhaps unwittingly) greatly enhances the horror effect (which otherwise is fairly tame). As stated previously, very often the transitions between scenes occur on close-ups rather than the standard establishing shots and disorient and unsettle. When they do not, they are marked by spectacular diagonal wipes that call attention to themselves such as, for example, the transition between the hospital scene and Juanito's birthday party (see Figure 1.2).

The birthday party scene also illustrates a unique—and disconcerting—attention to mise-en-scène: the oddly shaped clover leaf design on the floor, echoing the clover leaves on the back of each chair to suggest a very modern setting and somewhat of an obsession with luck. Peón emphasizes these elements with a disturbingly long and measured 360-degree pan around the table focusing on each child at the party. Yet, we later see that the home is

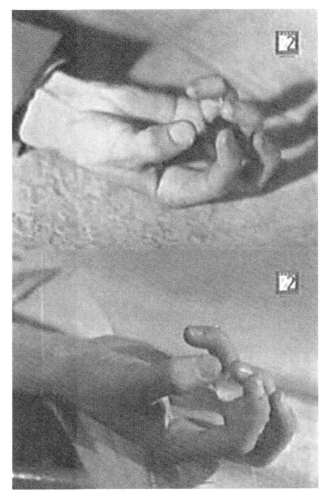

Figure 1.1 Clenched fists in *La Llorona*/The Weeping Woman (Ramón Peón, 1934).

actually a traditional home that has been in the family for centuries (complete with secret passages). Visually, the scenes in the present (with the exception of the birthday party) are 'realistic' in the gritty detective-film style of Hollywood films of the 1930s, but each flashback adopts a different tone: the colonial flashback is visually lush in the style of a historical reconstruction and filled with ornamentation and dozens of extras, while the conquest one is minimalist—most of it filmed against a flat unadorned backdrop—and almost surreal with an almost exclusive focus on la Malinche and/or her servant.

Lastly, one must mention the ghostly special effects, which are spectacularly lurid (see Figure 1.3) and, as García Riera put it, "indescribable"

Figure 1.2 A transition from *La Llorona*/The Weeping Woman (Ramón Peón, 1934)

(1993: 82). He is somewhat dismissive of the film ("not badly made and fairly amusing"), but I would argue that it represents an experimental milestone in the establishment of a full-fledged Mexican film industry and is also, to my knowledge, the first appearance of a masked menace in the Mexican cinema. Both the legend of La Llorona and masked characters played a significant role in Mexican exploitation cinema in subsequent decades.

Figure 1.3 Ghostly effects in *La Llorona*/The Weeping Woman (Ramón Peón, 1934).

Peón also directed *Sagrario*, Juan Orol's first production. Orol had little filmmaking experience but liked the movies and invested capital from the sale of land in a production company, Aspa Films (De la Vega Alfaro, 1987: 21–22). With a script by Quirico Michelena, he hired Peón to direct. Like *La Llorona*, *Sagrario* was generically innovative: it is the first film of the Mexican sound cinema to feature *both* adultery and incestuous relations (it was produced and released before *La mujer del puerto/The Woman of the Port*, 1934). Despite its *soupçon* of social aspirations (a working-class man who is wronged and jailed; a wife and daughter 'helped' by a kindly 'doctor' who makes the former his mistress and implicates the latter in symbolic incest), *Sagrario* was deeply marked by the melodramatic plot conventions of the by then booming *radionovelas*: illustrating the contradictions of the moralism of the times, female transgressions are splendidly—even luridly—aired but must be punished by either death or solitude. Unlike later *cabaretera* films in which performance and sexuality provided the women with agency (López, 1993b), here they are pawns and victims to the end.

Stylistically, *Sagrario* is much more conventional than *La Llorona*, despite a few timely placed double exposures that display inner thoughts and mark flashbacks (reminiscent of the ghostly specters of Peón's film), a spectacular beginning that visually conveys the stifling routine of the factory where Juan works, and lovely scenes of the lovers in Chapultepec park. Most interesting, however, is the nature of its melodramatic premises and its unprecedented success (90,000 pesos gross revenue in its first six months vs. 32,000 production costs). The explicit representation of extreme female transgressions as the dramatic nexus (adultery, intended incest), despite the inevitable tragic end of those who transgress, heightens the melodramatic pitch and infuses a new kind of salacious energy into the genre, which presages one of the most persistent characteristics of later mainstream and exploitation efforts.

Some months after the release of *Sagrario*, José Bohr began production on his Mexican directorial debut, *La sangre manda*. Bohr had arrived in Mexico in 1932, still interested in pursuing a film career—"We need pictures filmed in our language" (Bohr, 1987: 207)—and was enchanted by the opportunities in Mexico. Dissatisfied with the sound production facilities available (limited to the equipment used by the Rodríguez brothers for *Santa* two years earlier), Bohr went to Hollywood and bought a sound truck and cameras from a friend linked to a minor bankrupt studio (Tiffany Productions) (Bohr, 1987: 207–8). The filming of *La sangra manda* began in late 1933, with Bohr as producer/director, a script by Bohr and Eva "La Duquesa" Limiñana (his longtime partner) and Alex Phillips as cinematographer.

La sangre manda stands out among its contemporaries. While it exhibits very high production values, it is also the most indebted to the practices of the Hollywood Spanish-language films (not surprising, given Bohr's lineage), evidenced first of all by its setting: "in the world we live in, in contemporary times." The refusal to anchor the narrative in a real place, perhaps in an effort to achieve universal significance, undermines its impact, rendering its 'message' abstract and, in the end, distant and ethereal.

José (Bohr) plays the playboy son of the owner of an ironworks. The film begins with a sophisticated credit sequence using beautiful art deco font for the credits and a montage of busy office personnel as a backdrop. A close-up on a large clock of the Fundiciones Pedro Bolívar (Pedro Bolívar Ironworks) indicates it is 9:00 a.m. as owner Pedro Bolívar strolls in, noticing that his son's office is unoccupied. An hour later when he calls him, José is still in bed at home, drunk from the previous night's partying. This skillfully shot and edited opening sequence economically sets the dramatic stage for the film: the righteousness of work versus the irresponsible leisure of elites. That evening, the enraged Bolívar orders José to report to Chato López at the Ironworks at 7:00 a.m. to work as a laborer. José's arrival at the factory the next morning is nothing short of spectacular: he drives up in an elegant convertible driven by a black chauffeur, wearing tails and a top hat, and still visibly inebriated. This and other scenes shot on location at the foundry La Consolidada in Mexico City vividly capture the beauty of a steel plant and the harshness of working in one; simultaneously an ode to its symbolic modernity and an indictment of its effects (see Figure 1.4).

As José befriends the workers and falls in love with Chato's adoptive sister Lupe, he advocates for workers' rights (minimum salaries and collective bargaining), and convinces his father to provide funding for a library, day-care center, and theater in the Ironworks. Intending to marry Lupe, he withdraws from his family and former socialite girlfriend and moves in with her family. His relationship with Chato (who already calls him "hermano") is well-developed, especially via two long exterior traveling shots that follow the pair as they walk to the factory after boxing lessons.

Fully transformed into a member of the working class, José inaugurates the library and theater and continues his romance with Lupe. The rehearsals for the theater's inaugural performances and the inauguration are the scenes that Bohr is most comfortable with; not only in terms of his acting, but also in terms of the pacing and the actions of all the characters (Sara García makes her first appearance on film as a child performer's mother). However, in his own musical number, the specter of otherness that he had tried to suppress—his Chilean accent—bursts through in an all-too-jarring way as he sings cheek to cheek to Lupita.

That same evening, Chato's mother Amparo confesses on her deathbed that Pedro Bolívar is Chato's father and José's mother convinces Lupe to break up with José because of their social differences. When he loses his foothold in Chato's home and his loved one, José also seems to lose his class consciousness and in an argument with Chato at the factory, José angrily complains that the workers are usurping what his father amassed after years and that the workers have the same opportunity for growth

Figure 1.4 La Consolidada in Mexico City in *La sangre manda*/Blood Rules (José Bohr, 1934).

as his father had. A worker listening wryly remarks, "There is no cure, boys, blood rules." José gets into a fight with El Pesao and is spectacularly wounded when he falls near a foundry.

When José is finally recovered, during a soiree in his honor, the workers Chato has organized to reclaim his patrimony threaten to attack the Bolivar home. Carrying blazing torches when the police arrive, El Pesao pulls a gun on José; Lupe, who had gone to the house to warn José, jumps in front of the bullet and is killed. The workers and Bolivar strike an accord, the brothers reconcile, and José picks up Lupe's body and walks off screen, uttering the apocryphal words: "He is my brother."

As is evident in this analysis, after an inventive and promising beginning, the universalizing impulse takes over the narrative once José is inscribed into factory life. His magical conversion into a proletariat is as facile as his reconversion into a callous aristocrat after being wounded. Visually, however, *La sangre manda* is rather extraordinary for its time and comparable only to *La mujer del puerto* in visual achievement. Phillip's cinematography—beautiful chiaroscuros in the cantina, long traveling shots, and luminous close-ups—is simply spectacular. Overall, the film is very even-handed stylistically. For example, the juxtaposition of the luxurious life of the Bolivars with the clean simplicity of Chato's home and the poverty of another worker is vividly accomplished by the mise-en-scène but without jarring visual contrasts.

Although *La sangre manda* seemed an auspicious start, it was not especially successful and only lasted a week in a first-run theater. Not one to be easily dissuaded, Bohr immediately went into production for his second film, also cowritten with La Duquesa Olga—*¿Quién mató a Eva?*/Who Killed Eva?—which premiered in August 1934.

With *¿Quien mató a Eva?* Bohr found a more suitable genre for his talents, minus the social aspirations: the urban detective story. José (Bohr) is a young millionaire bored with his life. Returning from a gala in which he had just finished singing "I am so bored," José catches burglar Mario in his luxurious apartment and decides to join him in a burglary to inject some excitement into his life. Unfortunately, when they break into the house of famous actress Eva Orquiza, they find a squawking parrot and her dead body. José becomes the primary suspect after the police find his top hat in the scene and he goes 'underground' with Mario (disguised as Luponini, a gangster from Chicago), committed to finding the real murderer using rationality and psychology. The ambiance of the 'underground' provides Bohr with a fabulous setting to people with extraordinary types, ranging from ingénues led astray and a scheming vamp to a marvelous quartet of police detectives who often break into song. Singing is a common denominator among all: in the rooming house where Mario and José hide out, the denizens entertain themselves in the dining room by frequently breaking into song (all of which are shown in their entirety). As with *La sangre manda*, Phillips's cinematography is astonishingly beautiful, with expressive close-ups and many chiaroscuro shots, including a striking mirror shot of José during one of his escapades (see Figure 1.5). Without the narrative economy of a Howard Hawks in *The Big Sleep*, *¿Quién mató a Eva?* sustains a productive tension between José's search for Eva's killer, the mystery surrounding the characters of the underground, romance between José and one of the ingénues, and musical entertainment. The film was a worthy initiator of the detective/crime genre for the Mexican cinema.

Also in 1934, Orol partnered again with Peón to make *Mujeres sin alma/Soulless Women*. This time Orol played a much larger role in the creation of the film[5] and critics have argued that this film established the "Orolian" universe. Orol plays Julián, an honest chauffeur at the Consolidada Ironworks who ends up in jail when he is framed for theft by his boss Carlos, who is also the lover of his frivolous wife Olga. Olga's infidelities and unsavory life continue and lead to another tragedy: another worker is framed by Carlos and imprisoned; his wife (played by Adela Sequeyro) dies from grief and their children are left orphaned. Julián eventually escapes from prison, uncovers the truth, and kills Olga and Carlos. He is chased by the police and wounded, and runs to his mother's house to die in her arms. Although the film begins with ambitions of realism (again, as in *La sangre manda*, beautiful imagery of the industrial milieu of La Consolidada shot by the ubiquitous Phillips), it quickly settles into the most torpid of male melodramas following the formula that Orol himself would exploit often

Figure 1.5 A mirror shot in *¿Quién mató a Eva?/* Who Killed Eva?

later in his career: the loss of family values and female licentiousness cause the downfall of an honest man who, as a last recourse, must seek justice while never losing sight of his saintly mother.

Nineteen thirty-four was a significant year not only for the film industry (with total production increasing to twenty-three films that year) but for the nation. After a long campaign and despite the opposition of Calles, Lázaro Cárdenas was elected to the presidency and changed the shape of the nation, transforming the party of the revolution into a popular organization free from the control of Calles (Cárdenas forced Calles into exile in 1936). The political system established during his *sexenio* defined Mexican politics until the 1980s. During the Cárdenas *sexenio*, labor unions and *campesino* organizations were reorganized, urban and industrial workers gained unionization rights and wage increases, and the government finally fulfilled its revolutionary promises by expropriating and redistributing more than five hundred million acres to about eight hundred thousand *campesinos*. Under his leadership, the work of the Secretaría de Educación Pública and its socialist educational program focused on the empowerment and enfranchisement of rural communities also acquired renewed vigor (Knight, 1994; Vaughn, 1997). With a strong nationalist and populist agenda, Cárdenas had widespread popular support, which became almost unanimous when he masterminded the expropriation of foreign oil companies in 1938.

The new government also became interested in the burgeoning national cinema. Even before Cárdenas's inauguration, the Secretaría de Educación Pública financed the production of *Redes/Nets* in 1934 (released in 1936). About a group of fisherman near Veracruz who rebel against their exploiters, *Redes* reflected what the artistic intelligentsia—among others, noted composer Carlos Chávez, prominent Marxist Narciso Bassols (who had been at the head of the Secretaría de Educación Pública) and the progressive U.S. photographer Paul Strand—considered to be appropriate for the national cinema à la Eisenstein: *indigenismo* (faces, landscape, settings) and healthy—positive—doses of class struggle.[6] In January 1935, the Cárdenas administration promised via official decree to support the national industry and that same year provided railroad trains, a regiment, munitions, artillery, uniforms, and horses for Fernando de Fuentes's ¡*Vámonos con Pancho Villa!/Let's Go with Pancho Villa*, produced by the recently opened modern studios of the Cinematográfica Latinoamericana, S.A. (CLASA). Despite this official propitious climate (and their artistic achievement and subsequent fame), these films did not capture the public imagination: the biggest box-office hits of 1935 were directed by Orol and Bohr: respectively, *Madre querida/Dear Mother* and *Luponini (El terror de Chicago)/Luponini, the Terror of Chicago*.

Possibly inspired by Bohr's 1934 *Tu hijo/Your Son*, which initiated the 'cult of motherhood' films in the sound era but was not particularly successful with audiences or critics,[7] Orol adapted a sentimental story by Julián

Cisneros Tamayo and hit the mother lode with *Madre querida*. Released on the tenth of May to coincide with Mother's Day in Mexico (a day which had acquired great significance since its 'creation' in 1922),[8] the film was a resounding success, earning more than 500,000 pesos in the D.F. alone. In a sense, given its carefully arranged promotional angle, *Madre querida* could be considered the first Mexican film to be marketed with the panache and hucksterism later associated with exploitation cinema: in a later interview, Orol claimed that during the film's first theatrical run he handed out handkerchiefs as viewers bought their tickets, promising a complete refund if they were not used during the screening (De la Vega Alfaro, 1987: 30).

Madre querida begins with a long introduction by Orol himself, dressed in suit and tie, in which he dedicates the film to the *madrecitas* of the world who, as mothers, have suffered. With a still-thick Castilian accent and speaking like a radio announcer, Orol emotionally exalts motherhood as that which "makes men more human" contrasted with images of various monuments to motherhood. Again inspired by *radionovelas*, the film proper begins in an elementary school during recess: a group of boys talk about what they are going to buy their mothers for Mother's Day. Juanito complains that he has no money to buy a present and Luisito, a younger boy, gives him fifty cents because he has lost his mother. Having already established its melodramatic premises, the film completes the background of each of the two boys. Luisito is a spirited prankster from a wealthy family; his mother died in childbirth. Manuel, his lonely father, confesses to his uncle the reason for his perennial sadness (via two elaborate flashbacks which include three musical numbers—his loved one was a singer—two of them in a sad Baja California cabaret): he once had a great love in Cuba, his family kept them apart, and when he returned to Cuba he could not find her. Juanito, on the other hand, is serious and hard-working (selling newspapers and pumping gas) to help his humble single mother, Adela, make ends meet. After Luisito accidentally sets a gas station on fire when playing with fireworks, Juanito is accused of arson and, rather than betray his friend, accepts the blame and goes to a reformatory. Broken-hearted, Juanito's mother becomes gravely ill. The remorseful Luisito finally confesses the truth to his father, who tries to help Juanito and his mother. Of course, the dying Adela is Manuel's long lost love. She dies after telling Manuel that Juanito is his son. Meanwhile, Juanito has escaped from the reformatory to see his mother and, after learning of her death, takes to the streets. Finally, Manuel runs into Juanito at Adela's tomb, tells him he is his father and takes him home, where he eventually recovers.

As this plot synopsis demonstrates, Orol managed to create the urtext of maternal exaltation and sentimentalism. Dripping in melodramatic excess, the film required few stylistic flourishes beyond its already excessive narrative, although Orol seemed much taken with superimpositions, using them extensively to illustrate the ferocity of the fire Luisito accidentally ignites and Juanito's delirious dreams in which his mother comes to his beside as a ghostly apparition. Perhaps the key to understanding the film's success is to unravel its relationship to radio. *Madre querida* actually begins as an illustrated radio program and, building radio into the narrative itself, sustains a constant radiophonic vision and affect. Very early in the film, in the second flashback that explains the disappearance of Manuel's love in Cuba, he recounts that he learned that she had gone into radio to make a living and had later gone to Baja California. The flashback begins in the sleazy Baja nightclub, where Adela sings two numbers almost back-to-back in a decidedly radiophonic style: she stands frozen in front of a microphone, does not dance or emote, and barely acknowledges the audience. Later in the film, Luisito and his father sit by a large radio and listen to a radio announcer sending children a special Mother's Day message asking them to recognize the value of their mothers. Echoing Orol's sentiments and tone in the prologue, the presence of the radio positions the spectator into a similar heart-wrenching mode of spectatorship. Though cinematic, the experience translates into affective terms that would be instantly familiar and satisfying to audiences already well trained in—and in love with—the sentimentality of *radionovelas*.

The other big hit of 1935, *Luponini (El terror de Chicago)* took a very different approach to capturing the public's attention. Capitalizing on the popularity of Hollywood gangster films in the early 1930s and the fact that the post-1934 Production Code precluded the depiction of gangsters as tragic heroes, Bohr loosely adapted the story of notorious bank robber John Dillinger, who had been executed by the FBI in July 1934 as he was leaving a movie theater. In Bohr's version, Dillinger becomes Luponini (his character's alias in *¿Quién mató a Eva?*) who, in addition to having the physical agility that Dillinger had been famous for, is also a skilled singer and entertainer.

Once again exhibiting an excellent command of the medium, Bohr manages to take the more significant elements of the Dillinger story—his spectacular crimes and physical agility, the relentless taunting of the police, the daredevil escapes, the details of his death—and to embody them with a psychological motivation: Luponini, a somewhat frivolous bank teller with loose principles, wants to date the bank manager's daughter but is rebuffed because he doesn't have money. Later he marries another bank teller, Luisa, but after spending their first year of married life unemployed, she too rejects him to look for a man with money. At that crossroads, in a dramatic clenched-hand gesture that will become a leitmotif for the film (see Figure 1.6), Lupo (as he is called by his friends) swears that he will get money, lots of money, and will throw it in her face. Elegantly matching the clenched fist, the next shot brings us to the pool hall, where Lupo's criminal life begins with his friend "El Chato."

Lupo's life of crime is quickly established and documented by the detailed presentation of their first successful bank heist—eerily featuring only ambient sounds, which renders it essentially silent—and a frenzied montage of newspaper headlines and radio announcers breaking the news of yet another bank robbery committed by the man the press had dubbed *"el hombre mono"* (the monkey man) because of his physical prowess. The

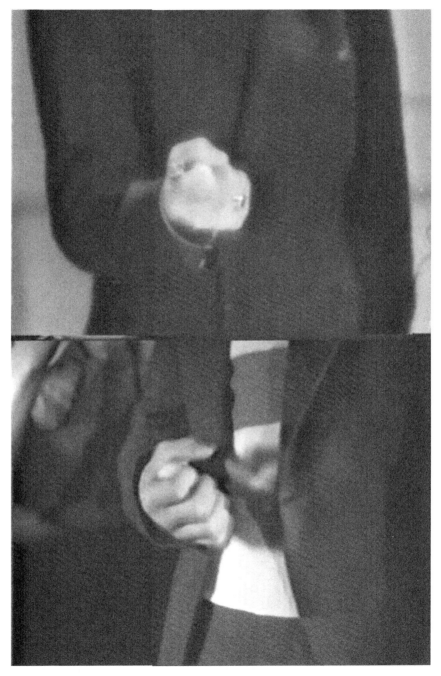

Figure 1.6 Clenched-hand gesture in *Luponini (El terror de Chicago)*/Luponini, the Terror of Chicago (Bohr, 1935).

crimes are, certainly by the standards of the Production Code–regimented
Hollywood cinema, lurid: Lupo and his gang are indiscriminate shooters
and have no qualms about killing anyone who stands in their way and/or
shooting at innocent crowds. Then, in another long scene also with only
ambient noises, Lupo robs the bank where he and Luisa worked. This heist
is complicated, but has been meticulously planned and timed, down to the
arrival of a gang member dressed as a motorcycle courier who struts directly
to the just opened bank vault, empties it into his valise, and smoothly drives
off with the loot. Another complication is that Luisa is still a teller in the
bank; in fact, she is the first to come in and be tied up. As he gets ready
to leave, Lupo grabs a fistful of money and, staring menacingly through
a bandanna that covers most of his face, throws it at her. That stare will
prove to be the beginning of his undoing: Luisa recognizes his eyes (see Figure 1.7) and, without thinking, yells out: "Those eyes . . . It's him!"

Although she doesn't hand him over to the police, Luisa is suspected
of helping "*el hombre mono*," loses her job and goes to Lupo at his new
place of employment: he has become an entertainer at a cinema and at El
Chato's new oddly decorated restaurant/cabaret. The bulk of the rest of the
film takes place in the milieu of this cabaret, where Lupo's new girlfriend,
La Maravilla, is a singing/dancing attraction, another old friend Isabel is a
hat-check girl, and Luisa becomes a tap dancer. The space of the cabaret,

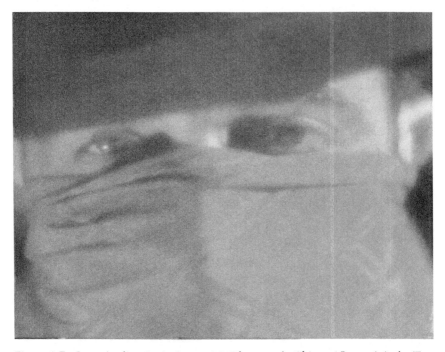

Figure 1.7   Lupo in disguise in *Luponini (El terror de Chicago)*/Luponini, the Terror of Chicago (Bohr, 1935).

as in later *cabaretera* films, is luxuriously baroque—a mood generated via mise-en-scène and Bohr's exemplary use of mirror shots to create depth— and a microcosm of passions: the women are always at each other's throats. In between several performances and rehearsals, the police very effectively incite Luisa and La Maravilla's jealousy to break them down; through an informer they are convinced Lupo is "*el hombre mono*," despite a history of rheumatism (for which he ostentatiously puts a wool glove on his right hand) and childhood accidents which render him less than agile. Lupo and his gang are planning one last heist of the nightclub itself, but when it sours they barely make it out after killing and wounding many and a spectacular chase ensues, chronicled by a montage of police calls and radio announcers and punctuated by spectacular shots of cars and motorcycles careening around curves. Finally Lupo throws his car down an embankment and manages to crawl away and disappear . . . in order to find a plastic surgeon to change his face.

Sporting his Asian new look, Lupo locates Luisa and Isabel's hideout, reads about La Maravilla's success in a newspaper, and decides to go see her. Simultaneously hounded by the police, Luisa cannot control her jealousy and, after a long interrogation punctuated by a cop knocking on a wood table relentlessly, gives up his identity and location at the Cine Esperanza, where La Maravilla performs.

The cops set up a trap at the theater, but as Luisa approaches Lupo to lead him out, he breaks down, confesses his love and asks her to remarry and go far away. In the lobby, with a big poster for *Delator* in the background (Spanish for John Ford's *The Informer*), Lupo swears his love. He is shot down spectacularly when he steps out of the theater and, after overhearing a report that Luisa has given up Lupo for 50,000 pesos, kills her, bemoaning "money always money." The last shot of the film is a dramatic close-up of a mirror reflecting the word "Fin," which is gradually covered in blood.

Obviously very familiar with the Hollywood gangster film, Bohr adapted the genre to address his own creative strengths and attempted to localize it. Though the film is set in "any country in the world" (Bohr was worried about potential censorship), the ambience is unmistakably 100 percent urban Mexican. And, as inevitable in any Mexican film of the era, its copious musical numbers mark it as the product of generic hybridization not only of Hollywood musicals but of the musicality of radio. Here too, different than in *Madre querida*, radio leaves its mark: the instant communication provided by radio announcers with "breaking news" enables the police to close in on Luponini and the diegetic public to learn of his exploits.

AFTER *RANCHO GRANDE*

In 1936, the eventual unexpected success of Fernando de Fuentes's modest production *Allá en el rancho grande/Over on the Big Ranch* radically changed the climate for filmmaking and introduced a new, uniquely

Mexican genre, the *comedia ranchera* (the rural comedy) (López, 1994). Over the next two years, the febrile pace and experimentation of the early sound entrepreneurs dissipated as it became clear that one 'formula' had risen above all others. Orol, Bohr, and Peón continued in the business, but their generic experiments lost their saliency. For example, Bohr produced another excellent crime film in 1936, *Marihuana, el monstruo verde/Marijuana, the Green Monster*,[9] but subsequently abandoned the genre, ostensibly looking for greater financial security, and jumped on the *comedia ranchera* bandwagon with *Por mis pistolas*/By My Guns (1937) and *Canto a mi tierra*/Song to My Land (1938), which introduced Pedro Vargas to the screen. In late 1939 he returned to Chile. Orol busily mined the suffering mother/wife genre with three films only to fall in with the *comedia ranchera* with *El derecho y el deber*/Right and Duty (1937). By 1938 he was in financial trouble and decided to look for other opportunities in Cuba. He only returned to Mexico in 1943 and his subsequent work is part of a dramatically different industrial environment. Peón, always somewhat of a director-for-hire, worked ceaselessly across genres: historical dramas, suffering mothers and wives (*No basta ser madre*/Motherhood Isn't Enough, 1937, enshrined actress Sara García as "the mother of Mexico"), detective dramas, and the *comedia ranchera* (*La madrina del diablo*/The Godmother of the Devil, 1937, introducing Jorge Negrete). In 1938, excited about new possibilities after the creation of a new national producer, PECUSA, he also returned to Cuba (Agramonte and Castillo, 2003: 99–106).

The legacies of Orol, Bohr, and Peón encompass many of the characteristics of the future exploitation cinema in Mexico. They made films quickly and inexpensively with often surprisingly good box-office returns. Their films reflected both national concerns as well as their own transnationalities and were thus among the very first Mexican films to attract international audiences. They were generically hybrid, combining the most spectacular elements of the cinema and radio, whether extraordinary sentimentalism or crime and violence, with that one mainstay of the early Mexican sound cinema that would endure: music, dance, and performance. Some of the generic mixes they pioneered—maternal exaltation, salacious melodrama—would become central to Mexican cinema. Others—horror, gangsters, and crime—would disappear almost entirely from the post-*Allá* 'Golden Age,' only to return, in the periphery as that which we now call latsploitation cinema.

NOTES

1. Since 1926, Mexican regulations required Spanish for all radio broadcasts, 25 percent Mexican music content, and banned religious programming (Hayes, 2000).
2. The first radionovela produced by XEW in 1932 was *Los tres mosqueteros* (The Three Musketeers) written by Alejandro Galindo and his brother Marco

Aurelio. See "Historia de W Rádio México," http://www.wradio.com.mx/historia.asp?id=196949, accessed July 1, 2008.
3. The D.F. or Distrito Federal was officially created on December 31, 1928.
4. That privilege has been reserved for the films of Fernando de Fuentes, Arcady Boytler, Alejandro Galindo, and, to a lesser degree, Juan Bustillo Oro, Gabriel Soria, and Miguel Contreras Torres.
5. In an interview with Alfredo Pelayo for the 1982 TV series *Los que hicieron nuestro cine*/The Ones who Created Our Cinema, Orol claimed that audiences laughed at moments when they were meant to cry. He reedited it and rereleased it in second-run theaters, where it apparently did much better (De la Vega Alfaro, 1987: 25).
6. Similar to *Redes* but independent of the State, *Janitzio* (1934, released 1935; dir. Carlos Navarro) also exalted the indigenous (and provided Emilio Fernández with his first starring role).
7. A contemporary critic called it "perhaps the least Mexican of the films made in Mexico" (De la Vega Alfaro, 1992: 110).
8. Orchestrated by the newspaper *Excelsior* in Mexico City in an effort to counter the very liberal initiatives promoting sex education and women's rights emanating from the liberal state of Yucatán (Acevedo, 1982: 8).
9. Although it is tempting to suggest a link between Bohr and the drug-abuse exploitation films making the rounds in the United States around this same time (such as Dwain Esper's *Narcotic*, 1933), there is no evidence that this was the case.

Part I

Latsploitation Beyond Borders

2 "Perversa América Latina"

The Reception of Latin American Exploitation Cinemas in Spanish Subcultures

Antonio Lázaro-Reboll

In its 1999 November issue, the Spanish fanzine *2000 maniacos* proposed to its readers the idea of a Trash Cinema "World Cup" ("Primer mundial caspa, 1999"). The essential criteria for qualification were . . . none and there were no rules (Liejas 1999a: 20). Spain as the host nation qualified automatically. Fifteen other countries made it to the finals. The strongest exploitation squads defended their countries with their most celebrated directors and stars: the United States, Mexico, Japan, France, Germany, the Philippines, Argentina, Turkey, Hong Kong, Italy, India, Indonesia, England, and Brazil. (The sixteenth country, the United Women of America, was invited purely for marketing and voyeuristic purposes.) In a patriotic act of celebratory fandom, *2000 maniacos* made sure that the winner was Spain. However, as one can see from the lineup, Latin America was well represented: Argentina, Brazil, and Mexico had a welcome reception on Spanish soil.

The final selection of players representing the individual nations does not present too many surprises. Mexico's manager, René Cardona, knowing a thing or two about fights, fielded Santo, El Enmascarado de Plata (The Man in the Silver Mask), who was flanked by two mexploitation directors, Federico Curiel and Miguel M. Delgado. On the bench were two very physical players just in case things got nasty, Wolf Rubinskis, aka Neutrón, and Murciélago (Bat) Velázquez. Argentina's formation was picked by Spanish Narciso Ibáñez Menta, who relied on the unpredictable vision of Armando Bó while León Klimovsky and Emilio Vieyra did the more mechanical work; Bó's secret weapons to distract the opposition were Isabel Sarli and Libertad Leblanc. What about the most imaginative team in the football world, Brazil? Player-manager José Mojica Marins/Zé do Caixão counted with Iván Cardoso to produce some magic and bury the opposition's efforts. If you want to know how Mexico, Argentina, and Brazil performed, you will have to read the match reports in the fanzine *2000 maniacos*.[1]

This chapter proposes to look at the general performance of Latin American exploitation cinemas, as well as their cultural meaning, in contemporary Spanish contexts of reception through an analysis of their circulation, consumption, and reception in very specific sites of exhibition and audience reception, namely, the Semana de cine fantástico y de terror de San Sebastián (Horror and Fantasy Film Festival) in its tenth and thirteenth editions and the fanzine *2000 maniacos*. The collaboration between the festival organizers and the fanzine's director and editor, Valencia, has yielded two issues devoted completely to Latin American exploitation cinema: "México loco superespecial. Chilli Terror" ("Superspecial Mad Mexico. Chilli Terror" issue 22) published in 1999 after the festival's retrospective on "Cine psicotrónico mexicano" ("Mexican psychotronic cinema") (see Figure 2.1) and "Bizarre latino" ("Latino Bizarre" issue 26) in 2002 following the retrospective "Perversa América Latina" ("Perverse Latin America") featuring a broader geographical and historical coverage of the continent's exploitation fare. Thus, the chapter looks at a localized cult response to Latin American exploitation cinemas.[2]

Subcultural products and ideologies such as fanzines and institutions such as film festivals provide the spaces and practices from which to make strategic interventions in the remapping of Spanish and Latin American cinematic histories and canons, with an emphasis on the inclusion of discourses and subgroups hitherto largely excluded from official accounts of film history and mainstream criticism. Fanzines like *2000 maniacos* escape critical scrutiny. They are hardly considered worthy objects of study for their ephemeral character and for their focus on specific subcultures. Whether considered as repositories of trivia or sites of marginalized subcultural ideologies, fanzines have been far removed from the center of cultural debates and excluded from histories of Spanish and Latin American cinema. The San Sebastián Horror and Fantasy Film Festival has been linked to fan activity since its first issue in 1989, screening the latest world horror production as well as classics, programming cult revivals and retrospectives, re-creating the American midnight movie craze, and allowing fans to express their affection for movies. Key players in contemporary Spanish horror production (for example, Jaime Balagueró, Nacho Cerdá, or Paco Plaza) have emerged among the festival regulars, who then went on to enter their shorts and debut feature films in the festival's official sections. Throughout the years it has also contributed to the dissemination of horror film culture by publishing books.[3] Furthermore, it enabled the creation of spaces and networks of communication such as the "Encuentro de fanzines" (Fanzine Convention), organized between 1996 and 2003, where fanzines have regularly presented their work to the horror fandom community and competed for financial reward.[4] By examining the collaboration between the festival and the fanzine, my aim is to acknowledge fan activities and practices as invaluable resources for studying the trajectory of Latin American exploitation cinemas in Spain. But the links between Spanish and Latin American exploitation cinema go beyond contemporary genre festivals and exploitation fandom for obvious historical, linguistic, and cultural reasons.

Figure 2.1 Poster for the San Sebastián Horror and Fantasy Film Festival's retrospective on "Cine psicotrónico mexicano."

TOWARDS A TOPOGRAPHY OF "TRASH-ATLANTIC" CONNECTIONS

A detailed topography of the transatlantic traffic of ideas, artists, and products between Spain and Latin American countries, with particular focus on the 1960s and 1970s, the heyday of exploitation filmmaking, is yet to be mapped out.[5] Coproductions, the cross-border movements of personnel, and the intercultural communication of images would enable us to understand the cultural geography of Latin American exploitation cinemas and their life beyond their respective territories. It is not my purpose here to provide a detailed narrative of coproductions (for instance, Ecuador and Spain in *El pantano de los cuervos/The Swamp of the Ravens* (Manuel Caño, 1973, and Mexico and Spain in *Santo contra el Dr. Muerte/Doctor Death/Santa vs. Doctor Death/The Saint vs. Doctor Death* (Rafael Romero Marchent, 1973) and *Navajeros/Dulces navajas* (Eloy de la Iglesia, 1980), directors who worked on both sides of the Atlantic (Argentinean Klimovsky), traveling actors and actresses (Alberto Dalbes, Perla Cristal, Rosanna Yanni—all from Argentina), or the almost impossible task of reconstructing the exhibition of El Santo's films which were screened in the double bills of the long gone *cines de barrio* (neighborhood cinemas), which attracted young audiences mainly,[6] but rather to identify and examine specific cinematic contact zones that enable us to draw parallels between Spanish and Latin American exploitation cinemas of the 1960s and 1970s: firstly, their marginal status in their respective filmic historiographies; and, secondly, their transnational status in the global culture of psychotronia.

The critical reception and exhibition of Latin American exploitation cinemas suffered the same critical fate as Spanish exploitation fare. In the same way that the officially sanctioned 'Nuevo Cine Español' (New Spanish Cinema) was privileged by specialist film magazines and mainstream film criticism, the New Latin America Cinemas of the late 1960s and early 1970s reached various spaces of exhibition (festivals and art-house cinemas) and sites of reception like *Nuestro Cine* and *Film Ideal*, whose critics welcomed Brazilian *cinema novo* as a kindred spirit for autochthonous oppositional filmmaking directors. While the festival and the art-house circuit enabled the viewing of New Latin American Cinemas, the films of Bó and Mojica Marins would not reach Spanish shores until the end of the dictatorship in 1975 and the abolition of censorship in 1977.[7] This means that Sarli's body was not exposed to Spanish audiences until 1977 with *Los días calientes/The Hot Days* (1965); *Fiebre/Fever* (1970) will have to wait until 1979, *Fuego/Fire* (1968) until 1980, and *Carne/Meat* (1968) a decade later. In the context of the Transition period, *Fuego*, as well as other Latin American subgeneric products, are packaged and classified under the short-lived category of Cine 'S'—a rating for adult films whose theme or content might offend the sensibility of the spectator, not just meant for softcore pornography but also for potentially violent and politically incendiary material.[8] But Sarli and other sex bomb Latinas, as defined by *2000 maniacos*, will only become erotic myths and, by extension, acquire cult status, in the contemporary context of psychotronic fandom at the turn of the twenty-first century. These specific contexts of reception reflect therefore different industrial, cultural, and technological moments in the recent history of Spanish cinema.

The critical reception of Latin American exploitation cinemas is a fairly recent and localized phenomenon. With the exception of coverage of individual directors Mojica Marins and Alejandro Jodorowsky in the horror and science fiction film magazine *Terror Fantastic* and the popular film magazine *Nuevo Fotogramas* in the early 1970s, the critical reception of Latin American exploitation was nonexistent. Journalist and fan Luis Gasca brought to the attention of horror aficionados the strange world of Mojica Marins in "Tropicalismo sangriento: el extraño mundo del brasileño Zé do Caixão" ("Bloody Tropicalism: The Strange World of Brazilian Coffin Joe," 1971) and "Mojica Marins: donde el instinto supera a la razón" ("Mojica Marins: Where Instinct Surpasses Reason," 1972), offering informative dossiers on the exceptional life of the director, his filmic production, and the exploitation of his alter ego Zé do Caixão in TV, comics, and merchandising. As for Jodorowsky, it is his avant-garde experimental theater work with the Grupo Pánico that is unorthodoxly and ingeniously reviewed by Pierrot (aka Antonio Gracía) in pieces like "Elucubraciones, desmayos y gritos sobre el Teatro-Pánico de Alejandro Jodorowsky" ("Lucubrations, Faints and Screams over Alejandro Jodorowsky's Panic Theater," 1972). These days both directors are cult staples in pyschotronic film Web sites, blogs, and online horror fans' message boards,[9] with links to information for the avid fan and the possibility of watching clips from many of these movies via YouTube.[10] Currently, Jodorowsky's appeal in Spain cuts across different audiences and tastes. On the one hand, his films have propelled him into auteur status in genre festivals, while, on the other, his varied literary and artistic production has made of him a key creative force in the world of Hispanic culture.[11] The cultural magazine *ClubCultura*, produced by FNAC España, and the Web site ClubCultura.com, which houses Jodorowsky's official homepage (www.alejandro-jodorowsky.com), consider Jodorowsky one of the most relevant contemporary Ibero-American authors, alongside, among others, Isabel Allende, Julio Cortázar, Ana María Matute, or Eduardo Mendoza. Canonized via membership in this literary club, Jodorowsky's is now right in the mainstream, appealing to middle-brow tastes.

Latin American exploitation cinemas were inaccessible and unobtainable for Spanish viewers and fans until the second half of the 1980s, when video stores and mail catalogue orders started to make them available. *2000 maniacos* editor Manuel Valencia reminisces in interviews about those outlets in his home town, Valencia, which have allowed him to build his film collection and provided him with the material subsequently reviewed in the first issues of the fanzine.[12] A look at any issue of *2000 maniacos* from 1989 to the present reveals a familiarity with "paracinema" publications: for instance, Michael Weldon's complete guides to psychotronic cinema *The Psychotronic Encyclopedia of Film* (1983), *The Psychotronic Videoguide to Film* (1996), and the cult movie fanzine *Psychotronic Video* (1989–2006), as well as B-movie specialist magazines *Video Watchdog* and *Filmfax*, and, more recently, volumes such as Pete Tombs's *Mondo Macabro: Weird and Wonderful Cinema Around the World* (1997), whose translation into Spanish in 2003 contributed further to the dissemination of Mexican, Brazilian, and Argentinean exploitation among Spanish exploitation fans. In fact, the visual aesthetics of *2000 maniacos* and other fanzine publications attests to a do-it-yourself ethic in its production—which is in itself a very exploitation *modus operandi*—since most of the graphic material has been poached from international catalogues and fanzines; likewise, the images of publicity posters are black-and-white or color reproductions from video and DVD covers, and stills are home-made photographs directly taken from the television screen. As Jeffrey Sconce (1995: 387) and Joan Hawkins have observed, "paracinema culture is heavily indebted to video technology" (Hawkins, 2000a: 34), mail-order video and DVD catalogues. In the reception of Latin American exploitation cinemas in Spanish subcultures, the transatlantic journey for these commodities is not the one you would have expected—Latin America–Spain—but rather United States–Spain via psychotronic film distributors (Video Watchdog, Sinister Cinema, Mondo Macabro), and, lately, via cyberspace, namely, through Internet file sharing and the online network YouTube, which have become a common everyday practice among fans for personal consumption and for trading with other members of the community.[13] Access to these films, whether through specialized outlets, paracinema catalogues, or the Internet, raises questions about the versions that fans have purchased and viewed since more often than not Latin American exploitation films have been seen through a foreign filter; furthermore, bootlegs, dubbed tapes, or uncut copies become part of the quest and consumption of these films. The reception of Latin American exploitation cinemas in Spain is therefore always mediated through fandom culture.[14] And *2000 maniacos* is arguably the best example of such fan practices. Let us focus on this fanzine and the ways in which Valencia and his collaborators write about and read Latin American psychotronic cinemas.

2000 MANIACOS: EXPLOITATION, GORE AND NUDITY

Taking its name from the classic exploitation pic *2,000 Maniacs* (Herschell Gordon Lewis, 1964), *2000 maniacos* published its first issue in August 1989. One hundred copies were produced and the price tag was a hundred pesetas ($1). Like any other fanzine publication, it has been unpredictable in its publication. However, it is approaching its third decade, which makes it possibly the oldest fanzine in Europe. There are two important turning points in the life of the publication: firstly, its distribution went national with issue 13 devoted exclusively to the porn queen Traci Lords; and, secondly, its 'official' association with the San Sebastián Horror and Fantasy Film Festival since 1992, with a special issue celebrating the retrospective on Italian horror cinema "Tutto Italia" ("All Italy"), has contributed to a much wider distribution (two thousand copies) and a quality far removed from the do-it-yourself amateurism of the original bundle of black-and-white photocopies (the price these days is 7 euros [$10]). *2000 maniacos* trades in horror, gore, porn, and exploitation, covering the low end of the horror market and the high and low end of the porn market. It provides its niche readership with a wealth of archival and collector information on international psychotronic culture. While Valencia is the main writer, there has been a number of regular collaborators whose names are well known in the subcultural field of the Spanish fanzine scene from the mid-1980s to the early 2000s: Jesús Palacios, Alex Zinéfilo, Sandra Uve, Borja Crespo, Charly Álvarez, and Casto Estópico, to name but a few.

Latin American exploitation cinemas have been the subject of two issues, "Chilli terror mexicano" (see Figure 2.2) and "Bizarre latino," though production from Latin America is covered in other editions.[15] The "México loco superespecial" issue opens with a star contribution: Guillermo del Toro "lays bare his hard-core fan heart" and writes "his very personal inventory of Mexican psychotronia" (1999: 5), providing a chronological overview of films and directors—from *La Llorona*/The Weeping Woman (Ramón Peón, 1933) and *Profanación* (Chano Urueta, 1933) to *Kalimán* (Alberto Mariscal, 1970)—and focusing on specific Mexican horror traditions and horrific creations (1999b: 5–11). Hailed as "one of us," in an echo of the famous line of Tod Browning's *Freaks* (1932), del Toro's fan kudos is reverentially acknowledged by Charly Álvarez (1999b: 59) and later complemented by an interview in which he displays once again his fan connoisseurship yet this time in his role as director (1999b: 52–59). The Mexican director's personal review is followed by an alphabetically arranged catalogue of "who's who" in Mexican horror and fantasy production ("México lindo y superloco" ["Beautiful and Crazy Mexico," Carmen Elisa Gómez and Pablo Herranz, 1999b: 12–21]), which functions as a series of encyclopedic entry points to the world of Mexican exploitation fare, and then a decalogue of reasons to "let yourself be snatched by Mexican fantasy cinema" ("10 razones para ser abducido por el cine fantástico mexicano" [Lieja, 1999b: 22–23]). For a fan of Mexican horror cinema and a compulsive list maker like me, Doctor P. K. Lieja's is preaching to the converted. But wherein lies the attraction for Mexican exploitation cinema? From a merely cultural and linguistic point of view, the playfulness and richness of Mexican-Spanish and the flouting of grammar conventions inscribed in many film titles are a cause for celebration for Spanish fans ("*¿Santo vs. las mujeres vampiro? ¿Santo vs. las mujeres vampiras? ¿Santo versus mujeres*

Figure 2.2   Cover of *2000 maniacos* (1999 issue 22).

vampiros?" [1999b: 22][16] seem to disarmingly disregard basic gender and number agreements); from a filmic tradition standpoint, these films are a prime example of exploitation practices at the level of production, distribution, and advertising: the moments of spectacle in the shape of "bellas sin alma" (soulless beauties), "luchadores enmascarados" (masked wrestlers), and "monstruos bajitos" (shortish monsters) (1999b: 22), the generic hybridity on display, the distribution of hot and cold versions for different venues and territories,[17] and, above all, the unique, colorful advertising tactics, which, in most cases, are "more thrilling than what is then seen on the screen" (1999b: 22).

Whilst del Toro, Gómez, Herranz, and Doctor P. K. Lieja present the *2000 maniacos* readership with the broader picture of Mexican exploitation cinema, Valencia enlisted connoisseurs from different fields of cultural production. Academic Eduardo de la Vega Alfaro sheds light on Fernando Méndez (1999b: 32–37); archivist and curator Rogelio Agrasánchez Jr., supplies inside knowledge about his father's productions (1999b: 48–51), together with an exuberant selection of popular film posters from the Agrasánchez Film Archives collection for the delight of readers (1999b: 76–77); journalist and novelist Mauricio-José Schwarz analyses wrestling superheroes El Santo and Superbarrio from a sociological perspective (1999b: 64–67); and Brian Moran, editor of American fanzine *Santo Street*, talks to Herranz about his fannish enthusiasm for wrestling women, Aztec mummies, and all things mexploitation (1999b: 40–43).[18] Added to these, a bibliography and a list of Internet resources, and even an index, give the fanzine a scholarly air. In fact, "Chilli terror mexicano" could be described as "the fanzine-as-dissertation," as "a site where academic knowledge may also circulate outside the academy" (Hills, 2002: 18) and therefore a contribution to the historical and cultural valorization of Mexican exploitation film history. In this respect, "Bizarre latino" functions as a second installment and contribution to the revision of Latin American exploitation cinemas, and, by extension, Spanish and Latin American cinematic encounters, histories, and canons.

A total of eleven films featured in the retrospective "Perversa América Latina" in the 13th edition of the San Sebastián Horror and Fantasy Film Festival, including a specific focus on films by Chilean Jodorowsky (*Fando y Lis/Fando and Lis*, 1967; *El topo/The Mole*, 1970; *La montaña sagrada/ The Holy Mountain*, 1973; and *Santa sangre/Holy Blood*, 1989) and Brazilian José Mojica Marins (*À meia noite levarei sua alma/At Midnight I Will Take Your Soul*, 1964; *Esta noite encarnarei no teu cadáver/At Midnight I Will Possess Your Corpse*, 1967; *Ritual dos sádicos/O despertar da besta/Awakening of the Beast*, 1969). The Bó-Sarli tandem (*Carne*, 1968) and newcomers Pablo Parés and Hernán Sáez (*Plaga zombie: Zona mutante/Zombie Plague: Mutant Zombie*, 2001) formed the Argentinean contingent, and the program was completed by a classic Mexican horror film (*El esqueleto de la Sra. Morales/Skeleton of Mrs. Morales* [Rogelio A. González, 1959]) and a contemporary Brazilian production (*O escorpião escarlate/The Scarlet Scorpion* [Iván Cardoso, 1998]). All the filmmakers and films present in the retrospective—and more—were colorfully covered in *2000 maniacos*: "84 colorful pages" on "Cuba, Brasil, México, Colombia, Argentina y mucho + bizarre LATINO" ("and much more

Latino Bizarre"). The fanzine offered a comprehensive journey through the uncharted territory of Latin American exploitation cinemas. Whether the retrospective's program depended on the availability of the films, the personal taste of the festival organizers, or the already existing cult status of Jodorowsky, Mojica Marins and Bó might be an important factor to take into account in discussing how these showcases function as seedbeds for cult revivals, and, by extension, participate in the construction of a Latin American exploitation cinemas canon. In a similar manner, *2000 maniacos* also contributes to this process of canon formation for access to these films as well as extratextual materials on Latin American films, directors, and actors, demarcates the writings published in this special issue. 'Knowledgeability,' rarity, and inaccessibility are common terms in fan accounts. Pedro Calleja's first encounter with Bó and Sarli, for example, is mediated through a photocopied version of Jorge Abel Martín's *Los films de Armando Bó con Isabel Sarli* (1981), which he borrowed from a friend back in the early 1980s (Calleja, 2002: 44); since then, his fanatical quest for Bó-Sarli films has proved elusive, Calleja confesses: "after 20 years of obsessive dedication to international exploitation, I haven't been able to watch half of their films" (Calleja, 2002: 45). As more films are released and become available through mainstream retailers and dedicated paracinema outlets, the reception of Latin American exploitation is subject to change. Equally, the screening of films in specialized festivals and the publication of material will create new reception contexts which will make us revisit provisional canons and historiographies.

The name of the retrospective, "Perversa América Latina," the title of the fanzine, "Bizarre latino" (see Figure 2.3), and the visual representation of the event via publicity materials work as discursive mechanisms which further frame and shape the exhibition, circulation, and consumption of Latin American exploitation cinemas for Spanish audiences. The retrospective's poster, which is reproduced in the back cover of *2000 maniacos*, is clearly linked to American exploitation exhibition practices and strategies, while at the same time it might be argued that it sets in motion a series of stereotypes on Latin America (see Figure 2.4). On the one hand, it promotes the image of a burlesque and sexploitative Eve; on the other, the promise of transgression is blatantly localized in the poster's play on the Latin American stereotype of the woman as "devourer" ("devoradora de hombres") and exotic. In its conflation of female sexuality, voluptuousness, sensuality, and danger (explicitly marked by the snake coiling around her body), Latin American exploitation cinema might be said to be represented as the exotic Other: gendered feminine, portrayed as wild, weird, and savage. This signaling of exoticism, I would argue, is more an invitation to peep at first and then stare at an overlooked body of Latin American cinema through the lens of exploitation cinema than an attempt to exoticize Latin American exploitation cinemas as cultural Other. Notwithstanding the unashamed use of the representation of woman as spectacle, what the promotional material mobilizes is a long-standing tradition of exploitation film advertising and the

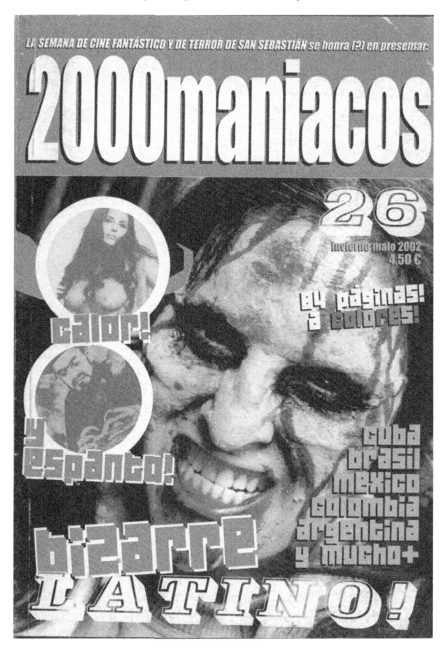

Figure 2.3   Cover of *2000 maniacos* (2002 issue 26).

belonging of Latin American exploitation cinemas to the "realm of bizarre cinema around the world" (Tombs, 1997: back page). Moreover, the quali-fication of Latin America's exploitation production as perverse knowingly

Figure 2.4   Poster for the San Sebastián Horror and Fantasy Film Festival's retrospective on "Perversa América Latina."

and ironically evokes the typical critical dismissal of exploitation cinema's attractions and perversions.

According to its brief editorial, issue 26 brings together "a wild bunch of maniacs" who "pay tribute and respect to the hottest and funniest Latin

America" because not only are they "the maddest, the most extravagant" but also "make pure psychotronic cinema" (Valencia, 2002: 4). Valencia and his contributors take the reader up and down the Latin American countries, charting exploitation "flicks," "chicks," and "freaks" (the Aztec mummy, the Brazilian bogeyman, the zombies from the pampas) and showing readers the ropes of trash aesthetics. *2000 maniacos* invites the reader on a journey ("travel with us to Latin America" [Valencia, 2002: 2]), promising "a tourist and crazy trip" and "a one-way ticket to the most vicious Latin America" (Álvarez, 2002: 20). The reader of paracinema catalogues and the potential buyer of products is usually, as Hawkins has noted in her analysis of exploitation fanzine culture and mail-order catalogue videos, "addressed as if he were a tourist" (2000a: 45). Psychotronic fandom is in a way the exploration and discovery of "every other historical manifestation of exploitation cinema" (Sconce, 1995: 372), a search for the obscure, the misunderstood, the uncharted. Psychotronic fans are also 'nomads,' always in movement, constantly advancing upon another text, appropriating new materials. Issue 26 is certainly this: an A to Z *à la* Weldon of Latin American psychotronia. It features interviews with star Isabel "Coca" Sarli (Calleja, 2002: 63), cult directors Jodorowsky (Palacios, 2002: 36–41), Mojica Marins (Zinéfilo, 2002: 30–33) and Cardoso (José Luis González Martínez, 2002: 70–71), new filmmakers Hernán Sáez (Valencia, 2002: 52–58) and Jorge Olguín from Chile (Sergei, 2002: 68–69), an auteurist overview of Bó (Calleja, 2002: 44–47), brief introductory articles on less known figures like Vieyra (Darío Lavia, 2002: 34–35) or Cuban Manuel S. Conde (Zinéfilo, 2002: 59–60), and more general articles on production across different nations and industries (Álvarez, 2002: 20–27), sex bomb latinas (Andrade, 2002: 64–67), Argentinean fanzine *La Cosa* (Valencia, 2002: 28–29) and Mexican subgeneric production (Herranz, 2002: 72–75). *2000 maniacos* offers therefore a wide-ranging overview of Latin American exploitation cinemas with its most representative players, genres, and films. It is to the films that I now turn, in particular to the ways in which the fanzine contributors write about Latin American psychotronic films, which, in the words of Valencia, have been "directly imported from mad and bizarre Latin American video stores" (2002: 14).

The film review section entitled "Graznidos tóxicos" ("Toxic Shrieks") provides us with a taste of the reading protocols one can encounter in the fanzine. By "reading protocol" here I understand not only the critical responses of the fans but also Sconce's textual category of paracinema, "a particular reading protocol, a counter-aesthetic turned subcultural sensibility devoted to all manner of cultural detritus" (1995: 372). The reading protocols in "Graznidos tóxicos" range from the auteurist to the historical to the purely pyschotronic, and the interpretive frameworks rely on intertextual references, generic conventions, transgeneric comparisons, extratextual information, and (sub)cultural connoisseurship. As Mark Jancovich argues in his analysis of *Film Threat* and *Psychotronic Video Watchdog*, "[e]ven within a single publication, the sheer eclecticism of the films discussed means that they are not read in one coherent way, but through a number of different and contradictory strategies which are constantly slipping into one another" (2002: 314). *2000 maniacos* is no different. The fifteen films considered follow the same format: the title of the film, a rating—which classifies films from "cult movie" to "um . . . interesting" to "abominable cataclysm"—screenplay credits, and the actual review. In the remaining space I will focus on those directed by Vieyra, René Cardona, José Díaz Morales, Enrique Carreras, Juan López Moctezuma, Jodorowsky, and Mojica Marins. Through an evaluation of these reviews I will be showing the ways in which fans write about the pleasures of exploitation and considering how fan discourses and academic discourses share conceptual and critical strategies which expose and challenge the limits of established Spanish and Latin American film historiographies.

The commentators' appreciation of the trash movie aesthetic comes to the fore in a number of reviews. In some cases reviewers perform ironic psychotronic readings celebrating the unintentionally bizarre or hilarious and wallowing in the unintentional artistic "brilliance" or "failure" of films. Thus, Susi Sexy's opening line for Cardona's *La horripilante bestia humana/Night of the Bloody Apes* (1968) succinctly introduces the film as "pure pyschotronic fare" (2002: 14). Its brilliance resides in its ingenuous titling and retitling in different territories (the classic horror title *Night of the Bloody Apes*, the openly exploitative *Horror and Sex*, or the more subgeneric *Gomar, the Human Gorilla*), a bizarre mad-doctor plot, and the explicit gore scenes which will please the trash film crowd. Valencia shares with us his viewing experience of *Profanadores de tumbas/ Santo contra los profanadores de tumbas/Santo versus the Grave Robbers* (Díaz Morales, 1964), writing with gusto about his particular psychotropic approach: the film "is a typical double-bill film . . . to be enjoyed at home, after a hangover, while you smoke some pot and leave your brain in stand-by" (Valencia, 2002: 15). Zinéfilo takes the reader through his more ordinary ritual: "I switch off the light, turn on the video, prepare some popcorn, grab a beer, sit comfortably, press play . . . and then disappointment sets in" (2002: 15). After having discovered Vieyra's *La venganza del sexo/The Curious Dr. Humpp* (1967), which he wholeheartedly recommended to *2000 maniacos* readers in a previous issue (1999a: 28–29), Zinéfilo acknowledges that he spent considerable time and financial effort in tracking *La bestia desnuda/The Naked Beast* (1967) and *Sangre de vírgenes/Blood of the Virgins* (1967) down. Unfortunately, *La bestia desnuda* turns out to be a failed, "unbearable homage to Dario Argento's first giallo" (2002: 15). There is only one scene that could be salvaged from the general "dullness and sloppiness" (2002: 15) which pervades throughout the film: a musical number whose homosexual undertones lend themselves to a queer reading and to speculate on Vieyra's sexual orientation. *Sangre de vírgenes* is another disappointment for this reviewer who wonders "how is it possible to produce a wonderful cult movie and two stinkers with the same core of collaborators?" in order to conclude that "'Vieyra's case' reaffirms once more the uncomfortable theory that the vast majority of cult movies are more the result of chance and fortuitousness than true cinematographic talent" (2002: 16).

But psychotronic appreciation (or despair) is not the only subcultural sensibility manifested in the reviews, for historical, generic, and aesthetic readings are performed by others. Herranz's reading of *Obras maestras de terror/Master of Horror* (1960) hardly addresses the formal and stylistic elements and focuses on the Spanish participation through the figures of Narciso Ibáñez Menta and his son Narciso Ibáñez Serrador, and their significance for both Argentinean and Spanish horror film and television histories. In his review of *Alucarda/Sisters of Satan/Innocents from Hell* (1975), Calleja reaches beyond its local context of production and positions López Moctezuma's film in relation to international horror traditions, namely, British (Hammer) and Spanish (Ibáñez Serrador). In addition to these intertextual subcultural references, Calleja also displays high intertextual cultural capital by explaining the filmmaker's relationship with the *Grupo Pánico*, in particular Jodorowsky, and with the surreal artist Leonora Carrington, and his involvement in the Mexican jazz scene (2002: 14).

Jodorowsky's cult auteur status seems to be at stake in two reviews which present a distinct difference in tone. An undoubted consideration of his auteur reputation sits next to a caustic view of his artistic persona and work. Whilst Ángel Vallejo ascribes auteur status to Jodorowsky through his reading of *El topo* and *La montaña sagrada*, Jordi Costa describes *Fando y Lis* (1968) as "a parodic auteur film" (2002: 19), and the filmmaker as "a trickster who has told the same story over and over again" (2002: 19). Vallejo interprets Jodorowsky's films through an auteurist framework by tracing a series of recurrent formal and stylistic concerns, which come to constitute a distinctive view of the world: the mystical and religious quest of the characters, who seek revenge and/or redemption, amidst a hallucinatory atmosphere (2002: 14). Such auteurist 'vision' is treated with aloofness and sarcasm by Costa, who, by way of an anthropological explanation, dismisses Jodorowsky's narratives of quest ("[his stories are] a rewriting of mythical accounts of self-discovery which are universal" (2002: 19); for Costa, Jodorowsky's films present us with an unavoidable choice between consecration or contempt: "*Fando y Lis* is . . . all or nothing. A fascinating piece of work or endless gibberish. Substandard avant-garde or pure poetry" (2002: 19). Mojica Marins's cult reputation, on the other hand, is unquestioned by Zinéfilo, who reviews the Brazilian director's 1960s productions (*À meia noite levarei sua alma, Esta noite encarnarei no teu cadáver* and *O despertar da besta*). Through his individual reviews, Zinéfilo unlocks some aspects of the strange world of Mojica Marins by striking a balance between the local significance of his films and his global cult status. *À meia noite levarei sua alma*, writes Zinéfilo, is a cult classic for several reasons: "its historical importance" since it was "the first horror film to be made in

Brazil" (2002: 17), its controversial impact in its country of origin since it transgressed contemporary cultural, social, and moral norms, and the vision of its creator since it is an exceptionally "personal, visceral, insulting, twisted, and refreshingly awkward" film (2002: 17), which combines transgressive, exploitative, popular, and avant-garde elements in a unique, frenzy manner. As the reviewer points out, the sequel, *Esta noite encarnarei no teu cadáver*, and *O despertar da besta* exploited both the popular success and controversy generated by the first film. The review of *Esta noite levarei sua alma* is structured around Mojica Marins's use of classic horror conventions and his psychotronic depiction of "hell in Eastmancolor" (2002: 18), whereas commentary on *O despertar da besta* pays special attention to the experimental and avant-garde elements of the film, concluding that the film is "a curious oddity halfway between American underground cinema (Waters, Morrisey, Kuchar . . .) and Latino surrealist cinema (Jodorowsky, Arrabal, . . .)" (2002: 19), which makes it partake of the counter-cinema aesthetics of the 1960s and 1970s. In his reviews, Zinéfilo is markedly sensitive to Mojica Marins's display of avant-garde, exploitation and trash aesthetics.

As most of these film reviews show, fan-writers display connoisseurship and a variety of reading strategies, and in many cases perform a "kind of dialectical cultural reading" (Hawkins, 2000a: 21) which cuts across high-brow, middle-brow, and low-brow references. These interpretive strategies do not differ from mainstream film reviewing and specialized film magazines' criticism. Furthermore, and put simply, fans and scholars do similar things, as current theorizations of exploitation cinema attest (see Sconce, 1995; Hawkins, 2000a; Betz, 2003). Fan subcultural production (*2000 maniacos*) and academic subcultural production tread similar critical territories. Although they occupy different institutional spaces—yet similar critical positions—within the field of exploitation, their discourses share expertise in (sub)generic and historical manifestations of exploitation cinema and set the agenda for a reevaluation of exploitation cinemas on both sides of the Atlantic. To acknowledge the critical intersections and interactions between various fields of cultural production—fan discourses, academic discourses, spaces for congregation—can only contribute to a richer picture of the cultural history of Latin American exploitation cinemas and to refigure related (Spanish and Latin American) film histories. Likewise, an institution like the San Sebastián Horror and Fantasy Film Festival, which has provided different generations of horror, exploitation, and psychotronic fans with venues not only to indulge in horror pleasures but also with networks where "fans from different walks of life gather together to share their fandom" (Hills, 2002: 61), must be written into the cultural history of Latin American exploitation cinemas. To borrow Hawkins's views on horror, fanzine culture and paracinema consumption are perhaps "the best vantage point[s] from which to study the cracks that seem to exist everywhere in late twentieth century [Spanish and Latin American] 'sacralized' film culture" (2000a: 28).

NOTES

1. Like many other fanzines, copies of *2000 maniacos* were flogged initially at gigs, fanzine and comic conventions, genre film festivals, or independent record and comic shops. My own collection certainly started that way. These days the fanzine is distributed to major comic shops in Spanish cities by DDT and can be obtained by contacting its editor Manuel Valencia (manolinv@inivia.es).

2. In this chapter I focus on the Semana de cine fantástico y de terror de San Sebastián and *2000 maniacos*. The International Week of Fantasy and Horror Movies held in Sitges since 1968 (the International Film Festival of Catalonia) was the first key player in the formation and maintenance of a horror fan culture in Spain. This festival provided the first space for the exhibition of Latin American exploitation cinema: Jodorowsky's *Fando y Lis* entered the official competition in 1969 and *Santa sangre* in 1989; so did the films of Mexican director Juan López Moctezuma in 1974 (*La mansión de la locura/The House of Madness*) and 1977 (*Alucarda*); Jodorowsky and Mojica Marins have been the object of tributes (the former in 1994 and again in 2006, the latter in 1997); and Mexican fantasy cinema was the subject of a retrospective entitled "Mad Mex" in 1991, which combined the work of exploitation filmmakers (Fernando Méndez [*El vampiro*, 1957], López Moctezuma [*Alucarda*], Alfonso Corona Blake [*Santo vs. las mujeres vampiro*, 1962], and auteurs Buñuel [*El ángel exterminador*, 1962, and *Simón del desierto*, 1964]; Arturo Ripstein [*La tía Alejandra*, 1978]). Likewise, there are a number of alternative publications and fanzines from the 1990s which have devoted some of their pages to Latin American exploitation cinema, El Santo and Mexican products being a favorite (see the film magazine *Ruta 66* (issues 47 and 108) or the now disappeared magazine *Flash-back* (issue 1, 1992) and fanzine *El grito* [issue 5, 1993]).

3. Since 1997 the festival has published several volumes on international horror film traditions: *Del giallo al gore. Cine fantástico y de terror italiano* (1997), *Cohen & Lustig* (1998), *Cine fantástico y de terror español, 1900–1983* (1999), *El cine fantástico y de terror de la Universal* (2000), *Cine fantástico y de terror alemán, 1913–1927* (2002), *Cine fantástico y de terror español, 1984–2004* (2005), and *American Gothic: Cine de terror USA, 1968–1980* (2007).

4. Among others, *Vampiria*, *Mudhoney*, *Dead Side*, *Sick Fun*, *Viva Poe*, *Mondo Brainless*.

5. As Alberto Elena has observed, "determining the number of Latin American films commercially shown in Spain, as well as their distribution by decade and context of production" is an arduous task (2003). Elena has been addressing the reception of Latin American cinema in Spain in a series of articles (1998, 1999, 2003) with particular focus on Mexican and Argentinean production.

6. The term *cine de barrio* can be translated as double-bill local cinema. Jordi Costa, for instance, recalls the repertory schedule of *cines de barrio* in a manner which sums up their role in the exhibition of popular genres in Spanish cinemas during his childhood and teenage years in the 1960s and 1970s: "we were used to watching a Santo, el Enmascarado de Plata film and a spaghetti western as part of the same double-bill" (Costa in Vallejo, 2006).

7. Jodorowsky's *Fando y Lis* was, at least, screened at the Sitges International Film Festival in 1969.

8. *Presidio de mulheres violentadas* (Antônio Polo Galante and Oswaldo de Oliveira, 1976) becomes *Aberraciones sexuales femeninas*, for example.

9. See Pedro Calleja's blog (www.pedrocalleja.blogin.com), who is a self-confessed fan of Sarli and Bó: "Isabel Sarli: La diosa neumática ¡Coca para todos!," "Entrevista con la Coca Sarli: la historia de AMOR más grande jamás contada" and "Carne sobre carne: El cine adulterado de Armando Bó', all of which have been published in *2000 maniacos*. See also "Isabel Sarli: Carne argentina de exportación" by Pablo Sapere in www.pasadizo.com, which also houses forums for fans.

10. See, for example, www.hellhammercito.blogspot ("José Mojica Marins [Zé do Caixão]"), www.cinefagia.com/terroruniversal ("El extraño mundo de Zé do Caixão"), or www.melanomafilms.net ("Maestros: José Mojica Marins").

11. Apart from the already mentioned 1994 and 2006 tribute in Sitges, Jodorowsky has received tributes and honorary awards at the Festival de Cine Iberoamericano held in Huelva (Spain) in 2001 and was awarded the Waldemar Daninsky Prize in the genre festival of Estepona (Spain), the Semana Internacional de Cine Fantástico y de Terror, in 2006. The 18th Horror and Fantasy Film Festival edition in San Sebastián in association with FNAC organized the screening of *Fando y Lis*, *El topo*, and *La montaña sagrada* as part of its parallel activities—the most recent instance of the circulation of Jodorowsky's work across specialized and mainstream audiences.

12. See "Entrevista a Manuel Valencia" in www.viruete.com (9 September 2005). He also admits that his publications on international porn cinema, *Videoguía X* (1994) and *Videoguía X* (II) (1996) would not have been possible without the role played by video stores.

13. International ventures such as the Mexican-American distributors Casa Negra Entertainment (www.casanegrafilms.com) provide for a very specialized market, namely, fans of classic Mexican horror. European and Spanish specialized also serve the Spanish fan community: for instance, London-based One-Eyed Film (www.oneyedfilms.com) define themselves as "horror and art-house specialist" in Latin American cinema, including in their catalogue the Ivan Cardoso Cult Collection and several Mojica Marins titles, and Madrid-based Phenomena DVD (http://phenomenadvd.eresmas.net) specializes in international cult cinema.

14. As part of the global consumption of psychotronia, a parallel could be drawn with the reception and consumption of mexploitation cinema in the United States: in the words of Syder and Tierney, "mexploitation has acquired a growing reputation in America among fans of cult and psychotronic cinema who in turn have their own sites of exhibition and sets of reading protocols" (2005: 50).

15. See, for example, issue 21 (1999a), which features an interview with Mojica Marins, or issue 34 (2005), a dossier on Isabel Sarli.

16. The grammatically incorrect *Santo vs. las mujeres vampiro* is the title of the film. But for the title to be grammatically correct, noun and adjective have to be in agreement; so it should read *Santo vs. las mujeres vampiras* (supposing vampire women to be feminine) or *Santo versus las mujeres vampiros* (supposing vampire women to be like generic vampires, masculine).

17. See Schaefer (1999: 73–75) for a description of "hot" and "cold" versions in the context of classical exploitation cinema. "Hot" versions would include graphic shots and nude scenes, whereas "cold" would not and would be mainly destined for exhibition in territories with censorship boards.

18. The contribution of Rogelio Agrasánchez Jr. coincided with the publication of his *Mexican Horror Cinema: Posters from Mexican Fantasy Films*.

3 Roger Corman Dis/covers Peru
National Cinema and Luis Llosa's *Hour of the Assassin/Misión en los Andes*

Jeffrey Middents

Director, writer, and producer Roger Corman has a fabled presence in the history of American cinema, directly responsible for beginning the careers of a number of notable American directors, including Francis Ford Coppola, Martin Scorsese, Jonathan Demme, Joe Dante, and Ron Howard. In addition to these, Corman produced a series of cheaply made genre films throughout Latin America and Asia under his production company Concorde-New Horizons throughout the 1980s. These produced very lucrative results, mainly because of an effective direct-to-video exhibition strategy in the United States. These films were made abroad primarily to capitalize on weak economies in countries which could nevertheless provide interesting natural settings. Given such low criteria, the rich location possibilities and the desperate financial downturn of the national economy in the 1980s, Peru was a natural choice for Corman's Concorde-New Horizons production company to exploit. In 1987, the first Corman-produced film was released: *Hour of the Assassin* starred former *CHiPs* heartthrob Erik Estrada as an assassin contracted by a corrupt government to assassinate the president-elect of the nonspecific Latin American country of 'San Pedro.' Continuing in 1989 with the futuristic, science fiction–crime film *Crime Zone*, Concorde-New Horizons would coproduce eleven films in Peru over the next seven years.[1]

Beverly Gray (2000) recounts an apocryphal story concerning how Corman found his original connection in Peru. According to screenwriter Fred Bailey, Corman was traveling sometime in the mid-1980s to Argentina to supervise a production when his plane had to land in Lima, Peru, due to inclement weather. Corman "got off the plane, took a taxi into town, opened up the yellow pages, and got somebody to find motion-picture production listings. [He] made a few calls asking who was the best filmmaker in Lima. . . . They all said, 'Luis Llosa.' [He] called him up, made a deal and was back on the airplane to Argentina in a couple hours." From Bailey's account, Gray concludes, "Corman, always on the lookout for exotic locales that would accommodate American filmmakers, *discovered* Peru" (2000: 171, my emphasis).

Gray's neocolonialist statement insinuates that Peru might be something of a virgin cinematic territory, ripe for exploitation—or, at least, exploitation filmmaking. In truth, a Peruvian filmmaking tradition had been active since at least the early 1960s with consistent production of short films since 1972 and of features since 1977. By the 1980s, Luis Llosa was a known figure within the media community, having produced and directed shorts for two very successful anthology films as well as some of the more innovative local television programming. By the end of the 1990s, Llosa would become the only Peruvian filmmaker to make it big in Hollywood, making such major studio films as 1994's *The Specialist* with Sharon Stone and Sylvester Stallone and 1997's *Anaconda* with Jennifer Lopez, Ice Cube, and Jon Voight. Yet when this last film earned more than $65 million, far more than any other Peruvian film, local film critics did not even mention this feat. In fact, in many written histories of Peruvian film, Llosa's work has been seriously undervalued in a national context, perhaps because his films have been entirely in English, or because they have dealt with low-brow topics and spectacle such as giant snakes. Ricardo Bedoya's book-length study of Peruvian film history, *100 años de cine en el Perú*, includes a small section on Llosa and Bedoya's exhaustive catalogue of films made in Peru (1995: 271–74). *Un cine reencontrado: Diccionario ilustrado de las películas peruanas* (1998) includes entries on Llosa's three movies made in Peru in the 1980s and 1990s. Nonetheless, Llosa is contextualized as 'a case apart,' with very little impact on the development of a sense of a Peruvian cinematic tradition. Subsequent discussions of the state of national cinematic production in Peru in any film-centric publications fail to discuss him in any manner, positive or negative.

Llosa's elision from Peruvian film history seems in part due to his sustained working relationship as producer and director with Corman, whose cavalier attitude in producing and acquiring cheaply made exploitation films around the world became renowned. That Corman is based in the United States exacerbates the problematic place of exploitation filmmaking within national cinematic contexts since these have in general been "habitually defined against Hollywood" (Crofts, 1998: 390). Indeed, the cultural and economic debate concerning 'cultural diversity' initiated by French diplomats during the 1993 talks concerning the General Agreement on Taxes and Tariffs is derived from concern about the audiovisual industry in the United States exacting a "domineering role in the cinematic and television world [to control] almost all national film markets" (Weber, 2004: 35). While not explicitly part of the Hollywood system, U.S. coproductions of exploitation cinema complicate the conventional view of how 'national cinema' is defined. Stephen Crofts has noted the emphasis "between the cultural mode of production, the modes of address of the art film—to the cultured, film-literate viewer—which characterizes art cinemas' distribution and exhibition channels, and art film genres," particularly characteristic of international coproductions (1998: 391). Andrew Higson has noted that this concept is often "used prescriptively rather than descriptively, citing what *ought* to be the national cinema, rather than describing the actual cinematic experience of popular audiences" (1989: 37). As a film that demonstrates a sense of *Peruvianness* both within the text as well as through exhibition practices, Luis Llosa's earliest feature challenges the traditional perspective of what constitutes national cinema. In examining the context of Peruvian production and exhibition practices in the mid-1980s, this paper reclaims Llosa's films made for Concorde-New Horizons, particularly *Hour of the Assassin*, within the Peruvian cinematic tradition and articulates why Peruvian critics and historians have been resistant to include him.

CORMAN'S LATIN AMERICA

Corman's comments concerning the explicit use of international locales to cut costs does much to support Tamara Falicov's argument that Corman's ventures in Argentina—and, by extension, elsewhere in places like Peru and the Philippines—were counterproductive to national traditions (2004: 31). She focuses on Argentine auteur Héctor Olivera, whose work ranges across three decades and includes powerful and award-winning testimonial films such as *La Patagonia rebelde/Rebellion in Patagonia* (1974), *La noche de los lápices/Night of the Pencils* (1986), and *El caso María Soledad/The Case of María Soledad* (1993). In contrast to these serious and well-respected dramas, Olivera made five films between 1985 and 1990 as coproductions with Corman's Concorde-New Horizons production company; two of these were sword-and-sorcery genre films, standard fare for the time ripping off the success of *Conan the Barbarian*, while the remaining three were what Argentine critics called "parodies" of original films made in Argentina. Falicov finds these films, *Two to Tango* (1988) and *Play Murder for Me* (1990), particularly damaging to the national cinematic identity, both for critics and for professionals who worked on these film. She concludes that "the [Corman-produced] films ultimately worked counter to the spirit of Argentine filmmaking due to either the absence of Argentina from the cinemascape or the distorted representations and/or stereotypes of Argentine culture in the few times it was depicted" (Falicov, 2004: 31).

I maintain that Falicov's assessment of the negative effects of Corman's exploitation ventures on Olivera and the Argentine industry is accurate, due primarily to two factors: firstly, the Argentine film industry had an established tradition, and secondly, Héctor Olivera, a key industry member, had produced his best films in the early 1980s, immediately *before* his association with Corman. Falicov notes how the Corman-produced *Two to Tango* was simply a denationalized (meaning: Argentina as a nation was largely written out and, as Falicov terms, "made for US audiences") version of the award-winning 1982 film *Ultimos días de la víctima/Last Days of the Victim* (Adolfo Aristarain) (2004: 35). The cinematic situation that Corman encountered in the mid-1980s in Peru was much different, with critics and filmmakers alike still defining what 'Peruvian cinema' meant. Although local production can be traced back to the silent period and included the founding of a studio in the mid-1930s, production halted with the coming of World War II and feature-length productions did not commence again until the 1960s; even then, feature films had only begun to be released with any regularity starting in 1977, and even ten years later only a handful of directors had been successful in producing and releasing a local feature film (Middents, 2001: 56–59).

Falicov calls for excluding movies from the Argentine cinematic tradition that do not seem to support conventional nationalist narratives, particularly when largely financed by and made for North Americans. When considering less developed national cinematic contexts such as that of Peru, where a varied tradition has not yet become evident, including these texts is both relevant and appropriate. Writing in the early 2000s, Gabriela Alemán argues for the necessary inclusion of exploitation films in the construction of the Ecuadorian cinematic tradition, particularly those made in the 1960s and 1970s cofinanced by Mexican or Argentine production companies, as a direct challenge to what is considered the art-house norm of most Latin American filmmaking: "What happens with those who not only produce little but reject or ultimately ignore what they do produce?" (2004: 97). The Peruvian cinematic tradition in the mid-1980s was caught between two extremes, characterized neither by the level of distinction, diversity, or ability that defined Argentine cinema nor the absence of tradition that marked Ecuadorian filmmaking. Adding exploitation coproductions with the United States therefore widens the perspective of national cinema.

PERUVIAN CINEMA IN THE 1980S

As with much of the rest of Latin America, film production in Peru began very shortly after its arrival on the continent at the end of the nineteenth century and developed a small tradition before celluloid shipments to South America halted during World War II, subsequently decimating nearly all local film production. Peruvian filmmaking reemerged slowly, with only a few scattered features made during the 1950s and 1960s. Production did not begin in earnest again until a film law sponsored by the Peruvian government in 1972 mandated that a locally produced short must accompany all foreign-produced feature films and that a percentage of the ticket sales must then go back to the Peruvian production company that made the short. This spurred a venerable short-film industry that produced several thousand shorts (of wildly varying quality) over the next twenty years and served as a training ground for Peruvian films, which were being released more regularly by the end of the 1970s.

Critics at the Peruvian film journal *Hablemos de cine* started discussing aspects of Peruvian national cinema from its founding in 1965, largely weighing their decisions not on thematic or political issues but on aesthetic concerns. This critique, modeled on the method established by fellow young critics at the French journal *Cahiers du Cinéma*, favored approaches that venerated an auteur approach to film directors and the formation and appreciation of genres. Thus, by the time a reasonable corpus of Peruvian feature films were released by the early 1980s, these critics identified (or, given the relative cultural capital critics have, instituted) a growing dichotomy between films set in the Andes and those set in more urban areas. Films set in the Andes, primarily associated with the Cuzco region, referred most closely to the early work of director Federico García.[2] In addition to being set in the Andes, García's earliest films followed narratives about poor, subaltern figures striving to overcome oppression, and employed script and aesthetic techniques more closely related to documentaries and neorealism.[3] Films set in more urban areas, exemplified by the work of Francisco Lombardi, privileged more linear narratives and cleaner visuals, often providing local variations on American genre films. For example, his most well-known film, *La boca del lobo/The Lion's Den* (1988), is a tense thriller concerning a hunt for a member of the contemporary terrorist organization Sendero Luminoso (Shining Path); considered one of the best Peruvian films ever made, it also borrows several narrative features from conventions of American war films, most explicitly from *The Deer Hunter* (1978).

The acceptance of genre productions goes somewhat against general perceptions of 'good' Latin American filmmaking, and yet both Augusto Tamayo's crime thriller *La fuga del chacal/The Jackal's Escape* and José Carlos Huayhuaca's sole feature directing effort, *Profesión: Detective*, were released earlier in 1987 to relatively respectable critical attention that often addressed how the films metaphorically spoke to questions of the national. Writing about *La fuga del chacal*, the single-named "Alat" noted that "in the perfect simplicity of the police drama, the film uncovers the crisis within Peru: the loss within contemporary society of the patrimonial figure" (qtd. in Bedoya, 1998: 270). Having rejected many examples of Peruvian filmmaking where strict attention was not paid to the mise-en-scène, the writers at the local film journals *Hablemos de cine* spent twenty years crafting ideas about what an acceptable 'Peruvian film' might be; their singular, loud praise for the work of Francisco Lombardi in the early 1980s indicated that what they actually favored was technically 'perfect' (to play on Cuban filmmaker and theorist Julio García Espinosa's concept of *imperfect cinema*) films whose narratives demonstrated a national spin on American typical genre filmmaking. Significantly, these so-called urban films like Lombardi's were not only favored by critics but also by Peruvian audiences in the 1980s: Tamayo's crime thriller *La fuga del chacal* broke previous box-office records with nine hundred thousand theatrical spectators. While also using traditional narrative themes and techniques more akin to documentary aesthetics espoused by the New Latin American Cinema, even the early features by the collective Grupo Chaski such as *Gregorio* (1985) and *Juliana* (1989) use relatively linear storytelling techniques and reference more global cinematic entities such as *Rambo* (1982).

CORMAN'S *HOUR OF THE ASSASSIN*

Hour of the Assassin was not conceived for Peruvian audiences, but for the lucrative exploitation home video market cornered by Concorde-New Horizons. Although none of Llosa's movies precisely fit the stylistic and aesthetic standards involving recycling and padding that Eric Schaefer (1999) identifies in classic exploitation films, Corman's more inclusive definition squarely identifies *Hour of the Assassin* as a prime example of exploitation cinema as articulated and produced by Concorde-New Horizons:

> Exploitation films were so named because you made a film about something wild with a great deal of action, a little sex, and possibly some sort of gimmick they often came out of the day's headlines. It's interesting how, decades later, when the majors saw they could have enormous success with *Big-budget* exploitation films, they gave them loftier terms—genre films or 'high-concept' films. (1998: 34)

It is not just the majors, however, who seem wary of the 'exploitation' term; local Peruvian critics also had a vested interest in distancing themselves from such terminology in favor of more 'acceptable' standards.

Hour of the Assassin explicitly recycled the plot of the 1973 Fred Zinnemann mainstream action thriller *The Day of the Jackal*, based on the popular novel by Frederick Forsyth. Written by Corman house scribe Jeff Leipzig, this version of the story stars Erik Estrada as an assassin named Martin Fierro contracted by a corrupt government to assassinate the president-elect of the nonspecific Latin American country of San Pedro. The entire movie follows him as he tries to collect weapons for the project while being pursued by governmental authorities (including a military specialist played by Robert Vaughan) who are looking to double-cross him. The changes from the unacknowledged source are significant: in this version, as the only people directly responsible for the deaths of other characters, the indistinguishable military officials are the only antagonists, leaving both Estrada's and Vaughan's characters coded as heroic.

Despite the high-profile source, *Hour of the Assassin* explicitly embraces its status as a simple genre picture, with numerous car chases and shoot-out scenes characteristic of any American action film, but few of the Americans involved felt this was a significant project. Of note, Estrada does not cite the film in his autobiography, dismissing in a single paragraph all the foreign productions he did during the 1980s as a sign of how bad things were that he had to trade on his *CHiPs* fame outside the United States (Estrada and Seay, 1997: 166). He mentions filming in Italy, Puerto Rico and Thailand; his Peruvian experience goes unconsidered. This was not what he told the Peruvian press: interviewed on his arrival to Lima, he noted that he was "thankfully impressed with both the shoot and the work being done by the Peruvian crew" and that Llosa was "a very intelligent director" (*Caretas*, 1986a: 45).

LUIS LLOSA'S *MISIÓN EN LOS ANDES*

Although *Hour of the Assassin* was explicitly filmed and marketed as a direct-to-video product for the United States market with all dialogue in English, the film functioned very differently in Peru, where it earned a commercial theatrical release under the title *Misión en los Andes* (literally, Mission in the Andes). The title change alone conspicuously ascribed a more identifiable regional and/or national identity than *Hour of the Assassin*, thus modifying the local audience's initial perception of the film as a Peruvian production. This invites a reading of the film focused more on the Peruvian elements, and necessarily divorces the film from its intended home video release in the United States.

Calling attention to the film's 'Peruvianness' also exposes Llosa's expertise with this kind of filmmaking in the first place: while Corman certainly had the capital and experience with internationally produced exploitation films, Llosa had established his own talents not on film but on local television, where he was already well-known for innovation and high production standards on several programs. By the end of the 1970s, the premiere television network in Peru, Panamericana Televisión, sought to distinguish itself from its closest competitor, América Televisión, by signing the primary filmmakers from the newly burgeoning Peruvian film tradition to create innovative programming for the channel. Having only made one short for the 1980 omnibus film *Aventuras prohibidas/Forbidden Adventures*, Llosa quickly became involved in two major innovations in local television programming for Panamericana (Vivas Sabroso, 2001: 226–27). The first, *La torre de Babel/The Tower of Babel,* was developed in conjunction with Llosa's cousin and internationally lauded Peruvian author Mario Vargas Llosa. The program crossed experimental documentary filmmaking with newsmagazine techniques and featured Mario interviewing a number of personalities as well as ordinary people throughout different parts of Peru as well as internationally; Luis Llosa often was the person behind the camera and in this way not only traveled extensively in country but also photographed diverse parts of Peru.[4] While *La torre de Babel* was a commercial failure, the second innovation, the police series *Gamboa* in 1983, succeeded during its three-year run. Evoking the early 1970s CBS series

The Streets of San Francisco, *Gamboa* moved a dramatic action series into the urban cityscape of Lima. Realizing by this point that he wanted to eventually make movies, Llosa (who produced and directed for the series) insisted on location shooting with a single camera, giving the gritty series a deliberately cinematic look and atmosphere unlike any previously seen on Peruvian television (Vivas Sabroso, 2001: 229).

The aforementioned apocryphal story that Corman picked Llosa's name from a phone book during a layover in Lima is instructive as to how Corman's 'Third World' dealings have been regarded, and perhaps why we are somewhat 'insulted' at the seeming 'lack of respect for local culture' in his internationally produced films. However, the reality of how Llosa came to Corman's attention speaks to the importance of television in establishing filmmakers in the 1980s in Peru. Llosa credits his big break to Livia Antola, a former buyer for Panamericana, who later moved to Los Angeles to acquire products for Corman's production companies. Since Corman was already producing in Argentina, Antola asked if he had ever thought of Peru as a possible location. When Corman expressed interest, she showed him an episode of *Gamboa* as evidence that potential filmmakers already existed in Peru—and could produce quality material on a very limited budget. Corman then called Llosa directly, offered the opportunity to direct a picture as long as it could be completed quickly; well versed with his experience in television, Llosa agreed to the terms and put the picture together in three months (Llosa, 2007).

The distinguishing Peruvian elements of the film lie in the multiple settings that local audiences would recognize, even if they had never seen movie-oriented action sequences in such locations. For example, the demonstration, first assassination attempt ,and subsequent car chase that begin the film all take place in the Lima suburb of Barranco, denoted by an unusual colonial square and cobblestone streets right by the ocean cliffs. Fierro goes to the titular Andes, where a local bar, a hostel, and particularly the streets indicate location shooting in Cuzco; Llosa may be credited for being one of the only directors from outside the region to film in Cuzco to not make the obvious choice of also filming Macchu Picchu, but this is probably also due to some effort to locate the film's narrative in a the fictional San Pedro as opposed to the very real Peru. Instead, a shootout is filmed in the nearby but slightly less familiar Incan ruin on Ollantaytambo, located within the Urubamba river valley. Fierro visits his father's grave during the Cuzco-shot sequence, which is accompanied by music from the familiar Peruvian *zampolla* pan-flute. Finally, the climactic inauguration sequence takes place in the central plaza of the southern provincial capital of Arequipa. Having Peru's second largest city stand for the capital city of fictional San Pedro might be seen by Peruvian audiences as amusing or even confrontational, as the city is historically known as a center for nationalism during the war for independence and even contemporary *arequipeños* will joke that their city should be the real capital of Peru.

Other elements of *Misión en los Andes* would resonate with Peruvian audiences differently than with the American viewers to which *Hour of the Assassin* was originally intended. As opposed to the assassin in the original *La fuga del chacal,* who turns into a dangerous loose cannon and becomes the antagonist of the picture, Peruvian audiences might ascribe a more heroic status to Estrada's character upon hearing the character's name: Martin Fierro evokes Argentine nationalism as the subject of a late nineteenth-century epic poem by José Hernández, who fights against encroaching Western traditions. While Peruvians do not have the same connection with the character as Argentines, Fierro as a figure would still be recognized by educated local audiences. The movie's antagonists, military officers bent on assassinating a democratically elected president, evoke recent Peruvian history: although each transfer of power was peaceful, the country had been ruled by the military governments of General Juan Velasco Alvarado and General Francisco Morales Bermúdez from 1968 to 1980, at which point the originally ousted president, Fernando Belaúnde Terry, returned.[5] Several Peruvian supporting actors known from other movies or, more importantly, from local television programs, including Orlando Sacha as Folco and Lourdes Berninzon as love interest Adriana, were used in billboard advertising for the film, even though costars Estrada and David Carradine would draw larger audiences. The novelty factor, particularly that an English-language American film was being made in Peru with the largest budget ever garnered by local standards, would also play significantly well for audiences.

Given trends in local filmmaking which favored other similar productions, *Misión en los Andes* netted over one million spectators to become one of the most theatrically viewed Peruvian films ever, a feat that remains true even at the beginning of the twenty-first century. Trends in Peruvian national filmmaking during this period, however, demonstrate that this movie was not an anomaly. On the contrary, the bigger budget (by Peruvian standards) offered more impressive special effects within an already-established Peruvian aesthetic in the 1980s. The large Peruvian audience clearly did not seem to mind that *Misión en los Andes* happened to be in English; in fact, the language combined with the improved technical qualities allowed viewers to compare the film with the American product that dominated national movie screens, which was what Peruvian audiences were already accustomed to. That local audiences could now recognize the locales and read other meanings into them only added to the film's entertaining appeal. Peruvian critics initially raved about Llosa's success. The venerated Isaac León Frías lauded the film in the newsweekly *Caretas,* noting particularly that "explosions and car chases like this have never been seen with this level of production values in a Peruvian film" (1987: 60).

Although he would later indicate that he cannot claim to be a nationalist-oriented director, Llosa explicitly referenced the possible impact of the film on national cinematic interests in publicity for the film. Quoted in an earlier *Caretas* article, Llosa noted that this "was not the type of film I would want to do, but it does give me the opportunity to make other movies closer to my heart. . . . I need government support . . . and I think that everyone understands that this film is an excellent way to erase the bad image the rest of the world sees in this country" (*Caretas*, 1986b: 46). Llosa indeed had little control over the script or the primary actors, both of which were furnished by Corman—but his geographic choices deliberately showcased Peru for both local and international audiences. The film's success would hopefully interest the Peruvian government in providing more financial support for national filmmaking opportunities. In my interview with him in 2007, Llosa said that even Corman thought that the visuals represented Peru in a broad and positive light. The expanse that Llosa brought to *Hour of the Assassin* on such a limited budget undoubtedly gave Corman the confidence to put more money into Llosa-produced projects in Peru.

CORMAN AND LLOSA IN PERU: *CRIME ZONE/ CALLES PELIGROSAS* AND BEYOND

Critical backlash began with Luis Llosa's second film, which did not fulfill the promise of being something "close to [his] heart." *Crime Zone* (1989) starred David Carradine and a pre–*Twin Peaks* Sherilyn Fenn in a posta-pocalyptic combination of *Bonnie and Clyde* (Arthur Penn, 1967) and George Orwell's novel *1984*. The story is more complex than *Hour of the Assassin*: officials in a dystopic police state must create criminals in order to justify and maintain its existence. Llosa combined a futuristic ambiance (created by neon lighting and shots of either postmodern-looking build-ings like the Museo de la Nación or metallic-fixtured shopping malls like the then-chic Centro Comercial Camino Real) with the inventive use of Lima's dusty urban blight of the late 1980s standing in for the aftermath of a nuclear war. With the exception of a car chase that follows down what is obviously the pedestrian area of Avenida José Pardo in Miraflores that captures some blink-and-you-miss-them shots of neon signs advertising the (now defunct) national airline Aeroperú, imagery that can be identi-fied as Peruvian is completely erased from this picture. Moreover, with a script entirely in English and the cast dominated by North Americans (including the supporting cast played almost exclusively by teachers and students from the American School of Lima), there was very little room to inscribe *Peruvianness* into the narrative. Llosa says that the approach to this film was based in art direction instead of dialogue and that shooting the large majority of the film at night covered many of the limitations the production faced.

Interestingly, Corman maintains a soft spot for *Crime Zone* as a notable Concorde-New Horizons production, perhaps because he claims to have come up with the film's concept himself (Gray, 2000: 173); among English-speaking genre critics, the movie has also fared relatively well. Peruvian critics, however, were not so kind, marking a shift from reception of Llosa's debut. Following a similar distribution strategy to *Misión en los Andes*, *Crime Zone* was released as *Calles peligrosas* (Dangerous Streets) in Lima in late 1989. This time, local critics, upset that Llosa did not fulfill his promise of the earlier film, decried the picture as not being Peruvian enough. A passage from José Carlos Huayhauca in *Posible* (September–October 1989) represents how several critics found fault with the film as a betrayal of national identity: "Barely present, Peru itself functions as much as an afterthought as the story and characters, subjugated to the action and special effects" (qtd. in Bedoya, 1998: 285).

The shift in critical opinion towards Llosa's film might be attributable to a change in local Peruvian consumption; after all, *Calles peligrosas* was released in Peru less than one year after two major critical and commercial successes from very different sources that did not reflect the trend in action-oriented genre films: Grupo Chaski's *Juliana* (1988), a film shot in documentary style following the life of a girl in a *pueblo jóven* shantytown, and Francisco Lombardi's *La boca del lobo*. The speculation that Peruvian tastes had been refined away from such genre pictures in the two-year interval, however, can be refuted since *Hour of the Assassin* was also released only a short time after similar films: Grupo Chaski's *Gregorio* (1985) and Lombardi's *La ciudad y los perros/The City and the Dogs* (1985), the adaptation of the Mario Vargas Llosa novel (called in English *The Time of the Hero*).

Corman and Llosa continued to function as partners through the beginning of the 1990s and several more Concorde-New Horizons films were made in Peru, but Llosa largely functioned as a producer on these films through his production company, Iguana Films. Several of these productions mark early work for directors who would later go on to bigger Hollywood careers, most notably Carl Franklin's submarine thriller *Full Fathom Five* (1990). Llosa himself only directed two more films for Concorde-New Horizons, now both recognized primarily for early nude appearances by American actresses: *800 Leagues Down the Amazon* (1993), starring Daphne Zúñiga from the later TV series *Melrose Place*, and *Fire on the Amazon*, an ecological thriller starring Sandra Bullock originally filmed in 1993 but not released until long after her ascent to Hollywood stardom with *Speed* (1994).

This is not to say that Llosa's career ended with his affiliation with Corman; instead, Llosa became a significant Hollywood director working in progressively larger action movies. In 1993, he released *Sniper* with Tom Berenger and Billy Zane, his first film made for theatrical release in the United States. Llosa's next two films, both made for budgets under $50 million, became worldwide financial successes: *The Specialist* in 1993, which made $170 million, and *Anaconda* in 1997. All of these films were coproduced by Llosa's Peruvian production company Iguana Films and one of the Hollywood majors (Columbia Pictures, Warner Brothers Pictures, etc.). Notably, despite the fact that Llosa's last Hollywood feature in particular is merely a big-budget exploitation film, none of these films was associated with Corman.

The only other Peruvian director who subsequently associated with Concorde-New Horizons was Augusto Tamayo, who started directing a film originally titled *Welcome to Oblivion*, starring Dack Rambo from the television show *Dallas*. Similar to *Crime Zone*, the story featured the dusty Peruvian desert as a background for another postapocalyptic science fiction crime adventure. However, Tamayo never completed the film and only a portion of the footage shot in Peru was eventually edited with material from other Corman productions by director Kevin Tent. The film was eventually released on video under the title *Ultra Warrior* in 1990 and credits both Tamayo and Tent as codirectors; unlike the earlier Peruvian coproductions, *Ultra Warrior* was not released in Peru at all.

LUIS LLOSA AS PERUVIAN DIRECTOR

Augusto Tamayo subsequently stopped making genre films, turning to period films such as *El bien esquivo/The Elusive Good* (2001) and *Una sombra al frente/Crossing a Shadow* (2007), both of which have more firmly and traditionally established him as a 'Peruvian filmmaker.' This is due both to the themes he addresses in the film's plots, the professional quality of his films and their more explicit connection to elements of 'art cinema' that tend to be associated with the concept of 'national cinema'; Peruvian film historians rarely bring up his association with Corman. This brings us back to why Luis Llosa has been summarily dismissed as a Peruvian filmmaker by most local critics and film historians. The obvious reason is because of his association with exploitation filmmaking, particularly as local critics traditionally rejected 'subquality' filmmaking generally associated with the genre. Yet, much like Alemán (2004) has done with exploitation films in Ecuador, some younger critics have reexamined the contribution of true exploitation filmmaking in Peru to the construction of national cinematic identity, particularly by Peru's only bona fide exploitation film specialist, Leonidas Zegarra. A member of the same graduating class from Universidad de Lima as Francisco Lombardi, Zegarra's movies explicitly cater to the mondo-trash market, with titles such as *Vedettes al desnudo/Un-veiled Models* (2003), *Poseída por el diablo (en las garras de Lucifer)/Possessed by the Devil (in Lucifer's Grasp)* (2006) and the most recent *300 millas en busca de mamá/300 Miles Looking for Mama* (2007). Local film publications have called attention to Zegarra, whose films "bring together the 'finest' local, commonplace celebrities [*el figuretti del chollywood*] with the trashiest crime stories," to consider his place within Peruvian film history (Wiener, 2003: 19). Web sites and blogs have also rallied to his cause, often written by young cinephiles entranced by exploitation.[6]

If Leonidas Zegarra is at least being discussed in the context of national cinema, why has Luis Llosa not received similar attention? His elision is perhaps because his films have been caught in between two cinematic categories that are generally considered to be antagonistic. As both a genre and production approach, exploitation cinema from the outset aims to deliver cheap, fast, formulaic product; as Corman defines it, the term is particularly apt when describing Llosa's films. The problem here is that, as Schaefer points out, exploitation films gain credibility precisely because they subvert easily readable narrative forms (1999: 14). Without the car chases, explosions, and dialogue in English and without support from Concorde-New Horizons, *Hour of the Assassin/Misión en los Andes* might otherwise figure as part of a trend of accomplished genre-oriented films made in Peru. Corman's name and international reputation may bring money to Peru but these also add the ideological coding of 'exploitation.' Llosa's early films are doubly damned, however, since these genre-oriented films of the mid-1980s have subsequently been considered in a more negative manner. This includes the work of Francisco Lombardi, Peru's most lauded director both nationally and internationally. Younger critics in the early twenty-first century have criticized what they call 'the Lombardi generation' of filmmakers for having created a stagnant cinema. If that is considered as a negative trend in national filmmaking, then Llosa's work—technically, if not thematically—is certainly part of that trajectory and further problematizes his potential status as a 'Peruvian filmmaker.' Zegarra, working outside this dominant local aesthetic, would not be considered as Lombardi's contemporary.

In addition to being associated with both Corman and Lombardi in the 1980s, Llosa's other problem stems from the relatively unchanged nature of his work since then, especially that he did not 'progress' away from exploitation cinema to the 'art films' which dominate conceptions of (Peruvian) national cinema. As such, *Misión en los Andes* has not had a lasting influence toward defining national cinema in a larger context. While several action-thriller films were produced in Peru before Llosa's subsequent Peruvian features, other directors do not continue this trend. Instead of "returning to films closer to his heart," as promised when filming *Hour of the Assassin*, Llosa embraced Corman's notion of exploitation filmmaking, one where the ability to make money superseded the notion of national cinema. Since Llosa's later films erased any and all cinematic markers of Peruvian national identity and since other Peruvian films were released that more explicitly embraced more traditional models of national cinema, critical discussion of national cinematic trends continued without including Llosa. Even when he turned away from action films in 2005 to adapt Mario Vargas Llosa's *La fiesta del chivo/The Feast of the Goat*, the subsequent English-language film about a lawyer returning to confront her past in the Dominican Republic does not register as a 'Peruvian' film outright, even though Llosa, Vargas Llosa, and screenwriter Augusto Cabada are all Peruvian.

When I asked him if he considered himself a Peruvian director in 2007, Luis Llosa replied matter-of-factly, "It would be unfair to say that. I am Peruvian, but I have nothing to do with Peru. The movies I made for Corman really only marginally reflect the reality of what actually happens in Peru. My body of work certainly does not reflect a Peruvian reality. The movies I have made have instead been international, commercial. That's the way it happened—it wasn't a conscious decision" (Llosa, 2007). His comments separating 'Corman's movies' from 'Peruvian cinema' indicate less about how he doesn't fit into the Peruvian cinematic tradition and more about how that tradition has been defined in a limited fashion. Including Llosa's *Misión en los Andes*, disguised as the Corman-produced venture *Hour of the Assassin*, in that tradition opens, enriches, and expands the definition of 'national cinema' to include films with more complex production and distribution strategies.

NOTES

1. The large majority of these films were directed by American directors with Llosa's production company, Iguana Films, providing services. Listed chronologically with all the alternate titles, the other nine films are: *Welcome to Oblivion/Ultra Warrior* (Augusto Tamayo and Kevin Tent, 1989/1994); *Heroes Stand Alone/Duncan's Dodgers* (Mark Griffiths, 1989); *Full Fathom Five* (Carl Franklin, 1990); *To Die Standing* (Louis Morneau, 1990); *Fire on the Amazon* (Llosa, 1991); *800 Leagues Down the Amazon* (Llosa, 1993); *Max Is Missing/Golden Warrior* (Griffiths, 1994); *New Crime City* (Jonathan Winfrey, 1994); *Watchers III* (Jeremy Standford, 1994).
2. García's early films include *Kuntur Wachana/Where Condors Go to Die* (1977), *Laulico* (1980) and *El caso Huayanay/The Huayanay Case* (1981) and the biopics *Melgar: Poeta insurgente/Melgar: Insurgent Poet* (1982) and *Tupac Amaru* (1984).
3. These characteristics also apply to much of Latin American filmmaking throughout the region from the late 1960s through the mid-1970s, known collectively as the *New Latin American Cinema*. Cuban filmmaker and theorist Julio García Espinosa (1997a[1969]) termed this type of filmmaking *imperfect cinema*, ascribing political valences to low-quality aesthetics and practices. Peruvian cinema in general, however, was never associated with the New Latin American Cinema and it should be noted that García's films are released in the late 1970s, nearly ten years after the most active period of the New Latin American Cinema (Middents, 2001: 185–208).
4. Mario later wrote about this experience in his novel-memoir *The Storyteller*, whose unnamed narrator "was responsible for a Peruvian television program called The Tower of Babel" and who worked with someone explicitly named "Lucho Llosa" (2001: 146).
5. It is tempting to read the references to Fierro and contemporary military regimes as a sign of a 'regional' Latin American identity in addition to a Peruvian 'national' identity, particularly as the diegetic location of the film

is the fictional country of San Pedro. However, both of these elements derive from the script written by American Matt Lepizig, and such regional markers are not necessarily extended through Llosa's use of mise-en-scène, which, more explicitly, points toward an underlying Peruvian identity. Distribution, in Latin America beyond Peru, might otherwise necessitate more 'regional' markers for distribution purposes, but it seems unlikely such a distribution strategy was envisioned.

6. See Montalvo (2004) and especially the comments at Servat (2008). Young cinephiles' embrace of exploitation cinema is a key element discussed by Sconce (1995).

4 "I Wonder Who the Real Cannibals Are"

Latin America and Colonialism in European Exploitation Cinema

Andrew Syder

In the late 1970s and early 1980s, a wave of European exploitation film-makers descended upon Latin America. The most common destination was the Amazon jungle, home to lost tribes of primitives in such films as *Emanuelle e gli ultimi cannibali/Emanuelle and the Last Cannibals* (Joe D'Amato, 1977), *Mondo cannibale/White Cannibal Queen/Cannibals* (Jesús Franco, 1980), *Cannibal Holocaust* (Ruggero Deodato, 1980), *Cannibal ferox/Make Them Die Slowly* (Umberto Lenzi, 1981), *Schiave bianche: Violenza in Amazzonia/Amazonia: The Catherine Miles Story* (Mario Gariazzo, 1985), *Nudo e selvaggio/Massacre in Dinosaur Valley* (Michele Massimo Tarantini, 1985), and *Inferno in diretta/Cut and Run* (Ruggero Deodato, 1985). The Spanish Caribbean also proved to be a popular location, with voodoo-cursed islands providing settings for *Zombi 2/Zombie/Zombie Flesh Eaters* (Lucio Fulci, 1979) and a sleazy series of Joe D'Amato films: *Papaya dei Caraibi/Papaya: Love Goddess of the Cannibals* (1978), *Orgasmo nero/Black Orgasm/Voodoo Baby* (1980), *Le Notti erotiche dei morti viventi/Erotic Nights of the Living Dead* (1980), and *Holocausto porno/Porno Holocaust* (1981).[1] A total of more than two dozen European exploitation films were set in Latin America during this period; almost all of them depicted the region as a primal, superstitious land filled with gut-munching cannibals or flesh-eating zombies.

These deeply stereotypical visions of Latin America were, of course, nothing new. The history of colonialism overflows with such ideas and discourses, ranging from the imperialist propaganda of Hans Staden's tales of cannibalism among the Tupinamba (1557) to anti-imperialist subversions of the cannibal metaphor by Latin American artists and theorists, such as Oswald de Andrade's *Manifesto antropófago* (1928). In this chapter, I examine how the cycle of European cannibal and zombie movies engaged with this history of colonialism in Latin America, investigating the function that the Latin American Other played in these films. I focus primarily on four of the most notorious and widely seen films of the cycle—*Emanuelle e gli ultimi cannibali, Zombi 2, Cannibal Holocaust,* and *Cannibal ferox*—and I employ three interweaving frameworks to structure my analysis.

The first framework is the institutional context of exploitation cinema in Italy, which was the central hub of the European exploitation industry from the 1960s to the 1980s and was the country that produced (or coproduced) almost all of the cannibal/zombie films. I examine how the colonial discourses in these films are inflected by the traditions of genre filmmaking in Italy and by the institutional shifts that occurred in Italian cinema during the 1970s. In particular, I argue that while all exploitation cinemas rely upon imitation, the practice is particularly central to Italian exploitation, making it an important lens through which to view the films.

The second framework is the history of Italian colonialism. While the topic of colonialism has been a focus of studies of these films, the specificity of Italian colonialism is absent from the debates that have emerged; colonialists are treated as a homogenous block and distinctions between different colonialisms are elided. By examining these films in the context of Italy's own, unique history of colonialism, we can tease out more nuanced understandings of the colonial encounters that the films enact and better comprehend why the representations of Latin America took the form that they did.

The final framework, more theoretical in nature, is a questioning of the role of exploitation films within discourses of national cinema and nationhood. The foundational theories and histories of national cinema were formed around the structural absence of the exploitation film, reflecting the taste distinctions of the academy and the historical evolution of film studies as a discipline, which spent many years arguing for the importance of film through such strategies as the auteur theory and the formation of canons of great works. In the Italian context, for instance, mainstay histories such as *Italian Cinema: From Neorealism to the Present* (Bondanella 1983) and *Italian National Cinema 1886–1986* (Sorlin 1996) simply ignore the country's expansive tradition of exploitation cinema, erasing from the records such prolific and influential directors as Lucio Fulci, Ruggero Deodato, Joe D'Amato, Umberto Lenzi, Sergio Martino, Enzo Castellari, and Antonio Margheriti. As a result, few theoretical frameworks exist for understanding the complex ways in which exploitation cinema contributes to the writing of a national culture. Yet, if, as Homi Bhabha argues, "the scraps, patches, and rags of daily life must be repeatedly turned into the signs of a national culture" (1994: 297), then surely we should pay particular attention to the "hodge-podge of cuttings and splicings" (Schaefer, 1999: 42) that make up a country's exploitation cinema. Or, to put it another way, what exactly do these scandalous cannibal and zombie films mean within the context of Italian national culture . . . and why did they pick on Latin America?

There are many reasons why European exploitation films have long been the problem children of academic discourses about national cinema: most of the films were aimed at international audiences, produced at the behest of foreign distributors; they were commonly shot in English, with American actors in leading roles; many of them were direct imitations of Hollywood hits, or were made to commercially exploit a popular trend; they were often shot overseas, wherever labor was inexpensive; and they operated outside the production and exhibition circuits of both highbrow art cinema and middlebrow entertainment. From the perspective of national cinema debates, all of these factors have been markers of the degraded nature of exploitation cinema, of its inability to contribute to a national cinema culture that is "positively yet critically seeking to engage with the multi-layeredness of specific socio-cultural formations" (Willemen, 1994: 212). In other words, the commercial, imitative, transnational, lowbrow qualities of European exploitation cinema have made it a square peg in the round hole of prescriptive discourses in the academy about the role of cinema in national culture.

It is precisely these qualities, however, that make European exploitation films such compelling exhibits of the "scraps, patches, and rags" of national culture. The Italian exploitation tradition, in particular, offers up a rich tapestry of interwoven film cycles that frequently used imitation and transnational dislocation as ways of engaging discourses of nationhood. The *poliziotteschi* cycle of violent crime movies from the mid-1970s, for example, responded to the lawlessness and domestic terrorism of 1970s Italy through a strategy of imitating and reworking the tough cop templates of *Dirty Harry* (Don Siegel, 1971) and *The French Connection* (William Friedkin, 1971). Likewise, the spaghetti westerns of the late-1960s refashioned Hollywood pioneering narratives at a time when Italy itself was going through a process of domestic expansion. This allegorical doubling of national and international spaces also permeates the *giallo* thrillers of the early-1970s, which were frequently built around fish-out-of-water narratives about foreigners in Italy or Italians overseas. As such, we should not simply dismiss Italian genre cinema for being imitative and trend-driven, but rather recognize this set of qualities as a dominant means through which ideas about nation circulated in these films. In the case of the cannibal/zombie films, their strategies of imitation link them back to two traditions that served as primary templates: adventure fiction and *mondo* documentaries. Both of these traditions were themselves deeply rooted in the narratives of colonialism.

Colonial adventure stories in the style of Edgar Rice Burroughs and Rudyard Kipling, in which white colonists encounter indigenous peoples while exploring remote regions of the world, provided the basic narrative formula for the cannibal/zombie films. Familiar characters and scenarios from such fiction recur throughout the cycle, with Latin America constructed as an undiscovered continent populated by explorers, anthropologists, missionaries, big-game hunters, superstitious locals, and tribes of dark savages. Umberto Lenzi, the director of *Cannibal ferox*, was himself responsible for popularizing these themes within Italian exploitation cinema. In the 1960s, Lenzi pioneered a cycle of colonial adventure movies with such films as *Sandokan, la tigre di Mompracem/Sandokan the Great* (1963), *I pirati della Malesia/The Pirates of Malaysia* (1964), *Sandok, il maciste della giungla/Temple of the White Elephant* (1964), and *Montagna di luce/Jungle Adventurer* (1965), many of which were based on the writings of Emilio Salgari, Italy's foremost author of adventure fiction. In 1972, Lenzi returned to the adventure genre with *Il paese del sesso selvaggio/Man from Deep River/Deep River Savages*, which resurrected the trope of a Westerner being held captive by a primitive tribe from such works as *The Captivity of Hans Staden of Hesse* (1557) and Herman Melville's *Typee: A Peep at Polynesian Life* (1846). Lenzi's film was immensely successful and, in true Italian exploitation fashion, became the prototype upon which many of the cannibal films were directly based. The nostalgic revival of colonial adventure fiction that followed such Hollywood blockbusters as *Indiana Jones and the Temple of Doom* (Steven Spielberg, 1984) and *Romancing the Stone* (Robert Zemeckis, 1984) also proved to be extremely influential on later cannibal films, reenergizing the cycle in the mid-1980s.

Mondo documentaries were similarly rooted in colonial traditions. The *mondo* cycle was initiated by *Mondo cane* (Gualtiero Jacopetti, Franco Prosperi, and Paolo Cavara, 1962), an extraordinarily successful film that documented shocking and sensational customs from around the world. Jacopetti and Prosperi continued the *mondo* formula with *La donna nel mondo/Women of the World* (1963), *Mondo cane 2* (1963), and, most infamously, *Africa addio/Africa Blood and Guts* (1966); others followed with such titles as *Mondo nudo/Naked World* (Francesco De Feo, 1963), *Mondo balordo/A Fool's World* (Roberto Bianchi Montero, 1964), and *Il pelo nel mondo/Go! Go! Go! World/Wicked World* (Antonio Margheriti, Marco Vicario, 1964).[2] The point of view these films presented was that of the tourist, sampling the exotic, titillating, or disgusting cultures of the Other through a consuming, colonial gaze. Advertisements for *Mondo cane* proclaimed, "it enters a hundred incredible worlds where the camera has never gone before!"—promoting the kind of sensationalist cinematic colonialism that would later become central to the pretense of discovering lost tribes of cannibals in the depths of the Amazon or zombies on remote Caribbean islands. (The *mondo* documentaries of the 1960s had themselves rarely ventured into Latin America, leaving the region ripe for exploitation by the cannibal/zombie cycle.) Shock footage of primitive social rituals and animal deaths in the cannibal films also derive directly from the *mondo* template, as does the cycle's frequent intermingling the authentic with the fabricated. *Emanuelle e gli ultimi cannibali* and *Schiave bianche*, for example, both deceitfully claim to be based on true stories. *Cannibal Holocaust* maintains a similar pretense through its use of faux documentary footage and through a warning to viewers during the opening credits: "For the sake of authenticity some sequences have been retained in their entirety."

How individual films of the cannibal-zombie cycle continued or built upon the colonial dimensions of adventure fiction and *mondo* documentary differs from film to film. Some, such as *Zombi 2* and *Emanuelle e gli ultimi cannibali*, embrace the colonial sensibilities in fairly uncritical ways; others, such as *Cannibal Holocaust* and *Cannibal ferox*, offer far more complex and ambivalent attitudes towards the project of colonialism.

Zombi 2 opens with a mysterious boat drifting in the New York harbor. Police board the vessel and discover a couple of flesh-eating zombies on deck. The boat owner's daughter, Anne Bowles (Tisa Farrow), teams up with a journalist, Peter West (Ian McCulloch), to investigate her father's disappearance. The trail leads them to the fictional Caribbean island of Matul, where a voodoo curse is bringing the dead back to life. Anne and Peter manage to escape the island alive, but to little avail: zombies have invaded Manhattan during their absence.

The film was made as an exploitative, unofficial sequel to *Dawn of the Dead* (George Romero, 1978), an American horror hit that had been released in Italy as *Zombi*. The two films, however, have very little in common; *Zombi 2* merely appropriated the title and took inspiration from several colonial adventure templates instead. The first was Tex Willer, the most famous adventure hero of Italian comic books. The film was initially conceived as a story of Willer discovering zombies, but when licensing rights to the character could not be secured, screenwriter Dardano Sarchetti kept the basic storyline intact and simply removed all references to Willer.[3] The second template was *I Walked with a Zombie* (Jacques Tourneur, 1943), a Hollywood horror classic from which *Zombi 2* derived its imperialist mythology of voodoo and zombies in the Spanish Caribbean. The deep nostalgia in *Zombi 2* for these colonial adventure stories is particularly pronounced when it is viewed in contrast to its ostensible progenitor, *Dawn of the Dead*. As Robin Wood (1986) has argued, the monster in 1970s American horror cinema was invariably of American origin and represented the return of the repressed. *Last House on the Left* (Wes Craven, 1972), for example, revealed the repressed violence bubbling under the surface of the middle-class American family, while *Dawn of the Dead* used shopping mall zombies as satirical metaphors for late-capitalist consumerism. By the end of these films, America has invariably destroyed itself: order is not restored, society is left in a state of crisis, and the monster has usually won. In contrast, *Zombi 2* identifies the monster as being of foreign origin, in keeping with older traditions of horror, such as *I Walked with a Zombie*, and consistent with colonial visions of the monstrous, ethnic Other. The scene of zombies crossing the Brooklyn Bridge at the end of *Zombi 2* is not an image of America being consumed by its own demons; it is an image more closely aligned with immigration and a fear of a Latin American invasion.

Emanuelle e gli ultimi cannibali offers a similar embrace of colonial adventure narratives. It opens with photojournalist Emanuelle (Laura

Gemser) working undercover in a psychiatric hospital, where she discovers a feral white woman who appears to have been raised by cannibals. Emanuelle decides to investigate and embarks on a journey into the Amazon with the assistance of anthropology professor Mark Lester (Gabriele Tinti) and Isabelle Wilkes (Mónica Zanchi), the daughter of a local colonist. Along the way, Emanuelle encounters a range of stock characters from adventure fiction (a big-game hunter looking for diamonds, a sister from a mission, etc.) and her expedition ultimately serves to affirm that, yes, primitive tribes of cannibals do still exist in the Amazon. The tribe that Emanuelle encounters is even identified as the Tupinamba, which was the tribe that Staden had associated with cannibalism back in the sixteenth century. The film similarly resurrects the age-old threat of white women being defiled by dark savages. It begins with Emanuelle discovering one such woman in a deranged state at the psychiatric hospital; and the narrative comes full circle at the end when Emanuelle saves another virginal, blonde, white woman (Isabelle) from the same fate. (Versions of this trope appear again in such films as *Mondo cannibale* and *Schiave bianche*.)

Β *Emanuelle e gli ultimi cannibali* was also an entry in the 'Black Emanuelle' series, an Italian sexploitation cycle from the late-1970s that sought to capitalize on the success of the original French film, *Emmanuelle* (Just Jaeckin, 1974).[4] The star of the series, Laura Gemser, was an Indonesian actress and her 'blackness' is sometimes used to playfully inject an element of colonial liminality into the films, such as when she pretends to be the cannibal tribe's goddess in order to save Isabelle. The character, however, is principally identified as a modern Westerner who has the privilege of traveling to foreign lands as a kind of erotic imperialist, a sophisticate who samples the sexual rituals of the exotic Other, and her blackness is primarily presented as a quality to be consumed by the film's voyeuristic audience.

Cannibal Holocaust and *Cannibal ferox*, in contrast, are much more outwardly ambivalent in their recycling of colonial narratives, with both films arguing that modernity is just as violent and as savage as the primitive world. *Cannibal Holocaust* revolves around an expedition by another anthropology professor, Harold Monroe (Robert Kerman), to find a crew of documentary filmmakers who went missing in the Amazon. At a cannibal village, Monroe locates the crew's eaten remains alongside their film canisters, and, upon viewing their footage, Monroe is appalled by the filmmakers' shocking acts of aggression towards the Amazonians. The film ends with the good professor walking off into the streets of Manhattan, asking himself, "I wonder who the real cannibals are." In *Cannibal ferox*, yet another anthropologist, Gloria Davis (Lorraine De Selle), leads an expedition into the Amazon as research for her doctoral thesis, which argues that cannibalism does not exist and is merely a myth concocted by colonialists. Soon after they enter the jungle, however, her group encounters two Americans who are on the run from cannibals. The situation then gets more complicated when Gloria learns that one of the Americans, Mike

(John Morghen), has an insatiable appetite for cocaine and has been torturing and killing the local tribespeople.

In both films, the acts of violence perpetrated by the cannibal tribes are framed as acts of vengeance for equally barbaric acts of aggression inflicted on them by characters from the modern world. Similar narratives of colonial comeuppance can be found throughout the cannibal/zombie cycle. In *Papaya dei Caraibi*, for instance, a cannibal queen seduces and kills a group of scientists who plan to use her island for atomic testing; and in *Le notti erotiche dei morti viventi*, an arrogant businessman falls victim to a zombie curse when he tries to turn a sacred island into a tourist hot spot. These critiques of colonialism have ignited a lot of discussion about the sincerity of the films' messages. While some have defended the films as anti-imperialist statements, most accounts have highlighted a strong undercurrent of hypocrisy. Phil Hardy, for example, makes the case that *Cannibal Holocaust* "pretends to condemn what it exploits" (1993: 334)—that is, the anti-imperialist message of the film is undercut by the fact that the filmmakers themselves had aggressively exploited the local peoples and wildlife, acting out imperial fantasies that ultimately reaffirmed myths of Latin America as a dark continent of savages. Unfortunately, much of the discussion of colonialism in this cycle of films has stopped here, leaving the films' apparent ambivalences and hypocrisies intact.

When these films are viewed in the context of Italian exploitation cinema and Italian colonialism, however, they take on a very different character. Relative to their antecedents in Italian exploitation, the films' critiques of colonialism, and their blurring of the modern and the primitive, do not appear as new departures. Quite the contrary: the juxtaposition of modern and primitive cultures in *mondo* cinema frequently served to question the customs of home. *Mondo* documentaries commonly featured an ironic narrator who would poke fun at the audience's salacious interest in the exotic Other, suggesting that 'we' can be just as strange and as shocking as 'them.' In other words, the colonial encounters with the Other served to blur boundaries and defamiliarize the home culture; or, as the U.S. poster for *Il pelo nel mondo* put it, the *mondo* tradition centered around "Primitive Rites—Civilized Wrongs."

This was, likewise, a prevalent theme throughout the history of colonial adventure fiction. In Melville's *Typee: A Peep at Polynesian Life*, for example, a British explorer is held captive by a Polynesian tribe that he fears are cannibals. The experience leads him to reflection: "The enormities perpetrated in the South Seas upon some of the inoffensive islanders wellnigh pass belief. . . . How often is the term 'savages' incorrectly applied!" (Melville, 1968: 26–7). Later, he continues, "I ask whether the mere eating of human flesh so very far exceeds in barbarity that custom [slavery] which only a few years since was practiced in enlightened England" (Melville, 1968: 125)—a statement remarkably similar to Professor Monroe's musing about who the real cannibals are. As such, we must question the extent to which films like *Cannibal Holocaust* and *Cannibal ferox* are expressing a political viewpoint or simply imitating and recycling the formulas of the literary and cinematic traditions upon which they are based. A closer examination of Italy's own history of colonialism can assist us in this endeavor, providing new perspectives on the cultural and political dimensions of the films' representations of Latin America.

Italy's colonial enterprises of the modern era peaked during the first half of the twentieth century with the conquests of four African nations: Libya, Ethiopia, Somalia, and Eritrea. Following defeat in World War II, Italy's colonial period ended abruptly when the 1947 Treaty of Paris stripped the country of its colonies. As a consequence, Italy did not go through the same processes of decolonization as other European nations. Angelo Del Boca, the leading historian of Italian colonialism, has described the resulting culture and history of Italy's postcolonial period as being characterized by silence, repression, and fabrication:

> During the war there was censorship. Afterwards, it suited all parties to hush things up. The Americans and British didn't want to push for prosecution of Italian war criminals as this would have risked the stability of the new state. They were horrified of a communist takeover. And the new Italy wanted very much to forget. It needed to heal the wounds. (quoted in Pankhurst 2004)

As such, Del Boca argues, "[t]he lack of debate on colonialism and the failure to condemn its most brutal aspects have promoted Italy's denial of its colonial faults" (2003: 19). He attributes this lack of public debate and the erasure of Italian colonialism from history books to the control that the ruling class exerted over documentation of the colonial period, barring from the colonial archives any scholars who were not part of the old imperialist lobby. As Patricia Palumbo notes, "the virtual inaccessibility of these archives made a probing, politically inflammatory investigation of the Italian colonial past impossible" (2003: 1). The government commission that controlled the archives instead produced a fifty-volume publication on the colonial period, entitled *L'Italia in Africa*, which Del Boca describes as a "colossal, costly, and almost incredible effort of mystification . . . a coarsely and impudently falsified account that aims to exalt Italian colonialism and underline its 'difference' from other contemporaneous colonialisms" (2003: 18). Absent was any mention of the use of concentration camps in Libya, Somalia, and Eritrea, the decimation of the Coptic church in which over 1,200 priests were killed, or the use of chemical weapons against the Ethiopians, which Italy did not officially recognize until 1996. Instead, the myth of *Italiani brava gente*— the good-hearted Italian—was promoted, as though Italian colonialism in Africa was somehow more benign than that of other European nations. Not until the 1970s did control of the archives begin to loosen, with significant critical histories first emerging in the decades that followed.

Irma Taddia argues that what differentiates Italy's relationship to colonial history from that of its European counterparts is the absence of an ideology of decolonization: "in Italy, no ideological current emerged in support of African and Asian decolonization, whereas other European nations promoted decolonization and helped shape political movements bringing African nationalist thought and ideology into contact with the ideologies of the West" (2005: 210). Viewed in this context, a profoundly different light is cast on attitudes towards colonialism within Italian exploitation cinema. In Lenzi's adventure films from the 1960s, for example, the gung-ho imperialism can be viewed as completely in step with the national culture's uncritical attitude towards colonization. In the *mondo* tradition, no film is a clearer illustration of this tendency than *Africa addio*, a film that, despite Jacopetti and Prosperi's declarations of neutrality, is a deeply nostalgic treatise on the African decolonization of the 1960s. This nostalgia is immediately evident from the film's opening narration—"The Africa of the Great Explorers, the huge land of hunting and adventure adored by entire generations of children has disappeared forever"—such that the *addio* of the film's title is in actuality a mournful farewell to this romanticized vision of Africa as a colonial playground. Indeed, nowhere in *Africa addio* is the project of colonialism criticized; the film's narrator consistently infantilizes the Africans, while criticizing the British and the French for timidly retreating:

> Europe is in a hurry to leave and on tiptoe even if, all things considered, it has given far more than it has taken. Europe, the continent that nursed Africa can no longer manage this big black baby that grew up too quickly, took bad company, and what's more, hates it because of its white skin. And so it is abandoned, still cranky and immature, just at the moment when it needs Europe the most.

This colonial nostalgia and apologism resurfaces in the cannibal/zombie films in a manner that reflects Palumbo's argument that "postwar historiographical neglect and obfuscation of the Italian colonial past is naturally matched by the blankness left by this past in the national culture" (2003: 11). This blankness lies at the center of the cannibal/zombie films through a double set of structural absences. The first structural absence is Africa. Out of all the Italian cannibal and zombie films of the 1970s and 1980s, none depicts colonial narratives that are set in Africa. They all take place in either Latin America or Asia, with the latter seen in such films as *Ultimo mondo cannibale/Jungle Holocaust/Last Cannibal World* (Ruggero Deodato, 1977), *La montagna del dio cannibale/The Mountain of the Cannibal God* (Sergio Martino, 1978), *Zombi holocaust/Zombie Holocaust/Dr. Butcher M.D.* (Marino Girolami, 1980), and *Mangiati vivi!/Eaten Alive* (Umberto Lenzi, 1980). The second structural absence is Italy itself. The films' protagonists are never Italian, identified instead as American or British. Moreover; most of the films' narratives are bookended in the United

States, as though America was home soil. *Emanuelle e gli ultimi cannibali,*
Zombi 2, Cannibal Holocaust, and *Cannibal ferox* all fit this pattern by
opening in Manhattan; the latter three conclude there too.

With this double absence, of Africa and of Italy, the cannibal/zom-
bie films elide any direct reference to Italy's own colonial past through a
series of displacements. The films transpose the lost colonial playground of
Africa onto Latin America, turning the jungles of the Amazon and tropical islands of the Caribbean into Africa's double. Latin America becomes
a space where colonial narratives and stereotypes can be replayed and
enjoyed at a safe distance from Italy's own terminated colonial project in
Africa, evasively using Latin America as a site for reinscribing an ideology of colonialism that is consistent with the nostalgic, apologist tradition
within Italian culture. In other words, it is a displacement that is both spatial and temporal. It is also notable that when the cycle of Italian cannibal/
zombie films is viewed as a whole, those set in Latin America and those set
in Asia are quite interchangeable; the function of these colonial spaces is
strictly generic and ahistorical, and the cultural specificity of each region is
of very little interest to most of the films.

The structural absence of Italy (and Italians) in these films further complicates these processes of ideological displacement. By having American
protagonists and by bookending the narratives in the United States, the
films maintain the voice and perspective of the colonizer. The point of view
is never that of the subaltern. Yet, by identifying the colonizer as American,
and not Italian, Italy itself is removed from the equation. This displacement
makes the cannibal/zombie films quite different from their antecedents in
mondo documentary and adventure fiction. As discussed previously, the
blurring of the line between the modern and the primitive in *mondo* cinema and in such adventure stories as Melville's *Typee* frequently served
to defamiliarize the home culture. Indeed, dating back to de Montaigne
(1580), the figure of the cannibal has been one of the most potent cultural
metaphors for losing one's sense of individuality and difference through
the process of being devoured by the Other. This blurring of modern and
primitive is certainly a central theme of the Italian cannibal/zombie cycle,
but with one significant difference: by identifying the modern world as
American, the films' home culture (Italy) is not directly implicated in any
way. As such, from the Italian perspective, the United States functions as
a kind of colonial Other, and the encounters depicted in the films are not
between home and Other, but rather between colonial Other and primitive
Other. Italy's own history of colonialism is never once addressed, relieving
the nation of any guilt or responsibility; nor is the myth of Italian colonial
'difference' ever called into question.

As a result, when critiques of colonialism are present in these films, the
finger is pointed at the colonial Other—at the United States—in much the
same way that the critiques of colonialism in *Africa addio* were directed at
British and French colonialism, but not Italian colonialism. Indeed, none of

the cannibal/zombie films is actually critical of the project of colonialism per se and they balance out their critiques of imperialism by having both 'bad' and 'good' colonialists in their narratives. The 'bad' colonialists are arrogant, irresponsible, and aggressive, and are punished for their actions at the hands (and mouths) of the cannibals and zombies. With great frequency and consistency, this punishment takes the form of graphic castrations: Mike in *Cannibal ferox*; Jack in *Cannibal Holocaust*; John in *Le Notti erotiche dei morti viventi*. The castration scenes cruelly undercut the films' overtly phallic representations of New York skyscrapers, as if the Italian filmmakers were gleefully cutting the Americans down to size. The opening sequence of *Cannibal Holocaust*, for example, explicitly connects the Manhattan skyline to American imperialism by coupling low-angle shots of the Empire State Building to voice-over narration from a TV reporter discussing man's omnipotence. This connection is then immediately undercut when the reporter moves on to talk about the barbaric jungles of the Amazon, but the images continue to show Manhattan street life—a deliberately ironic juxtaposition designed to deflate the achievements of American omnipotence. As the film progresses, it moves inevitably towards the 'bad' American imperialists (the missing film crew) receiving their comeuppances, with the most aggressive and immoral member of the team being shorn of his own phallus.

The 'good' colonialists, in contrast, are anthropologists and journalists who strikingly resemble the model of the *Italiani brava gente*. They uphold the official line on Italian colonialism by covering up and repressing the colonial faults they have witnessed—actions that run counter to what one expects of professional researchers. In *Cannibal Holocaust*, Professor Monroe is so appalled by the crew's documentary footage that he refuses to have anything more to do with it and petitions to have the evidence destroyed—hardly the act of an enlightened anthropologist! At the end of *Cannibal ferox*, Gloria preserves her doctoral thesis' argument that cannibalism does not exist, despite her personal evidence to the contrary. She does this to cover up the imperial aggression that was the cause of the cannibalism in the first place, and she ultimately wins an award for her contributions to the field. And *Emanuelle e gli ultimi cannibali* ends with Emanuelle asking herself if her research expedition was really worth all the deaths that it caused, leaving a note of uncertainty about whether she will publish her story or not.

The primary reason for this structural absence of Italy, and for the favoring of an apparently American perspective in the cannibal/zombie films, stems from economic and institutional factors and a domestic crisis in the Italian film industry. Throughout the 1960s and early 1970s, Italy's film industry was the strongest in Europe and second only to Hollywood in the global market. Italy saw a radical decline in its industry, however, in the second half of the 1970s. The national production average of close to three hundred films per year had dropped to ninety-eight films by 1978, and

513,700,000 domestic tickets sales in 1975 had plummeted to 276,300,000 by 1979 (Bondanella, 1983: 319). The reasons for this decline are many, including: the deregulation of Italian television, which led to the closure of many of the second-class theaters where exploitation films would play; the social-political uncertainty that hit Italy in the 1970s with the violent wave of terrorist bombings and kidnappings; and strategic changes made by Hollywood to strengthen its grip on the global market, including the withdrawal of funding from many European industries. With Italian exploitation cinema having always been anchored in imitation, the drive to replicate accelerated when the industry declined in the late 1970s and films were increasingly passed off as American product. New York City became the setting du jour of Italian exploitation cinema, with titles such as *Manhattan Baby* (Lucio Fulci, 1982), *Lo squartatore di New York/The New York Ripper* (Lucio Fulci, 1982), *1990: I guerrieri del Bronx/1990: The Bronx Warriors* (Enzo Castellari, 1982), and *2019: Dopo la caduta di New York/2019: After the Fall of New York* (Sergio Martino, 1983). Indeed, of the eight films that Fulci made between 1979 and 1982, six were set in the United States and only one was set in Italy.[5]

This strategy of imitation did more than simply dupe audiences into thinking they were watching a Hollywood film; it also had a huge impact on how Latin America was represented in European exploitation cinema. We can chart this impact by comparing the cannibal/zombie cycle of the 1970s/80s to the only other concentrated period of European genre filmmakers traveling to Latin America, which was in the late 1960s for such films as *Se tutte le donne del mondo/Kiss the Girls and Make Them Die* (Henry Levin, Arduino Maiuri, 1966), *Duello nel mondo/Ring around the World* (Luigi Scattini, Georges Combret, 1966), *Le carnaval des barbouzes/Killer's Carnival/Spy Against the World* (Alberto Cardone et al., 1966), *Ad ogni costo/Grand Slam* (Giuliano Montaldo, 1967), *Sette uomini e un cervello/Seven Men and One Brain* (Rossano Brazzi, 1968), *The Seven Secrets of Sumuru/The Girl from Rio* (Jesús Franco, 1969), and *Paroxismus/Venus in Furs* (Jesús Franco, 1969). The representation of Latin America in the two periods stand in stark contrast of one another. The 1960s films were crime and fantasy capers that took place in urban areas, usually Rio de Janeiro, and depicted Latin America as modern, chic, cosmopolitan, romantic, and vivacious—with carnival always in full swing. The films of the cannibal/zombie cycle, conversely, were set in a remote, isolated regions of a Latin America that was portrayed as prehistoric, menacing, dangerous, and cloaked in an atmosphere of death. This sweeping transformation of Latin America from a colorful carnival paradise to a green inferno nightmare can be directly linked to the industrial and economic changes that occurred in Italian (and European) exploitation cinema between the 1960s and the 1970s.

The 1960s had been a period of economic boom for both the Italian film industry and for Italian society as a whole. The cycle of films set in Latin America from this period reflect this affluence, most of which imitate a James Bond sensibility and feature globe-trotting narratives in which Rio is just one of several locations. *Ad ogni costo*, for example, moves between Rio, New York, London, Paris, and Rome; while *Le carnaval des barbouzes* takes us to Rio, Rome, Vienna, and San Francisco. The films' protagonists are equally international, such as the gang who pull off the diamond heist in *Ad ogni costo*, who are British, French, Italian, and German. The chic, urban Latin America of these films serves to reinforce a sense of European mobility and cosmopolitanism: it is an exotic Other to be conspicuously consumed, with Rio displayed as a series of vistas that mimic the covers of the *bossa nova* albums that had taken the world by storm in the mid-1960s.

By the late 1970s, with the tumultuous state of affairs in Italian life, the decline of the Italian film industry, and the increasing hegemony of Hollywood, the focus shifted away from displays of European wealth and mobility and towards an imitation of wealth and mobility from passing as American. The representations of Latin America transformed to support this shift, switching stereotypes from an exotic Other to be consumed to a savage Other that consumes you—its primitivism serving to bolster the identity of these films as a product of the modern 'First World.' It became common practice for Italian exploitation films to shoot a week or two of exterior shots in New York—usually without permits—and to hire local actors in order to sell the illusion of being an 'authentic' American film. Interestingly, however, the resulting representations of New York have a touristic quality, recalling how Rio was shot in the films from the 1960s. The city is not shot in the same way as it appears in American films of the period, in large part because of an insistence on displaying the skyline and famous landmarks whenever possible. In *Cannibal Holocaust*, for example, the television interviews with family members of the documentary crew all manage to energize the background space with familiar New York vistas. Likewise, a sex scene in *Emanuelle e gli ultimi cannibali* is staged in a vacant lot next to the Hudson River so that the Manhattan skyline can serve as a backdrop. Similarly, when Emanuelle and Professor Lester walk through the city, the camera pans up and down the tall buildings—a technique featured in similar montages in *Zombi 2*, *Cannibal Holocaust*, and *Cannibal ferox*. In other words, the conspicuous displays of Manhattan belie the films' efforts at appearing American, leaving a feeling of simulation rather than authenticity.

The net result of these various structural absences and transnational displacements is a certain kind of liminality, with the cannibal/zombie cycle occupying a series of in-between spaces. The films embrace colonial narratives about Latin America, but do so as a way of avoiding colonial memories of Africa. They pass themselves off as American productions, but are really Italian in disguise. They assume the narrative point of view of the colonizer, but do so as a means of defense against cultural and economic colonization from Hollywood. In other words, they are simultaneously colonizer and colonized. It is precisely this liminality, this in-betweenness, however, that makes the Italian cannibal/zombie films important artifacts in the writing of the nation—and points to why exploitation cinemas should be seen as significant "scraps, patches, and rags" within the fabrics of national cultures. Through their strategies of imitation and transnational dislocation we can see the films as responses to the tightening grip of American cultural imperialism, to the crises of the 1970s Italian film industry, and to the national culture's challenges in coming to terms with its own history of colonialism. In their simulation of American identities, and in their transpositions of Africa onto Latin America, the cannibal/zombie films slide ambivalently from one enunciatory position to another, creating a splitting and vacillation of national identity that recalls Bhabha's notions of liminality in the "double-writing" of nation (1994: 299). The films' various evasions, displacements, and doublings emerge as responses to the gaps and fissures of Italian colonial identity, and can be seen as attempts at reconciling the historical myths of Italian colonial 'difference' with the changing place of Italian society and culture in the global economy of the 1970s and 1980s.

From its vacillating position as both colonizer and colonized, it is perhaps not surprising that Italian exploitation cinema was so drawn to cannibals and zombies at that point in time. As literary figures, cannibals and flesh-eating zombies disrupt the interface of colonizer/colonized; their philosophy is one of erasing boundaries, of turning differences into sameness, as one culture is devoured by another. Oswald de Andrade wrote in his *Manifesto antropófago*, "Only Cannibalism unites us. Socially. Economically. Philosophically." He was speaking about the project of Brazilian modernism in the face of European and American imperialism, but the sentiment holds true (albeit with different inflections) for the Italian exploitation cinema of the 1970s and 1980s. As a strategy of dealing with the hegemony of Hollywood, Italian exploitation cinema itself practiced a form of cannibalism, eating up American cinema and spitting out a series of simulacra that were steeped in the pedagogical and performative discourses of Italian national culture. In looking at this cycle of Italian films about Latin American cannibals, we are left wondering, like Professor Monroe, who the real cannibals are—revealing a strange affinity between these European exploitation films and the Latin American stereotypes that they exploited.

NOTES

1. Most of the films discussed in this chapter possess a myriad of alternative titles, including overlapping uses of the same title by different films. I have used titles from the primary country of origin, consistent with the titles employed by the Internet Movie Database, including the most commonly used English language titles for each film, where appropriate.

2. The Italian *mondo* tradition was so popular it even reversed the usual pattern of imitation, with Americans jumping on the bandwagon with such films

as *Mondo Topless* (Russ Meyer, 1966), *Mondo Freudo* (Lee Frost, 1966), *Mondo Bizarro* (Lee Frost, 1966), *Mondo Hollywood* (Robert Carl Cohen, 1967), and *Mondo Mod* (Bethel Buckalew, 1967).

3. See the Dardano Sarchetti interview on the DVD of *Zombi 2* published by Shriek Show in 2003.

4. Other films in the 'Black Emanuelle' series include: *Emanuelle nera* (Bitto Albertini, 1975), *Emanuelle nera: Orient reportage* (Joe D'Amato, 1976), *Emanuelle in America* (Joe D'Amato, 1977), *Emanuelle: Perché violenza alle donne?* (Joe D'Amato, 1977), *Suor Emanuelle* (Giuseppe Vari, 1977), *La via della prostituzione* (Joe D'Amato, 1978), and *I mavri Emmanouella* (Ilias Mylonakos, 1979).

5. *Zombi 2* (1979), *Paura nella città dei morti viventi* (1980), *Quella villa accanto al cimitero* (1981), *Lo squartatore di New York* (1982), and *Manhattan Baby* (1982) all featured New York City; *E tu vivrai nel terrore—L'aldilà* (1981) was set in Louisiana. Only *Luca il contrabbandiere* (1980) was set in Italy.

Part II
Latsploitation Auteurs

5 Emilio Vieyra
Argentina's Transnational Master of Horror

Gerard Dapena

All major textbook accounts of Latin American cinema omit any mention of Argentinean filmmaker Emilio Vieyra.[1] For that matter, historians of Argentine cinema rarely bring up his name.[2] The latter exclusion is more surprising if we consider the longevity of Vieyra's career (forty-five years) and the wide-ranging eclecticism of his filmography, ranging from detective thrillers, superagent films, westerns, and action pictures to comedies, road movies, political dramas, and women-in-prison films. Furthermore, several of his films earned large sums of money and a few circulated outside of Argentina. A case in point would be the three musicals starring pop sensation Sandro: *Quiero llenarme de ti*/*I Want to Be Full of You* (1969), *La vida continúa*/*Life Goes On* (1969), and *Gitano*/*Gypsy* (1970); this triptych made Vieyra rich and Sandro a huge star all over Latin America.[3] After a hiatus of nearly ten years, Vieyra completed his last feature, *Cargo de conciencia*/*Guilty Conscience* (2005), a self-financed project, at the age of eighty-four. Given his lengthy and successful career, it is legitimate to wonder why Vieyra has been excluded from the canonic histories of Argentine cinema.

Although a popular cinema of genres has been the mainstay of Argentina's film industry since at least the 1930s, little attention has been devoted outside of Argentina to its popular cinema, even to the production from its classical period—the Golden Age. It is not surprising, then, that Vieyra's work is so unknown. As Dolores Tierney has pointed out, there are important political and cultural imperatives that have shaped the construction of film canons in Latin American cinema, both on a national and continental scale, resulting in the privileging of leftist political films vested in anti-imperialist discourses at the expense of popular cinemas (2004: 72). This bias helps explain the reasons behind Vieyra's exclusion. It is possible, too, that historians have been reluctant to deal with the eclecticism of his professional trajectory. Moreover, Vieyra's commercial orientation and his professed attachment to genre films have not helped his reputation in certain quarters committed to the defense of art cinema and auteurism.

Nevertheless, despite such neglect, Vieyra is finally achieving a measure of recognition. Ironically, this has come from paracinema fans, such as Argentine critic Diego Curubeto, who has recently discovered and celebrated a hitherto less heralded side to Vieyra's oeuvre (1996: 359–66). The Something Weird DVD release of *The Curious Dr. Humpp*, an English-dubbed version of Vieyra's *La venganza del sexo* (1967), followed by Something Weird Video's reissue on DVD of *The Deadly Organ*—one of several English titles for Vieyra's *Placer Sangriento* (1966)—and Mondo Macabro's subsequent release of *Blood of the Virgins/Sangre de vírgenes* (1967) have revealed Vieyra as a proficient and noteworthy master of horror cinema and highlighted his instrumental (and nearly solitary) role in carving a niche for this genre within Argentina's conservative film industry.

Vieyra's critical recovery is, however, not without its problematic aspects with respect to issues of national identity, authenticity, and authorial intentionality.[4] His newfound reputation rests on films that received limited commercial release abroad and were barely seen in their country of origin. In addition, only one of Vieyra's four films currently available on DVD is presented in its original Spanish-language track. Furthermore, the film that has single-handedly resuscitated interest in Vieyra's career, *The Curious Dr. Humpp*, is actually a heavily reedited version of *La venganza del sexo*, dubbed into English and featuring extensive sexually explicit scenes spliced into Vieyra's original cut.[5] Lastly, appreciation of Vieyra's work in paracinematic circles is often indebted to a camp sensibility that is heavily fraught with irony, balancing admiration for the films' bizarre plot twists, delirious fusion of sex and chills, imaginative camera work, and mise-en-scène with condescension for their technical and artistic shortcomings: occasional lapses in narrative logic, wooden performances, cheap makeup, and clumsy special effects. Although paracinema fans generally take these flaws as positive markers of style and authorial expression, they are still read as signs of artistic failure and incompetence; at best they are coded as acts of resistance to the dominant aesthetics (Sconce, 1995). Ultimately, Vieyra's "ineptitude" risks being read as a sign of Argentina's and his own underdevelopment.

Moreover, as the editors of *Defining Cult Movies* caution, exploitation films are generally accessed through viewing protocols and consumption practices that invest them with newfound value, often at the expense of the works' original meanings (Jancovich et al., 2003: 4). Thus, in the rush towards ever more rarefied assertions of unique personal taste and critical superiority, films like Vieyra's—products of a national film industry regarded as peripheral to the main trends of world cinema—run the risk of being reduced to exotic deracinated trash, fetishized for their double marginality: horror cinema from the so-called Third World. Given Vieyra's important contribution to Argentina's cinema, his work deserves to be considered within the historical context of its production and understood in relation to the social and cultural forces that impinged upon and shaped Argentina's film industry in the 1960s.

This chapter examines the nature of Vieyra's horror cycle on two separate but not entirely unrelated tracks. Firstly, it discusses these films' conception and circulation as transnational and cross-cultural commodities and probes the ways in which they interface between the local and the global. Vieyra's horror cycle is a unique occurrence both in his career and within the production history of mainstream Argentine filmmaking. Unlike most of Vieyra's other work, which was geared primarily, if not exclusively, towards domestic audiences, his low-budget horror movies sought to expand the population for Argentine popular cinema beyond the borders of the nation. In the process, he attempted to recover the international audiences that Argentina's film industry had lost since the early 1950s. By targeting the Hispanic market in the United States, which had only been sporadically receptive to Argentina's film production, Vieyra sought to gain a foothold inside the American market, even if this access was mainly limited to a marginal segment of the moviegoing public. Thus, at a time when most Argentinean directors, with the exception of Armando Bó (and, to a lesser extent, Leopoldo Torre Nilsson) had trouble accessing foreign markets, Vieyra, in collaboration with producer Orestes Trucco, perfected a model for international exhibition, devising filmic commodities conceived almost entirely for export.

Secondly, this chapter examines the manner by which these films mobilize and engage with important social and cultural issues that were specific to Argentina in the 1960s. Vieyra's horror movies offer openings through which one can detect traces of Argentina's ambivalent attitude towards the cultural and social effects of modernization. In fact, the films are remarkable for how they unfold in contemporary settings and dramatize conflicting responses to Argentina's confrontation with, pursuit of, desire for, and fear of modernity. Although the latter assumed a number of guises and its impact was felt in different spheres of Argentine life, modernity in the context of Vieyra's films is referenced through the new youth culture and in particular the so-called counterculture. Modernity for Argentina's youth was associated with positive experiences—change, mobility, advancement, freedom, the practice of nonconventional behavior—yet it raised fears among segments of society wary of its perceived deleterious effect on the social body. On the one hand, a cross-section of Argentina's younger generation used the trappings of Anglo-American youth culture—pop music, fashion, avant-garde art, drug consumption, gender fluidity, and sexual experimentation—as liberating tools for the construction of new identities. On the other hand, the church, the army and the state viewed these trappings as foreign, deviant, and in need of control and ultimately repression. Vieyra's fascination with youth culture was partly motivated by economic interests (i.e., the desire to tap into a niche audience in possession of disposable income and still loyal to the cinema as a key leisure activity) and partly by the desire to project an image of "hipness." Argentina's diametrical response to modernity underlies the latent ambivalence pervading Vieyra's horror films, whereby youth culture appears as a seductive lifestyle and a site for both the representation of the monstrous and the unleashing of violence.

After studying film at Columbia University, Vieyra returned to Argentina in the late 1950s. He founded a production company named Terceto and produced two features, *La madrastra/The Stepmother* (1960) and *Quinto año nacional*/Fifth National Year (1961), both directed by Rodolfo Blasco. Vieyra debuted as a director in 1961 with *Detrás de la mentira*/Behind the Truth, a low-budget police thriller notorious for its anticommunist slant. In 1965 Vieyra was approached by an American TV producer to direct a science-fiction picture, *Extraña invasión/Stay Tuned for Terror*, for the U.S. market. For economic reasons, filming took place in Argentina; the cast, headed by American actor Richard Conte, was mainly Argentine (although the story unfolded in the American South and the characters bore English names); Vieyra himself played a small part.[6] A well-crafted and eerie low-budget picture, inspired by the B-movie tradition, *Extraña invasión* signaled Vieyra's purposeful orientation towards the American market.[7]

Alerted by a friend that Puerto Ricans in New York liked horror films spiced with liberal doses of sex, Vieyra and his producer Orestes Trucco (Productores Argentinos Asociados) traveled to neighboring Uruguay to make *Placer sangriento* with a small advance of $10,000 from Pel Mex ("El rey del bizarre," 2005). Vieyra and Trucco were seeking to emulate the commercial success of *Testigo para un crimen/Violated Love* (1964), a film noir with erotic overtones designed as a star vehicle for Argentine bombshell Libertad Leblanc. After its initial run in New York's Hispanic theatrical market, *Testigo para un crimen* was acquired by the American distributor CIP, dubbed into English under Vieyra's supervision, and released, following the addition of a few erotic sequences, in the sexploitation circuit. *Placer sangriento*, shot quickly over the course of a week, opened in New York in January 1967 as an Azteca Films release. Vieyra's next horror feature, *La venganza del sexo*, was made in equally rushed and low-budget conditions; it opened in New York in May 1967, playing initially in a dozen Spanish-language theaters in Manhattan before making the rounds of screening venues in the boroughs. *La bestia desnuda* (aka *El monstruo asesino/The Naked Beast* 1967) arrived a few weeks later, opening in August across Hispanic theaters in New York and nearby New Jersey. *Sangre de vírgenes* was the last of Vieyra's horror movies, opening in New York on March 20, 1968.[8] *Placer sangriento* was the only film from Vieyra's horror cycle to have a timely premiere in Argentina, opening in Buenos Aires on November 22, 1967, almost a year after its New York debut. Vieyra's other horror films were not seen in his native country until the early 1970s, several years after their dates of completion, due to the strict censorship laws put in place by military authorities in the mid-1960s.[9]

While Vieyra was directing his first features, Argentina's cinema was experiencing a brief renaissance after the creation of the Instituto Nacional de Cinematografía (National Film Institute) and the passage in 1957 of a new cinema law favorable to domestic production. In the mid-1950s, Argentina's film industry was in profound decline; only one studio, Argentina Sono Film, remained active. Among the measures that revitalized domestic production were the concession of subsidies and prizes to filmmakers and producers and new guarantees of freedom of artistic expression. As a result, the number of Argentine films released domestically increased from fifteen feature films in 1957 to an annual average of thirty features between 1958 and 1967 (Calistro, 1984: 109–38). This period witnessed the emergence of the *Nuevo cine argentino*, a group of young filmmakers (including Manuel Antín, Fernando Ayala, Leonardo Favio, David Kohon, Rodolfo Kuhn) devoted to formal and narrative experimentation, in line with contemporary European trends, such as the French New Wave. Although short-lived as a movement, the directors associated with the *Nuevo cine argentino*, along with more seasoned artists such as Torre Nilsson, fashioned what might be considered Argentina's native brand of art cinema: intellectually complex, artistically sophisticated, reflective of an urban, modern, cosmopolitan sensibility. Their films, however, were better received by jurors and critics in international film festivals than by domestic audiences or even state film agencies.[10] Attacks came as well from the Left. Fernando Birri, a contemporary of these directors—and one of the key figures in the New Latin American Cinema movement—criticized their misguided penchant for a solipsistic "cinema of expression" that turned its back on the masses and lacked true revolutionary power (1997: 86–94).

Coetaneous with its birth and decline, Vieyra's cinema stands at the antipodes of the *Nuevo cine*, yet it hardly conforms to Birri's prescriptions for an antibourgeois and anticolonial cinema. If Vieyra's horror films from the 1960s are subversive, it is not because of their formal or ideological radicalism but rather for the challenge they posed to prevailing criteria of cinematic taste. Argentina's film industry had showed little inclination towards the development of a national horror cinema. It is not surprising, then, that the genre has traditionally endured a low repute among scholars and critics alike and has never achieved the prominence it found in other Latin American countries (Mexico, Brazil).[11] Clearly, Vieyra's turn to horror would have added little prestige to his career.

By today's standards, *Placer sangriento* is not a particularly frightening or erotically shocking film. The plot follows an investigation into the killings of several attractive young women who frequent nightclubs populated by shady characters and sexual deviants. The murderer, who conceals himself behind a monster mask, seduces his victims by playing a strange melody on an organ from a beachside cottage. Entranced by the music, the women deliver themselves into the hands of the killer, who injects them with a drug before intercourse, and later plunges a syringe into their torsos.

The women, portrayed as hedonistic and carefree, are at one point alluded to by the coroner involved in the investigation as "examples of modern youth" who are "all out of it" because of drugs, and therefore deserve to be murdered. As the killings mount and potential suspects are found dead, the police enlist a stripper (Gloria Prat) as a decoy to trap the assassin. Drawn by the trance-inducing organ music, she almost perishes but is saved by an inspector, who in turn slays the killer.

Placer sangriento displays several traits of Vieyra's horror cycle. Although it was made with little money, the film has a professional look far removed from typical exploitation fare. Its aesthetic virtues include atmospheric low-key cinematography by cameraman Aníbal González Paz, a moody musical score by Victor Buchino, and some complex camera work: a fondness for handheld shots, expressive close-ups and camera angles, subjective point-of-view shots, and startling contrasts of foreground/background spatial relations. These stylistic markers resurfaced to even greater effect in *La venganza del sexo*, a mad scientist tale that carries the subgenre's clichés to new heights of imagination and eroticism. As the film opens, a monster is on the loose, kidnapping teenagers in order to supply subjects for the experiments of Dr. Zoide (Aldo Barbero). Following the instructions of a talking brain preserved in a jar, Zoide wants to manufacture a serum obtained from the bodily chemicals released during sexual activity as a means to unlock the secret of eternal life. Horacio Funes (Ricardo Bauleo), a journalist, investigates the case alongside the police. After the monster kidnaps a stripper (Prat), Horacio manages to find his way into Zoide's hideout, but is discovered and subjected to the scientist's sexual tests. Managing to escape with the help of Zoide's nurse (Susana Beltrán), who has fallen in love with him, Horacio confronts Zoide in his laboratory, but just as the doctor is about to strangle him, the stripper stabs Zoide to death.

Neither *Placer sangriento* nor *La venganza del sexo* were kindly received by Buenos Aires' mainstream film critics. *La prensa*'s reviewer found the former lacking in anecdotal interest and decried its generic indeterminacy, neither truly horror nor a conventional crime thriller. He ultimately dismissed it as a mere excuse for the exhibition of female bodies in varied states of undress (*La prensa*, 1967). *La prensa*'s reviewer found *La venganza del sexo* puerile and lacking in suspense and deemed it a poor expression of the nation's cinema. Furthermore, he lamented that Vieyra's film was playing in a first-tier movie theater. Thus, not only was Vieyra's film regarded as an inappropriate representative of national cinema; it was seen as having "invaded" the exhibition space usually reserved for quality films (*La prensa*, 1971).

La bestia desnuda, the third horror feature in the Trucco-Vieyra partnership, treads on familiar ground. Ibañez, a young police inspector (Aldo Barbero), is assigned to the murder case of a chorus girl. His investigation leads him to interrogate the members of the theater revue where she danced. Through various narrative devices, camera movements and setups, and the use of suspenseful music, various characters are posited as suspects: the singer Rolo Borel (Rolo Puente); René, a costume designer (Osvaldo Pacheco); the theater's hunchback janitor (nicknamed Quasimodo); even the revue's director (played by Vieyra). As further assassinations raise the stakes for Ibañez, he persuades his girlfriend Sonia (Prat) to join the revue and help him track the killer through her inside knowledge. However, Sonia soon becomes the focus of the killer's obsessions.

Essentially a color remake of *Placer sangriento*, *La bestia desnuda*, in spite of its sensationalistic title, is the more pedestrian and least chilling of the cycle. It is also the least erotic, with few brief flashes of Prat's nude torso and a short scene featuring Beltrán's voluptuous naked body. On the other hand, it is the film that is most explicitly engaged with Buenos Aires' pop art scene, even if its depiction is trivialized and used mostly to add background color. The film's centerpiece is a musical sequence titled "Happening," edited at a frenetic pace to capture the sensorial impressions of a psychedelic trip. The scene capitalizes on the notoriety of Marta Minujín's famous happenings at the Instituto di Tella, arguably the most popularized among Buenos Aires' avant-garde events.[12] From an improvised stage in a villa at night, Rolo and René compel the crowd to live for the moment and escape from the emptiness of daily life by becoming a different person. As the song unfolds, the camera cuts to close-ups of different participants— lesbians, gays, cross-dressers, nymphomaniacs, pot smokers—donning outrageous costumes and wigs, awash in a sea of color. The scene concludes on a macabre note, with a staged guillotine execution.

Sangre de vírgenes, Vieyra's last horror film, and the bloodiest and most erotic of all, places another group of rabidly modern youth in harm's way. Unlike the predominantly somber interiors and night settings of earlier films, the first half of *Sangre de vírgenes* unfolds under the bright sun and blue skies of Argentina's Andes; repeated shots of crystalline lakes, tree-covered summits, and green meadows recall a tourist travelogue. A short nightclub sequence where our young protagonists consume drugs, go topless, and dance orgiastically sets the appropriately hip tone. Soon we are in familiar horror film territory, as a car breaks down in a deserted road at night, forcing the three couples to seek shelter in an abandoned lodge. The film's prologue, set seemingly in the nineteenth century, gives us the background story to the lodge's spectral inhabitants: Ofelia (Beltrán), the reluctant companion to the vampire Gustavo (Walter Kliche), who murdered Ofelia's husband Arturo (Miguel Angel Olmos) on her wedding night and then transformed her into a vampire. Weary of living in eternal damnation, she can only find a way out of her condition through sexual encounters with men. As Gustavo feasts on the female visitors, Ofelia seduces Raúl (Puente) and Tito (Bauleo). Liberated by her lovemaking, Ofelia kills Gustavo in his coffin with a dagger given to her by Arturo's ghost and then commits suicide.

Although it entailed an unprecedented move in the context of Argentina's cinema, Vieyra's turn to horror paralleled contemporary trends in international popular cinema. Coinciding with a resurgence of horror cinema in the 1960s, thanks to the success of the British-based Hammer Films, Roger Corman's AIP productions, and the work of Mario Bava, Vieyra's foray into this genre revealed a synchronous awareness of related enterprises in other Latin American national cinemas. In the mid to late 1950s, Mexico's film industry began a successful horror and fantasy cycle (including *Ladrón de cadáveres/Bodysnatcher*, Fernando Méndez, 1956), while, in the early 1960s, Brazilian José Mojica Marins made a string of low-budget horror films (including *À meia noite levarei sua alma/At Midnight I'll Take Your Soul*, 1963). Arguably, the manner in which contemporary practitioners of horror (particularly Hammer) were adding liberal amounts of highly suggestive eroticism emboldened Vieyra to test the boundaries of sexual permissiveness in his native Argentina; his films became notorious for their abundant nudity and their fondness for risqué subject matter (drugs, transvestism, homosexuality, nymphomania) traditionally avoided by Argentinean directors. The films' marketing campaigns, both in Argentina and in the United States, emphasized the interface of sex and violence.[13] In fact, their very audacity made their exhibition in Argentina nearly impossible.

Adam Lowenstein has argued for the need to examine gore and horror cinema's aesthetics of shock in connection with legacies of political and social violence. For Lowenstein, "the modern horror film may well be the genre of our time that registers most brutally the legacies of historical trauma" (2005: 10). Seemingly removed from the political turmoil of the times and designed with commercial intentions, Vieyra's films can nevertheless be read as representations inscribed with the indexical signs of Argentine society's encounter with violence and trauma. Their exhibition history in Argentina bears witness to a history of censorship and suppression and their on-screen bloodletting intimates at the Argentine state's increasing use of force against its citizens, a trend that would culminate in the brutal repression of the mid-1970s.[14]

After Perón's removal from power via a military coup in 1955, Argentina's traditional elites replaced his nationalist and protectionist agenda with a liberalization of the economy that led to the privatization of state firms and resources and the opening of the country to international financing. A wave of consumerism swept the middle classes and cultural endeavors took on a cosmopolitan cast. But Perón's followers and the disenfranchised working class continued to agitate and resist the dismantling of former populist policies through strikes, factory occupations, and, eventually, a clandestine guerrilla movement. State repression increased and widened its reach as the military took on a more prominent role in political and social life, especially after the onset in 1966 of the ruthless dictatorship of Juan Carlos Onganía. Under the latter's watch, students as well as workers became targets of state violence, censorship regulations were reinstated and reinforced, and the emerging avant-garde and related pop art scenes orbiting around the exhibition and performance space Instituto di Tella, among other Buenos Aires venues, came under intense scrutiny.[15]

Sergio Pujol (2002) describes the impact of Anglo-American rock music and its attendant fashions and countercultural attitudes in shaping alternative lifestyles among Argentina's urban youth. While Argentina's pop scene generally lacked a strong political dimension, under the rightward turn of Onganía's government, unconventional behavior in matters of clothing, personal appearance, sexuality, and leisure activities took on a contestatory edge that invited police intervention and punishment (verbal abuse and harassment, forced haircuts, beatings, police raids and closings of counterculture venues and publications, etc.) (Pujol, 2002: 49). Hippies, rockers, pot-smoking bohemians, and other countercultural types (the *psiconautas*, as writer Miguel Angel Grinberg called them) became objects of media fascination—witness the numerous articles in mainstreams weeklies like *Primera Plana*[16]—and were demonized by the Right, and ultimately co-opted by the mainstream culture industry (i.e., *El extraño del pelo largo/ The Stranger with Long Hair*, Julio Porter, 1969; *El profesor hippie/The Hippy Professor*, Fernando Ayala, 1969; and *La familia hippie/The Hippy Family*, Enrique Carreras, 1971).

Raymond Durgnat once remarked that the kingpin of the horror genre was "the rendezvous of eroticism and violence" (2000: 39). Vieyra's horror cycle fully subscribes to this formula, although the violence, with the exception of *Sangre de vírgenes*, is generally suggested rather than depicted and the sexual situations are less explicit than in contemporary American sexploitation films. Truth be said, it is sometimes hard to say with exactitude what Vieyra's point of view is on the sexually promiscuous and drug-taking youths that people his horror films; there is no overt message of condemnation, on moral or political grounds, nor is there a celebration of these subcultures. Following the mold of typical exploitation cinema, Vieyra's display of nudity, sexual licentiousness, and transgressive behavior foregrounds the appeal of forbidden spectacle; the striptease sequences in *Placer sangriento* and *La venganza del sexo* are good examples of this penchant for titillation. An ad for *La bestia desnuda* in the New York Spanish-language daily *El diario/La prensa* advertised the film as a peek into "a hallucinating world of drugs, sex, vice and pleasure" (1967). As Eric Schaefer points out in his groundbreaking study on this subgenre, exploitation films are often vehicles that symbolically articulate fear of difference and anxiety in the face of Otherness through the depiction of controversial and risqué subject matter (1999: 13). When we also consider Barry Keith Grant's claim that horror films mainly express the dread of bodily difference and negotiate the problematics of sexuality and gender roles, then Vieyra's horror cycle can be read as an exploration of the dual challenge to identity posed by modernity and nontraditional sexual practices (1996: 6).

The affinities between Vieyra's horror pictures and (s)exploitation are, ironically, more clearly revealed in *The Curious Dr. Humpp*. A few years after Vieyra's Spanish-language horror films had played out their profitable commercial runs, New York–based filmmaker and distributor Jerald Intrator obtained a print of *La venganza del sexo* which he proceeded to dub into English and, with the addition of visual material shot in the United States, released under the title of *The Curious Dr. Humpp,* an allusion to the popular Scandinavian X-rated art-house hit *I Am Curious Yellow.*[17] As Frank Henenlotter points out in the DVD's liner notes, Intrator integrated into Vieyra's original master over seventeen minutes of footage, preparing two different versions for theatrical distribution: one "hot" print with the erotic inserts and another "cold" print without for those locales with tough censorship laws (2003).[18] The inserts, which included separate sexual scenes involving two lesbians, a masturbating seminude blonde, and an orgy with four pot-smoking hippies, are dispersed evenly throughout the movie. The first of the two lesbian scenes appears a couple of minutes into the beginning of the film; it is connected to the plot through inserted close-ups of the monster's feet walking down a hallway and its hands turning a door knob. As it enters their room, we see a medium shot of the two women reacting in horror to its presence, followed by a close-up shot of the monster's grotesque face. This is the first time we see the creature, whereas in Vieyra's version its face is revealed much later, at the end of the striptease scene and just before the film's credits. Later inserts are similarly connected to the plot by means of various point-of-view shots, either belonging to the monster, to Dr. Zoide (now named Dr. Humpp), or to Horacio (now named George). A scene with the latter character is another good example of how Intrator's inserts are woven seamlessly into Vieyra's film. As Horacio/George wanders through the doctor's house, he opens various doors and peers into rooms. Vieyra's version featured over-the-shoulder shots of Bauleo looking at women asleep in beds, whereas Intrator's print substituted point-of-view shots of individuals engaged in sexual activity. In an ensuing scene, Bauleo hides from the monster behind a door as it enters a room; Intrator added shots of the hippie orgy as if they belonged to the monster's point of view, whereas in Vieyra's film the room is empty. Later, when Horacio and the stripper are forced to make love without touching, Intrator superimposed more explicit sexual images. He also made some alterations to the sound-track, adding lines of dialogue ("Go, Baby, Go" or "That's it!") along with groans and sighs that reference the sexual acts being depicted. Dr. Zoide/Humpp's dialog is altered so as to emphasize his obsession with sex and the sexual nature of his experiments; offhand remarks about hippies and lesbians serve to suture Intrator's inserts into the plot.

The Curious Dr. Humpp played the grindhouse circuit across the United States. With its aggressive sexual imagery and degrading portrayal of hippies, Intrator's print heightens the exploitative elements in Vieyra's original cut. For this reason, the portrayal of countercultural lifestyles and articulation of Otherness in *The Curious Dr. Humpp* are far less ambiguous. The representation of sexuality and its interaction with the

film's terrifying elements invoke even more clearly the dread of sexual difference that Williams (1996), Clover (1992), Berenstein (1996), and Creed
(1993), among others, see as constitutive of the horror genre. Titillating
shots of full frontal nudity and suggested sexual activity (masturbation,
intercourse) are quickly followed by shocking close-ups of the monster's
hideous face, pushing the viewer into a confrontation with the abject.
Furthermore, the extended duration of the soft-core passages destroys
Vieyra's calibrated balancing of narrative and erotic spectacle by favoring
the latter, while the added pulpy dialog heightens the story's overall zani-
ness, enhancing the film's camp appeal. Given the limited visibility of the
Spanish-language version, Vieyra's renascent reputation as a filmmaker
rests on the popularity of Intrator's print, which resurfaced in later years
on TV—excerpts were shown on *The Reel Wild Cinema* cable show on
the USA Network in the mid-1990s—and other specialized exhibition
circuits geared towards fans of psychotronic cinema. In fact, the fate of
La venganza del sexo is proof of how the hegemony of the 'First World'
in matters of cultural hierarchies and the circulation and consumption of
media still determines to some extent the recognition of filmic commodities from peripheral film industries like Argentina's and the conferral of
value onto marginal works of popular world cinema such as Vieyra's.[19]

Vieyra's horror cycle constitutes an interesting case study, in that it
allows us to examine the interface of center and periphery, the local and
the global within the arena of Argentina's popular cinema over the course
of four decades. Vieyra assimilates Hollywood and European visual, narrative, and generic conventions from the position of a filmmaker operating
inside a peripheral film industry, yet trained in the 'First World.' Despite the
films' obvious commercial elements, their affiliations to a critically disreputable genre and the political-cultural context surrounding their production
consigned them to a marginal status within Argentina. Yet these very deter-
minants enabled the films' initial entry into the 'First World,' albeit through
its peripheral markets: first Hispanic audiences, then English-speaking
exploitation circuits, and lastly the world of paracinema and psychotronic
film consumption.[20] These latter communities, firmly based in the 'First
World,' have been key players in the reevaluation of Vieyra's career.[21]

As occurred with cult filmmakers such as Ed Wood, Russ Meyer, and
Mojica Marins, paracinematic circles have laid the ground for potential considerations of Vieyra's oeuvre within the theoretical and critical
parameters of auteurship. However, authorship and authenticity have been
contested ideas in film studies for some time now. Hence, the notion that
the study of exploitation cinema can be carried out under auteurist terms
is extremely problematic. Indeed, much of the pleasure attained from the
consumption of paracinema rests on its rejection of the (initially auteurist) values used to define the cinema as a form of 'high art.' The exhibition
and distribution protocols of exploitation cinema often tended to preclude claims of authorship, as footage was freely lifted and plagiarized,

reappropriated and recycled in endless variations. Ultimately, exploitation films thrived on the levels of shock and titillation they were able to deliver, not on the recognition of a director's name. Intrator's unsanctioned commercialization of Vieyra's work illustrates the disregard for authorship typical of exploitation cinema's entrepreneurial spirit. And yet, in tension with this dismissal of authorial presence, there is an inevitable temptation to look at the dual operations of mimesis and recontextualization in works like *La venganza del sexo* as expressions of an idiosyncratic talent. And since Intrator's modified versions have been the basis for the current DVD transfers that have reestablished Vieyra's reputation, it is legitimate to at least raise the question of meaning and intentionality.

Although at first glance such moves would seemingly contradict Vieyra's loose and eclectic approach to genre and his likely lack of self-awareness as a so-called auteur, there are some grounds to validate these claims. Vieyra produced all of his films, which gave him creative control; he occasionally wrote some of his own story lines and screenplays and, during the 1960s, repeatedly worked with the same crew—notably with cinematographer González Paz and music composer Victor Buchino—and a small staple of actors (Bauleo, Beltrán, Prat, Barbero, Puente). Furthermore, the horror films all revolve diegetically around a police investigation, creating an interesting hybridization of horror and detective film. The theme of addiction and repeated references to drugs resurface in each of these works. Stylistically, the films demonstrate Vieyra's preference for a nervously roving handheld camera (often endowed with a high degree of subjectivity), tilted angles, wide-angle shots, and cuts to unsettling close-ups. They also exhibit a predilection for an anachronistic mise-en-scène inspired by the expressionistic aesthetics of Universal horror films and distill, at times, an uncanny visual poetry steeped in surrealism.

As Schaefer points out, cinematic forms that occupy marginal positions within a national film industry, such as exploitation cinema (and one might add horror and trash cinema), frequently deal with issues that are actually central to society (1999: 13). I argue that the same is true of Vieyra's horror cycle. The hostility and suppression that befell the reception of this body of work in Argentina is understandable not only from the point of view of taste and public morality but also cultural politics. One defining characteristic of Vieyra's horror movies is how implicated they are with the pulse of modernity, tapping into manifestations like pop culture, which were perceived and lived by sections of Argentina's society as both liberating and threatening. It might be helpful to compare a film like *La bestia desnuda* to the landmark agitprop documentary *La hora de los hornos/The Hour of the Furnaces* (1968), where left-wing filmmakers Octavio Getino and Fernando Solanas depict Argentina's avant-garde artists and counterculture types as the agents of imperialism. Party scenes and happenings are followed by a barrage of vacuous advertisements. Getino and Solanas present these youths as decadent hedonists whose consumerist embrace of pop art and the media commodities of the 'First World' place them at odds with the revolutionary process of national liberation and cultural decolonialization. Rather than embodying nonconformity, the adherents of Anglo-American youth culture are implicitly portrayed as symptoms of Argentina's neocolonial status and agents of cultural dependency.

In contrast, Vieyra's position on youth culture is not politicized; he does not treat modern art, pop culture, and the counterculture as threats to Argentina's sovereignty and cultural essences, but neither does he explicitly endorse the counterculture's antiestablishment spirit. References to these contemporary cultural movements were likely included to enhance the films' export value, while depictions of fringe sexualities and debauched behavior were meant to increase their prurient appeal to the target audiences. At the same time, these transgressive representations rendered the films as explosive cultural commodities set to rankle the conservative Argentine state. Through the depiction (and overlapping) of sexual desire and violence (kidnappings, rapes, brutal murders), Vieyra's films intersect the field of politics, or, at the very least, hint at a "political unconscious," to use Fredric Jameson's (1981) term. On the one hand, these images confronted and defied an implacable censorship apparatus and managed to elicit criticism both from the Right and the Left; on the other hand, these films were conceived with the knowledge that, regardless of their (in)visibility in Argentina, they would circulate and generate profits abroad. Is their local significance diminished in any way because of this transnational drift? [22] These films' suppression, first by Argentina's censors, film exhibitors, and critics and later by many of the film historians who have chronicled this era, certainly attests to the discomfort elicited by their presence; they do not happily fit into idealized notions of the national (cinema). Their lurid imagery and exploitation of countercultural sensibilities identify Vieyra's films as unmistakable products of Argentina's rebellious decade; their terrifying moments were mere preambles of further nightmares to come.

NOTES

1. John King, for instance, makes no mention of Vieyra in his section on Argentine cinema (2000: 79–97).
2. In her book on Argentine cinema, Tamara Falicov devotes two lines to Vieyra (2007: 44). Argentine film historians omit Vieyra's cinema altogether. See, for instance, J. M. Couselo et al. (1984). One exception is the multivolume history of Argentine cinema coordinated by Claudio España, which devotes a few pages to a profile of Vieyra's career (López, 2004: 250–52). There is also a discussion of Vieyra's and Trucco's collaboration with Libertad Leblanc in Gregorio Anchou (2004a: 452–54).
3. For details on the Sandro films, see Anchou (2004b: 426–27).
4. Daniel López dismisses Vieyra as a "hardcore reactionary" and berates Curubeto for having contributed to the growing cult around Vieyra's work (2004: 250).

100   *Gerard Dapena*

5. The reissue of *Placer sangriento* in the English-language version (*The Deadly Organ/Feast of Flesh*) is not as heavily compromised, although the dubbed dialog is badly dated.

6. Argentina's lower labor costs made it an attractive location for international film shoots. For a history of the relationship between Argentina's and Hollywood's respective film industries, see Curubeto (1993).

7. The film's production and exhibition history is somewhat obscure. Vieyra has spoken of an English-language version (with actors miming their words in English), but no information on an American release is available; plus, the only print in circulation today is a Spanish version (where, Conte aside, the actors' lips are clearly enunciating the dialog in Spanish). *Extraña invasión* opened in Buenos Aires eight years later, on October 10, 1974 (Curubeto, 1996: 362).

8. That the film played in New York City in a double bill, paired on one occasion with the Spanish musical *Carmen, la de Ronda* (1959), starring Sara Montiel and directed by fellow Argentinean Tulio Demicheli, suggests eclectic exhibition patterns among Spanish-language exhibitors.

9. Another reason for the delay is that Trucco, who was based in the United States, apparently did not have good contacts with Argentina's exhibitors. Eventually, *La venganza del sexo* opened in Buenos Aires on March 19, 1971, at the Metro theater; *La bestia desnuda* on March 25, 1971, at the Hindu theater; and *Sangre de vírgenes* on March 21, 1974. All three were released by Producciones Arroyo SCA, Vieyra's new production company.

10. For more on the *Nuevo cine*, see Aguilar (2004: 82–97).

11. For a history of horror and psychotronic films in Argentina, see Curubeto (1998: 128–35).

12. The weekly magazine *Primera plana* regularly covered Minujín's activities. For instance, see "Happenings. El gabinete de la doctora Minujín" (1966: 77) or "Happenings . . . y llegó el gran día" (1966: 20). For an overview of Argentina's art scene in the 1960s, see Giunta (2007).

13. An advance article in *La prensa* (21 March 1971) described *La bestia desnuda* as a work of suspense and terror against a backdrop of eroticism, while an ad announced that "the intimacy of the crime drew his victims, young and beautiful women, arousing in them lustful desires." An ad in the New York daily *El diario/La prensa* (20 March 1968) for *Sangre de vírgenes* capitalized on Beltrán's physique, as it warned readers of "sexual vampires drinking the blood of virgins."

14. On the topic of film censorship, see Maranghello (2004: 268–78) and España (2004: 336–37). For an understanding of Argentina's cycles of violence and repression, see Robben (2005).

15. For an introduction to the history of Argentina, see Romero (2002).

16. For instance, "Hacia la generación de la marijuana" (1967); "Unisexo. Chicas como muchachos que parecen chicas" (1966); "Alucinógenos. Viaje al centro de la historia" (1967); "Adolescentes. La bohemia de los fines de semana" (1966).

17. Intrator's trailer advertised Vieyra's film as "The Most Curious Picture of Them All." Later in 1971 Intrator would release an English-language version of *Placer sangriento* under the title *The Deadly Organ*.

18. For the distinction between hot and cold versions, see Schaefer (1999: 73–4).

19. In Argentina in 1994, Vieyra's horror cycle received renewed critical and public attention following a screening in Buenos Aires of all five films at the ICI, Spain's cultural center.

20. Ironically, the resurgence of interest among mainstream audiences towards exploitation films, spearheaded among others by Quentin Tarantino's and Robert Rodriguez's work in Hollywood and a parallel boom in academic and commercial publishing on the subject, has made Vieyra's once maligned and forgotten horror movies appealing to widening audiences; while the works of Fernando Solanas and Fernando Birri may continue to be admired by the few, these remain marginal to mass audiences and recent academic trends.

21. A week after its 1967 premiere in Buenos Aires' Sala Sarmiento, *Placer sangriento* was bounced off the screen to make way for a British horror film (*Frankenstein Created Woman*). Over thirty years later, a screening of The *Curious Dr. Humpp* on Britain's Channel 4 sparked a surge of interest in Vieyra's forgotten work. Psychotronic filmmaker Frank Henenlotter and the punk-rock band The Ramones are among Vieyra's most famous fans.

22. There were historic precedents to Vieyra's transnational experiment. Carlos Gardel in the1930s and later Libertad Lamarque in the 1940s and 1950s were Argentina's first transnational film stars; their films regularly played the Hispanic exhibition circuits in the United States. A classic like *Dios se lo pague* (*May God Reward You*, 1948) was a critical and commercial hit in the United States and was even considered by the Academy for a special award. Closer to Vieyra's time, the films of Torre Nilsson played well in Europe and a high number of international coproductions boosted Argentina's filmic output in the 1960s. But only director Armando Bó, leveraging the erotic appeal of his leading lady Isabel Sarli into box-office success, managed to secure continued distribution in foreign markets, including the United States, for over a decade. Not unlike Vieyra, Bó has been given at best cursory coverage in histories of Latin American cinema. Unlike Vieyra's films, Bó and Sarli's pictures did open in Argentina in a regular and generally timely fashion, albeit in tamer versions than those exhibited abroad (Ruétalo, 2004: 79–95).

6 Arty Exploitation, Cool Cult, and the Cinema of Alejandro Jodorowsky

Josetxo Cerdán and Miguel Fernández Labayen

MIDNIGHT MOVIES, EXPLOITATION, CULT, UNDERGROUND, *AUTEUR*, AND ART CINEMAS

Terms like *cult, exploitation, midnight* and *underground* movies or films have frequently been used as synonyms of a wide spectrum of minor, psychotronic, or paracinemas.[1] Although all these categories are closely related, they define diverse *sites* of cinematographic culture and refer to different features. Exploitation cinema, for example, is an industrial, thematic, and aesthetic category that mainly refers to particular circumstances of production, but it can also refer to a separate category of consumption and exhibition. Exploitation films are literally made *to exploit* the audience. Conversely, cult films may have a range of different production circumstances (from expensive studio films to poverty row quickies) and aesthetics (from classical to avant-garde) but are actually identified as 'cult films' by the audience. As Jancovich et al. have pointed out, the term *cult* refers to the ways in which films are classified in consumption. Generally, the fans self-consciously produce cult films as "cult" objects, irregardless of whether the director may or may not share the fans' subculture (2003: 1).

Chilean director Alejandro Jodorowsky may have been the first filmmaker to have successfully crossed over from exploitation to the mainstream making films that simultaneously embrace both cult and exploitation categories. Subsequent directors with similar beginnings in midnight or exploitation circuits (David Lynch, David Cronenberg, and Peter Jackson) have followed a comparable route, exceeding their marginal status by embracing much more mainstream and expensive productions and budgets. In the 1980s Lynch and Cronenberg made the leap from cult, sci-fi, and horror subculture (*Eraserhead,* 1977; *Shivers,* 1975), becoming art cinema auteurs (*Blue Velvet,* 1986; *Videodrome,* 1983). Similarly, in the 1990s and 2000s (and largely through the *Lord of the Rings* trilogy, 2001–2003) Jackson broke down the boundaries between his early exploitation/cult (*Bad Taste,* 1987; *Meet the Feebles,* 1989; *Braindead,* 1992) and later mainstream (*King Kong,* 2005) films and is now considered a mainstream auteur. This chapter will argue that Jodorowsky is an important precursor to these crossings between exploitation and art cinema. Taking a cue from Joan Hawkins, who looks at other

1960s artist-director-exploiteers (Andy Warhol and Paul Morrisey), this chapter will suggest that key to Jodorowsky's crossover is his simultaneous involvement with midnight movies, underground, art, and auteur cinema (2000a: 117–203). It will also explore how Jodorowsky relates cult cinema and exploitation cinema as 'taste subcultures' through similar textual and cultural strategies and, at the same time, how he manages to control all the tropes of auteur and art cinema, from the making of his films to the discourses surrounding them. Furthermore, this chapter analyzes how Jodorowsky aesthetically plays with cinema's myths, art world mystique, and mass culture idolatry, suggesting that he produces a multilayered cinema that finds its own place in contemporary cultural markets and categories. It will begin with a brief look at the self-image Jodorowsky constructs for his audience and cult fan base. Then it goes on to analyze the four films Jodorowsky made in Mexico to explore the place of these films within Mexican culture and their connection to Mexican cinema. The chapter ends with a consideration of Jodorowsky's exploitation strategies.

A SELF-MADE RUSSIAN-JEW-CHILEAN-FRENCH-AMERICAN EXPLOITEER

To understand Jodorowsky's exploitation and art cinema practices, one has to first appreciate his self-construction as an eccentric, extreme persona. Indeed, despite directing only six feature films (*Fando y Lis* ,1967; *El topo*, 1970; *La montaña sagrada/The Holy Mountain*, 1973; *Tusk*, 1980; *Santa sangre/Holy Blood*, 1989; *The Rainbow Thief*, 1990), his personal idiosyncratic character has led to a strong paracinematic following. The following quotation emphasizes how Jodorowsky creates himself as an excessive, unconventional egocentric, simultaneously a bourgeois intellectual, a spiritual mystic, and a freak fan:

> My parents were Russian. I was born in Iquique, a small town of 2000 people in Chile near Bolivia. I lived in the desert for ten years. The children didn't accept me because I was a 'Russian.' I moved to Santiago, the capital of Chile, where I studied Philosophy and Psychology. I worked in a circus as a clown. I acted in several plays and formed my own Marionette Theatre. I created a Theatre of Mime. I lived in Santiago for ten years. The young men didn't accept me because I was a 'Jew.' I went to Europe and lived in Paris. During that time I worked with Marcel Marceau and eventually became his partner. I wrote 'The Cage' and 'The Mask Maker' for him. I directed Maurice Chevalier. I founded the 'Panic' Movement with [Francisco] Arrabal and [Roland] Topor. I realized a Four Hour Happening which has been acclaimed as the best happening ever made. I lived in Paris for ten years. The French didn't

accept me because I was a 'Chilean.' I moved to Mexico where I directed 100 plays (Ionesco, Arrabal, Strindberg, Beckett, classical plays, etc.). I also wrote for the theatre (Zarathustra, Opera del orden, etc.). I wrote three books, as well as a comic strip. I directed my first films *Fando y Lis* and *El topo*. I lived in Mexico for ten years. The Mexicans didn't accept me because I was 'French.' I am married and have three sons and a daughter. Now I live in the United States where I am finishing my film, *The Holy Mountain*. The Americans think I am 'Mexican.' After ten years, I will move to another planet. They won't accept me because they will think I am 'American.' (Jodorowsky, 1973)

In this self-parodic statement, made as he was finishing *La montaña sagrada*, Jodorowsky briefly adopts (only to discard) the multicultural and transnational persona of a Russian-Chilean-Mexican-French-American Jew. He situates himself and his work in a complex web of references that simultaneously evoke highbrow European culture (Marceau, Ionesco, Beckett), exploitation transnationalism, and medium mutability (being from everywhere and yet nowhere at the same time; conceiving comic strips, making TV programs, writing self-help books, and acting in theaters). When he made this proclamation, Jodorowsky was being feted both as underground celebrity in the sophisticated, countercultural New York art scene and as auteur in the European art cinema circuit of the 1970s. *El topo* was still a big success both as one of the original 'midnight movies' of New York's East Village and as the best picture screened in London in 1973 by *Films & Filming* magazine (García Riera, 1996b: 283) and shown at the London Film Festival.[2]

META-MEXICO: *FANDO Y LIS, EL TOPO, LA MONTAÑA SAGRADA,* AND *SANTA SANGRE*

From his arrival in Mexico in 1960, Jodorowsky played a key part in contemporary Mexican culture. He staged for the first time in Mexico plays of Eugène Ionesco, Samuel Beckett, August Strindberg, and Arthur Schnitzler, directed the world premiere of *Penélope* by Leonora Carrington, and adapted for the stage works of Kafka and Nietzsche. Some of them provoked strong reactions, public scandals, and even censorship (Avedaño Trujillo, n.d.; González Dueñas, 2006: 297). To counter any further censorship attempts, Jodorowsky created the *efímero*, a concept similar to the *happening* in that it takes place only once (González Dueñas, 2006: 297; Jodorowsky, 2007: 328). He performed almost thirty *efímeros* before traveling to Paris in 1965, where he created the Grupo Pánico (Panic Movement), along with Spanish theatrical author Arrabal and French painter Topor. Pánico's work and its motto "humor, horror and simultaneity" evidenced its taste for surrealist inspired shock, discomfort, and cruelty (Jodorowsky, 2003).

Jodorowsky's theatrical work is key to understanding his later work in film. His dramatic endeavors in Mexico and Paris illustrate a mixture of European intellectualism, American (North and South) culture, and oppositional taste. Knowledge of these elements is necessary to understand Jodorowsky's exploitation universe, both in terms of its performativity and its quest for transgression and parody. His education in mime and experimental theater and his founding of an avant-garde movement in France are central to the Latin American exploitation aesthetic he develops, where *humor, horror,* and *simultaneity* are parts of the cultural practices associated with the continent. Shamanism, Santería, or Mexico's Day of the Dead are elements of Latin American popular culture that influence Jodorowsky's visions.

Given Jodorowsky's eclectic training and transnational identity, his arrival in Mexico happens at what is for him a particularly propitious moment of Mexican cultural redefinition. As Carlos Monsiváis points out, the Mexican public of the 1960s struggled to find a balance between cosmopolitanism and localism, favoring instead internationality and universalism (qtd. in King, 1990: 134). Jodorowsky's transnational films and other cultural production during this decade reflect Mexico's rejection of political localism in favor of a European and North American–dominated universal high culture (Agustín, 1990: 254).

Like many other exploitation auteurs, when he started to make films Jodorowsky found that he was at odds with the organized industrial system already in place.[3] To avoid further problems he founded his own production company (Producciones Pánicas) along with Samuel and Moisés Rosenberg, Roberto Viskin, and Juan López Moctezuma. With a budget of $300,000, *Fando y Lis* was shot on weekends from July to December of 1967. In 1968 it participated in the Muestra de Cine de Acapulco (Acapulco Film Festival), where it created such outrage that it was not released in the rest of the country until 1972. Both the press and some Mexican directors demanded Jodorowsky's exile for being a "pornographer and a foreigner" (García Riera, 1996a: 260).

A quick look at *Fando y Lis* reveals why the movie so offended the press and other Mexican directors. Not only does it start with Lis lying on a bed suggestively eating a flower (recalling Warhol's *Eat,* 1963) but also throughout the film there are explicit references to sexuality, death, and violence (e.g., the abuse of the girl onstage at the beginning of the film, including a metaphoric smashing of eggs by masculine hands). Jodorowsky also includes dream sequences and arty references (the body painting sequence structured as a performative representation), mixing them with exploitation elements. At one point, lusting girls chase Fando through the desert in a manner that recalls the cinema of Russ Meyer (a voluptuous woman dressed in black leather with a whip in her hand chases Fando down a hill).

A further point of contention for the press and other directors was the film's foreignism. Few elements connect it with Mexico or with its landscape. The actors (Sergio Klainer and Diana Mariscal) do not speak with

Mexican accents but are dubbed into a more neutral Spanish and play characters without any connections to previous or contemporary Mexican cinema. Settings are similarly non-Mexico specific. Fando and Lis's trip takes place in an extemporal, dislocated world, unveiling a universe closer to fairy tale than a realistic depiction of Mexico. Compared to another similarly kaleidoscopic Mexican film, Rubén Gámez's *La fórmula secreta/The Secret Formula* (1965), which does indulge in Mexican stereotypes, national symbols and traditions, *Fando y Lis*'s avant-gardism seems far from any discussion of Mexico itself. The avant-garde in *Fando y Lis* is more related to performance arts: Jodorowsky himself arrived in Mexico for the first time with the famous mime artist Marcel Marceau, from whom he learned about stage techniques and experimental methods. Through *Fando y Lis,* originally a play written by Arrabal and already staged by Jodorowsky in Mexico in 1961, the director finds a way to narrate avant-gardism, performance, experimental staging, and ties the film to the Pánico movement by means of aesthetics (Topor's images), narrative (Arrabal's text), and even the production company's name (Pánico Producciones). Equally importantly, Jodorowsky inserts references to previous *efímeros*, like the piano burning at the beginning of the film or the blood-drinking sequence. These events had already been staged; firstly as a ritual to honor Jodorowsky just before he left for Paris to found *Pánico* and secondly during Jodorowsky's intervention in Montezuma television (Jodorowsky, 2007: 339–40).

This search for international and extracinematic referents, exemplified in *Fando y Lis*, is, as Jodorowsky claims, a means of legitimating his artistic and commercial career. With little concern for the intellectual reaction produced by the film in Mexico, he emphasizes: "*Fando y Lis* was banned here, but we sold it to Cannon in the United States. . . . The film industry in Mexico had become closed off for me. But the scandal it created opened the doors for me" (1971). The movie opened in New York in 1970 in a version thirteen minutes shorter than the original and was sufficiently successful to allow Jodorowsky to find financial backing for his next film, *El topo*.

Unlike *Fando y Lis*, *El topo* revolves around the exploitation of Mexico. Made not quite on an exploitation budget ($400,000), *El topo* narrates the journey of a cowboy (el Topo, played by Jodorowsky) seeking spiritual inspiration through his encounter with three different masters and revenge for his wife's murder. Finally, el Topo ends up living in a cave underground inhabited by deformed citizens, who will be massacred in a massive shooting by the respectable and 'normal' inhabitants of the town.

The film plays self-consciously with the iconography not only of the western genre but also of Mexico, through Jodorowsky's use of an old U.S. western set. Mexico thus becomes a frontier, the space in which a journey takes place that is significant both in a religious and physical sense. The film displays an interest less in 1970s Mexican reality and more in a deliberate representation of images *associated* with Mexico as a border space, that is, the desert, the border village, and the Catholic mission. After his first national failure/international success with *Fando y Lis,* Jodorowsky became aware that the Mexican-based identity of his films could be exploited through both a metaphoric and geographical border ideal. The appeal of *El topo* to a metropolitan (and especially U.S.) audience was essentially that it offered an image of Mexico that centered on the notion of a spiritual quest, one balanced between baroque violence and sacred purity.

In *El topo* Jodorowsky plays with topical cinematographic representations of the Mexican landscape (the desert, the border village, or the Catholic mission in the middle of nowhere) and mixes in anarchic references to Zen philosophy.[4] If the first Master's advice to el Topo—"I don't try to win, but to gain perfect control"—embodies Zen idealism, el Topo's response as he kills the third Master—"too much perfection is an error"— defies Zen's idealism.[5] Jodorowsky's call towards anarchy is reflected in his culturally hybrid creative practices. He mixes the monstrous (populating his Mexico with dwarfs, the physically impaired, and 'freaks') with the sublime (his Mexico also has masters and muses). Despite some references to more obvious representations of Mexico (the mission or the border village), Jodorowsky rewrites (Mexico's) history in film by revising certain genre conventions. He takes the spaghetti western and parodies it, mixing it in with moments of 'hippie meditation' (e.g., the sequence at the lake when el Topo plays his flute). In *El topo* there is a strong dialogue between national culture (the bandits dressed as *charros,* the Colonel wearing a nineteenth-century Mexican army uniform) and foreign influences (beat counterculture, rock 'n' roll, drug subcultures), a mixture which ultimately gives birth to an identifiable subcultural group in Mexico called the "jipitecas" (Lerner, 1999: 20).

Jodorowsky's subsequent film, *La montaña sagrada,* like *El topo,* represents a journey towards immortality. This time it is a quest made by a group of thieves from all over the galaxy led by a guru (Jodorowsky). The first half of the movie is strongly influenced by Mexican iconography. We see a bloody representation of the conquest of America and a shooting of a group of students by the army, which references the 1968 Tlatelolco massacre.[6] These two historical moments are linked by a grotesque representation of Mexican public space. At the beginning of the film, a conquest sequence ironically comments on the 'touristization' of Mexican culture, by presenting it in the form of a toad and lizard circus show surrounded by tourists who, in turn, take pictures of or film, the circus show, the killing of youngsters by the military, and the rape of one of the tourists by a soldier as if these were interchangeable spectacles performed on the tourists' behalf.

These references to Mexico's history appear only in the first half of *La montaña sagrada.* The radical commentary of this first half contrasts with the decontextualization of the second half, in which the thieves struggle to become pure souls. However, the visual and emotional hook of the film lies, as it does in *El topo,* in exotic and baroque images of Mexico (the toad and lizard circus, the street stand selling Catholic souvenirs, women ironing blood-stained white clothes in the street, whores in the church). This exploitation of the country's geography and history is pursued both as a social commentary and an aesthetic tool. Although *El topo* had the production values and modus operandi of an underground movie, it is difficult to talk about *La montaña sagrada* in similar terms: it involved hundreds of extras, big painted sets, and lots of different locations. Indeed, these high production values were always part of Jodorowsky's cinematic vision. In 1965, whilst preparing his *efímero Melodrama sacramental*, he had declared that he wanted "to become the Cecil B. de Mille of *happening*" (Jodorowsky, 2007: 341). If de Mille used the Bible as an excuse to engage with entertainment and cinematic spectacle, *La montaña sagrada* plays a similar role in the Latin American exploitation universe. In what was his most excessive film to date, Jodorowsky exploits 'Mexicanness' to pursue a fantastic vision of redemption.

The problematic relationship of Jodorowsky with Mexican culture and its national symbols is again a point of discussion between critics of his next film, *Santa sangre*. Christopher Kelly Ortiz argues against scholars like Charles Ramírez Berg, who define Jodorowsky's work as *atypical* in Mexican film history. Ortiz posits there is a very definite link between Jodorowsky and Mexican cinema, suggesting that it fits explicitly "within the context of Mexican cultural and political ferment in the late 1960s." Ortiz goes on to say: "Jodorowsky's work can be seen . . . as very much part of and having origins in a specific cultural, historical and political moment within Mexican society" (1995: 225–27).

Santa sangre posits a binary relation between a father-U.S. (represented in the role of castrated Orgo) and mother-Mexico (Concha). In *Santa sangre*, Jorodowsky swaps the Zen spiritualism of his previous two films for a Latin American religious syncretism, substituting the Master for the Shaman. More than any other of his works, *Santa sangre* aggressively transfigures Mexican cultural elements, such as Mexican wrestling idol El Santo (who is transexually transfigured into *la Santa*) or popular songs like *Caballo negro* (Dámaso Pérez Prado), *Lágrimas negras* (Consuelo Velázquez), *Cucurrucú paloma* (Tomás Méndez), or *No volveré* (Esperón and Cortázar), which are used to illustrate violent passages of the movie.

In *Santa Sangre,* wrestling and popular music (Ortiz, 1995: 227) function as intertextual commentaries on Mexican traditional culture and national identity. In the Mexican mixture of *Santa sangre,* Jodorowsky uses cultural hybridization as a means of penetrating international markets. Jodorowsky's use of Mexican culture resembles that of Arturo Ripstein in films like *La mujer del puerto/Woman of the Port* (1991), where Ripstein "is less caught up with depicting social reality than with developing a brutal, even nihilistic but ultimately cinematic vision of Mexico. It is an approach that has shown strong appeal to European and North American audiences" (D'Lugo, 2003:

229). Jodorowsky's method of reaching international audiences is a similar rewriting of Mexican culture in metarepresentational and cultural (i.e., self-conscious use of Mexican culture and representation) terms.

EXPLOITATION STRATEGIES

Jodorowsky uses the simultaneously avant-garde *and* exploitative strategies of excess and shock as a means of questioning the norms of bourgeois cinephilia and "good taste" and blurring the boundaries between avant-garde and trash cinema (Hawkins, 2000a: 15).[7] Excess and shock are key elements in his cinema, which are intrinsically linked to a very specific mode of consumption. In particular, Jodorowsky uses spectacle (a key exploitation technique) as a means of challenging dominant Hollywood form.

Jodorowsky shares with the avant-garde movements of the twentieth century (particularly surrealism and Antonin Artaud's theater of cruelty) a desire to disrupt bourgeois values and morality. Like other artists from the 1960s (Kenneth Anger and Andy Warhol), he often does this by assaulting middle-class notions of 'good taste.' Jodorowsky's assault on middle-class 'good taste' includes all types of extreme representations, of violence, sex, or human deformity. Disabled characters/actors often make an appearance in his films; their 'deformities' are used to defy the normality of the status quo and filmic representation: Lis is paralyzed, el Topo's second wife is a dwarf, a limbless man joins the main character of *La montaña sagrada* during the first part of the film, and a dwarf plays a similar role in *Santa sangre*. There is also a recurrent utilization of blood in his films: from the final shooting of *El topo* to the blood pool in the church of *Santa sangre* or the explosion of frogs and lizards in *La montaña sagrada*. All depict human violence in the most grotesque and extreme way. Extreme representations like these draw Jodorowsky closer both to avant-garde and more popular forms of entertainment, such as the circus or carnival parades. Through these shocking strategies Jodorowsky's films are linked to a cultural tradition that shifts between twentieth-century artistic rewritings of 'beauty' and 'lower' entertainment forms.

Jodorowsky's excess is aesthetically embodied in the extreme use of blood, sex, and scatological motifs, a tactic that attracts both elite and subcultural audiences. For example, in *El topo* more than 3,000 (or 5,000, according to interviews) liters of artificial blood were used and three hundred white rabbits were killed (by Jodorowsky himself) in the fight sequence with the third master (Jodorowsky, 1971). With their strategies of shock, excess, and the spectacle of deformity, Jodorowsky's films are simultaneously welcomed by bourgeois intellectuals *and* subcultural audiences, who culturally distinguish themselves by the fact of having seen these films (often more than once).[8] As Hoberman suggests:

Repeat the mantra 'far fucking out' all you like but to fully appreciate the thing that is *El topo* you'd have to have been there 36 years ago, in the wee hours of the morning, stoned out of your gourd, in a run-down theater on lower Eighth Avenue. Even then, I assure you, Alejandro Jodorowsky's magnum opus was less kabbalah than cowabunga—albeit a triumph for theater owner Ben Barenholtz. (2006)

Hoberman's words on the rerun of *El topo* in New York in 2006 illustrate the importance both of a knowing (and generationally distinctive) consumption and contextualization of the film.

Psychoanalytic exploration of the unconscious is also re-elaborated by Jodorowsky's films. From the fetishism of the thieves at the beginning of *El topo* (one of them collects high-heel shoes, another one sketches a woman's body with stones and fakes intercourse with it, and the third slices a banana with his sword before eating it) to the oedipal narrative of *Santa sangre* (a story about liberation from maternal domination), psychoanalysis is always present in Jodorowsky's filmography. But it exists less in the high-culture avant-garde Buñuelian form and more as part of a 1960s popular rhetorical device. Psychoanalysis functions in Jodorowsky's universe as a means of introducing shocking material and disrupting the narration. In his early three features, the plot is constantly interrupted, either to temporally extend a moment of gory violence (as in the final killing of El Topo) or one of sexual contemplation (as in the body-painting sequence of *Fando y Lis* or the sex machine of *La montaña sagrada*) or to introduce characters and narrative threads that add nothing to the overall plot (as in Fando and Lis's drifting through Tar). In these films, plot is subordinated to spectacle by the adaptation of performative elements or narrative ellipses, which counteract the development of a meaningful narrative. The primacy of spectacle over narrative is, as Eric Schaefer argues, a key component of the exploitation film (1999: 68). Following the logic of spectacle (rather than one of narrative) is how Jodorowsky (and the exploitation film in general) challenges dominant, narrative-oriented classical form and Hollywood hegemony.

Another exploitation cinema technique Jodorowsky uses to challenge the hegemony of Hollywood is the mixing, subverting, and parodying of its generic and narrative conventions. For example, although *El topo* and *Santa sangre* can be rapidly ascribed to single genres, excessive cross-referencing to other generic modes questions such a rigid classification of the films. *El topo* is modeled exploitatively on the then current (at the beginning of the 1970s) spaghetti western (following the trend set by Sergio Leone), whilst *Santa sangre*, is modeled on the Italian *giallo* cinema of the 1980s following the dictates of Italian financing of the film and audience expectations of gore (a key part of 1980s cult film fan experience). *Santa sangre*'s generic interplay between psychotronic, subcultural, and Hollywood genres is a game of citation. Therefore, Fénix's impersonation of the invisible man while he watches on TV the James Whale film of the same name (1933) can be read as both a reflection of taste and changes in consumption, that is, the importance of 'home video' consumption as a potential act of filmic-televisual-videographical cult consumption.

Another way in which Jodorowsky engages citationally with his audiences is by creating genre and film references that are designed to elicit an exploitation-style shock. For example, in *El topo* he creates a grotesque John Wayne out of two deformed men. He describes, "I designed their costume from one I saw in the Encyclopedia of Film: a John Wayne costume. It was one costume, which I cut into two parts. I put the upper half on the man with no legs and the pants on the man with no arms. Two cripples [sic] make one John Wayne" (Jodorowsky, 1971).

Jodorowsky's films therefore use many strategies of contemporary exploitation cinema. However, what differentiates his films from other exploitation is their self-awareness about the relationship between underground counterculture exploitation and avant-garde cinema. Jodorowsky uses the tropes and modes of exploitation cinema to attract underground and cult audiences to his movies. In other words, Jodorowsky exploits the exploitation, adapting his works to contemporary of cinematic excess. But as the De Mille of exploitation, he offers more (more blood, more monstrosity) with an intellectual spin (more Zen, more—and 'higher'—cultural intertextuality).

Fando y Lis's international success created great expectations for Jodorowsky's future films. These led to a private screening of *El topo* at the Museum of Modern Art in New York. Ben Barenholtz bought the rights to exhibit the movie at the Elgin Theater in New York, where it premiered at midnight on December 18, 1970, after a screening of John Lennon and Yoko Ono's films, and ran continuously until the end of June 1971, making $4,000 a week. Through its placement in a time slot previously ignored (midnight), *El topo* became the first 'midnight movie' in film history, a cultural phenomenon that turned just the *exhibition* of certain films into cultural events in and of themselves (Hoberman and Rosenbaum, 1991: 77–109). The film was consumed in an environment shaped by underground and avant-garde shows. In this context, going to see a midnight movie became a ritual, with spectators watching the films over and over again in situations where drug consumption and sexual liberation were highly encouraged. *El topo* fits into these schemes. Even critics who dislike the movie observe the success of its late-night slot:

> I would have assumed that a film with this much underground reputation would have prompted cheers. There was some desultory applause, but most of the people around me seemed to want to be told whether it was good or bad, if not what it really meant. It's difficult, especially at three o'clock in the morning, to admit that you've been conned. . . . It would be a terrible mistake to show the movie at an earlier hour. (Vincent Canby in Hoberman and Rosenbaum, 1991: 94–95)

Behind Canby's rather negative description of the film's audience (that they watch *El topo* without knowing whether it is good or bad), we can detect a certain psychotronic mode of consumption (that they are willing to watch it and may even be embracing its 'badness') at these midnight screenings (Sconce, 1995: 390). Jodorowsky had suggested that audiences should "arrive stoned . . . to get high on the movie" (1971). For him, "*El topo* is endless. . . . If you're great, *El topo* is a great picture; if you are limited, *El topo* is limited" (Jodorowsky, 1971). The spectatorial freedom offered by the 1960s triplike, or 1990s psychotronic viewing modes is counterbalanced by Jodorowsky's endless references, so that *El topo* becomes a game of free interpretation, an idea that works as well for psychotronic fans as for 1960s avant-garde or experimental cinema followers.[9]

Jodorowsky's slippery position, of an intellectual turned into entertainer, an auteur who conceives engagement as a cultural artifact, troubles critics like Pauline Kael. In her review of *El topo* (entitled "El Poto"), she argues that "he's an exploitation filmmaker, but he glazes everything with a useful piety. It's the violence plus the unctuous prophetic tone that makes *El topo* a heavy trip. . . . Jodorowsky has come up with something new: exploitation filmmaking joined to sentimentality—the sentimentality of the counterculture" (1975: 339). It is the emotional appeal of Jodorowsky's films that Kael indicates, juxtaposed with his intellectual references, that gained him his reputation, that of an arty exploiter, a creator of cool cult. These detours between art, exploitation, and cult earn Jodorowsky the category of exploitation auteur with a great capacity to create surrealistic events out of his films that by far surpass a single viewing.

El topo became a crossover vehicle for Jodorowsky, a means by which he could move between the underground, avant-garde filmmaking, and cult cinema. As a consequence, the film's success allowed him to finance his next film, *La montaña sagrada*, a $750,000 coproduction between Mexico and the United States.

It was John Lennon who persuaded his manager, Allen Klein, to sign Jodorowsky on an exclusive contract for ABCKO Films after *El topo*'s success as a 'midnight movie.' But *El topo*'s career did not end with New York's midnight movie circuit. After an unsuccessful attempt in 1971 to make the movie into a more mainstream commercial success on Broadway, the film was shown at the London Film Festival (largely thanks to its links to the underground art scene in New York). Like *El topo*, *La montaña sagrada* was released in New York at the Waverly Theater on Fridays and Saturdays as a 'midnight movie' and elsewhere in the United States on a double bill with *El topo*. However, it was presented at the 1973 Cannes Film Festival as a U.S. (rather than a Mexican) film. What this exhibition history reveals is how Jodorowsky's films easily move between exploitation (midnight movie) and art cinema (Cannes Film Festival) circuits but do less well in mainstream commercial circuits. At the same time, during such mobility, *El topo* was banned in Mexico and not screened until 1975 (and even then in a version with twenty-one minutes cut from it). After a series of misunderstandings over future projects, Klein withdrew every print of *El topo* and *La montaña sagrada* from the market and turned down all subsequent requests to show them until 2004, when Klein's son authorized the films to be legally exhibited both at the *Cannes* and the *London* Film Festivals. Obviously, the absence of these films from the market for so long increased their cult status.

CONCLUSION: BEYOND EXPLOITATION

Like *La montaña sagrada*, *El topo* achieves the status of a cult film through its self-referentiality and through its multiple cultural references, all of which combine to elicit a particular kind of cult viewing experience from its audience. Jodorowsky reaches cult fans through exploitation strategies that reflect the different spaces and times of each film's production: 1970s Mexico of *El topo* and 1980s Italy of *Santa sangre*. *El topo* mines the 1970s' underground counterculture of the United States, whilst *Santa sangre* mines elements of the *giallo* genre. *El topo* channeled Jodorowsky's film through the midnight 'movie circuit'; *Santa sangre* channeled his films through video rentals. As times have changed, Jodorowsky has learned how to adapt to new models of film consumption.

In 2006, Jodorowsky's films were once again situated within the viewing category of French cinephilia when the digitally remastered versions of his main films (*Fando y Lis*, *El topo,* and *La montaña sagrada*) were released at the Cannes Film Festival. They were subsequently released in France (December 2006) and UK theaters (April, 2007). The three works have been commercialized in a six DVD pack (with the soundtrack of *El topo* and *La montaña sagrada*, and the found short film *La cravate/The Severed Heads* (1957)). Also in 2006, Jodorowsky obtained La Màquina del Temps (Time Machine) Award at Sitges (Festival Internacional de Cinema de Catalunya/ Catalonia Film Festival), one of Europe's first and most prestigious fantastic film festivals. To this list of recognitions we can add the Jack Smith Lifetime Achievement Award at the Chicago Underground Film Festival in 2000. By exploiting many different sources (exploitation cinema, Zen philosophy, film history, psychoanalysis, popular culture, theatrical avant-garde techniques, Mexican identity) Jodorowsky and his films have achieved social recognition in vastly different areas of cinematic culture, such as the European *auteur* tradition, psychotronic fandom, and the cinematic underground. Because of this worldwide recognition, Chilean President Michelle Bachelet awarded him the Orden al Mérito Artístico y Cultural Pablo Neruda on April 27, 2006. Jodorowsky's exploitation of exploitation cinema, among other cultural sources, demonstrates that it is not only a subcultural film category. As his career exemplifies, exploitation can (and has) led to social recognition, cultural credibility, artistic consideration, and institutional authority.

NOTES

1. The term *psychotronic* derives from Michael Weldon's cult movie fanzine *Psychotronic Video*. As for *paracinema*, see the groundbreaking work of Jeffrey Sconce (1995), who coined the term. An interesting discussion of the concept of "minor cinemas" related to avant-garde, art cinema, and other marginal film practices can be found in David E. James (2005).
2. Garcia Riera (1996b: 284) also recounts that the film was screened at the Cannes Film Festival, but no other sources provide details about this screening.
3. For example, when he tried to shoot his first film in Mexico, *Fando y Lis*, he needed the approval of the Sociedad de Directores, an organization that worked with the Sindicato de Trabajadores de la Producción Cinematográfica (the Union of Workers of Cinematographic Production). The union agreed to work with Jodorowsky but he had to shoot the film as an episode movie, making each of the parts with different crews as if they were independent short films.
4. Jodorowsky's "Fábulas pánicas," a comic strip that was published in *El Heraldo* from 1967 to 1969, is a formidable example of the director's progressive implication in Zen principles and his visualization of Eastern philosophy (2006b). As Rita González and Jesse Lerner recall, Jodorowsky admitted that "I tried to make a western and ended up with an eastern" (1998: 69).
5. For Jodorowsky, "accidents always appear like shadows; theatre people fight against them because they consider them 'imperfections,' a misunderstanding that makes them ignore the real essence of theatrical language: the provocation of accidents" (Jodorowsky, 2007: 328).
6. In August 1968, government troops opened fire on students and workers protesting in a Mexico City Square, Tlatelolco. Hundreds and some say thousands were killed. The massacre testified to the increasing rift between an authoritarian government and an alienated populace.
7. That there can be such a congruence between avant-garde and low (exploitation) cinemas is something Hawkins has pointed out (2000a: 15).
8. Significantly, the second film after *El topo* to enjoy a successful midnight run in New York was Tod Browning's *Freaks* (1932).
9. "You can read the clitoris. You can read the anus. You can read anything you want. Because every body part is like a book . . . Everything can be read. Everything is a book. You can read a hat, shoes . . . an umbrella" (Jodorowsky, 1971). This allegiance has been critiqued by James Peterson in relation to the U.S. avant-garde and especially Stan Brakhage's work, under what Peterson has labeled the "liberation theory," one that falsely "encourages us to think of (the American avant-garde) cinema as part of a single, transhistorical avant-garde predicated exclusively on the rejection of an oppressive tradition" (Peterson, 1994: 6). In this way, Jodorowsky's words about his films clearly align him to liberation theory in an era when semiotics and poststructuralism were advocating for the importance of signifiers, connecting him with countercultural practices of the 1960s.

Dolores Tierney

José Mojica Marins's peers have called him a primitive artist, an "idiot savant," and even a Brazilian Buñuel (Barcinski and Finotti, 1998: 122). However, despite such accolades, and the fact that he was very productive and successful in the 1960s, major English-language accounts of Brazilian cinema during this period ignore Mojica's films and focus instead on *cinema novo* and the related movement *cinema do lixo* (garbage cinema).[1] This is despite the fact that Mojica was a contemporary and, according to Rogério Sganzerla, director of the cinema do lixo classic *O bandido da luz vermelha/Red Light Bandit* (1968), avowed "father" of the latter movement (Barcinski and Finotti, 1998: 14). Mojica's low-budget gore and drug films *À meia-noite levarei sua alma/At Midnight I will take your soul* (1963), *Esta noite encarnarei no teu cadáver/This night I will possess your corpse* (1966), *O estranho mundo de Zé do Caixão/The Strange World of Coffin Joe* (1966), and *O despertar da besta/Awakening of the Beast* (1969) were unprecedented in Brazil, and like *cinema novo*, also made use out of an 'esthetics of poverty.'

Latin American film criticism might have overlooked Mojica but in the United States he has found a new fan base. His 1990s' surfacing has come about due to the increasing popularity of 'trash' or paracinema. This is largely thanks to the release of his films on Mike Vraney's Something Weird label, and to the 1999 Sundance-awarded documentary *Maldito, the Strange World of Coffin Joe* (André Barcinski and Ivan Finotti).[2] Mojica's fame had reached the UK several years ago where two of his films, *Esta noite encarnarei no teu cadáver* and *O despertar da besta*, as well as Barcinski and Finotti's documentary, were included in the Channel 4 series "Mad Auteurs." Indeed, as stated in Barcinski and Finotti's 1998 biography of Mojica, *Maldito*, it is precisely his success abroad in alternative viewing circuits like those of paracinema or Channel 4 that has sparked a renewed critical interest in him back in Brazil as well as alerting popular culture commentators to the monstrous neglect this incredible Brazilian auteur has suffered in his own country (1998: 124).

Of course, as is the case with many critically neglected directors in many countries, Mojica has always been a popular success in Brazil and occupies a very prominent position as a popular personality. Mojica is such a recognizable figure that he is frequently asked to kiss babies on the streets of São Paulo and has even appeared at the head of a samba school in the Rio Carnival (Tombs, 1997: 117, 126).[3] A recent article by Eva Bueno, a U.S.-based Brazilian academic, on the work of another critically neglected, yet highly popular, Brazilian actor and filmmaker, Amácio Mazzaropi, suggests that what is played out in such cases of critical neglect is a struggle over the terms and structures that define national culture (1999: 34). Bueno argues that, because of the way Brazil was colonized and developed—largely by the establishment of cities on the East Coast—the terms of Brazilian national culture have similarly been colonized by the East Coast city-dwelling elites (1999: 34). In the case of Mazzaropi, "one of the most celebrated Brazilian artists of all time" (Bueno, 1999: 33), making commercial comedies for an audience that is largely rural or recently arrived from the countryside, his films are deemed outside the paradigms of metropolitan 1960s' cultural concerns. *Cinema novo*, on the other hand, is considered to embody these concerns—even to the extent that its perspective on the *sertão* (Brazil's northeastern backlands) comes from the city (Bueno, 1999: 34). However, Bueno highlights the inconsistencies and classist assumptions that potentially trigger the critical disdain with which Mazzaropi is held. She explores how his films respond to issues (rural displacement to the city, working class poverty and powerlessness) equally as important as those addressed by *cinema novo* (underdevelopment, poverty, hunger and racial tension) (Bueno, 1999: 47; Johnson and Stam 1995: 68).

What Bueno's approach makes clear is that this hegemonic narrative of Brazilian culture in the 1960s, which allows one cinema (*cinema novo*) to dominate over others, needs to be challenged. As to why Mojica has gone unrecognized by both established criticism in Brazil and 'Third World' criticism, it appears that the keepers of Brazilian culture and also 'Third World' film theorists, who often reproduce national cinema discourses, operate according to cultural politics which champion not all marginal filmmakers, but only a *certain* kind of marginality. That Mojica's films, although excluded from the main accounts, actually share many characteristics with Brazil's avant-garde *cinema novo* of the 1960s further underscores the contradictory nature of the cultural politics of 'Third World' film criticism.

BORN TO BE BAD

Mojica's beginnings in cinema reflect Brazil's position in the world cultural economy—potentially more so than those of one of the renowned auteurs of *cinema novo*, Nelson Pereira dos Santos (*Vidas secas/Barren Lives*, 1963; *Como era gostoso o meu francês/How Tasty Was My Little Frenchman*, 1971). Whilst Pereira dos Santos attended the Centro Sperimentale in Rome, birthplace of neorealism, Mojica left school at the age of thirteen and learned the art of filmmaking by going to the cinema.[4] As a self-taught filmmaker with no higher education, he is seemingly more typical of Brazil, a country with one of the lowest literacy rates in South America. Furthermore, as a self-taught filmmaker, his biography also explains his particular cinematic leanings, as it reads like that of an exploitation director *and*, I suggest, the 'ideal' (rather than actual) radical Latin American filmmaker.[5] The son of Spanish immigrants, Mojica grew up in a cinema that his father managed in a suburb of São Paulo. At the age of twelve he refused the offer of a bike for his birthday, preferring instead an 8mm camera, which he put to good use making horror shorts. His initial forays into feature filmmaking were disastrous. With his first attempt at a feature, *Sentença de Deus/ God's Sentence* (1953), three successive actresses playing the lead either died or lost limbs. In 1959, his third, and ultimately successful, attempt at feature filmmaking, *A sina do aventureiro/The Adventurer's Fate*, took him on location. However, when he returned to São Paulo he discovered that his wife had miscarried and much of the footage shot on location was out of focus (Tombs, 1997: 117).

But it was really Mojica's fourth film and the first ever horror film to be made in Brazil, *À meia-noite levarei sua alma* (1963), that began to establish him as a director with popular appeal and a distinctive style. Set in upstate São Paulo, the film tells the story of Zé do Caixão (Coffin Joe), a nihilist undertaker who terrorizes a small town in his search for an ideal woman to bear him a child. Surprisingly, to create his monster Mojica did not draw on any of the horrific figures which exist in Brazilian culture: the *homen marinho* (merman) or the *jaracara* (a vampire snake) (Tombs, 1997: 118). Instead, like other gothic auteurs (Mary Shelley and Wes Craven), Zé do Caixão, the cloaked and taloned bogeyman Mojica created and played for this film and its sequels, was the product of his own nightmares—with a little help from Universal's horror cycle (particularly *Dracula*; Tod Browning, 1931) and *Nosferatu* (F. W. Murnau, 1922). Indeed, it has been suggested that Zé do Caixão is actually the manifestation of Mojica's dark side. This slippage is reflected in criticism that often conflates Mojica with the malevolent character he plays (Tombs, 1997: 121). Potentially the cause for such a conflation is one of Mojica's ultra-low-budget production strategies. To save money, Mojica would often use real 'creepy crawlies' in his films. Hence, when Zé do Caixão kills his barren wife Lenita with a poisonous spider, critics have read as real not only the fear seen in the actress's eyes but also the glee in Zé/Mojica's eyes as he watches her suffer.

À meia-noite levarei sua alma was a popular success amongst urban film audiences but received mixed reviews from contemporary critics. Some of those who praised the film suggested that its immoral, indiscriminately cruel protagonist Zé do Caixão was in fact a reflection and criticism of the arbitrary state violence that was on the increase in Brazil from the military coup in 1964 onwards (Barcinski and Finotti, 1998: 119). Other critics marveled at the film's black humor, originality, and expressionist style (Barcinski and Finotti, 1998: 118). But what is interesting for the purposes of this chapter is not just the fact that established criticism largely rejected and criticized the film, but the precise terms which they used to do so; namely, its poverty and "*subdesenvolvimento*" (underdevelopment) (Barcinski and Finotti, 1998: 119) because these are the precise terms on which both *cinema novo* and the other radical filmmaking theories and practices of New Latin American cinema are based and valued. What is also interesting is that it points out an initial inconsistency in 1960s' accounts and their criteria for inclusion and exclusion of filmmakers.

Furthermore, as a self-educated filmmaker with no formal or theoretical training, Mojica could be the ideal candidate for the utopia envisaged by one of the key theorists of New Latin American Cinema, the Cuban Julio García Espinosa. In "For an Imperfect Cinema" (1997a [1969]) García Espinosa suggests that in a revolutionary society the artist/filmmaker would not be an intellectual, but a worker (like Mojica?), for whom filmmaking would be a continuation of his working life (1997a: 73–74).[6] García Espinosa's essay calls for a revolutionary future where filmmaking would be democratized, where the categories of "artist" and "intellectual" and the elitist assumptions that underlie them would be eradicated (1997a: 75, 77). And yet, despite such rhetoric, not all Latin American film criticism and practice have followed García Espinosa's theoretical lead. Whilst the Cuban Revolution *has* facilitated the democratizing of filmmaking practice in its establishment of film training, programs or schools at the ICAIC (Instituto Cubano de Arte e Industria Cinematográficos—of which García Espinosa is both founder and sometime director) the ISA (Instituto Superior de Arte) and the Escuela International de Cine y Television (International School of Cinema and Television)[7]—as far as its limited economic resources would allow—other New Latin American cinema theorists only paid lip service to dismantling the barriers between art and life whilst at the same time underscoring and perpetuating their own privileged access to film production and status as artists. For example, Glauber Rocha claimed, "if commercial cinema is the tradition, *auteur* cinema is the revolution" (Stam and Miller, 2000: 5).

TRASH CINEMA BRAZILIAN STYLE AND 'IMPERFECT CINEMA'

García Espinosa also suggests in his essay that technically or stylistically perfect cinema cannot be an aim in itself in an underdeveloped country because, in the commercial cinemas of the metropolis, these values have become irredeemably superficial. Hence, the transparent surface of classical cinema becomes a way of lulling the audience into passive consumption. He suggests, on the other hand, making an *imperfect cinema* that shows the conditions of technical impoverishment and awakens the audience to critical consciousness. That *imperfect cinema* has often been misinterpreted as an apology for deliberately making bad films[8]—suggests its link to 'badfilm' practice, another kind of 'imperfect' filmmaking. Indeed, in many ways the avowed strategies of 1960s' Latin American filmmakers like García Espinosa and also Glauber Rocha, which seek to make a discursive strategy out of the material conditions of poverty and underdevelopment, are concepts that also have currency (albeit of a different kind) within this quite different filmic arena. As Jeffrey Sconce points out in '"Trashing' the Academy":

> [R]ather than explore the systematic application of style as the elite techniques of a cinematic artist, paracinematic culture celebrates the systematic 'failure' or 'distortion' of conventional cinematic style by 'autuers' [sic] who are valued more as 'eccentrics' than as artists, who work within the impoverished and clandestine conditions typical of exploitation cinema. These films deviate from Hollywood classicism not necessarily by artistic intentionality, but by the effects of *material poverty* and technical ineptitude. (Sconce, 1995: 385, emphasis mine)

The study of exploitation and the related fields of trash and cult film has developed as an extension of an already existing film studies arena—the exploration of film practice beyond Hollywood commercial orthodoxy and the mainstream national cinemas. In the U.S. academy the study of exploitation and its related field (cult and trash) is gaining considerable critical momentum and even institutional legitimacy through books from high-profile university presses, Eric Schaefer (1999) and Sconce (2007), both from Duke, and a flourishing of film courses at various universities in the United States and the UK. These studies of 'trash' or 'exploitation' cinema have begun to reevaluate the terms on which these cinemas have been classed as 'bad' and critically dismissed. This move in the U.S. academy leads us to also reevaluate exploitation cinemas beyond the United States such as that of Mojica in Brazil. Within trash cinema paradigms, rather than consider technical primitivism (or 'underdevelopment') as failed sophistication, as the term 'bad' implies, or as lacking substance, as the term 'camp' (often applied to these films) implies, exploitation cinema studies examine amongst other things the way these films offer resistance (whether deliberate or unconscious) to a repressive and homogenizing mainstream (Schaefer, 1999: 13).

In the United States the terms 'badfilm' or 'trash' cinema are used with increasing frequency to refer to all that which dominant culture discards or disregards as unimportant. This practice describes *both* Mojica's films—a mixture of Marvel comics, Universal horror films, and *Tales from the Crypt* and also a Brazilian 'trash' cinema of a very different cultural pedigree, one which the critical establishment has more tastefully labeled as "cultural detritus" (Stam, 2000: 83).

Cinema do lixo or 'trash' or 'garbage' cinema is actually a reaction against *cinema novo*, but is considered a part of its 'third stage.'[9] The first phase of *cinema novo* (1960–1964) was idealistic. Its Rio-based filmmakers—

Rocha, Pereira dos Santos, and Rui Guerra—believed that a new cinematic language, an "esthetics of violence," was the only way to make the nation aware of the neocolonial cultural system and Brazil's position within that system. The second phase of *cinema novo*, sparked by the 1964 coup, was plagued with self-doubt as the left-leaning intellectuals examined the failures of their utopian project. The third and last phase of *cinema novo* begins with the 1968 coup within the coup. This phase is part of/aligned with the artistic and intellectual movement Tropicália and typified by films like dos Santos's *Como era gostoso o meu francês*. The films of the tropicalist phase are still anti-imperialist but are aimed at a much broader (domestic) audience than the hermetic, avant-garde films of the first and second phases of *cinema novo*. Hence, instead of the disruptive style and narratives of the early period, exemplified by *Deus e o diabo na terra do sol/Black God, White Devil* (Rocha, 1963), they adopt (for the most part) classical story telling and editing techniques and incorporate popular strategies with popular appeal— love stories or comedy.

As we can see from the previous description, the credentials on which *cinema novo* becomes representative of Brazilian cinema in the 1960s depend on the critical templates of 'Third World'/'First World' opposition. It is because *cinema novo* tells the narratives of anti-imperialism, of revolutionary, political 'movements' that studies of 'Third World' filmmaking are invested in telling that they form a canon of 'landmark' films. Mojica's films, on the other hand, are excluded because they are considered lowbrow exploitation, fodder for the 'masses' which would seemingly preclude their connection to issues of cultural or political import. Furthermore, given their roots in Universal horror films and their borrowing from U.S. comic traditions, Mojica's films present some problems with respect to the discourses of postcolonialism on imperialist domination and ideological hegemony.

MAPPING THE RELATIONSHIP BETWEEN ART CINEMA AND EXPLOITATION CINEMA

However, in recent critical work on U.S. exploitation film by Joan Hawkins, Schaefer, and Sconce, much has been written about the way "high culture trades on the same images, tropes and themes which characterize low culture" (Hawkins, 2000b: 15), thus challenging the existence of a binary opposition between art cinema/the avant-garde and exploitation cinema (Schaefer, 1999: 332–31).[10] We find this to be the case with Mojica and the tropicalist/garbage esthetic of late 1960s Brazil.

Brazil's *cinema do lixo*, also known as the *Udigrudi*—a Brazilian pronunciation of the word *Underground*—emerged as Mojica began work on *O despertar da besta*. As 'third stage' *cinema novo* was deciding to reach out towards the audience with a more commercial, accessible cinema, the *Udigrudi* wanted to "slap" it in the face (Johnson and Stam, 1995: 311).

As *cinema novo* moved away from the disjointed alienation of the "esthetics of hunger" towards technical polish and high production values with films like *Macunaíma* (Joaquim Pedro de Andrade, 1969), *cinema marginal* (marginal cinema), as Udigrudi was also called, demanded a radicalization of the esthetics of hunger, rejecting the codes of a well-made cinema in favor of "dirty screen" and "garbage" esthetics. Taking their name from the Boca do Lixo district of São Paulo where the movement was based, Sganzerla, Ozualdo Candeias (*A margem/The Margin*, 1967), Júlio Bressane (*Matou a família e foi ao cinema/Killed the Family and Went to the Movies*, 1970), and others argued that a "garbage style" was appropriate for a 'Third World' country forced to pick through the leavings of an international system dominated by 'First World' capitalism (Johnson and Stam, 1995: 312). (We note here the similarities with the definition of Trash cinema and that the dominant vs. counterculture opposition is transposed onto a 'First World' vs. 'Third World' opposition.)

Although the Udigrudi were purposely marginal, identifying socially downward with rebellious lumpen characters, they were also *marginalized* through harassment by the censors and boycotting from the exhibitors (Johnson and Stam, 1995: 39). But whilst the Udigrudi only *aspired* downwards to the lumpenproletariat, with Sganzerla's anti-intellectual *O bandido da luz vermelha* trashing the esthetics of European art films like *A bout de souffle/Breathless* (Jean-Luc Godard, 1960) as a *gesture* against elitism, it was Mojica who actually made films *that appealed to* the lumpenproletariat and also *from* the lumpenproletariat, casting his films from vast numbers of working-class volunteers (Barcinski and Finotti, 1998: 124). Furthermore, although the censors harassed the Udigrudi, Mojica was actually the director most censored by the military government after the 1968 coup within the coup. In fact, the censors ordered so many cuts from *O despertar da besta* (originally titled *Ritual dos sádicos/Sadistic Ritual*) that the film had to be withdrawn, effectively banning it until the softening of the regime in the mid-1980s when it was released until the new title. Furthermore, Mojica was arrested because the film was believed to have subliminal political messages. This suggests Mojica and his films were perceived as a radical threat to the military authoritarianism which then ensued and, potentially, that the avant-garde *cinema do lixo* and the more commercial and mainstream *cinema novo* were not. (Although this is not to suggest that *cinema novo* of the third phase abandoned its radical political stance. To avoid rigorous censorship, *cinema novo* films of this period adopted allegorical strategies and forms, as in *Macunaíma* (Johnson and Stam, 1995: 38).

Although there is no explicit political agenda in Mojica's films, as there was with Rocha's films and those of other *cinema novo* directors, in the sense of treating film as praxis in the struggle against neocolonialism (Johnson and Stam, 1995: 33), there is an attempt to deal with contemporary issues and to probe societal tensions. Mojica's *O desperta da besta*, for example, attempts to deal with the subcultural dimensions of the 1960s drug culture.

Although the film might titillate with sexual excesses of drug taking in the manner of typical exploitation fare, it also alludes to police brutality and torture. In different scenes it shows a number of people being bundled into the back of police cars.[11] Furthermore, like the tropicalist or prototropicalist masterpieces that make up the canon of Brazilian cinema in the 1960s, *Terra em transe/Land in Anguish* (Rocha 1967) and *O dragão da maldade contra o santo guerreino/Antônio das mortes* (Rocha 1969), the sadistic fantasies of the acid-dropping characters in *O despertar da besta* can also be attributed to the atmosphere of intensified repression and censorship (Armes, 1987: 177), particularly when it turns out that their horrific hallucinations were all self-induced and not drug related.[12]

Therefore, inasmuch as they appeal to the masses, and are a threat to authoritarianism, on a thematic and social level Mojica's films ostensibly have countercinema credentials. This problematizes their exclusion from the surrounding avant-garde film movements that make up the Brazilian film canon as it is presented in English-language critical material. On an esthetic level we find that Mojica also challenges our assumptions about the differences between avant-garde experimental films (i.e., *cinema do lixo*, tropicalism, and *cinema novo*) and exploitation cinema.

According to Robert Stam, the garbage or tropicalist esthetic advocates shocking bourgeois sensibility, the exaltation of bad taste, and the use of self-reflexivity (2000: 84–85). Given these criteria, *O despertar da besta* could be described as Mojica's most tropicalist film. It begins with a highly self-reflexive episode: Mojica the filmmaker defends himself and his films before a television People's Court. The television footage actually comes from a program Mojica was invited to take part in, *Quem tem medo da verdade?/Who is Afraid of the Truth?* (1969). Here he was subjected to questions by a panel of 'experts' to determine whether or not he was a 'fake' (Tombs, 1997: 122). Later on in the film, Mojica attends a (staged) roundtable discussion on the effect of drugs on society. As part of this roundtable, a psychiatrist recounts his experience with four volunteers who take part in an LSD experiment. The LSD experiment revolves around the fictional Zé do Caixão. Like contemporary LSD films from the United States such as *The Trip* (Roger Corman, 1967), *O despertar da besta* attempts to simulate the altered perception of these trips through the use of a number of different cinematic devices which also correspond to further features of tropicalism: the use of color as opposed to the gritty and alienating black and white of earlier *cinema novo*'s *Deus e o diabo na terra do sol*. Firstly, as the characters begin their respective trips the film switches from black and white to gaudy color. Then different grotesque tropicalist monsters—including a group of menacing aliens—terrorize the volunteers. That some of these 'aliens' turn out to be a row of human buttocks with features painted on them, including mustaches, would be hilarious were it not for the hellish context in which they are placed (see Figure 7.1). The 'buttocks-as-aliens' functions simultaneously as a tropicalist piece, shocking bourgeois sensibility and defying the

Figure 7.1 "Buttocks-as-aliens" in *O despertar da besta/Awakening of the Beast* (José Mojica Marins, 1969).

parameters of avant-garde taste and at the same time as paracinema, appealing to an audience that delights in such bad taste extremes.

Further evidence of how Mojica's paracinema can be read in avant-garde terms is through his use of gore. Hawkins points out that the use of excessive physical horror, although considered to be so, is not solely a technique of exploitation cinema and is equally found in art cinema: for example, Stan Brakhage's 1972 autopsy film *The Act of Seeing with One's Own Eyes* (2000b: 16). She suggests that in both cases, whether it is called exploitation thrills or "artistic shock treatment," it is designed to break the spectator's esthetic distance by creating an excessively physical response. Mojica's *À meia-noite levarei sua alma* makes innovative and early use of gore contemporaneously with American exploitation director H. G. Lewis (*Blood Feast* 1963). In one scene, Zé slams a bottle down on the hand of a man who dares to defy him, cutting off several fingers.

Of course, as Hawkins points out, the distinguishing criteria between low genres like Mojica's gore and highbrow genres like Brazil's cinema do lixo/cinema marginal is that they supposedly use their material differently. For the cultural elite, avant-garde cinemas have a cultural purpose, seeking to instruct or challenge the spectator, which in the case of *cinema novo* (and the rest of New Latin American Cinema) takes the specific form of cultural decolonization and consciousness raising. Low-genre exploitation films, on the other hand, are supposedly intended to simply titillate and excite the spectator with forbidden spectacle, which in the case of Mojica's films means scenes of nudity, gore, and horror (Hawkins, 2000b: 16–17). But Hawkins also points out that this is not a hard and fast distinction— high culture and low culture can often elicit the same spectatorial pleasure. In one scene from a famous early *cinema marginal* film, *Os cafajestes/The Scoundrels* (Rui Guerra, 1962), for example, the camera circles around a naked woman trapped and harassed on a beach. This Brazilian avant-garde film replicates the point of view of the eponymous antiheroes who mercilessly drive around her. Similar sadistic treatments of women within the frame as well as an unblinking camera appear in Mojica's second horror film, *Esta noite encarnarei no teu cadáver*. Zé has now found his perfect woman to bear him a son, but as he consummates the deal he watches as the scantily clad rejected hopefuls are dispatched in a snake pit conveniently situated by his bed.

Furthermore, as Hawkins also points out, "it is not so clear that low genres seek only to titillate, low genres can also be analyzed for serious content and purpose" (2000b: 17). Like *cinema novo*, Mojica's films also deal with the problems facing the rural and urban lumpenproletariat: starvation, violence, religious alienation, and economic exploitation. In *À meia-noite levarei sua alma*, Mojica's Zé do Caixão is a sacrilegious atheist who continually challenges the Catholic beliefs of the small town where he lives. In his long soliloquies about free will and destiny, as well as his open defiance of religious practices (eating meat on Good Friday and going out on All Souls night), he suggests that the church peddles fear and superstition as a means of social control. As such, *À meia-noite levarei sua alma* seems not so different to the early *cinema novo* masterpiece *Barravento* (Rocha, 1962), which illustrates what happens when "religion prevents a fishing community from understanding the real conditions in which they live" (King, 2000: 108).

To a certain extent what has happened with Mojica has happened elsewhere. Other great exploitation auteurs have 'disappeared' from film history only to be 'rediscovered' by the paracinematic community—H. G. Lewis, the "wizard of gore," was recently 'rediscovered' by Quentin Tarantino. Hence, such erasure is by no means limited to the developing world. However, with the developing world there are certain political and cultural imperatives which further complicate the construction of film canons and dictate the historical erasure of certain directors and not others. For example, for those who wish to argue within postcolonialist perspectives for a country's autonomy or even successful escape from colonial ideological hegemony (as most criticism of Latin American film has wished to argue), it is important to emphasize the extent to which these countries have been successful in developing their own cultures. (Mojica's Marvel comic esthetics and *Tales from the Crypt* mise-en-scène, even his Universal Studios/

Nosferatu Zé make him an easy target for erasure.) This often means, however, that the cultural production of the country in question is measured in terms that easily translate into the international discourses of high art and high modernism—even though these are considered the products of the colonial nations (France, Germany, United Kingdom, United States). Stam's admirable work advocating Brazilian cultural production offers an example of such cultural critique. His strategy in one article is not to talk about Latin American modernism and postmodernism on their own terms, but to introduce them as fully formed movements *avant-la-lettre*, prior to the birth of these movements in Europe (Stam, 2000: 83), which still places Europe as an important cultural signpost for understanding Latin American culture. Similarly, in an introduction to Brazilian countercinema tellingly entitled "On the Margins: Brazilian Avant-Garde Cinema," Stam begins: "Like the United States, Brazil displays a vital avant-garde cultural tradition" (Johnson and Stam, 1995: 306). Hence, in order to argue for cultural legitimacy on a world stage, the cultural politics of 'Third World' film criticism emphasizes first the developing country's similarity with the 'First World' and second its relationship to what is easily translatable as culturally prestigious—avant-garde esthetics.

Therefore, and as even this attempted nonelitist analysis of Mojica's films makes clear, part of the difficulty with Latin American film criticism, as part of a broader culture of 'Third World' film criticism, is that it is too easily ruled by the values of elite/prestige/art cinemas. Furthermore, and somewhat paradoxically, because of the way it circulates in Europe and the United States in art cinemas, university courses, and film journals, the New Latin American Cinemas simultaneously belong to whilst nominally rejecting 'elite' culture, that is, their explicit anti-neocolonialist and antibourgeois position. Hence, there is a cultural capital not in marginality itself, but in a *certain kind* of marginality. This paradox, arguing for cultural autonomy from the culture of the Western metropolis in terms that nevertheless reveal the prejudices of the Western artistic institution, is a problem that has been discussed by the various reevaluations of the different achievements of Latin America's new cinemas in the 1980s. It has similarly been acknowledged that this is also the problem with its most prominent filmmakers, who not only belong to a group of often European-educated white men but also, despite their attempts to reject the elite culture of which they are a product, make hermetic, oblique films which appeal only to this same group (Johnson and Stam, 1995: 34).

It is with this in mind that Mojica's paracinema appears as a more successful refusal of 'elite' culture than the New Latin American Cinemas. As a filmmaker without professional training or higher education of any kind, and as someone excluded from the list of canonical cinematic works, Mojica remains successfully outside the realm of elite culture. However, even this chapter published in an academic anthology potentially compromises Mojica's countercinema credentials. This is a problem which Sconce identifies when he points out that, even with paracinema the highbrow/low-brow split is increasingly difficult to define. With recent retrospectives, film courses and increasing critical attention, paracinema has begun its ascent into elite culture, to infiltrate (or trash) the academy (Sconce, 1995: 373).

But whether this will mean compromising exploitation cinemas, by seeking to respectabilize them through avant-garde or more culturally legitimate criteria much in the same way the critical field has sought to do with the modern horror film, remains to be seen.[13] This chapter began by suggesting that the struggle to define Brazilian cinematic culture of the 1960s is a battle between a group of popular-film fans (the larger paracinematic community and the Brazilian audience) and an elite group of would-be cinematic tastemakers (*cinema novo*, established national film criticism, and 'Third World' film criticism). But the process of arguing for Mojica's place within the canon—which has taken the form of showing how his exploitation cinema trades on the same social concerns, tropes, and esthetics valued in the canon of Brazilian avant-garde cinema of the 1960s—seems to reveal that the argument for Mojica's inclusion/exclusion is not a question of opposing sides but really the fragmentation of a single "taste culture" (Sconce, 1995: 372).

There are therefore certain problems posed by the argument for Mojica's inclusion in the canon. As Stephen Jay Schneider and Tony Williams point out (2005), the trouble with arguments like the one rehearsed in this chapter is that, while problematizing the opposition between art cinema and exploitation cinema, we effectively refigure it in terms of an equally deceptive opposition between Hollywood and non-Hollywood filmmaking practices whether it is called marginal, imperfect, or exploitation cinema (Schneider and Williams, 2005: 2). What this results in is a critical disavowal and potential erasure of the very important differences between trash/exploitation filmmaking and the New Latin American Cinema avant-garde. Therefore, while searching for a way to critically examine Latin America's rich and diverse exploitation cinemas we must be careful not to fall into this trap. We must also consider that, although avant-garde and exploitation cinema both resist Hollywood commercial orthodoxy as repressive and homogenizing, at the same time exploitation cinema offers its own form of resistance to the bourgeois excesses of the avant-garde.

NOTES

1. Randal Johnson and Robert Stam's *Brazilian Cinema*, the major English-language text for Brazilian Cinema, includes a two-line reference to Mojica in a list of names from the *Udigrudi* (1995: 40).
2. Mojica's films are now becoming more and more accessible to the extent that they are available in such mainstream arenas as Tower Records (in an attractive 3-DVD coffin-shaped set) and on Amazon sites worldwide.
3. Two of his films attest to this self-avowed media ubiquity. Some show him as a well-known personality often on the television, or recognized in the street.

Other films explore a darker side of his ubiquity with characters' subconscious minds being inhabited by Zé do Caixão, the character he created, and his nightmarish world. In *O despertar da besta*, drug experiment candidates, featured on a 'real-life' TV show in which Mojica appears, fantasize about his character Zé do Caixão whilst (supposedly) tripping on LSD—supposedly because, unbeknownst to them, they are in fact injected with distilled water. (In a continuity error worthy of only truly bad [i.e., great] exploitation films, Mojica has people injecting LSD when it is common knowledge that the drug is in fact ingested.) In *Delírios de um anormal/Hallucinations of a Deranged Mind* (Mojica Marins, 1977), a psychiatrist becomes convinced that Zé do Caixão is after his wife. Doctors bring the filmmaker Mojica to the hospital to persuade the patient that Zé is only a fictional character. However, the film ends ambiguously with the suggestion that Zé do Caixão might indeed be a malevolent presence that exists and exerts influence extra-diegetically (i.e., outside the film world).

4. Many other New Latin American Cinema directors studied at the Centro Sperimentale in the 1950s, including Argentinean Fernando Birri, Cubans Julio García Espinosa and Tomás Gutiérrez Alea, and Colombian Gabriel García Márquez. Many of these went on to adopt neorealism as an esthetic model.

5. Exploitation directors are usually autodidacts: consider Doris Wishman in the United States (Mike Quarles, 1993) and Armando Bó in Argentina (Rodrigo Fernández y Denise Nagy, 1999). Popular film culture is also romantically invested in the idea of learning by watching as embodied in the 'video store clerk to Hollywood director' myth of Quentin Tarantino.

6. We could perhaps call Mojica this kind of worker rather than artist, given that filmmaking was one of a number of activities he used to support himself and his family, including photonovels, comics, a makeup line, and even records.

7. The EICTV was founded in 1986 by the Foundation for New Latin American Cinema headed by García Márquez. Its first director was Argentinean filmmaker Fernando Birri, famous for one of the earliest New Latin American films, *Tire dié/Throw Us Ten* (1958).

8. A fact which García Espinosa had to refute in an essay written fifteen years later, "Mediations on Imperfect Cinema" (1997b [1983]).

9. In its initial phase (1960–1964), *cinema novo* developed through the different practices of young filmmakers living in Rio in the early 1960s: Glauber Rocha, Nelson Pereira dos Santos (who was also one of the precursors to *cinema novo* with *Rio zona norte/Rio Northern Zone*, 1957, and *Rio 40 graus/Rio 40 Degrees* 1955), Rui Guerra, Carlos Diegues, and Joaquim Pedro de Andrade. Their early work shared certain common features: an idealist assumption that, not only were their films a radical expression of Latin American 'otherness' in the face of a neocolonial cultural system, but also that they could serve to make the public aware of their position within this system and also of their own poverty. *Cinema novo* attempted to create a political cinema, one which would be popular not in terms of mass commercialization but in the sense that it was "for the people" (King, 2000: 108).

If the first phase of *cinema novo* was characterized by a certain optimism, the second phase of *cinema novo* (1964–1968) was plagued with self-doubt. Sparked by the military coup d'etat that overthrew João Goulart in 1964—the left-leaning intellectuals of *cinema novo* were thrown into a crisis of self-examination. The military takeover destroyed the illusions of the leftists who had imagined themselves a vanguard leading the marginalized masses away from alienation and towards freedom. It forced the progressive elite to see both its own powerlessness and recognize its own elite status. The coup forced a reconceptualization of leftist filmmaking strategies where films attempt to explore the reasons for the failure of the left-populist project. Thus Rocha's *Terra em transe/Land in Anguish* (1967) forms a critical portrait of the leftist intellectuals.

10. Schaefer notes the similarities between the foreign art film and the exploitation fare in terms of offering forbidden spectacle in the form of nudity and sex acts (1999: 333).

11. Although it receives less critical attention than the Southern Cone 'dirty wars,' Brazil also had a 'dirty war' contemporaneous with those waged in Argentina, Chile, and Uruguay through the late 1960s and 1970s. It has been suggested that the reasons Brazil's dirty war is less discussed have to do with the fact that this war was more social than political and also that it is effectively still being waged on the streets of the major cities against all forms of 'marginals,' street kids, and so on.

12. See note 3.

13. Indeed, it could be argued that if 'Third World' paracinema goes the same way as the modern horror film in terms of its treatment by the critical establishment, that is, displacing study away from what is unacceptable on grounds of taste (i.e., the mise-en-scène of violence) towards other more "respectable" issues such as philosophy, politics, and sexuality, this represents little progress (Brophy, 1983: 4–5).

8   More Than Simply Cowboys, Naked Virgins, Werewolves, and Vampires?

The Transatlantic Cinema of León Klimovsky

Andrew Willis

León Klimovsky was a stalwart of the European commercial and exploitation cinema of the 1960s and 1970s working across a range of genres including: westerns; horror; comedy; war films; historical epics; psychological thrillers and melodramas. Whilst still best known for his genre work in Europe, he had initially made his name writing and then directing 'respectable' films in his native Argentina. As an example of a transatlantic director, Klimovsky's work raises a number of important issues in relation to the academic study of such commercial work on both continents. In this chapter I want to consider a number of Klimovsky's films in relation to the shifting Argentine and European contexts in which they were produced, suggesting ways in which they might be read that refuses to simply celebrate their oft cited marginal status as 'cult,' 'trash,' and 'exploitation' as much of his work has previously been, instead reading them politically as 'popular' products of their times, acknowledging, as Jeffrey Sconce does, that such cult films or "paracinema" are not necessarily a "uniformly 'progressive' body of cinema" (1995: 383). Indeed, it is through placing Klimovsky's work firmly into these contexts that we can begin to see them as far from examples of progressive cinema and in fact often highly reactionary.

Klimovsky was born in Buenos Aires in 1906 and died in Madrid in 1996. He is variously credited as having initially trained as a dentist, but rejected that career for one in the cinema, beginning work in the Argentine film industry in the 1940s. Domingo Di Nubila states that he had worked as a film critic for Radio Belgrano and formed Cine Arte, a specialized film club, in 1941 (1998: 345). His first professional work in the film industry was as a scriptwriter, and it was in this capacity that he contributed to *Se abre el abismo/Descent into Hell* (1944), a feature that was directed by Frenchman Pierre Chenal. It was critically well received and actress Judith Sulián was awarded a Silver Condor for her supporting performance by the Argentinean Film Critics Association, indicating that at this early stage in his career Klimovsky was involved in projects that were seen as having some level of artistic significance. This cultural status seems to have continued when Klimovsky made his debut feature *El jugador /The Player* (1948), an adaptation of Fyodor Dostoyevsky. Following this first directorial work, Klimovsky quickly built a reputation as a reliable director and one who would significantly be associated with the field of literary adaptation. In a similar vein, he went on to translate a range of other critically lauded or popular novels for the big screen. These included, most notably, screen versions of Ernesto Sábato's *El túnel/The Tunnel* (1952) and Alexander Dumas's *El conde de Montecristo/The Count of Monte Cristo* (1953).

Films such as *El túnel* and *El conde de Montecristo*, whilst drawn from established literary sources, remain at what might best be described as the middlebrow end of the commercial Argentine cinema of the time. If, as Octavio Getino (2005) suggests, Argentine cinema at this moment is usually divided into two trends, the bourgeois and the popular, Klimovsky's work with its literary origins would certainly be associated with the former. However, whilst his work often draws on literary pieces, the choice of works such as *El conde de Montecristo* also suggests that at the same time at least one eye was also on the commercial potential of these works. The fact that many of his Argentine films straddle Getino's division is today largely forgotten due to the much higher profile and wider awareness of his later popular and generic European films. It is this position outside the usual binary opposition evoked by writers concerned with Argentine film that may explain why Klimovsky remains a peripheral figure in most of the subsequent histories of the country's cinematic output. His films of this period have certainly not been seen as operating at the highbrow end of cinematic practice of the period, and, whilst making a number of highly professional works, Klimovsky is rarely discussed in terms of his potential status as an auteur like other directors of the era such as Luis César Amadori, Francisco Mugica, or even Mario Soffici. Perhaps reflecting his position as a maker of middlebrow rather than high-status films, Jorge Miguel Couselo notes that Klimovsky's well-received adaptation of *El túnel* did not benefit from "the prestige of film society exposure or serious criticism" that would usually meet the release of better respected works (1988: 32).

Another issue raised by the status of Klimovsky's films is the fact that some of his Argentine output of this period might, on first encounter, seem to fall more clearly into the exploitation arena than his later European work, particularly those films made in the late 1960s and 1970s that he is so closely associated with. This has meant that when critics do approach his work they have simply looked for connections with these later works in his early films, rather than focusing on the differences. This may go some way to explain why the most well-known film of Klimovsky's Argentine period internationally is the drug warning tale *Marihuana* (1950). This feature would seem to be in a tradition that links it to U.S. works such as *Tell Your Children* (aka *Reefer Madness*, 1936). *Tell Your Children* was originally conceived by its church backers as an educational tool that would warn parents about the dangers marijuana posed to young people. The original was quickly bought and recut by notorious exploitation producer/director Dwain Esper, who introduced more salacious material and released the new version on the exploitation circuit. Like the original *Tell Your Children*, Klimovsky's *Marihuana* had been intended as a serious warning about the drug and its ill effects, and on closer inspection its cultural status would seem to be much more ambiguous than perhaps the marketing of the film might suggest (see Figure 8.1). For example, even though it is now to be found rubbing shoulders with all sorts of exploitation movies in the pages of the catalogue of Something Weird, a leading U.S. cult video and DVD distributor, *Marihuana* was initially seen, in Argentina at least, as a serious attempt to warn people of the dangers of the drug and, as César Maranghello states, had been through some slight edits and changes in line with governmental edicts that films should "reflect the high level of culture, customs and ideology of the Argentine people" (2005: 96). Once this had been done, the film was officially supported, which is certainly reflected by the fact that it was selected for and shown as an Argentine representative at the prestigious Cannes International Film Festival in 1951, something that also reinforces the idea that at this stage in his career, and in some circles, Klimovsky's work still carried some cultural kudos even when today the subject matter of his work would seem a little 'sleazy.'

Figure 8.1   Mexican advertising of *Marihuana* (León Klimovsky, 1950).

POLITICAL CONTEXTS

On the surface, Klimovsky's position as something of a middlebrow director combined with his growing reputation as a highly skilled professional
might explain why he was able to move quite easily from Argentina into
the European commercial film industry. However, alongside this professionally based transatlantic transition, the historical moment within which
Klimovsky was making his early films should not be forgotten, as this can
provide an essential context within which we might begin to further understand his shift from Latin America to Spain. Perhaps the most significant
factor is the political climate in Argentina at the time. Juan Perón was
elected in 1946 and served two presidencies before being removed from
office in 1955. John King offers an explanation of the impact this had on
the film industry and the practitioners working within it, arguing that:

> This period of 1946–55 was viewed as one of cultural obscurantism by
> most intellectuals and artists. Films for example, fell under the control
> of the Sub-secretariat for Information and the Press, which acted as a
> form of propaganda ministry monitoring newspapers, radio broadcasts
> and the cinema . . . few intellectuals and artists supported Perón in this
> period. (1988: 10)

This latter fact meant that a number of people associated with the film industry, such as actress Libertad Lamarque, who was said to have angered Eva
Perón, and director Luis Saslavsky, left Argentina during the Perón period,
many for political reasons (Falicov, 2007: 29). Klimovsky, however, did not
leave for Europe until 1955, the same year as the government fell. One reason
for his exit at that point might be the rapid decline experienced by the film
industry as protection was removed and profits from foreign imports were
free to leave the country. As Ana M. López explains, "Even though Perón's
film protection laws had not been entirely successful, their sudden abolition
gave the *coup de grâce* to an already weakened film industry and essentially
ended studio-system production in Argentina" (1988: 50).

   However, another reason for Klimovsky's exit might have been the fact
that one of the studios he was closely associated with, Argentina Sono Film,
where he had made some of his best-known works such as *El túnel* and *El
conde de Montecristo*, had very close links to the Perón government. So,
whilst King may argue that "few intellectuals and artists supported Perón
in this period," a number of those within the film industry clearly did or
at the least had strong sympathies with it as Argentina Sono Films' reputation reflects (1988: 10). Maranghello (2005) points out that after the coup
d'etat of 1955 the new government identified all the recent productions of
Sono Film with the Peronist Party. This was not the first time the company
had been identified as having strong political associations. Tamara Falicov

quotes Vincent de Pascal from a 1941 edition of *The Hollywood Reporter* where he states that there were claims that Argentina Sono Film was partly financed by the German Embassy through the *Banco germánico*, that its series of newsreels, *Noticieros panamericanos*, had a Nazi flavor, that German organizations were promoted in its films, and that those running the company as well as its artistic and technical personnel were Naziphiles (2007: 21–22). While there have been no studies to fully substantiate this claim, the newsreels in question during this specific period of the company were directed by "Raúl Alejandro Apold, a film critic at *El mundo* who became head of publicity at Sono Film in 1941. Apold was later to become the most hard-line, right-wing censor in Perón's administration" (Falicov, 2007: 22). Clearly, this history and association would put pressure on directors such as Klimovsky, who worked closely with Argentina Sono Film. Consequently, such figures might fear that the 1955 change in government would lead to their careers coming under threat for political reasons. His close connection to a company with links to the previous government, amidst a highly politicized period in Argentine history, raises speculation and might even further explain why Klimovsky felt it might be best to continue his career in Europe. While the connections between the political context in Argentina and the production of Klimovsky's films are not so clear, there is enough evidence to at least question a simplistic "progressive" reading of films such as *Marihuana*. Further research about Klimovsky's Argentine work needs to be conducted within the context of Argentina, given Klimovsky's clear ideological positioning within the context of Spain, as will be argued following. Unfortunately, this is beyond the scope of this chapter.

It is certainly true that within many of the histories of Argentine film the importance of certain trends of cinema is marginalized. Enrique Colina and Daniel Díaz Torres argue that films of the 1930s and 1940s, such as melodramas, were examples of a "reactionary populism" where "God, Fatherland and Home make up the inseparable trinity of social equilibrium" (qtd. in King, 1990: 38). King suggests that their dismissal is problematic as it rejects the whole melodramatic genre of the period en masse and he offers a brief reassessment of some key examples in his study of Latin American cinema (1990: 38–40). This rethinking of the previous wholesale rejection of an era of popular filmmaking is of course valuable, but we should not lose sight of the original criticism in a rush to embrace popular cinema. This is particularly so in the case of Klimovsky, as some of the caution offered by Colina and Díaz Torres is worth remembering when looking at a director whose work does indeed offer reactionary perspectives on the world, as I will argue next. His later European exploitation films are certainly no exception to this, and for this reason a reevaluation of Klimovsky's Argentine phase should be undertaken since it is possible to see the seeds of a rather conservative worldview in Klimovsky's Argentine films.

KLIMOVSKY, THE AUTEUR?

As already noted from the mid-1950s Klimovsky continued his filmmaking career in Europe. At this point the volume of his output seemed to increase as he found a place for himself within the more commercial parts of the Spanish film industry. During this highly productive period he was able to reveal that he could turn his hand to most popular genres of the day. Indeed, as his filmography developed it would include a wide variety of films, from comedies to melodramas to war films, with as many as three or four titles a year bearing his name as director. Typical of Klimovsky's output during this period, and his ability to work quickly in a commercial context, is the 1956 comedy *Viaje de novios/Honeymoon*. This film was shot in color for Agata Films at the Ballesteros Studios just outside Madrid and is a farcical comedy set in a hotel for newlyweds. The film starred the young actors Fernando Fernán Gómez as Juan, a young man who had spent the last few years in Africa, and Analía Gadé as Ana, who is fresh off the plane from Argentina when they first meet each other. At the start of the film the pair are brought together by Federico, who quickly whisks them off to a luxury hotel for their honeymoon. As the central couple at first do not know each other at all, what follows is a very typical light farce comprising many awkward moments and mistaken intentions, many based around Juan's lack of social skills. *Viaje de novios* is a very self-contained film with a small number of repeated locations around the hotel and an equally small number of characters, and is shot in a rather anonymous style that highlights the dialogue and comedic action. The one interesting thing that might be drawn from the film occurs at the end of the story; Ana ultimately sees the good in Juan and the pair finally realizes that they do in fact love each other. The key moment that reveals Ana's change of heart occurs when a newly assertive Juan demands that she repair a missing button on his jacket, something we had previously seen him attempting to do himself. Ana, from Argentina of course, decides that if she is to find a place for herself in Spain with Juan she had better just agree to do what he says. It might be a little far fetched, but one could argue that, like Ana, Klimovsky was able to see how best to fit into Spain upon his arrival from Buenos Aires, in his case by becoming invisible and making commercial films. The rather anonymous visual style of Klimovsky's films might be seen to reflect that invisibility, and it is this factor that has made it difficult for critics to make a convincing case for the director as an auteur. Again, this may offer another reason why his work has been overlooked by many of those writing about both Argentine and European cinema.

However, the vast amount of films directed by Klimovsky in both Argentina and Europe, many in the latter context on the equivalent of poverty row budgets, might be linked together in a traditionally auteurist manner. For example, there are recurrent visual moments across his work such as a repeated use of striking tracking shots which can be found in, for example, the opening of the 1969 war film *No importa morir/Legion of No Return*, the western *Pagó cara su muerte/Tierra Brava* (1969), and the horror film *La noche de Walpurgis/The Werewolf's Shadow* (1971). This, along with the repeated use of slow motion alongside a distorted soundtrack, offer perhaps the most obvious contributions to what might be constructed as a Klimovsky 'stylistic signature.' Even if one can make a case for Klimovsky the auteur based on the visual style the director employed, any such approach still has to face the fact that for all these visual and aural links the most consistent element in his films is that, today rarely evoked, mark of the auteur, his 'worldview.'[1] It is within this realm that there is certainly a consistency, but it is one that shows quite starkly the reactionary side to León Klimovsky's work, and this aspect is something that should not be ignored in favor of a somewhat safer, depoliticized, and purely aesthetic approach to his films. In fact, when one considers Klimovsky's work in more detail it becomes somewhat troublesome for someone like me who has sought to find the potentially radical and oppositional in the exploitation cinemas produced across the globe. With an example like Klimovsky it is hard to look beyond these reactionary facets and these, I would argue, force us to ask some other rather searching questions about how we might approach exploitation and cult cinema beyond identifying what is ultimately a rather vague notion of 'alternative auteurs.' Therefore, before considering what I consider to be the more reactionary side of Klimovsky's cinema in more detail, I want to discuss the approach of some writing about cult cinema and how it raises a number of important questions when looking at the director at hand.

THE DANGERS OF CULT FILM CRITICISM

Exploitation cinema has increasingly been championed as an alternative and even oppositional cinematic form. This is, of course, in some instances true, as the work of writers such as Jim Hillier and Aaron Lipstadt (1980) on U.S. exploitation cinema indicates. In a number of pieces they carefully identify the liberal tendencies in a number of Roger Corman's New World films and cycles of the 1970s. What is so vital about their approach is the fact that they were very specific about the films they are discussing in the construction of their argument: *Caged Heat* (1974), *Dynamite Women/The Great Texas Dynamite Chase* (1976), *Lady in Red* (1979) are combined with a considered look at the U.S. film industry of the period, alongside an acknowledgment of the independence offered by the economic situation at New World. In other words, their work never loses sight of the historical, industrial, and cultural specificity of the films at hand.

The anchoring of the radical potential of exploitation cinema in specific economic, historical, and national contexts remains a vital component of any analysis if we are to see any form of exploitation cinema as more than just throwaway, commercial 'trash.' In relation to Latin American cinema, Dolores Tierney (2004) does exactly this in her study of Brazilian maverick director José Mojica Marins, placing her subject into a number of essential contexts that assist in an understanding of how the director and his work engages with and can be read as offering a challenge to them, and in doing so might be read as oppositional and radical. However, whilst Tierney offers an informed and anchored approach, others are not so careful, and on occasion the simple celebration of exploitation cinema as somehow essentially radical by its mere existence is offered by other writers in the field. For example, in their introduction to the collection *Unruly Pleasures: The Cult Film and its Critics*, Xavier Mendik and Graeme Harper assert, "by linking the cult movie with the uncontrollable force of the orgasm, this volume views the cult text as a potentially subversive medium," before going on to state:

> While the cult movie can take many generic forms, its depictions are frequently aligned (as with the orgasm) to excessive, dangerous and even distasteful types of display, which impress themselves on their audience as distinct from the viewing patterns that make up our everyday cinema consumption. (2000: 11)

For me, this approach, and its assertion of the radical potential of cult films, is not without problems because it does not draw on any kind of historical and cultural specificities. The meaning of a variety of cult films, each produced and consumed in very different contexts, seems to be condensed into one grand alternative experience. However, the specific industrial and cultural questions are all the more important when we are discussing works such as those of Klimovsky produced in the first instance to make a quick profit in a competitive commercial environment.

Klimovsky's films *can* easily be assimilated into the general assumption or argument that exploitation and trash cinema offer some kind of radicalism per se—that is, that such films are challenging and oppositional by their sheer existence. This is basically the argument put forward by Joan Hawkins when she states, in relation to Jess Franco's films:

> The existence of these films is extraordinary, given the social and political climate of the time. Even the tame, domestic versions of Franco's films hint at illicit sexuality, lesbianism, and other activities officially designated as perversions by General Franco's government. (2000a: 93)

In some ways of course it is extraordinary that such films were made in that environment. However, one must be careful when arguing that the mere presence of images that might be problematic for the state censors means that such works are automatically politically progressive in that context. As I will now go on to argue, the films of Klimovsky reveal that such potentially transgressive images can in fact be utilized in a very conservative and ultimately reactionary way.

KLIMOVSKY'S REACTIONARY CINEMA

It is essential to remember that when he left Argentina Klimovsky went to Spain to continue his filmmaking career. Whilst language would of course make this a logical step, it is also worth recalling that Spain was a country being run at that time by General Francisco Franco's National-Catholic right-wing dictatorship. It is also of note that in the late 1960s and early 1970s, the period of Klimovsky's production that will focus on here, Spanish censorship became 'harsher' in comparison to the *aperturista* (open) climate of the early to mid-1960s as the "regime felt under attack from the increased demands for democratization and liberalization" (Triana Toribio, 2003: 95). A detailed consideration of some of the films Klimovsky produced in Spain reveals a willingness to embrace what might best be described as a reactionary politics. Of course, this in turn meant his work was somewhat in tune with the National-Catholic ideology (celebration of the peasantry, *Hispanidad* [Spanishness], a united, Catholic Spain, anticommunism, and a particular idea of Spanish womanhood) of the Francoist government. Once one acknowledges this, examples of Klimovsky's work that on the surface might seem to have little connection, existing as they do in a wide variety of genres, can be drawn together by a right-wing, even Francoist, perspective on society and the way in which it functions.

Klimovsky's exploitation cinema certainly is not an example of the 'challenging just by their existence' that some might wish of marginal and cult work of the period. A film such as *El mariscal del infierno/The Devil's Possessed* (1974) is interesting in this light. On the surface it presents the story of an evil medieval lord who oppresses his people as he searches for wealth by employing an alchemist, this in turn leading the peasants to rise up in defiance. However, rather than offering a radical and subversive image of a heroic underclass resisting the corruption of the aristocracy (for this might seem like celebration of the 'wrong' kind of peasant, i.e., the politicized landless Aragonese or Extremaduran defeated in the Civil War [Triana Toribio, 2003: 41]), the poor in Klimovsky's world have to await the arrival of another nobleman to lead them to victory with the cry of "May the Lord help us." Thereafter they must live a life within the existing system rather than creating an alternative fairer one that their uprising may have created. It is just this kind of utopian, idealistic ending that popular genre films of this period could offer because they often operated outside the dominance of social realism; and it is that sort of perspective that Hillier and Lipstadt championed in their work on the New World films of the 1970s mentioned earlier. Not here though, in the case of *El mariscal del infierno* the film's attempt at realism operates as a constrictive mode of practice. The film was shot on striking Spanish locations to create its medieval world rather than re-creating a less realist and more mythic past in the studio that may have allowed the story to develop in a less restrained and more radical way.

With this reading of *El mariscal del infierno* in mind, it is not surprising that even the most unknown and seemingly throwaway works from the Klimovsky filmography, such as his 1969 war film *No importa morir,* can also be seen to offer a very Francoist, and in this instance an anticommunist, perspective. An Italian-Spanish coproduction between Leone Film–Daiano Film of Rome and Atlantida Films, Madrid, here the cold war is injected into the Second World War as Tab Hunter plays a tough GI called Richards who is ordered to lead the top secret mission to blow up a bridge over the river Elba before the Soviet soldiers arrive. The film is a mix of *The Magnificent Seven* (1960) and *The Dirty Dozen* (1967), and on the surface might seem like nothing more than a cheap, commercially minded, rip-off. However, the film shifts from the generic conventions of most World War II films in that, whilst the enemies guarding the bridge are the familiar German soldiers, the real enemy and those who must be stopped are the Russians. Hunter's Richards is starkly informed that at all costs the Soviets must not reach a position where they are able to cross the bridge. He, quite rightly, observes that "it all sounds a bit like politics, sir," but is quickly rebuffed by his Major, who asserts that "we can't afford to reflect on politics now." This suggestion, of course, is exactly what we should be doing when we come to analyze such films, and with a politically informed perspective we are able to identify the way in which the finale of *No importa morir* confirms the film's more general right-wing perspective. As the Russian tanks with their impressive firepower arrive at the destroyed bridge, their commander seems unconcerned by the destruction he sees before him and states that "all we have to do is reach the Elba and use it as a division between two Germanys: East and West." In a neat twist the film manages to imply that, whilst the Germans were bad, they might not be as bad as the Soviets, who had been planning the division of Germany throughout the war. On reflection, with this sort of political sentiment it is not surprising that the film had no problem getting made in Spain even with its strict censorship.

In a similar fashion, less progressive political elements but ones that fit explicitly within Francoist ideologies can be identified as recurring in other Klimovsky genre films. One of the most easily identifiable is the repeated use of priests or religious figures in key roles. As Klimovsky would become closely associated with the horror genre in the 1970s, these might be explained away in that context as stock generic characters, but it is more likely that they are in keeping with National-Catholic ideology imposed throughout the dictatorship. However, they are traditionally less visible in European or spaghetti westerns. A priest appears in a significant scene in the 1968 film *Un hombre vino a matar/Rattler Kid.* Here, a soldier called Tony Garnett is falsely accused of murder and the only person who believes that he is innocent is the fort priest. A telling scene in this film has that same priest asking God to help him do the right thing when faced by the kid's false imprisonment. Having reflected and prayed long and hard, he decides to let the kid go and responds to his asking how he will explain his action by saying, "I have my conscience and above all my faith." The trajectory of the film's narrative is the drive to prove that the priest, and through prayer God, were correct about Garnett. With those odds it is little surprise that by the end their faith is proved well founded and that finally the kid acts properly.

In 1971 Klimovsky directed *Reverendo Colt/Reverend Colt*, a film in which a well-known bounty hunter reappears in a dusty frontier town, having become a priest and now claiming he wants nothing more than to build a church for the inhabitants and bring God to the Wild West. Whilst the film delivers the expected western elements of wagon trains, frontier towns, shoot-outs, tenderfoots, ambushes, renegades, and posses, Klimovsky seems most interested in the scenes that explore the gimmick of the gunfighter turned priest. When he is accused of taking part in a rob- bery and is about to be hanged by a lynch mob, the Reverend states that whatever happens to him it "will be God's will." Later, when a bad guy attempts to shoot him but misses, the Reverend forgives him, and later still as he plays cards with a hardened gambler he says that the stakes will be "dollars against psalms for your soul." In a flashback, similar to those in *Once Upon a Time in the West* (1968), and again supporting the beneficent image of the Catholic church imposed during Franco's regime, the audience learns that as a sickly child he was taken care of by a kind priest who he also witnessed being killed by bandits. The absolute goodness of the church and its representatives are at the absolute center of the story and the central character's road to redemption.

These National-Catholic religious images are perhaps less surpris- ing than they first seem when one discovers hidden amongst Klimovsky's 1960s output a film called *Aquella joven de blanco/Bernadette de Lourdes* (1965). This feature, starring Cristina Galbó, is another telling of the story of Bernadette of Lourdes and takes a deeply serious, even reverend, attitude to its subject matter. The film's opening shows the thousands of people who visit the shrine from all over the world in a documentary fashion utilizing actual footage of pilgrims before going on to present the story of the young girl who has a vision of the Virgin Mary. Much of the film is almost neore- alist in style, and the reverential approach adopted by Klimovsky reveals a filmmaker seemingly happy to make a pious account of this most important Catholic tale.[2] Here, then, is a film that perhaps offers a key to many of Klimovsky's religious characters and the fact that throughout the Franco years he had no problems working on projects in Spain. However, if one only looked at the excessive cult films, such as his horror output, that Kli- movsky was responsible for, this one, so important in understanding his work, might easily be overlooked.

Perhaps not surprisingly, even the more seemingly progressive and chal- lenging oddities of Klimovsky's filmmaking career prove to be less than radical, and wholly consistent with right-wing Francoist gender politics, when one looks closely at them and places them alongside his other output. The 1974 film *Odio mi cuerpo/I Hate My Body* is certainly one of his stranger offerings. Set in Germany, safely outside Spain most likely for censorship reasons, it tells the tale of a successful brain transplant performed by an ex-Nazi surgeon played by Narciso Ibáñez Menta. The swap is between a man and a woman, and the film explores how mentally different the sexes are and how if a woman behaves too much like a man trouble logically follows. *Odio mi cuerpo* contains a clear swipe at feminism, another of the perceived enemies of Francoism, in a scene in a factory where a group of women explicitly referred to as "feminists" are shown to be naïve and misguided in their demands for equality. But its anti–women's liberation sentiments are perhaps best shown in the finale of the film. As the central character is raped by three sailors, she, using her masculine brain, decides to fight back; however, she is easily cast aside by the burley men, hitting her head on a nearby pile of wood and dying. In keeping with the Catholic ideal of a woman, proper to Francoist marriage manuals, in which woman's "fundamental characteristic" is preferably submission (Smith, 2000: 53–54), the film suggests, rather reprehensibly even by 1974 standards, that if only she had laid back and enjoyed it as the sailors suggest she would have survived. The sheer bizarreness of the storyline combined with Klimovsky's occasionally disorientating visual style and striking use of point-of-view shots does not prevent the overall impact of the film once again being deeply conservative. Here, we have a film that initially may seem a little 'out there' and certainly challenging, tackling something that mainstream cinema would, at the time, certainly have shied away from, but that, once one considers the sexual politics of Spain in this period, and in particular the nationalist constructions of womanhood, is designed to be a warning not to Nazi surgeons but to women who want to act like and be treated the same as men. Ultimately, this is a warning that in its conservatism seems once again in line with the reactionary politics of Klimovsky's cinema and something that would not be out of step with much of the thinking related to women's issues in Franco's Spain. Whilst at first it may be difficult for champions of exploitation and cult films such as myself to admit it, León Klimovsky and his films are perhaps typical rather than atypical of the work that appeared in such production contexts as Spain at these particular historical moments. Rather than being awash with the radical and subversive images that Mendik and Harper (2000) might desire, the low-budget commercial and exploitation cinema of Europe in the 1960s and 1970s is more likely to throw up films that are more conservative than subversive and radical in their perspectives on issues such as the politics of class, race, and gender. In light of this, the work of Klimovsky in this period also offers the opportunity to redress some of these more problematic tendencies within cult film criticism as well as the opportunity to grapple with fan cultures critically rather than in a celebratory fashion.

Linked to this, much has recently been made of the "academic fan," but, as Joanne Hollows (2003) and Jacinda Read (2003) suggest, we should not let that rather uncritical category lead us into an academic cul-de-sac. Perhaps our job as 'academic critics' is not to simply be a fan and repeat the approaches and excesses of fan culture but to continue to engage critically with the ways that much cult fan culture operates around films such as those of Klimovsky.

Finally, it is important to remember that those films that do actually offer a challenge to dominant ways of thinking within exploitation production contexts can only be seen as radical and alternative if one is willing to acknowledge the reactionary nature of the majority of the works churned out by those industries in both Latin America and Europe. It is not a film's mere existence within an exploitation or cult context that makes it somehow challenging but the way in which it engages with the historical and cultural specificities of its often shifting moment of production and consumption. Without this contextualization we will be destined to roam forever from screening to screening arguing that the exposure of a naked breast in a European or Latin American exploitation film from the 1970s was somehow heralding the end of capitalism as we know it, even if that exposure of flesh brought significant financial profits for its producers and distributors, or that our presence in front of such works in cinemas or on DVD marks us out as consumers in 'opposition to the mainstream,' whatever that may be.

NOTES

1. Discussions about authorship and cinema are presented in a very useful fashion in John Caughie (1981).
2. The importance of the Catholic religion to the Franco regime and its idea of the Spanish nation cannot be underestimated and is explored in some depth in Stanley Payne (1984).

Part III
Politicizing Latsploitation

9 Made in South America
Locating *Snuff*

Glenn Ward

As a formative influence on the dissemination of the snuff movie legend from the mid-1970s on, *Snuff* (Michael Findlay, Roberta Findlay, 1976) continues to have an afterlife in excess of its textual properties. The unusual circumstances surrounding the film's production, reputation, and cultural legacy have been widely reported: Johnson and Schaefer (1993), Kerekes and Slater (1993), and Petley (2000) are all informative sources. The majority of accounts deal with *Snuff*'s significance in debates about media violence, pornography, and censorship. Most quote the infamous advertising tagline, used in American and British campaigns and still used on the currently widely available DVD: "the film that could only be made in South America—where life is CHEAP!" Few discuss how 'South America' functions here. This essay looks at how competing notions of 'South America' operate in the film and in the discourse around it. I argue that while many of the film's constructions of the region in which it is set manifest a 'neo-colonialist' point of view, they by no means do so uniformly or without internal contradiction. Certain images of place and space, for example, are sited within a sometimes perplexing geography that resists containment by 'Latin American' stereotypes. I also suggest that the financially led decision to transplant a 'North American' story to Latin American soil—along with the rough-and-ready assemblage of this "exquisite corpse exercise in filmmaking" (Hawkins, 2000a: 136)—creates textual ruptures and tensions which menace the binary model of the colonizer's hegemonic vision pitched against, and successfully silencing, the subaltern Other. Many aspects of *Snuff* and its marketing practices clearly invite this model, but it does not go unchallenged in the film.

Snuff started life in 1970–71 as *The Slaughter* (*El angel de la muerte*), a low-budget mixed-genre feature by the exploitation filmmaking team of Michael and Roberta Findlay. Shot over four weeks mainly in Argentina for $30,000, with a postdubbed cast of "largely Argentinean actors who spoke very little English" (Hawkins, 2000a: 136), *The Slaughter*—along with a whole cycle of exploitation films of the period—sought to capitalize on contemporary publicity surrounding the Charles Manson murder case. Inspired both by the Manson cult's killing of the pregnant film actress

Sharon Tate, and by the public's salacious interest in it, the Findlays' convoluted and shambolic narrative hopscotches around Argentina and Uruguay as it follows the escapades of a gang of young hippie/biker women who plot to kill a pregnant starlet and her associates. Under the drug-fuelled influence of their charismatic Mansonesque leader, Satán (Enrique Larratelli), the gang embarks on the campaign of slaughter promised by the title.

If the Findlays' ramshackle but timely feature was hastily put together to catch the public's fascination with Manson and his 'family,' their efforts were not rewarded. Reports vary as to whether the film was ever shown theatrically, but it was shelved shortly after being made. All accounts agree with Roberta Findlay's own assessment that it was too "awful" to be released (Peary, 1978: 30). Any fan of 'paracinema' or 'badfilm'—including the Findlays' other features—might be surprised to hear of an exploitation film being deemed too incompetent for exhibition. In fact, Findlay also implies that the other trouble with *The Slaughter* was that it was too sympathetic or "favorable" to Manson (Peary, 1978: 30).

Another stumbling block may have been *The Slaughter*'s failure to deliver on genre expectations. Compared to the Findlays' own equally inept *Flesh* trilogy (1967–1968), it was, for all its gestures towards topicality, behind the times. Its attempted spectacles of sex and violence are unlikely to have impressed audiences in 1971. With lackluster soft-core writhing, skinny-dipping and toplessness sharing screen time with hippies, drugs, and light torture, the film was doubtless too mild for the gore/ghoulie market and too tame for the roughies/kinkies trend that the Findlays themselves had helped to define.

In October 1975, the distributor Allan Shackleton decided to blow the dust off this cinematic failure. If *The Slaughter* had been an outmoded sexploitation action film, Shackleton now sought to align his film with contemporary genre developments. From North American kinkies and roughies to European Sadeian erotica, sleaze cinema from the late 1960s on had begun to hybridize the codes of horror and pornography into often unsettling new shapes, either by highlighting the sexual undercurrents of horror or foregrounding the violent implications of sexploitation. On the back of relaxed censorship, the rise of gory shockers, and what Johnson and Schaefer characterize as a brief middle-class flirtation with hard-core 'porno-chic,' the mid-seventies witnessed a deepening of these trends and provided the conditions for Shackleton to reinvest in and update his material.[1] Motivated by rumors about the existence of 'snuff' films, Shackleton commissioned the shooting of some fake 'snuff' footage and had this attached to the end of *The Slaughter*. The whole was released early in 1976, complete with the incendiary new title *Snuff*, but minus any cast or crew credits.

The sources of these reputed snuff films and the sources of the rumors remain open to conjecture. Making no mention of the geographical origin of the films, the legendary exploitation distributor and producer David F. Friedman claimed in 1986 that the snuff myth originated "back in the

1970s" when the Campaign for Decency through Law had alleged that "the X-rated industry was torturing and killing performers on camera" (Hebditch and Anning, 1998: 330). Kerekes and Slater for their part propose that Shackleton's catalyst had been provided by renewed interest in Manson after the attempted assassination in September 1975 of President Gerald Ford by a former 'family' member. As Petley and Brottman point out, Ed Sanders's bestselling book about the Manson case, *The Family* (first edition 1971), had initiated a rumor that the cult had in their possession 'home movies' in which murder—'snuffing out'—was captured on celluloid. Shackleton grasped the opportunity to rework and rename his Manson-based dud (Petley, 2000: 205).

While the old *Slaughter* had hedged its bets by relocating its Stateside bogeyman to Argentina and Uruguay, the new *Snuff* and its publicity now compounded the North/South mixture by (con)fusing hearsay about Manson's murder footage with stories of South American snuff. In a 1978 interview, Roberta Findlay acknowledged Manson as the direct inspiration for *The Slaughter*, but saw the impetus for its reinvention as *Snuff* as coming from further afield: the former "just sat around until the distributor read about these 'snuff' things in South America" (Peary, 1978: 30). According to several accounts, Shackleton was moved to act "after reading an article in the New York Times about the possible existence of a 'snuff' movie smuggled into the US from South America" (Vale and Juno, 1986: 193). Some sources—such as, from very different perspectives, Lederer (1980), Williams (1990) and McNair (1996)—stress the 'pornographic' content of the alleged material, while Petley suggests that these "snuff things" were reputed to be "records of the torture and murder of political prisoners of the oppressive regimes" in the Southern Cone (Petley, 2000: 205). Hebditch and Anning's exploration of the porn industry, though skeptical about the existence of snuff pornography (in which a woman is murdered at the climax of a sex act), define snuff as "documentary footage . . . showing real brutality and atrocities" filmed by "military torture teams" in the region (1988: 337). It certainly seems likely that Shackleton saw these and other events as a useful 'tie-in' for the Findlays' film. Hebditch and Anning are unsure of the extent to which *Snuff* itself was directly influenced by such verité materials, but implicitly repeat the urban legend that fragments of authentic snuff footage—imported this time from Central America—are incorporated into Joe D'Amato's *Emanuelle in America* (1977) (1988: 337).

It is unclear precisely how much *Snuff* and its "made in South America" tagline were responsible for—rather than merely making hay with—the myth of the 'South American' snuff film. The antipornography anthology *Take Back the Night* (Lederer, 1980) seems to have played its part in cementing the notion that 'South America' was the origin of both snuff and *Snuff*. Brottman adds that some protestors against the film outside cinemas in New York waved a placard bearing the words "We Mourn the Death of our Latin American Sister," even though the actress in question was "quite clearly North American" (2005: 84). Though the details vary from version to version, the release of *Snuff* just three months after the emergence of South American 'snuff' reports in the press is unlikely to have been simply opportune. In an ethically dubious but ingenious bit of marketeering, Shackleton seems to have primed the public for his largely Argentinean product by fuelling, if not fabricating, the myths himself (Johnson and Schaefer, 1993: 44). Brottman elaborates that Shackleton leaked insinuations to the press that *Snuff* "had been produced in Buenos Aires and involved the murder of a 'real woman' " (2005: 8). Deep inside this hall of mirrors, Shackleton and *Snuff* seem to have been responsible for crystallizing the idea of 'snuff' films as a South American phenomenon.

Roberta Findlay says that "the choice of Argentina for shooting and setting was simple"; assuming that a combination of "violence and exotic locations" would prove enticing to potential investors, the Findlays "thought and thought of an exotic place and picked Argentina. I always wanted to go to Argentina" (Peary, 1978: 30). A touristic opportunity for Findlay, the choice was also economic. Since the film was made there "to avoid union costs" (Kerekes and Slater, 1993: 11), much of the crew were hired locally. As Findlay explains, "actors were cheaper. An assistant cameraman made about fifty dollars a week," so the investors could "get triple or quadruple [their] money's worth" (Peary, 1978: 30). *The Slaughter* was made at a time when national cinema was a keenly debated issue within Latin American intellectual circles. With the idea of a militant Third Cinema—possessing an autonomous identity beyond both Hollywood and the European art house—gaining support in Argentina alongside Brazil's *cinema novo* and Cuba's *imperfect cinema* (King, 2000), 'First World' use of 'Third World' resources was increasingly regarded as a neocolonialist enterprise. In this context, the Findlays' location of the film in the area seems a product of colonialist domination in the region and its film industry. Discussing a number of low-budget and mainly straight-to-video coproductions made by Roger Corman and Aries Cinematográfica Argentina in the 1980s, Tamara Falicov has outlined some of the "unequal power dynamics" that can plague such practices (2004: 31). Unlike Corman, the Findlays did not marginalize Argentine actors or use "the Argentine landscape . . . as a backdrop and double for forests in medieval Europe" (Falicov, 2004: 31). But just as Corman's search for cheap labor can be seen to result in 'Third World' dependency (Falicov, 2004: 36), so Findlay's explanation that *The Slaughter* was made in Argentina "because everything was so cheap" and "exotic" there (Peary, 1978: 30) reveals the power imbalance characteristic of economic and ideological imperialism.

With peculiarly circular logic, *Snuff*'s crystallization of 'South American snuff' myths helped to lend credence to the violence and gore of its infamous climax. In other words, the film's South American-ness seemed to guarantee the veracity of its final scene. Hence, contrary to the way Corman's 1980s productions sought, according to Falicov, to disguise their

Argentinean identity, Shackleton and the Findlays' assemblage advertised its South American credentials while concealing its North American origins. That Shackleton's rumormongering successfully primed the audience to buy into the "Made in South America" claim suggests that 'First World' audiences were already apt to believe that life—and not just cast and crew—was "cheap" there. Both *The Slaughter* and *Snuff* displaced North American anxieties about itself (clustered around and scapegoated in the figure of Charles Manson, as Brottman argues) on to South America, the more 'civilized' America believing that such an atrocity 'could only' be made in the 'dark continent' south of the Central American isthmus.

The blithe invocation of foreign, usually 'South American,' origins as implicit evidence for the existence of snuff films has reverberated down the years since Shackleton's masterstroke. Hence a British tabloid review of *Falling Down* (Joel Schumacher, 1992) quoted by Kerekes and Slater refers to "the most odious [film] I have seen since someone showed me a South American snuff film" (1993: 302). Julian Petley, writing of a mid-1990s reprisal of Britain's early 1980s 'video nasties' scare, cites another newspaper: "the first 'snuff' video found in this country . . . was apparently shot abroad." A *Guardian* report of the same year quotes a trading standards officer: "these videos show genuine killings. . . . We suspect that they come from North or South America where missing persons are more of a way of life" (in Petley, 2000: 216). 'Foreign' location apparently lends credibility to atrocity footage, no matter how patently fake; in a clear case of cultural projection, it would appear that nothing is too savage or monstrous for 'abroad.' Thirty years after *Snuff*'s original release, the British antiporn campaigner Julie Bindel has written of watching "a snuff movie" in the early 1980s: "one of the activists had gone into a porn shop in England and asked if the owner had something 'really extreme.' He gave her a film of a woman in South America being raped, tortured and murdered. As a finale, her hand was sawn off. . . . We had proved that snuff existed" (*The Guardian G2*, 2006: 18). As well as inadvertently echoing the overheated ballyhoo around the material against which she protests, Bindel repeats the tactics of Lederer's *Take Back the Night*—she refers to "activists in the US who were fighting the same battles"—by conflating Shackleton's fiction with snuff the 'fact.' (In *Snuff* the severing of a prosthetic hand appears during but not 'as' the finale.) Her recourse to the entire South American subcontinent is as vague and homogenizing as that of Shackleton, and perhaps even more so than the film itself; in the absence of evidence, the rhetorical impact of 'South America' here relies on the readers' preconceptions, and on their absorption of the South American snuff myth.

As well as being a matter of exoticism and economics, the Findlays' decision to shoot primarily in Argentina took advantage of 'First World' perceptions of South American brutality. Argentina and Uruguay stand in the film less as specific countries and more as metonyms for the Southern Cone. The specific settings for much of the film's action can be difficult to identify, but are cross-nationally triangulated across Punta del Este, Montevideo, and the province of Buenos Aires. According to Diego Curubeto, actual locations included the Tigre, the Ezeiza Airport, and the Ciudad deportiva del club Boca Juniors (1996: 339). Film producer Max Marsh (Aldo Mayo) and his starlet fiancée Terri London (Mirtha Massa) arrive at Buenos Aires airport from New York via—as a PA announcement makes clear—Miami, Lima, and Santiago; their LAN Chile flight is bound for Rio via Montevideo. Terri is soon whisked off to Punta del Este by her old flame, the jet-setting German playboy Horst Frank (Clao Villanueva). Little sense of distance exists in the film's elliptical psychogeography; Frank observes that Buenos Aires is "two hours away" from Punta del Este by boat (in reality it is 212 miles away), and Terri—playing prima donna in a strange land—complains about the heat and about having to wait all day to be connected to Frank by telephone. Yet at other points Buenos Aires seems to be but a short ride from Montevideo by motorcycle, and crossing the world's widest estuary by speedboat appears effortless. While cities are occasionally mentioned in the dialogue by name, countries are not; if Shackleton's boast that *Snuff* was 'made in South America' was suitably nonspecific, so the film in many ways erases borders. In some respects the leaky quality of national borders in the film has a 'real-world' basis. People, goods, and ideas have, for example, long flowed between the major cities of Buenos Aires and Montevideo, with the former arguably identifying with the latter more than with its own rural provinces. But hazy and porous boundaries also generate a geographical confusion that is par for the course in horror and exploitation cinema. Eddie Muller and Daniel Faris refer to the "topsy-turvy world geography" of 1940s 'goona-goona' movies in which "hunters on the veldt were often surprised by Bengal tigers suddenly leaping through tall grasses" (1997: 46), while David Skal recalls *The Wolf Man*'s (George Waggner, 1941) "geographically indistinct" pastiche of Europe in which "'[b]oundaries and credibility were . . . blurred" (1993: 215). *Snuff*'s imaginary geography acts as a synecdoche for generalized and endemic subcontinental barbarity.

The permeability and fluidity of national borders presented in *Snuff* enables the film to gesture towards any number of historical events within, and ideas about, Latin America, while loosely playing upon generic notions of omnipresent brutality and lawlessness. As scriptwriter for *The Slaughter*, Michael Findlay may have seen in his locations a chance to make his film broadly redolent of social upheavals in several different South American countries. The Southern Cone countries were in fact still relatively stable and democratic before the turn of the 1970s; that *The Slaughter* could nevertheless equate the area with savagery and Otherness indicates the degree to which the film's imperialist gaze conflates the Southern Cone with the rest of South America. The film therefore allows for a generalized sense of random violence and social breakdown that could later be drawn upon by *Snuff*'s "made in South America" claim.

As Roberta Findlay fairly dismissively commented, "Michael, being one of those Upper West Side liberals, added all these political implications" to *The Slaughter* (Peary, 1978: 30). The Findlays' film makes no overt reference to the institutionalized violence used against insurgents by the right-wing sectors of society which began to seize power across Argentina, Chile, and Uruguay from the late 1960s; nor are any possible political subtexts handled with the least conviction. A businessman is stabbed to death in a restroom in Buenos Aires Airport, in a scene entirely lacking cause or consequence; a child-abusing farmer shoots Angelica's father with a loaded pistol he happens to have handy at his bedside. These and other scenes can, perhaps charitably, be read as the Findlays' attempts to evoke a sense of omnipresent violence and mayhem, while attempting to make a virtue of their cavalier approach to continuity and motivation.

From his perspective in the mid-1970s, Shackleton may in turn have used more recent events and revelations to retrospectively add shades of topicality to the Findlays' Manson-inspired plot. Reports of widespread 'disappearances,' on-the-spot executions, and random violence at the hands of the military junta in Pinochet's Chile; repression and torture in President Juan María Bordaberry's Uruguay; and the eradication of subversive elements at the behest of General Rafael Videla and the Argentine Anticommunist Alliance in Argentina (Feitlowitz, 1998; Corradi et al., 1992) formed a bloody new context for the release of *Snuff* in cinemas in the mid-late 1970s and on home video in the 1980s.

Perhaps it is a testament to Shackleton's business savvy that *Snuff*'s opportunistic release could lend possibly unintended connotations to the Findlays' mise-en-scènes, and that Argentine locations in particular might bring to the mind of a 'First World' viewer a political situation in which "kidnappings, executions and random violence made everyone vulnerable" (Feitlowitz, 1998: 6). Thus, the derelict factory that Satán and his gang use as their headquarters—and in which the first torture and would-be erotic initiation ceremony take place—may stand for the abandoned film set in Death Valley used by the Manson family (Brottman, 2005: 90). But, depending on the knowledges and competencies of the audience, it may equally evoke a sense of Argentinean socioeconomic decline, or the extra-legal punishments, disappearances, and "torture in secret places" (Fagen, 1992: 53) that haunted the country from the 1970s to the early 1980s.[2] Related connotations may linger around a makeshift outdoor police station—a desk in a rural setting, normally interpreted as a symptom of the Findlays' budgetary constraints and incompetence—that bewilderingly appears at one point. A rusted and weeded-over steam locomotive outside the factory building enjoys iconic status in the film, and, while no doubt chosen merely as a striking feature in a 'middle-of-nowhere' location, can also be taken to symbolize the erosion and collapse of Argentina's once booming agrarian-export and post–Second World War industrial economy. Given that mainly British investors, bankers, and railway engineers had been sufficiently involved in building Argentina's infrastructure for the country to be referred to by British diplomats as the 'sixth dominion' of the British Empire (Rock, 2002: 4), the derelict engine may be a sign for post-'imperial' decay.

Despite these potentially available sociohistorical implications, neocolonialist practices and xenophobic discourses are manifested through the figuring of Roberta Findlay's "exotic place" as an object of both fear and desire. Apparently self-contradictory, this fascination constructs the Other as at once vibrant and violent. A protracted and abruptly inserted scene involving Max and Terri visiting carnival demonstrates the dual nature of the dominant South American stereotype. Besides helping to pad the film out to feature length and providing readymade, low-cost spectacle, the footage seems intended as a familiar trope with which to guarantee the film's 'South American-ness' while offering documentation of supposedly 'local color' to the viewer's virtual tourist gaze. Just as Shackleton's "made in South America" boast fed off—and into—newspaper stories in order to hint at the authenticity of its 'snuff' footage, so the stock material aims to insert the reality effect of documentary into *Snuff*'s portrayal of the area. Borrowing from the ethnographic filmmaker's claim to deliver "indexical representation[s] of patterns of culture" (Hansen et al., 1991: 201) that are notably absent elsewhere in the film, the footage perhaps asks to be seen as an unmediated record of 'colorful natives.' As Hanson, Needham, and Nichols have argued, ethnographic documentary's reality effect trades on the "evidentiary status" of a representational code which promises knowledge of other places and cultures (1991: 201). Ironically, this 'knowledge' is provided in *Snuff* through a geographical displacement. Multiplying the film's spatial confusions, the footage clearly shows carnival in neither Buenos Aires nor Montevideo but the samba rhythms and large organized street parades in Rio. The error would be obvious to most Latin American viewers, but the images doubtless act as ready signifiers of 'Latinicity' for the 'First World' gaze. Max and Terri are in any case spectators-in-the-text standing in for the intended viewer's eroticizing, curious eye; the fact that we see them in insert shots on film stock of patently different quality to the carnival footage underlines their isolation and distance from the spectacle. "Stereotypes of the other propose a rogue's gallery of the forbidden" (Hansen et al., 1991: 204–5), and that which is forbidden is by definition desirable. At one point Terri declares this carnival to be "ten times better than Mardi Gras," but the revelry quickly shows its ugly side: lack of inhibition descends into savagery, and chaos emerges from behind the masquerade as Angelica somehow finds Max and stabs him, before disappearing back into the mass. The scene's trajectory from tourist spectacle to murder encapsulates Max and Terri's metaphorical function as 'great white hunters,' with carnival performing the same role as the Amazon in countless 'atrocity,' mondo, and cannibal movies.

Yet even here the film suggests a degree of self-consciousness regarding the Findlays' positionality. Recalling the anti-imperialist rhetoric of late 1960s New Latin American Cinema, London and Marsh combine and equate the filmmaker, the tourist, and the colonizer. Substituting for Roman Polanski and Sharon Tate, but also acting as self-portraits of Michael and Roberta Findlay (the former often directed under the pseudonym Julian Marsh), the couple soon meet the dreaded fate of jungle explorers in many a colonial narrative, as they encounter the murderously vengeful tribe in the form of Satán and his women. The colonizer's anxiety becomes utterly hyperbolic in the notorious climax commissioned by Shackleton. Wearing a T-shirt with the slogan 'Vida es muerte' to assure us that we are still in Latin American territory, the on-screen filmmaker fatally 'penetrates' a apparently North American production assistant (filmed in New York, the sequence has much better synchronization of North American voices to actors than is apparent in the rest of the film). The murderer compensates for *The Slaughter*'s soft-core failure to penetrate girl or jungle by eventually waving her innards triumphantly in the air. An obscene fantasy seems to be fashioned from the anxiety of reverse colonization. It would perhaps be stretching the point to read the murders of Marsh, London, and the production assistant as inchoate fantasies of atonement for the involvement of the United States in training Latin America in interrogation techniques and counterinsurgency operations; to be sure, Michael Findlay's politics are, as Roberta put it, "very confused" (Peary, 1978: 30). But the reflexivity of the killings might at least problematize any assumption that the film takes up its colonialist perspective consistently or without question.

In spite of spatial compressions and ellipses possibly indicative of the filmmakers' lack of geographical knowledge, *Snuff*'s map of the region is not quite as undifferentiated as one might expect. Low-budget filmmaking no doubt finding rural shooting considerably more convenient, urban centers of modernity like Punta del Este, Montevideo, and Buenos Aires are heard of but only obliquely glimpsed. But pragmatic choices often have ideological effects and the very sidelining of the metropolitan supports an image of Latin America as a backwater full of "evil or chaos, excess greed or indolence" (Hansen et al., 1991: 205), and reinforces the myth of a feral 'Third World' region populated by idle drunks, trigger-happy predatory peasants, and so on. Yet, whether in an attempt to recognize that "[t]he development of capitalism . . . only deepened and complicated the existing structural heterogeneity" of the Southern Cone (Lechner, 1992: 28), or more simply in a spurious effort to "justify the violence" through "a small amount of rhetoric about killing the rich in revenge for the sufferings of the poor" (LaBelle, 1980: 273), the film presents the area as deeply economically and socially divided. Shots of Marsh and Frank lounging by their swimming pools or driving through the suburbs in convertibles—complete with easy listening bossa nova soundtrack—are often contrasted with images of rural poverty and decline, such as Angelica's flashback to her troubled rural past, some shooting in local stores, and the opening images of a long-abandoned steam locomotive.

Rather as certain locations may recall political violence and economic decline, the Argentinean and Uruguayan settings seem to have moved Michael Findlay to touch on his 'liberal' politics by roughly grafting together Manson-as-counterculture-figurehead and Satán-as-South-American-insurrectionist. Like the "rumor-panic" about snuff films (Brottman, 2005) of which the film took advantage, Satán is a hybrid of North and South American sources of anxious fascination. Perhaps distantly influenced by memories of Che Guevara and the Cuban Revolution of 1959, Satán is readable in part as an antiestablishment class warrior commanding his "guerrilla-esque looking" women (Margold in Hebditch and Anning, 1988: 338) to mount attacks on a ruling class epitomized by Horst Frank's "very bad, spoiled rich boy," as he describes himself, and his arms-dealing German father. The latter is heard boasting of having just sold arms to an "Arab" nation; Terri says she feels uneasy about Germans selling arms "to Arabs to kill Jews" and, in an echo of the widespread disquiet over former members of the Third Reich reportedly finding refuge in Latin America, Satán calls him a Nazi. In the climax of *The Slaughter*, Satán's gang raids the Frank estate and murders him, a 'swinging' couple, and Terri. Presumably to represent the degeneracy of the ruling class and the film industry, Terri is in bed with Frank's father. Though its chief purpose is to imply that Satán is "an outlaw because he killed off the German family" (Peary, 1978: 30), the arms-dealer/Nazi subplot can be seen as a disavowal of Charles Manson's own white supremacist sympathies (he appeared at trial with a swastika inscribed on his forehead). This "outlaw" is also of course a monstrous oppressor; that the *Snuff* campaign capitalized on reports of extreme right-wing violence against leftist rebellion typifies the film's inconsistent politics and illustrates the double standards within much exploitation cinema.

Similar tensions and mixed messages attend to the portrayal of Satán's women. While Terri is shown to be the more modern and relatively stylish female character—she is, after all, from New York and is named London—*The Slaughter* struggles to balance the gang's more 'primitive' characteristics with their trappings of modernity. Tying the film into the subgeneric likes of *Satan's Sadists* (Al Adamson, 1969) and *She-Devils on Wheels* (Herschell Gordon Lewis, 1968) as much as *Easy Rider* (Dennis Hopper, 1969), they ride motorcycles, wear headbands, do drugs, carry guns with aplomb, and are ushered into the film with a clear 'homage' to the ostinato from Steppenwolf's version of "Born to be Wild." They are creatures of nonplace belonging to road, river, and dilapidated factory, raiding but not inhabiting the conurbations. But the narrative and ideological need for their primitiveness demands that the film downplay the women's modernity in much the same way as it marginalizes cosmopolitan urban space. Paralleling the initial use of the carnivalesque to present a reassuring image of

Latin American spontaneity and exuberance, intermittent outdoor sexploitation scenes centered on the frolics of Satán's women offer a scenic marriage of eroticism and exoticism for the dominant 'First World' imaginary. Located in landscape settings, these scenes of soft-core sex al fresco and nude bathing in sunlit glades partake of exploitation cinema's characteristic perspective on 'forbidden' spectacle. Both salacious and Edenic, the film's use of the 'nudes in a landscape' trope embodies a colonialist mode of visuality which evinces fetishistic curiosity for the native in her habitat, and attempts to naturalize the construction of "the 'primitive,' 'exotic,' 'sexual,' backwards and romantic savage" (Foster, 1999: 3). The film's problem is then to offer some sort of explanation for their violence. On the one hand, these are naturally "bare-foot [and] sexually liberated" women, as Brottman prefers to see them (2005: 90). On the other hand, Angelica's would-be harrowing flashback into her underprivileged past offers a brief excursion into the sociology and psychology of abuse as she tells us that "ever since I was a little girl I've always been in bondage." Abused by an impoverished farm owner whenever her drunken father was "away in town," by the age of seventeen she had become "a regular whore" drawn to powerful and cruel men. Far from being 'born to be wild,' Angelica informs us that "all my life I've been in bondage of one kind or another. I'm not saying that I like it: I have to have it." The class-based tenor of the scene suggests that Angelica's psychosexual enslavement is a metaphor for political repression: this is social bondage.

It is a measure of the film's inability to take an idea very far that implicit sociopolitical critique tends to be cut short by evocations of the shamelessness of the savage innocent. Effectively equating foreign flesh and foreign land, these scenes produce both as objects of desired "carnal knowledge on the one hand, cultural knowledge on the other" (Hansen et al, 1991: 203). In so doing they are continuous with imperialist discourses found in—but by no means limited to—classical-era exploitation subgenres like the jungle picture (e.g., *Wild Women of Wongo* [James L. Wolcott, 1958]; *Captive Wild Woman* [Edward Dmytryk, 1943]), as much as later soft-core sex films (e.g., the *Emmanuelle* series of the 1970s). Hence sexploitation au naturel offers only the more benign side of the imperialist desire/fear fantasy-formation. In Angelica's flashback, Luis hangs up her dead father's disembodied hands "for all to see"; Angelica's brother then follows Luis into what she describes as "the jungle," strangles him, and throws him in the river. Here the film attempts to create a dramatic contrast between the watery glade as site of soft-core pleasures and as location of senseless violence. Echoing the way in which the chaos of carnival allows and conceals Max's murder, the colonialist's untamed wilderness swiftly becomes the "corrupt jungle" (Foster, 1999: 36) which harbors torture, rape, and, of course, slaughter.

In its mobilizations of stereotypes, mixed-up geography, and imperialist narrative tropes—and even in its use of dubbed dialogue which literally prevents the actors from 'speaking in their own voice'—*Snuff* manifests the "erasures, excisions, reifications, and objectifications that exist throughout the locus of seeing and being seen" (Rogoff, 1996: 189). But these representational practices do not tell the whole story. The film's contradictory and confused treatment of place and space can disturb the dichotomy of neocolonialist subject/subaltern object. Dolores Tierney has criticized the historical tendency in Latin American film scholarship to limit analysis to "paradigms of cultural dependency" (2004: 63). In a different context, Irit Rogoff has likewise warned of "the vagueness, not to mention the stultifying binarism that is brought by designating as 'other' all that is not self" (1996: 190). A certain cultural essentialism can lurk in accounts of the empowered representing subject and the disempowered misrepresented Other, with either side of the rift being hypostatized as a pure identity. The suggestion, for example, that "[w]hat remains unrepresentable is the Other's difference. The Other . . . rarely functions as participant in and creator of a system of meanings, including a narrative structure of their own devising" (Hansen et al, 1991: 205) arguably assumes that the 'speaking subject' is an autonomous site of self-identical agency, and that self-representation by the Other might somehow be free of power or ideology. The failures, confusions, and tensions in Shackleton's/the Findlays' composite beast imply, however unintentionally or clumsily, that the dominant enunciative position is neither homogeneous nor uncontested.

Rogoff has argued that excessively binaristic subject/object models can be challenged by a "locational politics" which addresses the cultural contexts in which representations become "intelligible" for differently located audiences (1996: 190). Where *Snuff* is concerned, such an approach might entail consideration not just of how images of 'jungle,' carnival, makeshift police station, rusted locomotive, and so on might function for the hegemonic 'First World' imaginary, but of how these features could signify to differently competent viewers in diverse sites of consumption. A locational politics that asks what is intelligible to whom and in what context might also address both the situatedness of the critic's attempts to 'decode,' and the filmmaker's attempts to 'encode,' places. How, for example, might my position as a white British viewer inform what I comprehend and fail to comprehend in *Snuff*'s mise-en-scène? How might the subaltern 'speak' through locations that appear to me insistently specific (as opposed to generic), differentiated (as opposed to homogenized), and difficult to read (without being mystifyingly inscrutable)? As an exploitation quickie, *Snuff*'s hurried and often haphazard staging means that, unlike countless other more respectable movies and in spite of the efforts of a few key scenes, it fails to leave a lasting impression of milieu and locale. The opening 'Easy Rider' shots and their accompanying soundtrack lead us to believe that we are watching a North American biker flick; it quickly becomes apparent that we are not, but in its haste the film makes little attempt to tell us precisely where we are or to provide any 'background information.' No signposts are provided and the film is parsimonious with establishing shots and obvious visual locators. Of course these lacunae can be seen as weaknesses in storytelling or proof of the filmmakers' geopolitical blind spots. But the legibility or otherwise of the films' spaces and places also foregrounds the problem of cultural competence by confronting viewers with gaps in knowledge, denying us the "ultimate pleasure of knowing the other" (Hansen et al., 1991: 225) and suggesting the possibility of a cultural politics of *un*intelligibility.

NOTES

1. Johnson and Schaefer (1993) add that Shackleton took advantage of 'porno chic' by giving the film an 'X' rating, thereby enabling the film to be confused with hard core by prospective viewers.
2. The Findlays' *Touch of Her Flesh* (1967) similarly made much play with an unused industrial building as an off-the-peg image of desolation against which to juxtapose seminaked women.

10 Based on a True Story
Reality-Based Exploitation Cinema in Mexico

David Wilt

Real-life events like notorious crimes, disasters, and scandals, presold to audiences via exposure in the daily press, have long been prime candidates for cinematic exploitation. Along with other examples of popular media—tabloid newspapers, popular songs, comic books, and so forth—reality-based exploitation (*rbe*) films can be viewed as a kind of social document of their time period. There is a universal fascination with crime, scandal, and disasters, but the topics selected for film treatment and the manner in which they are depicted on-screen are revealing. Hollywood films based on such topics have been quite common, but in Mexico, this type of motion picture was relatively rare prior to the 1970s. This chapter will examine the manner in which Mexican *rbe* movies reflect (and distort) the facts, why they became popular in Mexico in the 1970s and beyond, and what the public and official reaction to *rbe* films has been.

Although there are many formal similarities between U.S. and Mexican exploitation films, the motion picture industry in Mexico was significantly different than in the United States. Eric Schaefer largely defines the "classical exploitation film" in terms of the nontraditional nature of its production and distribution (1999: 4–6). While 'class' distinctions between films (and theaters) existed in Mexico, there was no alternative exhibition circuit for 'exploitation' movies as would be the case in the United States. From the 1930s through the 1980s, very few Mexican features were made outside of the 'official' film industry. Only with the establishment of the nontheatrical *videohome* market in the mid-1980s did a distinct underclass of movies—identifiable by budget, intended audience, and subject matter—come into existence.

Not all Mexican reality-based films are 'exploitation' movies in the American sense. From the 1970s through the 1990s there was a fairly clear distinction between 'quality' cinema (such as the so-called *cine de denuncia* of the 1970s and 1980s) and 'commercial' films, with exploitation pictures squarely in the second category. The *cine de denuncia* and exploitation movies both utilize real-life events as topics, and at times—particularly in the area of promotion and advertising—the line between the two types of films is blurred, but clear distinctions can still be drawn. *Cine de denuncia* was mostly made by young, independent filmmakers (Arturo Ripstein, Felipe

Cazals, José Estrada); exploitation cinema came from veteran, commercial producers and directors. *Cine de denuncia* films and the real-life events that inspired them were often separated by a number of years; exploitation movies were generally made quickly, to capitalize on public interest in their topic. Many examples of *cine de denuncia* took liberties with the facts and changed the names of the protagonists; exploitation films may have embellished the facts but could not veer too far from reality (since audiences were already familiar with the story), and the use of real names (even if only in the films' titles) was an important exploitation factor. Finally, although exploitation movies may have paid lip service to some higher purpose, their basic *raison d'etre* was the financial exploitation of a notable event; *cine de denuncia* used the re-creation of actual events as a vehicle for a broader criticism of societal problems.

Mexican reality-based exploitation movies may thus be identified primarily by the circumstances of their production, their content, and the manner in which the real-life basis of the films is exploited to attract audiences. The films use an actual, well-known person or incident as their central focus. The majority of Mexican *rbe* movies are based on Mexican events, although some notable exceptions deal with internationally notorious topics. Schaefer notes, "In many instances, exploitation movies were able to piggyback on topical stories in the news or on editorial pages" (1999: 114): since *rbe* movies were openly based on famous real-life events, this promotional 'hook' did not have to be falsified for the films' advertising. The publicity identified the original event being re-created on the screen, promised additional information on the incident, and hinted at the revelation of details heretofore unseen. Even though potential viewers would already be familiar with the 'plot' (from coverage in other media), promotional phrases such as "Know the Truth!" (*Guyana, el crimen del siglo/Guyana, the Crime of the Century/Guyana—Cult of the Damned*, René Cardona, Jr., 1979), "The Truth Will Surprise You!" (*Las muertas de Juárez/The Dead Women of Juárez*, Enrique Murillo, 2002), and "What No One Dared to Tell" (*Lo negro del Negro/The Dark Side of Blackie*, Angel Rodríguez Vázquez and Benjamin Escamilla Espinosa, 1987) assured audiences the movie versions of notorious events would show them 'more.'

Although reality-based exploitation films are produced and marketed on the assumption that audiences have some familiarity with (and interest in) the subject matter, the filmmakers must meet certain expectations as a result—not deviating too far from the known facts of the case—but are also permitted to utilize a kind of cinematic shorthand, given the audience's prior knowledge. When this goes too far, however—as in the case of *Lo negro del Negro*—such movies may be unintelligible to viewers unfamiliar with the incident or individuals involved.

Formal attributes of *rbe* movies constitute a code connecting the on-screen content with reality and bolstering the films' claims to verisimilitude. These links include the use of real names (or homonyms) and actors who resemble the original players; voice-over narration, printed titles, and insert shots of newspaper headlines; documentary footage of the actual event; re-creation of original settings and images (such as famous photos). The publicity claims of veracity are echoed in the movies themselves: at the beginning of *Supervivientes de los Andes/Survive* (René Cardona Sr., 1976), the narrator says, "This is the definitive story . . ."

Mexican movies overtly based on real-life events (excluding histori-cal subjects) were fairly rare prior to 1970. This is not to suggest there was no public interest in such topics before this decade: the *nota roja* (crime news) has long been a popular facet of Mexican journalism, and books, plays, songs, and other media were not hesitant to exploit noto-rious current events. As Carlos Monsiváis writes, "crime stories were supposed to transform tragedy into spectacle, spectacle into moralistic warning, warning into fun ('relajo'), and fun into the stories of a collec-tivity" (1997: 148). Indeed, the reality-based exploitation film in Mexico is in many ways the cinematic counterpart of the *nota roja* and tabloid press. *Alarma!*, Mexico's most successful and notorious tabloid, was first printed in 1963, but publications focused on crime and scandal date back to at least the 1930s, and many mainstream Mexican newspapers also contained special *nota roja* sections. In recent years, tabloid journalism in print has been joined by electronic tabloid journalism such as *Ciudad desnuda* (Naked City) and *Fuera de la ley* (Outside the Law): these two ground-breaking TV shows of the mid-1990s, although canceled due to political pressure, were quickly replaced by similar programs (Hallin, 2000: 268–269). The *nota roja* and reality-based exploitation films share some important connections. Each is a highly visual medium serving a mass audience interested in sensational crimes, scandals, and disasters (it is not surprising the events depicted in *rbe* films are among the most notorious contemporary tabloid stories). *Rbe* movies often pay tribute to their print counterparts—especially *Alarma!*—by using tabloid-style pro-motional art and catchphrases.

The history of Mexican *rbe* films dates back to the early years of cin-ema in Mexico. *El automóvil gris/The Grey Automobile* (Enrique Rosas, 1919) was "the most ambitious and perhaps the most important picture of Mexican silent cinema" (Dávalos, 1996: 34), and also the country's first reality-based exploitation movie, inspired by "the most important criminal episodes of the [early twentieth-century] period" (Monsiváis, 1997: 149). In 1915, criminals disguised as soldiers committed a series of robberies in Mexico City, using false search warrants to gain entry to their wealthy victims' homes. Enrique Rosas filmed the execution of some of the gang members in December 1915, and four years later made *El automóvil gris*, combining his documentary footage with newly shot scenes. The movie was produced by Azteca Film, allegedly with General Pablo González—the military official in charge of Mexico City when the Grey Car Gang was captured—as a silent partner.

Many characteristics of *rbe* films are already present in this seminal work: it is based on a well-known case, includes documentary footage, and one of the real-life participants (a police official) re-creates his role on-screen. Slightly altered versions of real names are used and an on-screen title states the new scenes were filmed where the actual events occurred. Contemporary publicity pointed out the movie was "Based on the sensational case . . . that so affected metropolitan society and reverberated throughout the whole country" (Torres San Martín, 1993: 23), and lobby cards for the movie promised the audience will "see the authentic execution of the accused." However, *El automóvil gris* is not a documentary, and deviates from the historical record for its own purposes. Pablo González had presidential ambitions and the movie tries to "exalt . . . González, since in the series he appears responsible for the apprehension and exemplary punishment of the malefactors . . ." (Dávalos, 1996: 35).

The next major *rbe* film was based on a notorious kidnapping. In early 1945, María Elena Rivera abducted two-year-old Fernandito Bohigas Lomelí, the youngest son of a family for whom she worked. Rivera did not attempt to collect a ransom, intending to raise the boy as her own son. After seven months, in October 1945, the police arrested Rivera and returned Bohigas to his family. In May 1946, *¡Ya tengo a mi hijo!*/I Have My Son Now! (Ismael Rodríguez) went into production with Fernandito playing himself. The Bohigas kidnapping received a considerable amount of protracted media attention and the film was released in August 1946 (quickly by contemporary Mexican standards) to capitalize on the publicity.

However, these two films were the major exceptions to the rule in the pre-1970 period. There are multiple reasons for the cinema's reluctance to exploit newsworthy subjects: censorship (and fear of censorship), legal issues, the structure of the industry itself, and the fact that certain popular and dominant screen genres (such as *comedias rancheras*) were not necessarily conducive to reality-based adaptations.

Official film censorship began in Mexico in 1913, but usually focused on political issues. The 1949 Film Law—which remained in effect until the early 1990s—may have served to dampen producers' enthusiasm for reality-based exploitation movies.[1] A 1952 amendment to the law (Article 69) states a film's exhibition could be prohibited if it contained an "attack on or disrespect of [a person's] private life." Such attacks included exposing a person "to hate, contempt, or ridicule, or when one's reputation or interests could be damaged," and "When, in making reference to a civil or criminal topic, false acts are mentioned or the truth is altered, for the purpose of causing damage to a person" (García Riera, 1993: 15).

In the 1960s, a new generation of Mexican filmmakers began to emerge, whose ranks included Arturo Ripstein, Jorge Fons, Felipe Cazals, Alberto Isaac, José Estrada, Jaime Humberto Hermosillo, and so on. Beginning in 1970, these filmmakers were emboldened to address controversial topics—and to use real-life events as the basis for their movies—by new president Luis Echeverría's open invitation for more political and social discourse in the cinema (Mora 1989: 120; Treviño 1979: 26). The government also helped finance motion pictures through a system of loans and established three state-run production companies. Of course, the result was not absolute freedom of expression. Films which failed to conform to the government's ideology did not receive funding or—if they were produced anyway—were *congelada* (frozen) or *enlatada* (canned) or released with little or no marketing support. Echeverría was succeeded in 1976 by José López Portillo, whose administration was notably more conservative, but the genie could not be put back in the bottle, and movies based on actual events and people continued to be produced. However, under the López Portillo administration and later, a number of films with political or social content were banned outright, held up from release, or 'dumped' on the market in unfavorable circumstances.[2]

The earliest beneficiaries of the Echeverría *apertura* (openness) were the new directors such as Arturo Ripstein, Felipe Cazals, and José Estrada. Working on what became known as the *cine de denuncia*, they used motion pictures to examine social and political issues. Ripstein (*El castillo de la pureza/The Castle of Purity*, 1972), Cazals (*Canoa*, 1974; *Las Poquianchis*, 1976; and *Los motivos de Luz*/The Motives of Luz, 1982) and Estrada (*El profeta Mimí/The Prophet Mimi*, 1972) all made movies based on real-life incidents (specifically, notorious crimes). Ripstein and Estrada's pictures were traditional, dramatic narratives with strong fictional components, while Cazals experimented with film form more extensively, adding elements of documentary filmmaking to his re-creations of actual events. As noted earlier, these were not strictly reality-based exploitation films; however, commercial filmmakers were not slow to follow the trend, even if their reasons for utilizing actual events as the basis for their movies were less altruistic than those of the *cine de denuncia* filmmakers.

One such commercial filmmaker who exploited this new freedom of expression was René Cardona Jr. In the late 1960s, Cardona Jr. began exploring the possibility of internationalizing Mexican cinema. Cardona Jr. produced films—some directed by himself, some by his father René Cardona Sr.—calculated to reach a wider audience than the usual Spanish-language product. Cardona Jr. successfully saw that *La horripilante bestia humana/Night of the Bloody Apes* (1968), *Robinson Crusoe* (1970), *La noche de los mil gatos/Night of a Thousand Cats/ Blood Feast* (1970), *Tintorera!/Tiger Shark* (1976), and other titles received significant international distribution. These films each have 'hooks' to appeal to wider audiences: international performers in the cast (Anjanette Comer, Stuart Whitman, Gene Barry, Donald Pleasance, etc.), a tie-in to a literary name (Jules Verne, Daniel Defoe), a recognizable genre (spy thriller, horror, western), or an imitative link to another popular film (for example, *Tintorera!* and *Jaws*). Beginning in the mid-1970s, Cardona Jr. added reality-based plots to his list of exploitative elements.

Cardona Jr.'s first 'based on a true story' movie was *Supervivientes de los Andes*, written and directed by his father René Cardona Sr., adapted from the book *Survive!* by Clay Blair Jr. On 13 October 1972, an airplane carrying an amateur rugby team and other passengers crashed in the Andes Mountains. Sixteen survivors were rescued on 23 December, after two of the men trekked through the mountains to reach help. The story became even more sensational when it was revealed the men had eaten human flesh to survive their ordeal. *Supervivientes de los Andes* changes the passengers' names and alters some details of the story, but the movie remains closely focused on the crash and the passengers' struggle to survive, eschewing melodramatic subplots or flashbacks. Although some critics considered the movie distasteful, the cannibalism aspect used to exploit the film is not very graphically depicted in the movie itself. The major 'name' performer is Cardona Jr. regular Hugo Stiglitz, but he is simply another member of the ensemble cast, not the 'star.' *Supervivientes de los Andes* was released in a cut and dubbed version as *Survive!* in the United States by Paramount and was financially, if not critically, successful.

Guyana, el crimen del siglo was based on the case of the Reverend Jim Jones and the "Jonestown Massacre" of over 900 people in November 1978. Just three months later, René Cardona Jr. was re-creating the events before his movie cameras. While exploitative on the surface, the picture is actually a fairly somber and accurate retelling of the facts. Although the names of the protagonists were slightly altered—Jim Jones becomes "James Johnson," Leo Ryan is called "Lee O'Brien," etc.—the visual representation of the protagonists and the "Johnsontown" sets (re-created near Acapulco, although there is some footage of Georgetown, the Guyanese capital, which may have been shot by a second unit) are very faithful to reality. One facet of the movie which is not entirely accurate is the racial identity of Jones's followers: while nearly two-thirds of those who died in Jonestown were African-American (although most of Jones's confidants were white), the cast and extras in *Guyana, el crimen del siglo* are mostly (but not entirely) white or *mestizo* in appearance. Unlike *Supervivientes de los Andes*, which sold internationally solely on its exploitative subject matter, *Guyana, el crimen del siglo* also had 'star' names for non-Mexican audiences: the major roles were taken by Hollywood actors like Gene Barry, Stuart Whitman, and Joseph Cotten. Universal picked up the movie for U.S. theatrical release—retitling it *Guyana, Cult of the Damned*—cutting nearly half an hour of footage, replacing the music score, and adding voice-over narration. The U.S. version concludes with red-tinted news photographs of the mass suicide's aftermath (intercut with fictional flashbacks).

While René Cardona Jr.'s reality-based exploitation movies received worldwide exposure in large part because he intentionally selected internationally known events as their basis, other Mexican *rbe* movies were oriented more towards local audiences, concentrating on domestic scandals and featuring no foreign performers in their casts. One of the most notorious of these local films was based on a best-selling book entitled *Lo negro del Negro Durazo*/The Dark Side of "Blackie" Durazo, published in 1983 in Mexico. Written by José González González, a former member of Mexico's secret police, the book detailed the corrupt administration of Arturo "Negro" Durazo, chief of police in Mexico City from 1976 to 1982. Durazo, a childhood friend of then-president José López Portillo, fled the country when Miguel de la Madrid took over the post of chief executive. González's book consists of anecdotes about Durazo's corrupt career and even lists the amounts of money stolen by the police chief and his cronies during the López Portillo *sexenio*. The book probably owes its popularity to its willingness to 'name names' and to some mildly sensationalistic references to extramarital sex, drug and alcohol abuse, torture, and even murder. A flood of imitations, sequels, and knockoffs followed.

The film version of González's book, *Lo negro del Negro* (1984), was codirected by Benjamín Escamilla Espinoza, then publisher of the crime tabloid newspaper *Alarma!* (Ironically, as part of the same *renovación moral* (moral renovation) policy that drove Durazo into exile, the *Alarma!* tabloid was suppressed by the government from 1986 until 1991). If the original book was a loose collection of anecdotes, the film adaptation is little more than a series of cinematic illustrations of selected sections of the book. Some of the episodes were significantly altered in the movie, for reasons which can be guessed at. For example, Durazo's son, angry over a failing grade, once shot up an automobile owned by his teacher. In the book, the school's directors (a group of Catholic priests) complained to Durazo and were appeased by cash and expensive black-market electronics; the film changes the deputation to one man, not a priest, thus removing any possibility of church complaints.

Although González's book is credited on-screen, real names are never used in the film: González is only referred to by his nickname of "Flaco," Durazo's assistant, Francisco Sahagún Baca is "Paco," Durazo's son "Yoyo" becomes "Lolo," and so on. This demonstrates the differing levels of restriction (or self-censorship) between filmmakers and publishers, since nonfiction books and even comic book depictions of Durazo and his cronies were not at all hesitant to 'name names.' It might be noted, however, that Durazo won legal judgments for defamation of character against some publishers and at least one of the comic book titles was officially suppressed, so perhaps the producers of *Lo negro del Negro* were wise to be cautious. Escamilla employed look-alike actors for the main roles, including Ricardo de Loera as Negro and Juan Peláez as Sahagún; a double for president José López Portillo appears in one sequence, unidentified by name or office but instantly recognizable to Mexican audiences. In fact, *Lo negro del Negro* as a whole makes little sense to viewers unfamiliar with the actual case, effectively limiting its market to Mexico.

Mentioned in passing in González's book and depicted in a vague fashion in the movie is the story of a gang of bank robbers who operated under the orders of Sahagún and were later tortured and murdered by the police in 1982. Ismael Rodríguez Jr. later made *Masacre en el Río Tula*/Massacre in Río Tula (1985) based on this incident. Neither Durazo nor his right-hand man Sahagún are impersonated or referred to by name, but the movie still ran into censorship problems and was not shown in Mexico City until 1991. At least one source suggests the problem was the film's oblique reference to the 1984 murder of investigative journalist Manuel Buendía—who in print blamed the Río Tula killings on Durazo's police and was researching official corruption—rather than the political sensitivity of the Río Tula case itself (Estrada, 2007). Like a number of other *rbe* films, the poster for *Masacre en el Río Tula* imitates the cover of crime tabloid *Alarma!*, reminding potential audiences of the movie's factual basis.

The Durazo story on film came to an end with *Durazo, la verdadera historia*/Durazo, the True Story (Gilberto de Anda, 1988). Arturo "el Negro" (who, despite the film's title, is never identified by last name in the movie itself) is portrayed as an honorable, brave police official who goes undercover to defeat arms smugglers and guerrillas, and shoots it out with Colombian drug dealers before his (unnamed) childhood pal becomes president of Mexico and appoints him head of the Mexico City police department. Aside from Durazo (and references to José López Portillo, referred to only as "the President"), no actual individuals are identified and the movie contains none of the usual *rbe* codes such as on-screen time/date/place titles, nor is there any attempt to re-create the actual time period (the early 1970s) of the events. The film concludes with animated jail doors closing in front of Durazo's face, suggesting he was unjustly accused. Shot in May 1988, *Durazo, la verdadera historia* wasn't shown until 1991, another example of the government delaying the release of a movie with 'sensitive' content (Estrada, 2003).

Another notorious incident made into an *rbe* film was the Camarena case. On 7 February 1985, Drug Enforcement Agency agent Enrique "Kiki" Camarena was kidnapped in Guadalajara, Mexico. After several days of torture and interrogation, he was killed and his body buried in a rural area, where it was discovered on 5 March. His murderers were presumably members of a drug cartel. *El secuestro de Camarena*/The Kidnapping of Camarena (Alfredo B. Crevenna, 1987) re-creates the same basic events, but the differences are significant: the main character is named *George* Camarena; the movie is not set in Guadalajara; a subplot involves Camarena's unhappy, childless marriage (the real Camarena was happily married and had three children). *El secuestro de Camarena* adds completely fictional incidents such as the kidnapping, rape, and murder of Camarena's niece and a romance between Camarena and a female Colombian drug courier. The movie also eschews the usual reality-linking devices: there are no date/time/place titles, no narration, and no inserts of newspaper headlines. Consequently, the standard printed disclaimer—"the characters and events in this film are fictitious; any similarity with real-life characters and events is purely coincidental"—is in this instance largely true, if rather ingenuous (the title of the film makes it obvious what real-life incident is being referred to, even if the details of the story have been significantly altered). However, this did not mean *El secuestro de Camarena* would avoid censorship problems.

Filmed in August and September 1985, less than six months after Enrique Camarena's body was unearthed, *El secuestro de Camarena* played successfully in Spanish-language theaters in the United States (publicity materials exist with the English title *The Kidnapping of Camarena*, suggesting a dubbed version may have been distributed as well). The Mexican government authorization number indicates this film was reviewed and approved in 1985 or 1986, but it was not shown in Mexico City until May 1991, and then as *El secuestro de un policia*/The Kidnapping of a Policeman—the posters had a paper 'snipe' hastily pasted over the original title (Quezada, 2005: 704). Why was *El secuestro de Camarena* 'frozen' for six years and finally shown in Mexico City cinemas (the country's largest market) in a retitled and possibly censored form? The reasons for withholding a film from exhibition are rarely public, but the government may have frowned on *El secuestro de Camarena* because the picture alluded to an incident which did not reflect well on Mexico, that is, the torture and murder of a foreign law enforcement agent by a drug gang, possibly with the complicity of Mexican police. Thus, the producers' attempt to exploit the real-life Camarena case backfired, and the film—when belatedly screened, shorn of its original title—was indistinguishable from many other fictional 1980s action films.

Although infamous crimes and scandals inspired numerous *rbe* films, disasters—earthquakes, fires, shipwrecks, airplane crashes, mine collapses, etc.—also provide ample opportunity for cinematic exploitation. However, relatively few Mexican films have been made on such topics, probably because disaster movies tend to be expensive to produce. *Supervivientes de los Andes* is one exception, as is *Trágico terremoto en México*/Tragic Earthquake in Mexico (Francisco Guerrero, 1987). The Mexico City earthquake of 16 September 1985 is the greatest natural disaster ever suffered by Mexico, providing a historic and personal touchstone for everyone who lived through it. Constructed on the site of a lakebed, Mexico City is an unstable metropolis at best. The 1985 earthquake was not the first seismic event the city had suffered, but prior to this no film had been made specifically about an actual Mexican earthquake, although a real earthquake on 29 July 1957 served as a *deus ex machina* at the conclusion of *Señoritas*/Young Ladies (Fernando Méndez, 1958), and the Mexican-Guatemalan coproduction, *Terremoto en Guatemala*/Earthquake in Guatemala (Rafael Lanuza,1976) used the real-life Guatemalan earthquake (including documentary footage of the aftermath) of 4 February 1976 as the basis for its plot.

Although at least five other contemporary movies refer to or depict the disaster, *Trágico terremoto en México* is the only major feature film dealing exclusively with the 1985 earthquake.[3] Filmed in February–March

1987, the picture concentrates on a small group of characters living in a single *vecindad* (apartment block) and the rescue operation mounted at a nearby hospital which collapses during the earthquake. Unlike *Supervivientes de los Andes*, a fairly straightforward re-creation of the facts, the characters and situations in *Trágico terremoto en México* are fictional. The first half of the film introduces the characters and sets up the melodramatic conflicts which will be resolved in one fashion or another during and after the earthquake.

What differentiates *Trágico terremoto en México* from other fictionalized disaster movies such as *Earthquake* (Mark Robson, 1974) and make it a reality-based exploitation movie are its coded reality links. For example, *Trágico terremoto* includes news footage from September 1985 and some of the fictional scenes were shot in buildings ruined by the disaster. Television personality Óscar Cadena appears both in videotape shot on the day of the earthquake and in re-created scenes. The script inserts factual incidents into the dramatic story, such as the tale of 'miracle babies' rescued from the ruins of a maternity hospital, and depicts the well-publicized collective rescue efforts of ordinary citizens. Also present throughout the first half of the film are onscreen reminders (printed titles, repeated shots of clocks, watches, etc.) of the time and date, in essence counting down to the moment of the earthquake, a time fixed in the memory of Mexican audiences who lived through the actual event.

In addition to theatrical productions, *rbe* films also appeared in the direct-to-video market. Beginning in the mid-1980s, the Mexican film industry began producing large numbers of direct-to-video productions to feed the home video market in Mexico and (especially) the United States. Although some of the so-called *videohomes* were ambitious in nature, these productions were quickly marginalized due to their low budgets and narrow focus (the vast majority were either lowbrow comedies or formulaic action pictures). The *videohome* became a populist cinema for the working class, and as a result has been very responsive to tabloid staples such as the Gloria Trevi scandal, the murder of TV host Paco Stanley, the *chupacabras* monster, satanic sects, narcotics-related violence, and various permutations and combinations thereof.[4]

Among other sensational real-life cases subjected to *videohome* treatment are David Koresh and the Branch Davidian cult in Waco, Texas (*Tragedia en Waco, Texas/*Tragedy in Waco, Texas, Fernando Durán Rojas, 1993), the assassination of Cardinal Jesús Ocampo in Guadalajara (*La muerte de un cardenal/*The Death of a Cardinal, Christian González, 1993), and even such politically sensitive topics as the 1995 killing of *campesinos* in Aguas Blancas (*Aguas Blancas, pueblo sacrificado/*Aguas Blancas, Sacrificed Town, Angel Rodríguez Vázquez, 1997) and the 1997 Acteal massacre in Chiapas (*El guerrillero de Chiapas/*The Guerrilla of Chiapas, Juan José Pérez Padilla, 1999), although the latter incidents were presented in very oblique fashion to avoid possible repercussions from censors.[5] The low-budget nature of such productions (usually shot on 16mm with small crews) allows them to be made quickly, to capitalize on current events. For example, *La caída de un dictador*/The Fall of a Dictator (Alberto Cano Jr., 1990) began shooting in March 1990, only two months after the actual capture of Manuel Noriega in Panama by U.S. troops. The serial killer known as "La Mataviejitas" (the Killer of Old Women) was arrested in April 2006, and at least two *videohomes* (*La Mataviejitas*/The Old-Lady Killer, Christian González, 2006; *La Mataviejitas: Asesina serial*/The Old-Lady Killer: Female Serial Killer, Miguel Marte, 2006) were rapidly released on the topic. These 'instant films' are the cinematic equivalent of the tabloid press; although—wary of legal issues—most recent examples contain at least a token disclaimer.

One early reality-based exploitation *videohome* dealt with a 'narcosatánico' cult. Cuban-American Adolfo Constanzo parlayed his personal religion into money and influence in Mexico, with clients including police officials, politicians, drug lords, even actress Irma Serrano. The 1989 discovery of more than a dozen mutilated corpses—among them a U.S. college student—buried on the "narcosatánicos" ranch in Matamoros forced Constanzo into hiding. Trapped by police in a Mexico City apartment, Constanzo ordered one of his own henchmen to kill him. Although the Satanic cult and drug-smuggling aspects were newsworthy, the fact that a youth from the United States was one of the cult's victims drew even more media attention. At least five books were published in the United States about the case; both Geraldo Rivera and Oprah Winfrey devoted television programs to it. The Mexican tabloid press contributed as well, with Constanzo's prominent friends providing additional spice to the tale.

A flurry of movies about Satanic sects appeared shortly after the case came to light, but most merely exploited current interest in the topic and had little or nothing to do with Constanzo. The direct-to-video *La secta de la muerte*/The Sect of Death (Román Hernández, 1989) adheres more closely to the facts. The video box art features a newspaper headline reading "Secta Satánica en Matamoros" (Satanic Sect in Matamoros), and the box copy says "A real life act! An event that has affected the world!" Cuban-American Fidel leaves Miami to found his own Satanic religion, rents a farmhouse near Matamoros and goes into the drug business, 'thanking Satan' for his patronage with human sacrifices. Fidel becomes the associate of a Peruvian drug baron, but when the police raid his new, lavish home, Fidel and his aide kill each other. *La secta de la muerte* ignores major parts of the real story, including Constanzo's stay in Mexico City, his influential clients, and the abduction and murder of the U.S. college student. Some of the omissions may have been a result of the movie's low budget, but producer Ismael Rodríguez Jr.—whose *Masacre en el Río Tula* had yet to be released theatrically due to government disapproval—may have been wary of outraging the censors yet again. In the 1980s, Rodríguez Jr. and his father, famous director Ismael Rodríguez, specialized in exploitation films masquerading as social commentary—*Corrupción*/Corruption (1983), *Pasaporte a la muerte*/Passport to Death (1986), *Noche de buitres*/Night of Vultures (1987), *Traficantes de niños*/Traffickers in Children (1989), and others—but seem to have avoided overt reality-based exploitation after their *Río Tula* experience.

The history of reality-based exploitation films in Mexico illustrates the tightrope act Mexican filmmakers performed (and continue to perform) between their desire to make popular movies on the one hand and the threat of government intervention on the other. Despite the obvious exploitation possibilities in films based on famous real-life events, filmmakers did not take full advantage of this until the 1970s. Fear of censorship problems and legal challenges were probably the primary reasons for the small number of *rbe* movies produced prior to Luis Echeverría's presidency (1970–76). Echeverría's willingness to allow examination of social and political topics in the cinema opened the door for both serious and commercial movies dealing with actual people and events. Subsequent administrations were less liberal and both censorship and legal problems resumed, yet the Mexican film industry continued to make reality-based films throughout the 1980s and into the early 1990s. Since that time, the direct-to-video market has increasingly become the home for this type of production, given that *videohomes* can be produced quickly and economically in response to exploitable news events, and the level of government oversight is significantly less than for theatrical features. Furthermore, with most screen time devoted to imported blockbusters (mostly from Hollywood), there is little market for low-budget exploitation movies in Mexican theaters. Regardless of the format and market, *rbe* films continue to serve as a reflection of contemporary popular interests. Skirting the edge of good taste and risking the censor's ire, exploitation filmmakers strive to convert real-life drama into profits via the medium of motion pictures.

NOTES

1. Failure to receive government authorization for exhibition resulted in "frozen" films like *La sombra del caudillo*/The Shadow of the Leader (Julio Bracho) (produced in 1960, released in 1990), and *Rosa blanca*/White Rose (Roberto Gavaldón) (shot in 1961, released in 1972).
2. For example, *La viuda negra*/The Black Widow (Arturo Ripstein, 1977) was not released until 1983 because it was deemed potentially offensive to religious sensibilities. The political satire *La ley de Heródes* (*Herod's Law*, 1998) nearly suffered the same fate, but a public outcry allowed director Luis Estrada to buy the film back from the government and release it commercially, with considerable success.
3. *El día de los albañiles 3*/Day of the Bricklayers Part III (Gilberto Martínez Solares, 1987), *El otro crimen*/The Other Crime (Carlos González Morantes, 1988), *Derrumbe*/Collapse (Eduardo Carrasco Zanini, 1985), *El niño y el Papa*/The Boy and the Pope (Rodrigo Castaño, 1986), and *Ciudad de ciegos*/

City of the Blind (Alberto Cortés, 1990) re-create the event and/or depict its aftermath.

4. The *chupacabra* (goat-sucker) monster allegedly attacked livestock (notably goats, hence its name) in rural areas of Mexico. Paco Stanley was shot to death in Mexico City in 1999, possibly as a result of drug connections (the direct-to-video *La muerte del Paco "eSe"*/The Death of Paco S re-created the event in 2000). Pop singer Gloria Trevi and her manager Sergio Andrade fled Mexico in 1999 after allegations they abused adolescent girls in their entourage. *Videohome* versions of this case include *Bienvenida al clan*/Welcome to the Clan (Carlos Franco, 2000), and *Gloria, víctima de la fama*/Gloria, Victim of Fame (Enrique Murillo, 2000).

5. In June 1995, a group of *campesinos* from the town of Aguas Blancas, Guerrero, on their way to a demonstration, were ambushed by police and more than a dozen were killed. The event was captured on videotape, fueling the controversy. The Acteal massacre occurred in the state of Chiapas in December 1997. Forty-five church members were murdered by paramilitary forces that believed the victims were affiliated with the Ejército Zapatista de Liberación Nacional. Many Mexicans are convinced the government was complicit in both events, but films on the topics make no overt claims in this regard.

11 *Con amor, tequila, y gasolina*
Lola the Truck Driver, and Screen Resistance in cine fronterizo

Catherine L. Benamou

Little by little the confederate flags painted on the back of trucks are being replaced by the image of the Virgin of Guadalupe. Transmissions by radio or CB frequencies can now be heard in Spanish as well as in English. One no longer sees hearts bearing the face of Marilyn Monroe or patriotic slogans on the doors of their [truck] cabs. Today, Hispanics [drivers] have their names stamped on them. Tiny flags from their countries of origin hang from truck interiors and all day long they tune into Spanish-language radio or listen to recordings by Vicente Fernández, Los Tigres del Norte, La Orquesta San Vicente of El Salvador.

Miguel Vivanco, El Pregonero[1]

. . . With her mere presence, this woman has already won half the battle. The other half she wins with the charisma she has in front of the cameras, especially when she interprets that character that has brought her so much luck, that of the woman of great principles, who drives gigantic trucks, who loves life, wages a fight against drugs and defends women's rights. All without giving up her femininity.

Josué R. Rivas, El Diario/La Prensa, upon meeting Rosa Gloria
Chagoyán[2]

This chapter is devoted to a critical exploration of the public and screen personae of Mexican action star and community activist Rosa Gloria Chagoyán, and the politics of gendered and national representation in the larger body of *cine fronterizo* or Mexican border cinema of which she was a vital part, as exemplified in her *Lola la trailera*/Lola the Truck Driver action series (1983–1991). In this series, which follows an epic road movie format spiced up with action sequences and musical comedy, the daughter (Chagoyán) of a semitruck driver seeks to avenge her father's death at the hands of narcotraffickers, after he refuses to hide their cocaine shipments in his fresh Mexican produce cargo destined for the border. To do this, she herself must get behind the wheel and infiltrate the operation up to its highest levels of command; she is assisted in this task by an undercover cop, played by her husband in actual life, Rolando Fernández (also the series producer of this and her next film, *Juana la cubana/*Juana the Cuban, 1994, in which she doubles as a disillusioned revolutionary Comandante Zeta and a sensuous nightclub performer a la *Tropicana*). Significantly, Lola remains steadfastly in the driver's seat, and it is she who delivers the most in the manner of pyrotechnics and gunshots, saving her boyfriend cop's life on more than one occasion.

This chapter emphasizes the sociocultural and aesthetic dimensions of Chagoyán's rise to iconic status through these films as a sensuous, late-twentieth-century *soldadera*, or woman warrior, capable of carrying the nation's burden on her shoulders, just as *cine fronterizo* began to reinvent itself, finding new outlets on videocassettes, on late-night television, and on the World Wide Web. While it is impossible to chart here the full extent of Chagoyán's film career from the early 1970s to the mid-1990s, let alone the ongoing circulation of her personae on stage, television, and in cyberspace, its pinnacle (achieved when Chagoyán left romantic sex comedies to become engaged in *cine fronterizo*), together with its developmental gaps and limitations, provide a reliable vehicle for examining the significance of exploitation cinema, strictly defined,[3] in reconfiguring the stakes and terms of national and social identity during a series of hairpin turns in the Mexican political economy, the Mexican film industry, as well as in Mexico's *and Mexicans'* relationship to the United States.

Chagoyán's pushing of the social and moral boundaries of women's roles and gender relations in these films prompts us to revisit both the issue of art cinema taking the cultural lead in the revision of gender roles and relationships and the periodization of neoliberalism in Mexican cinema and society, usually pegged to the Salinas de Gortari presidency (1988–1994) and the advent of NAFTA, to focus more on the period corresponding with Mexico's 'debt crisis' in the late 1970s and 1980s, a period which witnessed what can be termed the reprivatization of the film industry (leading to a zigzagging of production levels), a sharp decline in citizens' purchasing power (by 50 percent between 1976 and 1985), the steady closure of small, neighborhood theaters and movie palaces in both Mexico and the United States, and a corresponding decline in movie attendance (Rosas Mantecón in Garcia Canclini, et al., 2006: 264, 266, 272, 278; see also de la Mora, 2006: 140–41; Ramírez Berg, 1992: 50–54). During this same period, a bill—initiated by President Luis Echevarría in 1974—was passed granting women equality under the law and in the workplace (Ramírez Berg, 1992: 55), yet women also began bearing a heavier burden within the Mexican household as male migration to the United States accelerated.

Key to this inquiry is the adoption of a transnational frame of analysis, which will allow for a more accurate depiction of Chagoyán's fields of activity and reception as an exploitation star, her scope of influence as a border-crossing icon of *mexicanidad* or Mexicanness (following in the footsteps of the more virginal *Guadalupe*); as well as for insight into the tense, yet dynamic and sustained relationship between the commercial cinemas of Mexico and the United States, which has operated simultaneously as a hegemonic source of mass media texts and techniques, and as an expanding, lucrative market for Mexican media, thanks, in large part, to the steady (e)migration[4] of the Mexican working class. Indeed, it is thanks to this market that Chagoyán's popularity has been able to thrive and that a unique cottage industry relying on low budgets, multitasking personnel, and the double advantages (in terms of currency, purchasing power, and avoidance of censorship and union labor) of a border location was able to develop.

In the process, this chapter foregrounds the complexity of the politics of gender representation and reception generated (respectively) by Chagoyán's casting, agency as a protagonist and offscreen activist, and fetishization linked to the commodification of her image. Chagoyán's unique combination of patriotism and social irreverence, her affection towards the deviant and the less fortunate, her skilful maintenance of feminine agency and independence while in character—as reflected in dialogue, bodily action, and focalization within the mise-en-scène of her brand of *cine fronterizo*—are constitutive of, rather than parallel or supplemental to, the politico-cultural status and effectivity of exploitation as a viable form of national cinema; and the discursive repositioning through this mode of cultural construction and consumption of the Mexican working class in the wake of neoliberalism and immigration crackdowns. Hence, tied to the project of cultural retrieval and revaluation that tends to be associated with scholarship on exploitation films (Benshoff, 2000; Greene, 2005; Holmlund, 2005; Kraszewski, 2002; Ramírez Berg, 1992: 125–136; 155–174; 190–210; Schaefer, 1997 and 1999; Sims, 2006; et. al.) is an assessment of the relevance of *cine fronterizo*, via Rosa Gloria Chagoyán's gynocentric contributions, to the reconstruction of Mexican modernity along the lines of social justice and ethical conduct, such that a productive role can be found for subaltern subjectivities, long silenced by, folklorized, or belittled by the state and corresponding cinematic discourses (de la Mora, 2006; Ramírez Berg, 1992), and mistreated and marginalized in the United States by exclusionary immigration policies and opportunistic agents of exploitation.

ROSA GLORIA, QUEEN OF HEARTS: 100 PERCENT BRUNETTE AND MEXICANA

It is near the eve of the new millennium on *Cristina*, a popular weekly talk show broadcast internationally by Univisión, the largest Spanish-language television network in the United States. A handful of attentive viewers who mailed their wishes to the host, Cristina Saralegui, have been chosen to have their dreams fulfilled courtesy of corporate broadcasting, on this episode, aptly titled "Soñando contigo" or "Dreaming of You." Among the lucky few is a short, stocky, and modestly dressed middle-aged man, whose only wish is to have a moment alone with his idol, Rosa Gloria Chagoyán, best known to her fans as "Lola la trailera" or "Juana la cubana," her most popular screen roles in recent memory. Saralegui swiftly ushers the devotee onto a specially decorated set—a romantic 'honeymoon' suite—where, upon seeing Rosa Gloria, he swoons backward onto the satin-covered bed, much to the delight of the studio audience. After regaining his composure, the man vigorously embraces the star who, in typical "Lola wear"(spare jewelry, (in stark contrast to other "Cristina" guests), a lightly sequined, V-necked blouse, knit pants, tight at the waist, and boots made for walkin'), towers over him by nearly two feet. Although it has been nearly a decade since Chagoyán appeared in her iconic "Lola" series, and she has done little to conceal her age—save a girdle, hair dye, or spandex hose[5]—she is still naturally buxom, hefty-hipped, yet slim-waisted, with a firm jaw, yet sporting a delicate smile, still coiffed in a cascade of dark curls, and to all appearances, content to assume the role of 'dream lover' in this not so private and unconsummated tryst.

Beyond the marked disparity in height that casts a comic light on the talk-show 'couple,' along with the distinct impression that Chagoyán's desirability resides in her ability to proudly embody Mexico's *everywoman*, rather than beauty pageant 'perfection,' other, intriguing incongruities rise to the surface of this scene and contemporary reports on Rosa Gloria's cross-border activity—also invoking the special powers of Lola—in the Spanish-language press (cited previously). From these incongruities, a series of paradoxes emerges that invites clarification and disentanglement:

Paradox 1: Why is it that Chagoyán, who evidently enjoys a broad fan base among U.S. Latinas/os—large enough to prompt the not-so-random choice of this man as wish recipient on a show broadcast to millions—is treated here as a *sideshow gimmick* rather than as a full-fledged talk-show guest star who is accorded a 'grand entrance' down the studio runway, and a detailed biographical probing by the equally middle-aged, albeit less attractively full-figured, diva host? Surely, it cannot be because she has refused to go 'blonde' like so many others (J.Lo, Mirka Dellanos, Kate del Castillo, Paulina Rubio) who have graced Cristina's couch? Perhaps, notwithstanding the grouping of Spanish-language media under the umbrella of popular 'lowbrow' entertainment, one can still find discursive fissures and tensions predicated upon matters of 'taste' and power, such that network- (and ultimately 'state'-) endorsed star ambassadors and models of beauty and valor, such as Thalia Sodi (married to Sony recording magnate Tommy Mottola) and Angélica Vale (who starred in Televisa's version of *Ugly Betty*, *La fea más bella*, 2006–2007), are guaranteed a central spotlight, while those deemed less marketable within the Hispanic mainstream are kept cautiously at the margins, and reeled in on occasion to 'spice up' the act? If so, then why did Saralegui invite her good friend Andrés García, who, like Chagoyán, achieved stardom through Mexican exploitation action thrillers of the

1980s, to cohost her ten-year anniversary show? How is it that Chagoyán's popularity has benefited from the commodification of her image, her screen persona cultivated largely through commercially driven border production, yet she still stands in tenuous relation to prime-time television?

Paradox 2: How has Chagoyán managed to cultivate and retain her sex appeal and popularity among male spectators (gay and straight) when the two roles she is best known for in Mexican cinema—a *norteña* semitruck driver and a 'Cuban' revolutionary, respectively—show her as much in active combat, killing and maiming men, as in seductive poses speaking softly? Is this simply a function of a sadomasochistic dynamic at play in the viewing practices of (mostly migrant) working-class men? Or should one interrogate more thoroughly, placing in broader sociocultural context, this female screen persona that falls within an action, rather than emotion-driven, category of cinema, and therefore deemed by filmmakers and programmers alike to appeal mainly to male audiences (hence the programming of these films on late-night television)? Is the circulation of Chagoyán's image working at cross-purposes when it ranges from YouTube clips that highlight her fighting prowess, to the inclusion of stills and frame enlargements privileging her physical attributes on fan sites that feature star pinups targeting male Web surfers?[6] Finally, what sense can be made of Chagoyán's open defense of women's rights—and especially of her self-management of body image and sociopolitical identity—precisely during a period when not so subtle attempts are being made to refurbish Mexican masculinity on screen by way of action films, along with other forms of transnational television programming (including *telenovelas*), starring icons of *machismo*, and combining amped-up dosages of bare-chested sex appeal with male-perpetrated violence? How can Chagoyán retain her sex appeal behind the wheel, without posing in the nude (in voluntary compliance with the "teaser, but not porn," strictures of exploitation cinema) (Schaefer, 1999: 8) in an era of increased Hispanic access to the driver's seats of trailer trucks in the United States (where porn can be had in abundance), thanks to the intensified U.S.-Mexican trade spurred by NAFTA and the retirement of Anglo-American truck drivers in the United States?[7]

LOLA, LA REINA DEL NACOTRÁFICO (LOLA, QUEEN OF TACKY TRAFFICKING): ON THE ROAD TO A PARAMODERN AND POSTFEMINIST ETHICS OF ENGAGEMENT AND AFFIRMATION

In answer to the first paradox, extensive fissuring, shaped by an insidious politics of taste and social clout, is to be found within commercial televisual discourse, but not so exaggerated as to strain the limits of the timeworn populist paradigm of representation that informs nearly all U.S. Spanish-language network programming. Chagoyán is indeed popular enough to attract a massive diasporic audience, and she is still capable, judging by the *Cristina* studio audience response, of eliciting viewer pleasure; yet her continual opening up of discursive and ideological boundaries that have been carefully preserved in the mainstream through genre-coded gender conduct, namely, the division between gynocentric emotional forms (*telenovelas* and talk shows) and phallocentric action forms (crime thrillers, boxing films, and recycled *cine fronterizo*), prevent her from qualifying for media appearances that are mass-, rather than regionally, promoted. What Chagoyán's apparent 'demotion' on *Cristina* does is to call attention to the double standards characterizing the dominant paradigm, by underscoring how, by embracing her screen persona, Lola, who is clearly 'of the people' (*del pueblo*), and whose demeanor and sartorial style oscillate between kitsch seductress (vamp, action) and modest yet proud *ranchera* (cowgirl, emotion), Chagoyán's public presence does not conform with the multilayered binary terms of that discourse. She is neither a member of the enchanted globalized and globe-trotting Hispanic celebrity circle populated by more conventional female stars, and by those, like Saralegui, who mediate between them and the viewer; nor is she reducible to a lumpen member ('queen for a day') of the Latina/o on-screen audience. Moreover, Chagoyán's stardom, while indisputable, was also achieved mainly with respect to a *transfronterizo* or cross-border circuit of distribution, targeting what can be called greater Mexico (as of 2005, a sector equaling one-fifth of the Mexican national population lived in the United States), rather than the borderless, less nationally rooted global sphere of the Spanish-speaking world. Her persona does not fit neatly into gender- and class-bound genre parameters because she is the modern Mexican embodiment of the Aztec Coatlicue, a powerful feminine archetype, who, as the "first god of Aztec mythology," predates the mother/whore dichotomy and is the "creator and destroyer of all matter and form" (Ramírez Berg, 1992: 58).

This smaller-scale transnationalism is thus partly a function of the discourse of cultural authenticity—and hence rootedness in Mexican regional culture—which Chagoyán projects, and which, more than any marketing strategy, is key to her popular appeal, especially for a borderlands or migrant audience that is intensively engaged in U.S.-controlled economic activity (licit and illicit) and experiencing social fragmentation and cultural discontinuity as a result. Across the gamut of her public personae, ranging from sex kitten and nightclub diva to uncompromising undercover enforcer and community activist, Chagoyán unabashedly wears the twin badges of regionalism (*norteña* in both appearance and character) and nationalism in the face of U.S. cultural and economic hegemony, while successfully cultivating and blending elements of cultural authenticity and aesthetic hybridity; in doing so, she straddles the boundary within media discourse between modernist/national and postmodernist/global constructions of cultural identity and aesthetic politics.

Chagoyán's interstitiality with respect to the populist, globalized media paradigm, and hence her ineligibility for the prime-time red-carpet treatment, can also be traced to her idiosyncratic career itinerary. The waning of the low-budget, fast-turnaround *cine fronterizo* cycle in the late 1980s, early 1990s (owing to U.S. restrictions on foreign companies operating in U.S. territory,[8] *de facto* Mexican currency devaluation, along with the decline in theatrical attendance described above) hardly spelled the end of her active career: in addition to the feature-length *Juana la cubana*, released in 1994, Chagoyán continued to deliver live and televised performances in both Mexico and the United States. Shortly after making her cameo appearance on *Cristina*, Chagoyán performed at a nightclub (Centro Nocturno Chibcha) in Queens, New York (Rivas, 1999b: 25), and she made regular appearances at the ACE (Asociación de Cronistas de Espectáculos) Awards ceremony in New York (Rivas, 1999a: 24; Inclán, 2002) both as entertainer and as awards recipient. In 2000, she invited Telemundo network to interview her in her home, and even in her bedroom (a sly exploitation move) for its *Cotorreando* show (*La Opinión*, 2000), and also launched a Mexican radio program titled *Aventuras de Lola la trailera/Adventures of Lola the Truckdriver* (Inclán, 2000). A few years later, she could be spotted performing on "Despierta América," Univisión's daily morning show, in front of the Alamo in San Antonio (Jakle, 2002: 6B), as well as in a special televised concert for the Día de los Hispanos, August 4, 2002, at the Ringling Brothers Circus in Dallas, Texas (Churnin, 2002: 4C). In 2004, Chagoyán was the recipient of a *Defensoras del Folklore* (Defenders of Folklore) award at a music festival in the heart of Mexico City (Inclán, 2004). And in 2008, a musical appearance by Chagoyán at the grassroots Mesquite Festival in Las Vegas, Nevada, was videotaped by a fan and posted on YouTube (*Lola la trailera*, 2008).

This activity stands in sharp contrast to the careers of her male *churro* counterparts, which either ended with the dissipation of *cine fronterizo* in the late 1980s, or were electronically recycled on national and transnational television. The exceptions belong to screen *charro* (cow and bull handling) star Antonio Aguilar, who has experienced partial reincarnation through his son Pepe's musical career; and the aforementioned Andrés García, whose films rarely appear now on U.S. Spanish-language television, yet, having reinvented himself as an older *galán* (male romantic lead) in *telenovelas* and miniseries (*Mujeres engañadas*/Women Who Have Been Cheated, 1999–2000, and *El pantera*/The Panther, 2007–2008, both produced by Televisa), then trying his hand at corporate advertising, appears to have fully crossed over into the mainstream, capitalizing on his sex symbol past, yet turning his professional back on the vernacular forms and venues that enveloped it. Chagoyán's adamant refusal to "get out or sell out," the fact that no venue in her view appears to be too small or too 'local' (see Rivas, 1999b: 25), speaks to a different kind of cultural politic.

The continued adherence, *via* Lola, to a discourse of cultural authenticity centered on overt claims to, and the championing of, *mestiza* working class and Mexican *norteño* identity also holds important clues to the social (gendered reception) and ideological (gender politics) dilemma (paradox 2) posed by ambiguities embedded in her performance of her sexy warrior "Lola/Coatlicue" persona. Of course, it can be argued that, through her engagement in a marginal, regionally focused cinematic practice, Chagoyán has been free to fold into her persona (seasoned as it has been by her zigzagging itinerary between screen, radio microphone, television set, and stage) characteristics and behaviors that would be filtered or excluded from the construction of a more mainstream Latina star image, especially bearing in mind the dichotomizations between 'clowns' (Lupe Vélez, Carmen Miranda, Rosie Pérez) and sex goddesses (Rita Hayworth, Salma Hayek, Penelope Cruz) that have preceded and surround her. Part of this freedom could be due to the relative absence of critical and state scrutiny given to border *churros*, as compared to their U.S. (rated "M" or "R") counterparts. While the Bolivian American actress Raquel Welch initially forged her own star persona with the superficial melding of vixen warrior traits, it is clear that in terms of the reception of her persona, sexual attractiveness trumped rebelliousness, which, instead of being given a line of 'serious' development within the actual character or the plot, was used simply to market sexploitation films in the late 1960s. (In this sense, although it predates Chagoyán's starring roles by over a decade, Welch's screen persona is much more postmodern in its blending of forms and departure from the historical real than Chagoyán's, which takes contemporary border life as its referent).

Thus, Chagoyán has been able to expose in her 'sexy-warrior-avenger' image (whether or not it was originally conceived [Orso, 2001] by her husband, costar and producer Rolando Fernández), a range of social positions and sensibilities which, if not always available, are conceivable and potentially desirable for modern regional women, notwithstanding their dichotomization or absence in more mainstream or 'art cinema' representations. Precisely because these dimensions can lead to contradictory positions, both socially and ideologically, one finds that, beginning with *Contacto chicano/The Chicano Connection* (1979) and threading through the *Lola la trailera* series and *Juana la cubana*, the doublevoicedness of Chagoyán's persona—her inexhaustible power to attract and effectively repel the masculine sex—is usually woven into a broader social or moral struggle engaged in by her characters. This struggle, occurring on a secondary plane of reference and decodification for the culturally prepared spectator, is manifested as a physical struggle in the diegesis both *across* Chagoyán's physiognomy (displaying her skill as an actress) and *between* authentic *mexicanos* (or *cubanos*, in the case of *Juana la cubana*) and various traitors and evildoers; a struggle, which, in its visible and audible excess, partially derives from the difficulty of integrating these sensibilities—desire and righteous resistance—and expressing them from a decidedly female position in a still patriarchal, socially intolerant universe.

Thus, it isn't a question of eliminating the potential for contradiction in the sexy-warrior persona, or of insisting that a distinction should be made (as a 'vulgar' feminist reading might have it), between 'progressive' images of feminine resistance *versus* 'conformist' or 'compromising' (and even 'repressive') images of women as sexual objects. And is sexual attractiveness, Rosa Gloria/Lola seems to ask, always tantamount to objectification? The sociocultural effectivity of Chagoyán's screen persona resides in the dramatic license to take up an intermediary and unresolved position between the two; meanwhile, as Adrienne McLean has suggested in her revisionist reading of Rita Hayworth's career, the mainstream channeling of women's performance into sexual or sensual spectacle might overshadow or delay the expression of resistance, but need not extinguish or preclude its emergence in less obvious forms. What McLean observes regarding feminist-informed, scholarly criticism of a star like Hayworth could easily apply to Chagoyán:

> The risks of ignoring this 'both/and,' the conditions under which historical audiences engaged with, learned from, or interrogated the wide spectrum of information about Hayworth produced by various mass-media outlets, is that we might also be ignoring the implications of a woman's star image as having material effects in the social world, conflicted and ambivalent and *unexpected* effects, that can be participating in the formation of a feminist consciousness rather than only keeping patriarchy in place. (McLean, 2004: 6; italics in original)

At the very least, McLean suggests, and, without stopping short of recognizing female stars' discursive agency (an easy task in the case of Chagoyán), we should try to appreciate the *labor* of their performance, opening the possibility for an assessment of "competence and ability," in addition to the more gender-oriented task of locating, and following the vectors of, visual pleasure (2004: 9–10). Chagoyán herself has asked us to consider the work of performance and its attachment to agency:

> Economically, I don't need to work, but emotionally, yes. I don't use stunt doubles in movies. During one film shoot, I almost died. I had an accident in which I was unconscious for three days, but as soon as I came to I went immediately back to work. I work because it gives me pleasure. (From the Spanish original quoted in Rivas, 1999b: 25)

The question of the 'material' and psychosocial effects of Chagoyán's performances within the cultural universe of *cine fronterizo* will be addressed momentarily. A more immediate challenge involves the location of her multidimensional—yet professionally consistent—persona within the culturally specific context of the transnational region in which her films and most of her live performances are produced and circulated. This will bring us closer to reading her action films, not withstanding the degree of artifice and imperfection that remove them from transparent realism, in light of the linkage of cross-border or *transfronterizo* cultural activity to "a mode of life characterized by a continuous interaction among individuals and institutions belonging to two distinct socioeconomic structures (in this case, nations) in the region where they share a common border" (Ruiz, 1998: 105).

A place to begin this discussion is the memorable 'chick fights' in at least two of Chagoyán's films, *Contacto chicano* (1979) and *Lola la trailera III* (1991). One might interpret these fights (hair-pulling, slapping, scratching, knee pushing, with Chagoyán's character inevitably emerging as the disheveled victor) as a means of neutralizing not just the 'enemy' in the plot, but also, in ideological terms, the feminine attack on patriarchal power structures. After all, 'chick fights,' a staple of late 1960s and early 1970s sex- and blaxploitation films, as well as mexploitation *lucha libre* films, often appear to be designed for heterosexual male vicarious pleasure, especially given the loss of the combatants' composure (the undoing of the hairdo, smearing of makeup), the linkage of physical movement to irrational urges (rather than calculated vengeance or meting out of justice), and the unusual, 'private' glimpses at, and positioning of, female body parts that can occur as a result. At the same time, the narrative positioning of the fights and the cultural and social identity of the combatants in these films prompt an attempt at a more culturally situated interpretation. Such a cultural, rather than strictly psychoanalytic, reading is reinforced by the placement of the fights at the climax of the film's plots, as if to underscore the importance of Chagoyán's role in resolving the central conflict, which in both cases only superficially pivots around the commission of felony crimes.

In *Contacto chicano*, the fight occurs near and in the backyard swimming pool of a Chicano diamond trafficker (Armando Silvestre) who has been living the 'good life' in 'San Francisco' with a blonde 'French' woman (Livia Michel) while posing as an Italian under the pseudonym Gino Valetti. The cover of Chagoyán's character, Linda Lince, and partner, Tony Andrade (Gerardo Reyes), who, as Mexican undercover contraband agents, have been investigating the murder of a Mexican deep-sea diver who worked as a mule for the Chicano and his 'real Italian' Mafia bosses, has just been blown. With Linda and Tony's lives in clear danger, an African-American female FBI agent posing as a maid (uncredited) emerges from the house and shoots 'Gino' with a handgun, but not before revealing his true name—Carlos González—and Chicano identity, and receiving a mortal wound herself. With the FBI agent incapacitated, and Gino/Carlos near death, the Mexican pair takes hold of the operation, although for some inexplicable reason, Linda does not have access to a gun, and goes after Ivonne, Carlos's lover, who is clearly implicated in the criminal scheme, bare-handed. Although one can note a hesitancy on the part of the director (Federico Curiel), screen-writer (Augusto Novaro Vega), or producer (Arnulfo Delgado), to further empower Chagoyán's character by arming her in this scene, her ability to sustain a fight to the finish, *mano a mano*, with a corrupt European enemy on U.S. soil still serves as an indication of her cultural pride and valor. How-ever, the most unwieldy enemy in symbolic terms, if not the most socially powerful, is Gino/Carlos; like Linda and Tony, he is socioculturally posi-tioned between the subaltern African-American and the European gangsters to whom the Americas are but a convenient location to do business; yet he chooses to sell out, and even kill, his Mexican brothers—before aiming his gun at Tony, he offers a lame disclaimer, "lo siento hermanito" (I'm sorry little brother)—in exchange for money, a showcase house, a trophy lover, and the possibility of assuming a European, 'white' identity.

The momentary disempowerment of Chagoyán, the undercover cop in *Contacto chicano*, has given way in *Lola la trailera III* to the conscious *choice* of Rosa Gloria, here cast as Lola the Truck Driver, to fight a 'blonde' U.S. female opponent (who is dressed, dominatrix style, in studded black patent leather clothing and stiletto heeled boots) bare-handed, instead of with the semitruck cab and machine-gun artillery she has used in a previ-ous scene to eliminate the male members and guards of a U.S.-run contra-band ring. The visual excess generated by the extended sequence, in which the women climb a warehouse scaffold and Lola succeeds in throwing her blonde opponent to certain injury below, prolonged by the use of slow motion and freeze frame of Lola in the final shots of the sequence, under-scores the contrast not only in color between brunette Lola's fire-engine-red and the blonde *gringa*'s evildoer black garments (recalling the contrast between Linda's bright red and blue sunsuit and Ivonne's deceptively white sundress in *Contacto chicano*), but in national origin, with Lola success-fully defending Mexican sovereignty over its resources from foreign incur-sions and leakages achieved with corrupt Mexican cooperation.

Critically attending to this allegorical level of signification, according to which subaltern subjectivities and Mexican nationality in particular are able to prevail over imperialist powers, makes it possible to see the con-tinued relevance of these films for the *transfronterizo* viewer, whether a "fourth-generation Chicano[s]" or a "new immigrant[s] from the state[s] of Mexico's indigenous south" (Ruiz, 1998: 105), male or female, not only because of the range of sociocultural identities woven into the formation of their characters but also because of the projection onto the lived space of the cross-border region (depicted in these films as Baja–Northern Cali-fornia and northern Mexico, respectively) of two imaginary scenes simul-taneously—a quasi-sexual fantasy that develops through performative and audiovisual style and syntax, into an act of cultural affirmation and show of political strength. The narrative ambiguity and polysemy within the mise-en-scène that allow for this cultural identification in active tension with gendered voyeurism and vicarious pleasure are facilitated by the niche

182   *Catherine L. Benamou*

occupied by these films within *cine fronterizo*: an artisanal mode of practice that is itself situated on both sides of the border, 'clean' enough to be
shown in neighborhood theaters and on late-night television, yet marginal
enough to be free from the representational pressures of technical perfection and respect for the socioeconomic status quo that are characteristic of
more 'metropolitan' Mexican art cinema and national prime time televisual
programming, respectively.

". . . BUSCANDO JUSTICIA DE AQUÍ A LA FRONTERA, LA REINA DE LOS HOMBRES Y DE LAS CARRETERAS":[9] THE POLITICAL POTENTIAL— AND LIMITS—OF *CINE FRONTERIZO*

Much of Chagoyán's filmography has been misremembered, incorrectly documented, or relegated to the film historical dustbin, owing to its association
with a body of filmmaking—*churros* (in Mexican slang, exploitation films:
a pastry that is sweet and filling, but offers little nourishment)—judged to
be of low technical quality, produced mainly for profit, opportunistic (or at
worst exploitative) in relation to border labor and location conditions, and
perhaps most significantly, released without being vetted by those who have
the nation's cultural and social interests in mind. Indeed, while Chagoyán
herself claimed in a 1999 interview that she had appeared in fifty films,
imdb.com lists only forty-one produced between 1973 and 2002.

   While the acknowledgment of the efforts to produce these films at the
margins of a state-supported and -promoted film industry, as well as their
popularity, can be considered a contribution to the study of national popular culture (rather than film history), to attribute social meaning and political effectivity to Chagoyán's films on the basis of her vernacular-modern
gynocentric politics might be perceived as tantamount to critical and cultural heresy—but only if one is using the national art cinema, most of which
has been state produced, or coproduced with the Hollywood studio and
European cultural fund systems (with the multiple ambitions and agendas
that entails) as a standard of measurement, as so many critics, in reviewing cine fronterizo, have. Viewed from the standpoint of such criticism, it
might be easy to dismiss *Juana la cubana* with these words: "The pathetic
ideological confusion of this abomination is only surpassed by the porten-
tous ineptitude of the filmic result" (del Diestro, 1994: 38).

   To give a fair and contextualized critical reading to Chagoyán's film corpus, as I have attempted here, does not necessarily mean overlooking the
many-layered stigmata (*sic*) stuck across it by critical derision and scholarly neglect, or ignoring the gaps in visual and plot continuity, the lack of
perfect sound-image synchronization, of unadjusted color balance—which
themselves contribute, it can be argued, to the productive ambiguity of the
action, and perhaps to an alternative poetics (as contrasted with a plot-based

reading) in the course of decipherment. Instead, it means allowing the possibility that creative casting, choreography, unintentional excess, accented language, and the labor of performance and persona-mongering themselves are suggestive of a cultural semantics that is sociohistorically grounded, yet capable, through the magic of fiction and generic repetition, of defying the experiential and distribution barriers imposed by geopolitics, the vagaries of a neoliberal economy, even the aging—beyond normative limits—of the female sex goddess–warrior body. Whether or not the allegorical dimension came through (although I sustain it has been inscribed in these films just as much as it was in blaxploitation) and notwithstanding the hastily crafted artifice, *cine fronterizo*, including Chagoyán's films, has seemed more 'genuine' to those who have also experienced state neglect or, because they tried their luck across the border, experienced growing disenfranchisement. If I have tried to encourage a holistic, intermedial reading of Chagoyán's Lola/Coatlicue persona, it has been partly to underscore the need to assess sociopolitical effectivity in the dynamic space between screen and public sphere (how else to understand Chagoyán's appearance, Lolita semitruck in tow, to support Mexican truck drivers during a protest of NAFTA-driven restrictions in 2001?). To simply dismiss the discursive potential of *cine fronterizo* and its straight-to-video avatars based on a centrist, institutionally dictated scale of cultural values a priori, and without testing the waters of the wider geocultural sphere in which it has been consumed, begs the question of why, indeed, an allegorical road movie such as Alfonso Cuarón's *Y tu mamá también* (2001), critically judged as an art film and nominated for various international awards, including the coveted Oscar for Best Foreign Language Film, should be considered as *intrinsically* more 'political' than the kitschy allegorical journey of Lola behind the wheel of a Mexican semitruck?

NOTES

The author wishes to thank Kristy Rawson, Ph.D. student in Screen Arts and Cultures at the University of Michigan, for her expert research assistance throughout July 2007; Leo Ogata for his assistance with economic calculations; as well as the editors of this volume, Victoria Ruétalo and Dolores Tierney, for their helpful suggestions and collegial support throughout the crafting of this chapter.

1. Vivanco, 2006: 12. This and all other translations from the Spanish (with the exception of official distribution titles for certain films) are my own.
2. Rivas, 1999b: 25.
3. I will be using Eric Schaefer's definition, as set forth in Schaefer, 1999: 3–8, with some adjustments to reflect the shift in national context(s) of production and distribution.
4. Increasingly, given current restrictions on immigration to the United States, as well as on the terms for obtaining and retaining temporary work permits, the exodus of millions of Mexicans across the border can be characterized more as an act, albeit mostly involuntary, of *emigration* rather than of migration, which was characteristic of the Bracero period (1942–1964) and post-Bracero period (1970s and 1980s).

5. See the blog: "Rosa Gloria Chagoyán diva del cine mexicano," at http:/archivohose.blogspot.com/search/label/Rosa%20Gloria%20Chagoyan. As for her age, no information exists on fan sites or on imdb.com; however, the thirty-year span of her career suggests she is probably well past forty.

6. See, for example, the contrast in mode of address and graphic composition between *El secuestro de Lola (Clip 3)*, posted by películas1 on YouTube April 4, 2008, http://www.youtube.com/watch?v=ce9_bZMOOlI&feature=related, accessed September 15, 2008; *Lola la trailera (Clip 5)*, posted by películas1, YouTube, April 4, 2008; http://www.youtube.com/watch?v=1CNTP-tOPNU&feature=related, accessed September 15, 2008; *Juana la cubana (Clip 8)*, posted by películas1, YouTube, April 10, 2008; http://www.youtube.com/watch?v=RsRL6, accessed August 20, 2008.

7. See Vivanco, 2006. A similar phenomenon has occurred in the construction trade, allegedly owing to the dangers associated with that type of work. Both professions are celebrated in coporate advertisements circulating on Spanish-language television.

8. Iglesias Prieto, 1989: 119; in 1988, border films could be shot in four weeks, and the average cost was 250 million [old] pesos (Iglesias, 1989: 111), or around US $80,000.

9. "Seeking justice from here to the border, the queen of men and highways." From the lyrics to the corrido "Lola la trailera," written by Francisco Brancamontes and performed by Conjunto Internacional Michoacán in the original *Lola la trailera* (1983).

12 The *Naco* in Mexican Film

La banda del carro rojo, Border Cinema, and Migrant Audiences[1]

Adán Avalos

> Modern cinematic technology has become a weapon in the struggle
> for social justice . . .(Cine-Aztlán, 1992: 275)

My childhood memories sometimes seem unsettling to other people. I remember helicopters hovering overhead as I labored in fields of fruit, spending the night in a sleeping bag in the hallway of a two-bedroom apartment shared by my thirteen family members, storing all of my earthly belongings in a *cajón* (cardboard box), watching two of my sisters get caught by the INS as I hid in an orchard, sitting terrified in a moving vehicle after my cousin jumped out of the driver's seat and ran into a field of corn to avoid *la migra* (U.S. Border Patrol). When asked, I always answer that I had a happy childhood. Movies, particularly Mexican cinema, provided a rich refuge for me and for my imagination. I vividly remember a family trip to a dilapidated movie theater in Fresno, California. For the price of admission, my parents got free or reduced-rate counsel from a paralegal in an upstairs office next to the projectionist. While my parents and other Mexican *illegal* immigrants obtained assistance with the challenge of legalizing their status in the United States, we children were captivated by the film being screened—*La banda del carro rojo*/The Red Car Gang (Rubén Galindo, 1976)—a film about four Mexican men struggling to survive in the United States with limited financial, social, and cultural resources. As one of eleven children of a Mexican family of migrant workers, I could well understand the desperation of these four characters that fight by all means necessary to attain a better standard of living, a life free from the hardships of racial or class prejudice, what you call a Mexican immigrant or migrant version of the 'American Dream.'

Although my family did not turn to a life of crime, as did the characters of *La banda*, this and other films like *La mafia de la frontera*/Border Mafia (Jaime Fernández, 1979) and *Asalto en Tijuana*/Armed Robbery in Tijuana (Alfredo Gurrola, 1984) captured elements of our experiences on the Mexico/U.S. border, experiences that make many other Americans uncomfortable. Looking back, I realize how meaningful it was for me to see filmic representations of my family's journey on the big screen. My ten brothers and sisters and I eagerly consumed such Mexican films as *Maldita miseria/* Damn Misery (Júlio Aldama, 1979), and *Perro callejero/*Street Dog (Gilberto Gazcón, 1980), with actors such as Valentín Trujillo, Rosa Gloria Chagoyán, and Mário and Fernando Almada. These Mexican movies of the 1970s and 1980s, belonging to a genre referred to as border cinema (a subsection of exploitation cinema), often detail the lives of recent Mexican immigrants in the United States and focus on the Mexico/U.S. border region. My family is just one example of the type of audience drawn to these films—an audience of recent immigrants, mostly from Mexico but also from other Latin American countries. This largely ignored audience predominantly works in the service industry as farm laborers, mechanics, maids, gardeners, janitors—people not often represented in American popular culture.

Much critical work on Mexican cinema focuses on the Golden Age (1940–1955), a period that reflected the emergence and development of a state-sanctioned 'national cinema,' and which participated in defining Mexican national identity (Mora, 1982; Paranaguá, 1995; Noble, 2005; Tierney, 2007). In recent years, more critical attention is given to what's being called the 'New Wave' of Mexican cinema, created by filmmakers such as the former directing/writing team Alejandro González Iñárritu and Guillermo Arriaga (*Amores perros*, 2000), Alfonso Cuarón (*Y tu mamá también*, 2001) and Guillermo del Toro (*El espinazo del diablo*, 2001). This Mexican cinema of the past ten years has captivated international audiences, won critical acclaim in international festivals, and given much deserved attention to cinema south of the border.

In spite of these current trends in Mexican film scholarship, the border cinema, which so captivated me and other migrant audiences, is currently being ignored by both film critics and the academic community. While acknowledging the popularity of these films with recent immigrants, critics and scholars tend to focus on the genre's low production values, stock characters, stilted performances, rampant sexism and misogyny, cheap and fast production processes, and straight-to-video distribution as indications of its limited cultural and artistic value. Film scholar David Maciel, who has done extensive research on Mexican and border cinema, rightfully points to the fact that the private producers of border cinema are motivated by profits, " . . . with little regard for creativity, aesthetics, or even professional standards" (1990: 29). Prominent cultural critic and film scholar Norma Iglesias confirms Maciel's assessment of border cinema and also maintains that it "tends to standardize forms of representation, thus avoiding the complex cultural, social, and political realities of the border region" (2003: 211–212). Even in Mexico, this border cinema is considered to be *naco* (a derogatory term which I discuss later).

In writing about Mexican popular films, Maricruz Castro Ricalde brings up the issue of "worthiness"—noting that most Westerners reserve the word *art* for what is considered the 'best' and "most worthy" (2004: 195–196).

Ricalde addresses the inherent hierarchy of culture, one in which in the case of popular and thereby exploitation films occupies a low position. In her discussion of María Elena Velasco's (La India María) films, which she uses as a case study of popular films of the 1970s and the 1980s, she notes the manner in which public taste takes a back seat to media reception; it is the critics, she argues, that determine aesthetic achievement, not the box-office records (2004: 196–97).[2] Exploitation films are equally ignored by the privileged classes and the academic elite, who construct their own "mediating imaginary" that excludes the popular classes (Ricalde, 2004: 210). Ricalde's concerns share a point of contact with Andrew Higson's work on national cinemas. He argues that the context of consumption is as important to the discussion of national cinema as the site of production, and that we should focus our attention more "on the activity of national audiences and the conditions under which they make sense of and use the films they watch" (Higson, 1989: 36).

I agree with Ricalde's analysis that it is a serious mistake for critics to lose sight of the popular audience, and to dismiss the importance of popular genres such as exploitation cinema. While agreeing with Maciel's argument that the focus of the producers of border cinema is profit-motivated, I disagree that this in and of itself justifies his conclusion that "it is difficult to find many artistic, cultural, or social values in these contemporary films" (1990: 29). Furthermore, I take issue with Iglesias's statement that "the manner in which border cinema has simplified and decontextualized a complex border reality and the migration process, has served to stifle border residents' critical engagement with their reality" (2003: 198).[3]

In this essay, I reclaim the controversial term *naco* and apply it to the genre of border cinema; specifically, films produced from 1976 through the present. The term *naco*, as previously defined, was originally used as a slur against Indians, peasants, or anyone who stood for the provincial backwardness and who could only be redeemed through an international culture (Lomnitz, 2001: 111). Although I acknowledge the rampant violence and misogyny—hence the term exploitation—of the *naco* genre, I re-semanticize this negative valence to challenge the conventional understanding of a marginal cinema that is disavowed and derided by dominant critical discourse. I define *naco* cinema as a transnational cinema that reflects and creates the identity of recent Latino immigrants into the United States, a group that is constantly transgressing established boundaries. From here on in, I will refer to border cinema as *naco* cinema. All *naco* movies are mass-produced quickly, cheaply, and primarily for profit. As such, *naco* cinema belongs to the genre of exploitation cinema, and encompasses many subgenres, among them: action, western, comedy, brothel (*cabaretera*), horror, science-fiction, wrestling, and fronterizo films.

Following Ricalde's footsteps, I hope to contribute to the agenda of cultural studies in democratizing the study of culture by revaluing the 'low genre' of *naco* cinema, and reevaluating it critically. The very fact that these films are so wildly popular with recent Mexican and Latino immigrant audiences, the fastest growing demographic in the United States, suggests that it is worthwhile to undertake a second look at the genre.[4] Studying these films can give us a means to access the histories, dreams, and realities of the audiences that consume and find meaning in them. These films, much like the *corridos*, as María Herrera-Sobek has argued, "will yield valuable information as to the ideology, world view, political, economic and social situation of the Mexican people" (1979: 49). By exploring how these films represent immigrant stories on the Mexico/U.S. border region, we can gain a more complete picture of the audience's experience as new immigrants in the United States. Furthermore, we can learn about the ways in which *naco* cinema speaks to migrant communities' " . . . struggle for social justice . . ." (Cine-Aztlán, 1992: 275).[5]

This chapter focuses on those *naco* films belonging to the subgenre inspired by *corridos* (traditional ballads) and *narcocorridos* (drug ballads), specifically films based on the songs of the Mexican-American superband *Los Tigres del Norte*. I begin with a brief historical overview of the origin and development of *naco* cinema, starting with what I will refer to as the first phase (from the Golden Age to 1976), which saw the emergence of '*naco* taste,' followed by the second phase (1976–1989), which consolidated the genre, and finally, the third phase (1989–present), which saw the genre transform in new ways. As a case study, I will revisit the classic *naco* film *La banda del carro rojo*, a film seminal to the genre of *naco* cinema and formative in the development of my own identity as a new immigrant, and later, as a Chicano thinker. I will explore how audiences read films such as *La banda del carro rojo*, and others. I argue that rather than being cursorily dismissed, *naco* films such as *La banda del carro rojo* should be validated and seen as important cultural documents that merit serious academic inquiry.[6]

SETTING THE STAGE: THE BIRTH OF *NACO* TASTE IN CINEMA (1950–1976)

This period, which I refer to as the birth of *naco* taste in cinema, began towards the end of the Golden Age. During the Golden Age, Mexican national cinema showed the country as a glorious developing nation with romanticized peasants and campesinos (e.g., Emilio 'El Indio' Fernández's *María Candelaria*, 1943, and Fernando de Fuentes's *Allá en el rancho grande/Out on the Big Ranch*, 1936). These films and others like them were made to build national character and to educate citizens. Mexican national cinema was the political and cultural re-visioning of a national identity alongside the development of the vibrant cinema industry (Hershfield, 1999: 81). However, due to the withdrawal of U.S. financial support post-1946 and the aggressive competitive tactics of the Hollywood film

industry, which forced the Mexican state to recant on some of its protectionist measures, by 1950 Mexico's state-sponsored cinema was in crisis,
and it took twenty years for any major changes to occur (Tierney, 2007:
160–161). A new period of Mexican cinema was ushered in by the governmental policies of Luis Echeverría's *sexenio* (1970–76). Filmmakers like
Felipe Cazals, Jaime Humberto Hermosillo, Arturo Ripstein, and others
of the *Nuevo cine* movement switched to a more realist and less idealized vision of the country (Ramírez Berg, 1992: 46–52). It was during this
period that Mexican filmmakers moved into previously unexplored territory that would take them further and further from the centralized, romanticized idea of the nation.

Towards the end of the 1940s, in an attempt to save the film industry,
private producers began making low-budget genre films that placed the plot
in an urban setting (De la Vega, 1999: 166). What was born in this transitional period was a model of production that was cheap, fast, and made
primarily for profit. Film scholar John Mraz has referred to this as the
development of the *churro* in the early 1950s. A *churro* is a cheap, mass-
produced, sugary, fried pastry—in Mexican film it describes any piece of
work hastily made, poorly done, and created purely for the "fast buck"
(Mraz, 1984: 23). Although *churros* alienated the Mexican middle-class
audience, who turned to Hollywood movies instead, they were very popular with the urban working populace (De la Vega, 1999: 167).

These genre pictures were comedies, romances, melodramas, adventures, and musicals (Ramírez Berg, 1992: 7). They were characterized by
their heroes (Mario Moreno 'Cantinflas,' German Valdez 'Tin Tan,' and
'El Santo' the masked wrestler). These popular heroes were outsiders and
reflected the same characteristics of the audience who eagerly consumed
their films. El Santo physically wrestled with the oppressors whilst Cantinflas and Tin Tan (in films like *Ahí está el detalle/Here is the Point*, 1940;
El rey del barrio/The King of the Neighborhood, 1950) outwitted them
through verbal sparring. These new heroes challenged and unmasked the
social problems of Mexico's inner city (inequality) and also addressed
global fears (the cold war, etc.).

Although the abovementioned films were sponsored by the state, they
were made according to the new model of film production, and reflected
the emergence of the themes that would come to characterize *naco* cinema.
These themes were a direct result of the influx of working poor into the
cities due to the accelerated process of industrialization that had begun
years earlier (De la Vega, 1999: 166). Films that dealt with these themes are
Ismael Rodríguez's two huge melodramatic successes *Nosotros los pobres*
and *Ustedes los ricos* (*We the Poor*, 1947, and *You the Rich*, 1948) as they
showcased the famous Pedro Infante but without his trademark *charro*
(cowboy) outfit and his horse, which had gained him immense popularity and a place in national identity. He now wore clothes and spoke like
the vast majority of new arrivals in the city. His singing still matched his

persona in the film, but he was now depicted as a poor working-class hero, living in a Mexico City slum where most of the inhabitants have to deal with the daily struggle of survival.

Several factors led to the consolidation of the *naco* genre in the mid-1970s. One was the beginning of video production and later straight-to-video cinema, which changed the established traditional forms of production and distribution. But the most significant were the governmental policy changes made after President Luis Echeverría Alvarez left office. The gains that the industry saw during Echeverría's tenure were wiped out when President José López Portillo came to power in 1976 (Ramírez Berg, 1992: 30). Portillo considered Echeverría's term a disaster, both to the country and to the film industry, and he began reversing the trends of his predecessor by eliminating the state's direct involvement in the film industry (Ramírez Berg, 1992: 51). By 1977 the private sector's production of *naco* film was already much greater than that of the state-sponsored sector. At this point most themes of low-budget film productions had moved from Mexico City to the northern parts of the country, particularly to *la frontera*, following the large population migration to the northern border region.[7] Even though most of these seasonal workers made the trip back home to towns in rural Mexico, many stayed in the border region. Here they found work and maintained hope for alternative ways to enter the United States. The increased population in the lawless border region made the area ripe for corruption. Recent arrivals from the countryside were often naïve and gullible. Another group of new arrivals came to take advantage of the country folk—drug smugglers and *coyotes* (guides taking people illegally across the border). There had always been corruption, but the increased population and opportunity for dishonesty pushed the problem into the open, making corruption an expected part of daily life. Corruption ran rampant in the government as well, from federal officials to police on the street. The border thus became a transitional area or a 'holding cell' for Mexicans hoping to eventually settle permanently in the United States. As migration became more and more a part of the reality of Mexico's poorer class—and as people moved from the south to *la frontera* (the border)—their lives were characterized by new experiences, new problems, and new dreams. It was these new experiences of people on the border that provided the foundation for a great majority of themes in *naco* cinema's second stage.

THE *NACO* IN MEXICAN FILM, 1976–89: *LA BANDA DEL CARRO ROJO*

By the mid-1970s, with the consolidation of the genre of *naco* cinema, the plots of *naco* films focused on the hardships of leaving home, corruption, city life, working in a foreign country, drug and alcohol, and other struggles of day-to-day addiction. The dark subject matter offered an element of realism combined with exaggerated glamour and violence. Like in *telenovelas* (soap operas), emotions in these *naco* films ran high and tensions are built up with soundtracks engineered to evoke suspense. The films popularized during this period were action movies revolving around drug dealing and the border as a place controlled by the drug cartels. This period also saw the direct merger between *corridos* (traditional ballads) and films. Many narratives were based upon and driven by *corridos*. Popular musical groups sang about common drug dealers in *corridos*, catapulting them to the status of local and regional heroes. The audiences of this *naco* cinema could identify directly with the experiences depicted on screen; the narratives were contemporary to their own. While the viewers may have been far removed from drug trafficking and other illegal activities, they certainly experienced crossing the border, racial prejudice, and financial hardship. Audience members may have known family members or friends that experienced the dramatic stories of this early *naco* cinema; this was a world familiar to them that was unavailable in mainstream cinema.

Starting in the mid-1970s and continuing through to the present moment, many *naco* films base their plots on the lyrics of *corridos* and especially on a subgroup of ballads called *narcocorridos*, which celebrate and eulogize the life of drug traffickers on the border. Beginning in the mid-1970s, the popular Mexican-American band *Los Tigres del Norte* (The Tigers of the North) sang *narcocorridos*, which became the foundation for a series of *narco* films (*La banda del carro rojo, Treinta segundos para morir/*Thirty Seconds to Die (Rubén Benavides, 1981), *Un hombre violento/*A Violent Man (Valentín Trujillo, 1986), *La jaula de oro/*The Golden Cage (Sergio Véjar, 1987), *La camioneta gris/*The Grey Pickup (José Luis Urquieta, 1990). The audience's familiarity with the songs made these films easy to follow, since they were primarily functioning as an extended video to accompany the music.

La banda del carro rojo is the first *Los Tigres narcocorrido* to be made into a film. The film follows a plot outlined in the *corrido*, but adds elements to fill out subplots. There are four principal characters, or *nacos*, in the film that make up the red car gang. At first, each seems to follow the stereotypical formula of this genre, but a closer reading of the characters reveals that they are much more complex. The audience may not only identify with each character in the way they dress and talk but also in the ways they think and react when confronted with life-changing decisions. They are open to reading depth into these characters even though each character was created according to a stereotype, and within a formula that remains the same throughout most of these films. Because many audience members have personally shared the experiences of the characters, or at the least know of someone (a loved one, friend, relative) who has, the audience is not simply passively enjoying the entertainment or easily manipulated by the stock characters and formulas; I argue that this audience is actively engaging and ascribing new meanings to situations and characters on the screen.

In the film *La banda del carro rojo*, the character Pedro, played by Pedro Infante Jr. (the son of Golden Age actor Pedro Infante), is a naïve and newly arrived illegal immigrant to the United States. While the actor's father had huge critical success and was seen as a national icon, Pedro Infante Jr. can be seen as an *un*official national icon, representative of the experiences of displaced Mexicans. Unlike his father, he is ignored by the critics because of his participation in *naco* films. In this film, Pedro exhibits all the dreams of the first-generation migrant: he expects easy wealth and fame to fall into his hands. Pedro insists that in the United States "they recognize talent" and he believes that he will successfully become a Hollywood actor. When we first see Pedro, he is wearing the typical and simple outfit of a humble Mexican worker (worn-out jeans, T-shirt, and tennis shoes), but through the course of the film, he abandons them and instead adopts entirely new attire, consisting of hat, boots, and three-piece suit that display a northern influence. The audience may quickly read his new American attire as a sign of his loss of national identity. While Pedro may have seemingly acquired the external trappings that would signal he has achieved the financial success part of the 'American Dream,' there is a high price to pay for the fortune he made through drug money. By acting illegally, Pedro has in fact betrayed the honest principles of the 'American Dream.' But the audience can nonetheless still share, enjoy, and vicariously rejoice in his material success, without having to compromise its own honest identity.

The character Rodrigo, played by Fernando Almada, is a Mexican immigrant who has been in the United States for many years and is already disillusioned with the possibility of ever achieving the financial stability and well-being enshrined in the idea of the 'American Dream.' He is in debt and cannot afford to pay for the medical treatment of his terminally ill daughter. He argues with his brother in the film and declares that he is an honest man, but his brother Quintana counters with "what has honesty and hard work given you, a life of misery, a ranch that you can't afford, a wife that abandons you and a sick daughter. You call that progress?" After some deliberation, Rodrigo decides to help his brother smuggle 100 kilos of cocaine into the United States. He hopes that with the money he can take his daughter to the best hospitals and to the best doctors who can find a cure for her disease. In an earlier scene, Rodrigo and Pedro's ideologies clash during their conversation. Pedro believes that Rodrigo has 'made it' because he has cars and a ranch but Rodrigo counters that he owns nothing and that he cannot even pay for his daughter's treatment. Rodrigo refers to his own story, a life of hard work resulting in very little wealth or upward mobility.

The character Quintana, played by the very famous Mário Almada, is familiar to many in the Mexican immigrant community. Mário Almada is one of the most successful working actors in *naco* cinema, having made well over three hundred films. He has worked with respected Mexican directors like Arturo Ripstein and has had critical acclaim. The great majority of the films that he has starred in have always dealt with social issues, even though most critics find fault with the films for being too simplistic in their approach. In this film he plays the leader of the red car gang who feels forced to venture into illegal business to get out of debt. Although his gambling addiction may make him unsympathetic to American viewers, many Mexicans from the lower socioeconomic strata interpret his behavior as an act of desperation and relate it to his quest to achieve the prosperity that is supposedly available to all (if they work hard) in the United States (i.e., another aspect of the 'American Dream'). His trajectory during the film traces an arc from an honest citizen with a gambling problem, to a drug trafficker, to a dead man. Quintana illustrates the difficult position of desperate, poor immigrants with few avenues for upward mobility, who make the wrong choices and are forced to pay a high price.

The character Boom represents a Mexican-American, or better yet, a *pocho* who is deeply entrenched in the criminal element.[8] He may be interpreted as a product of Chicano alienation caused by the unassailable consumer culture of the 1960s and 1970s that recent immigrants could not participate in. As a response, many lower-income Mexican-Americans, frustrated and enraged by the impossibility of ever having the money to actively participate in the consumer culture through honest means, turned to wage-earning endeavors that involved crime (Limón, 1994: 109). Boom operates as a *coyote*, ferrying desperate Mexicans across the border. In this act, he exploits others from his home country, charging exorbitant rates for a voyage that may not even be successful. His drug addiction also makes him unreliable and selfish. Boom has long since discarded the idea of making an 'honest' living in favor of making a lucrative income by any means necessary.

What the four characters have in common is their deep desire for freedom. Driven by different motivations into a life of crime, they hope to evade the authorities and make money in order to get out of debt, pay for medical treatment, or simply just for narcissistic reasons. When it becomes clear that their pursuit of money through crime is not sustainable, and the Texas Rangers pick up their trail, they decide to avoid capture at any cost. In the film's climactic finale, when they find themselves surrounded by the Rangers, they decide to take a last stand and die with a pistol in their hand. Feeling victimized by society their entire lives, they decide to take charge in their moment of death. In their eyes, death as free men is better than spending the rest of their lives in prison.

The *corrido*, as well as the film *La banda del carro rojo*, illustrates many of the themes of Mexican immigrants' cultural experiences, beginning in the 1970s and continuing to the present, including social inequality, the struggle of migration, the expectations of quick success, the temptation of drugs, limited access to power, and the differences between first- and second-generation Mexican-Americans. The narrative deals with an experience common to immigrants to the United States: the hope of achieving the 'American Dream' quickly destroyed by the realities of discrimination, alienation, and exclusion. New immigrants who enter the United

States illegally are immediately criminalized. They are uncomfortable with authority and feel excluded from the social arena. Some internalize a feeling of criminality. The lack of education and opportunities for social mobility lead people to the drudgery of low-wage jobs and desperate frustration. Often the frustration is centered on the inability to pay for or access basic human needs such as health care. For some, this frustration pushes them towards a life of crime—the only way they feel able to gain control of their destiny.

The characters in *La banda*, who deal with the same feelings of exclusion and disempowerment, choose to empower themselves through crime. They act out the subconscious fantasies of the audience—who get to see themselves mirrored on screen—powerful and courageous, standing against the system. Even if the character dies at the end, at least he has died after his moment of glory. Though most migrants do not lead lives of crime, either because their repressed rage against the system keeps them disempowered or because their religious beliefs warn them against it, they are responsive to the story of *La banda*, and other *naco* films like it. Thus, what appears at first glance to be a simple and uncomplicated narrative that is based on a two-minute song can actually be read as a profound reflection on the complexity of the immigrant experience.

THE NEW *NACO*: 1989 TO THE PRESENT

By the 1980s, most *naco* movies were made by small independent companies and shot on video. Independent producers slashed costs by relying on family members for casting, sets, and crew. Shooting took place on local ranches owned by relatives. The actors often wore their own clothes, and props consisted of whatever objects were available on site. Producers sometimes filmed two movies simultaneously to save costs. Most films took approximately three to four weeks to shoot at a cost of $50,000 to $85,000 per film (Ramírez Berg, 2002: 226). Cheap and quickly made, the films were characterized by low production values and nonprofessional acting. When the VCR became widely accessible in the mid-1980s, many *naco* films became available on video in local Latino markets in the United States. Advertising for these films replicates the flashy nature of the films themselves; posters are very colorful and designed with images of guns, cars, women, and drugs. People could purchase a tape for approximately $10 to $20 and rent them for around $3.

Films of the third stage of *naco* cinema continue to reflect the political, economic, and industrial conditions of the period. They reflect the oppressive daily life in the border region, and explore misery, violence, overcrowding, and promiscuity. The plots of the films continue to deal with the experiences of their intended audience, the recent Mexican and Latino immigrants in the United States, largely poor and lacking in formal education, who cross to the United States to work for little money in *el norte.* We can determine a direct line of influence between these *naco* films and the Mexican films that garnered such critical acclaim in recent years. For instance, *La banda de carro rojo* and Robert Rodríguez's *El mariachi* (1992) both comment on the financial crisis of the 1980s, the war on drugs, NAFTA, and the fortification of the U.S./Mexico border. As the United States stepped up actions against the new migrant class, the resentment in the films became more pronounced. As the frustrations of new Latino immigrants increased, the *naco* films became more violent and unrepentant. In the decades after *La banda del carro rojo* was produced, both *narcocorridos* and *naco* films based on them became progressively more violent, showcasing machine guns, omnipresent swearing, and female degradation. What's more, while the characters in *La banda del carro rojo* pay for their crimes at the end of the film (they all die), the criminal characters in the more recent *naco* films often do not pay for their crimes. The character of the drug dealer in the *naco* films has become more of a cultural icon—a cruel modern hero *never* defeated by the system.

With their low production values, unprofessional acting, shoddy sets, melodramatic plots, gratuitous violence, and sex, these films do not have much merit according to the standards of traditional film criticism, which dismisses the importance of films made primarily for profit and mass consumption. Iglesias writes that the films I have dubbed *naco* films are created solely as a response to commercial interests (2003: 211–12). Although producers may have the mighty dollar in mind when making *naco* films, critics are misguided in their quick dismissal of this film genre or in ignoring the films merely because they can be read as 'low' culture. For, in doing so, they fail to see the true value of these films as important social and cultural documents that represent the struggles and dreams of a group of people.

In this essay, I have argued that *naco* films are worthy of the scrutiny of academic study. These *naco* films are cultural documents of social transformation that attest to the developing identity of the migrant class of Latinos. Once one understands the context in which these films are created, and to whom they are addressed, one can begin to appreciate their cultural importance and relevance. When defining Mexico, particularly in the context of today's political and economic climate, it is important to look at all aspects of the cultural spectrum, not simply concentrate on the most palatable ones. *Naco* cinema addresses the unpleasant realities of many immigrants living on low wages outside of their home country.

I would even go so far as to argue that many of the descendants who were born in the United States of recent immigrants privilege *naco* films above mainstream American and Mexican films because they deliberately offend middle- and upper-class aesthetic values. *Naco* films do not attempt to create lasting artistic polemics or deep philosophical thoughts, nor are they interested in capturing a large percentage of the box-office market or Oscar nominations. Audiences celebrate these films because they discard the typical goals of most moviemakers. By deliberately patronizing 'low' culture, audiences chip away at the dominance of the mainstream. By watching the latest *naco* film on DVD, audience members take a small amount of money from big-name directors and the Hollywood circus. This immigrant film consumers seem to take delight in the fact that they are not funding 'high' art when they watch *naco* films; they enjoy participating in the 'low' end of the standard artistic film hierarchy. This economic and social move remains subtle and unrecognized by almost all but the participants, but it does signal a deliberate choice (Avalos, 2007–2008).

It seems that my childhood memories of a low-income Mexican family living on the border of the United States and Mexico have become compelling subject matter for the critically acclaimed 'New Wave' of Mexican films, such as *Babel* (González Iñárritu, 2006). However, it is important to remember that these stories have been told for decades to a largely ignored audience of migrant workers. Academia and popular culture recognize the public's interest in these 'new' stories and in this 'new' form of storytelling, but may not understand its ancestry. I would like to give credit to the *naco* films as part of the foundation for this new movement. I believe that this new cinema is not entirely 'new' but relies upon a foundation of quickly produced, critically dismissed *naco* movies: both share attention to the border region, as a place of opportunity and self-invention; both feature grainy, low-quality film style and high melodrama. In an investigation of *naco* films, we may trace a continuum between the Golden Age and the current crop of incredibly popular Mexican directors. Instead of a cultural desert during the last half of the twentieth century, we observe a trajectory of films leading to a 'New Wave' of Mexican Cinema, first exploring the underside of Mexico by focusing on struggle and strife in urban centers, then in the border region. By examining the *naco* film era, we may observe the evolution of the aesthetic celebrated by the Mexican auteur directors of today.

NOTES

1. I am grateful to the editors for their helpful suggestions for revisions. Thanks also to Curtis Marez, Pierrette Hondagneu-Sotelo, Amy Bouse, Susana Chavez-Silverman, Ilana Lapid, and Gabriel Avalos, who read and commented on various drafts of this chapter.
2. Originally developed for television in the early 70s, María Elena Velasco's character quickly became a sensation and the subject of more than twenty films. Some of her film titles are *Tonta, tonta pero no tanto* (*Dumb, Dumb but not that Dumb*, 1972), *El coyote emplumado* (*The Plumed Coyote*, 1983), *Ni de aquí, ni de allá* (*Neither from Here nor from There*, 1988). The character is portrayed as a typical southwestern Mexican Indian who dresses in traditional costume consisting of ribbons on her braided hair and colorful native blouse and skirt. Her films are socially conscious, slapstick comedies about a woman out of her element.
3. In my own experience, these border films spoke to me and to my brothers and sisters. Instead of 'stifling' us, they engaged us because they reflected our

experiences and concerns as a working-class migrant family dealing with issues of displacement in a foreign country. Unlike other films available for our consumption, they told stories from the perspective of people we could relate to—the undocumented, the marginalized, and the disenfranchised.

4. Another aspect to consider about exploitation films is the fact that when there are only a few production people to please, the director enjoys a great deal more freedom in artistic choices. As Jeffrey Sconce points out, in his well-read essay on cinematic tastes, Hollywood films require endless meetings with lawyers, accountants, and corporate boards, while low-budget films may become wildly eccentric, even presenting unpopular and politically incorrect views (1995: 381–382). The filmmakers may also approach current and unusual subject matter: the taboos that scare Hollywood away from unpopular and radical views do not hold the same power over producers who do not expect to see their films reviewed in national newspapers and academic journals.

5. For instance, Ricalde sustains that these films often tell the stories of working- and lower-class characters exhibiting resistance to and negotiation with dominant cultures, but Mexican critics largely ignore this resistance (2004: 199).

6. In doing so, I hope to echo the reappropriation of a word once used to express disapproval. There is a long history of this: the term *impressionism*, first coined in 1874, expressed the critics' disfavor with the emerging painting style; 'impressionism' first denounced the short attention span of the painters, who are now among the most beloved in art history. Once a term of derision, *impressionism* now conjures up the most popular and well-known movement in art of the nineteenth century.

7. This demographic shift was due in part to the end of the U.S. Bracero program in 1964. Begun in 1942, it is estimated that this program contracted more than four million guest workers during its twenty-two year period (Alba, 1989: 22). Another factor that pushed people northwards was the Border Industrialization Program that the Mexican government began in 1965 to encourage companies to move to the border region. The government wanted to assert control of the 'wild' border provinces by building industry, including the maquiladoras (sweatshops).

8. Generally, a *pocho* is a derogatory word used to describe a Mexican who was born in the United States but has rejected or has no sense of his Mexican heritage or the Spanish language.

Part IV

Sex, Sex, and More Sex

13 Temptations
Isabel Sarli Exposed

Victoria Ruétalo

The 1957 production of *El trueno entre las hojas/Thunder among the Leaves*, featuring the first full frontal nude scene in Argentina, became an instantaneous box-office hit that would unveil a new star sensation: Isabel Sarli. Director Bó's adaptation of a socially motivated story, written by critically acclaimed author Augusto Roa Bastos, about the abuse of indigenous groups and workers in the Paraguayan jungle was not the basis for the ensuing controversy surrounding the film. Rather, it was the one scene where the soon-to-be cleanest woman on Argentine celluloid disrobes and dips into the high Paraná River, astounding a mostly Catholic nation. What was meant to be a supporting role for Sarli became the beginning of a scandalous career and the creation of a national sex symbol. Audience response to the film and huge lineups at the theaters caused Bó to bump Sarli from third place in the credits to star billing, and so the Bó-Sarli partnership that would eventually make twenty-seven films and span almost three decades began. In an interview, Bó admits: "She [Sarli] herself earned her own spot as the film's main star" (qtd. in Martín, 1981:18) and indeed, the rest is history.[1] Sarli would become a Latin American pinup desired by men everywhere regardless of their class, race, or age.

Richard Dyer's 1981 book has become the benchmark theory on how to approach the topic of stardom. Through the examination of films, promotional material, publicity, and criticism, Dyer analyzes the historical, ideological, and aesthetic meaning of film stars, in what he calls the 'star image.' Following suit are pioneers in the growing field of Latin American star studies, scholars such as Ana M. López, who explores the careers of three Latin Americans who starred in Hollywood during the Good Neighbor policy films.[2] By tracing the shift in Hollywood's ethnographic view of Latin America, López identifies the role of three female stars, Dolores del Río, Lupe Vélez, and Carmen Miranda, and assigns agency particularly to Miranda, who "does not burst the illusory bubble of the Good Neighbor, but by inflating it beyond recognition . . . highlights its status as a discursive construct, a mimetic myth" (López, 1993a: 78). In a parallel fashion, the present chapter looks at the many myths that construct Sarli's star image and highlights some of the contradictory discourses that surround these same myths to show that the star's image was confined by both class and gender stereotypes directly linked to the sociopolitical situation in Argentina.

Similar to Mexico, Argentina did not establish a star system until after the arrival of sound. Even Hollywood's Spanish-language production attempts failed in part due to their inability to feature an internationally explosive icon. Tango singer Carlos Gardel would be the only one to come close to achieving such stature, but his sudden accidental death precipitated an early end to a fast-growing celluloid career.[3] With the triumph of Argentina's national film industry, during the establishment of the studio era in the 1930s and 1940s, new stars were born. Nini Marshall, Luis Sandrini, Tita Merello, and Mirta Legrand were a few of the most noteworthy of the period. The most beloved figure of all, tango singer and actress Libertad Lamarque, would go on to capture the hearts of fans throughout the Spanish-speaking world. On the set of *La cabalgata del circo/The Circus Cavalcade* (Eduardo Boneo and Mario Soffici, 1945), a film starring the actress alongside Hugo del Carril and coincidently enough Bó, Lamarque would make an enemy of supporting actress Eva Duarte. Many myths surrounded this confrontation between the diva and the soon-to-be first lady of the nation. The only thing certain was Lamarque's fate: once Perón rose to power she self-exiled to Mexico, where her career would continue to blossom. Many other artists and filmmakers followed the same path as the dreamy-eyed brunette. This and other factors such as the collapse of the industry studios would heavily impact the star system in the nation.

None of these early actresses, despite their popular appeal, would attain the distinction of national sex symbol. In fact, Argentina desperately lacked a sex symbol, a role destined for overnight sensation Sarli. What allowed Sarli to assume this role were precisely the same reasons that would retain Lamarque as Argentina's reputable sweetheart. While Lamarque was representative of a much earlier period and different cinematic scene, the two icons embodied opposites that were irreconcilable throughout the 1950s and 1960s. Lamarque, from respectable upper-class pedigree, was cast in high-production-value roles playing young naïve women who always dreamed of becoming mothers and wives, but somehow "were tricked or forced by circumstances into successful careers as singers" (López, 1993b: 157). Sarli, unable to shake her working-class upbringing, performed in low-budget roles that would problematize in new ways the characteristic stereotypes of the old classical cinemas found in the mother-whore dichotomy. Her exuberant physical appearance would overshadow any onstage talent that she may have had to offer. By examining closely Sarli's on-screen (films) and offscreen (promotional, publicity, and critical texts) star persona I hope to expose some of the ideological, historical, and aesthetic contradictions found in the myths surrounding her stardom. Simultaneously ostracized and adored, Sarli promotes a contentious figure, much like her idol Eva Perón, locked within the lumpenproletariat class who will succeed to break through many gender-specific taboos yet still confined within gendered roles. In essence, to read Sarli's stardom is not to salvage the dark-haired beauty as the embodiment of a progressive text but to acknowledge how she both reacts to and reflects the anxieties, needs, and desires of a stifling Argentine society wanting to overflow beyond its borders.

QUINTESSENTIALLY 'POPULAR'

As a model, Sarli won the Miss Argentina pageant in 1955 and became an instant subject of media attention. Strangely enough, during one of these conversations with the press the most beautiful woman in the nation inspired headlines that read: "Miss Capital is *not* a Sophisticated Beauty: A Conversation with Isabel Sarli" (my emphasis) (*Mundo radial* 1955: 4). The beauty queen's upfront confession about her fascination with English literature, describing how she devours the pages of Lord Byron, Milton, Oscar Wilde, and even Shakespeare in their *original* language, did little to reinforce her simplicity. As easily as the reporters dismiss Sarli's erudite hobbies, they emphasize her "flaming" appearance and confident demeanor conducted with the "sobriety of those who know where they are going and what they want" (*Mundo radial*, 1955: 5). Consequently, what most bothers these journalists is Sarli's failure to conform to what is expected of high-society ladies. This initial exposure, well before the launching of her sensationalist film appearances, situates Sarli within the parameters of the popular class, where she will remain for the rest of her career.

As fate would have it, Sarli's inauguration into the spotlight with her 1955 victory gave her the opportunity to meet General Juan Domingo Perón before traveling to the United States to represent the nation at the Miss Universe pageant. This meeting between the bombshell and the president took place shortly before Perón was dethroned by a coup and exiled. Conversely, Perón's message to Sarli inculcates her into the Peronist ideology. She recalls his words with pride: "You are worth twenty Ambassador Paz [Argentine Ambassador to the United States at the time] because you represent the beauty of the Argentine woman and you carry a message of good will to all in the universe" (qtd. in Romano, 1995: 31). Ironically, it would be the "immoral and obscene" content of her films that took the brunt of the attacks by the Triple A, the right-winged faction of Peronism threatening her and Bó in 1974, despite her own personal political allegiance to Perón (Romano, 1995:131).[4]

As the stardom of Sarli developed into its popular incarnation, the more severe became the tone responding to her on-screen performance. Many of her critics were unable to differentiate between her on-screen roles and her offscreen persona. An example of this incapacity of the press to separate between image and person is apparent in another key interview, which appeared in *Satiricón*, a humorous magazine targeting the nation's sociopolitical situation. The title itself, "Isabel Sarli: The Two Main Reasons for her Career," already predicts the mocking path that the note will take. The star's voluptuous physical appearance, referred to as "vulgar" (Gallotti, 1972: 27), assumes a much harsher description than "not sophisticated," more reminiscent of the tone the censors would undertake as they argued that Sarli's body was "too provocative and ostentatious" for upholding the morals of Argentina (Fernández and Nagy, 1999: 144). While there is no denying that Sarli originated from a working-class family background, raised solely by her mother, the press never allows her to shed her past. A combination of her nude scenes, believed to be 'vulgar in taste,' and the characters that she played in her films (surrounded by factory workers and members of the proletariat, men defined by animal instincts) may be responsible for always grounding the star's image within the attributes of a lower social class. On the one hand, Sarli's films reenact and exalt the Peronist politics of the period as they sought to represent truly 'national and popular' portrayals of the people, unleashing the suppressed Peronist desire that was construed as ideologically threatening at the time.

FEMALE, FEMININE, FEMINIST?

Sarli's instant success can in part be attributed to her natural coyness, a trait that would both complement her overall charm and excuse the audacity of her on-screen performances. From the very birth of her career, Sarli presents an offscreen image that is diametrically opposed to her on-screen characters. Her Catholic and strict educational background are often highlighted by both promotional materials and media coverage of the films. She is posited as shy and reserved, "nothing like the image she sells" (Fontán, 1974: 61). This more 'proper' Sarli clashes with the on-screen Sarli, who is unable to escape her own sexualized body. Many of the anecdotes surrounding the films themselves concur with the image of Sarli as a naïve female who accidentally stumbled upon her career choice by performing a scene where she distances herself from the intervening intimacy of the camera. Bó's initial deception in the infamous first nude scene in *El trueno entre las hojas*, which would spark her star phenomena in the first place, exposes both his conscious manipulation of Sarli and her innocent state of unawareness and lack of preparedness. Bó explains:

> I had told Isabel that she would bathe in the river with a skin colored suit . . . She hysterically started crying . . . Of course, I became an asshole. And I insulted and screamed at her, because she wanted the skin colored suit I had promised her. And the suit did not exist, because I had never thought of filming her wearing it. After much arguing we came to a resolution. 'I will film you from afar,' I told her. 'You will appear very small.' Then I put the camera on a mountain, Isabel came up and looked through the lens. But at this moment the camera had a

35 mm lens and she was satisfied and appeared nude with no hesitation. But when she descended I changed it to a 150 mm lens. (qtd. in Martín, 1981: 18)

While focusing on this account all books and references to the duo neglect or overlook other aspects of the film that deconstruct Bó's details or in the least leave behind unanswered questions. For instance, if Sarli was so resistant to the lustful camera, then how did Bó shoot another scene in the same movie that would reveal a medium shot of Sarli's breast? Prior to the contentious unveiling, Sarli's character Flavia tantalizes husband Max during a malaria-induced hallucination by slowly opening her blouse, exposing herself, and fondling her breasts. Although Sarli seems apprehensive in her performance, this scene, albeit not as risky as its more controversial counterpart, would be rather burdensome for a shy Catholic girl raised in stern surroundings. Furthermore, additional analysis of the bathing scene itself reveals inconsistencies with Bó's version of how it was filmed. The highly edited montage presents a series of shots cut together to capture Sarli 'playing in the water.' While Sarli is consciously cautious in this appearance, her movements coincide with those of the water only to unveil the most essential part of her body: her bosom. Her actions are quite clearly staged and the actress seems rather aware of the close presence of the camera's eye. More complexly, there are two radically different angles juxtaposed through montage in this scene. One coincides with Bó's aforementioned proud description; a high angle taken from the top of a mountain with a 35-mm lens capturing a long shot and the deceptive medium shot from the same angle taken with the 150-mm lens. Alternatively, there is another angle, which would have been impossible to shoot from afar given the natural mise-en-scène of the space. This straight-on angle captures Sarli directly leveled with the eye of the camera (See Figure 13.1). There is no doubting the camera's close vicinity to the star. Whether Sarli was misled, as both parties claim, or whether she was complicitous in the execution of the scene remains to be determined.

While playing a bashful role behind the camera's glare, within her films, Sarli's characters solidify a contradictory and complex variant of one of the feminine paradigms quite familiar in Latin American cinema from the classical era: the devourer. Neither a vixen nor a saintly mother, Sarli's on-screen characters will incur their own paradigm, mirroring traits of others found in classical Latin American film, but consisting of Sarli's unique trademark produced in part by the camera shots featuring the star. The Sarli-Bó films highlight two specific camera shots that will work towards constructing the star's on-screen predominance. Sarli's first appearance to the audience in *El trueno entre las hojas* is through a picture gazed at by husband Max, as he desirously awaits her arrival in the Paraguayan jungle. The camera closes in on this image of Flavia before it dissolves to Flavia's in-person arrival. In this frame her midriff is the center of attention as she

Figure 13.1   Isabel Sarli's first frontal nude scene in *El trueno entre las hojas/Thunder among the Leaves* (Armando Bó, 1957).

descends from the boat when finally the camera settles on the characteristic Sarli medium shot. Interestingly enough, the medium shot flatters and functions to better market Sarli's attributes: her breasts. Bó admits: "She [Sarli] knows that a low neck line sells, that her attraction is a medium shot. I always film her with a 50 mm lens so that the shot features her face and bust" (qtd. in Martín, 1981: 81). The medium shot politely invades the star's most cherished features without exposing a detailed focus on her face, thereby not clearly exhibiting her expressions or gestures as much as a close-up would. Some would argue that the medium shot is ideal, for it hides Sarli's 'unrefined' performance. Nonetheless, the fragmentation described in the aforementioned scene during her premiere on celluloid appears more frequently in other films where her most prized body parts are indeed the focus of the gawking camera. For example, . . . *Y el demonio creó al hombre/ . . . And the Devil Created Men* (1960) opens with a shot following its star's lower body, highlighting her legs. Despite the fragmentation and focus on other body parts, the camera prefers to center on Sarli's breasts hidden under low-cut dresses tailor-made by designer Paco Jamandreu, via the consistent use of the medium shot.[5]

Serving only one purpose, the long shot, the other preferred framing technique exploited in the first part of her career, integrates the main character, Sarli, into her surroundings. Since one of the most glaring attributes of these Sarli-Bó productions is the exploration of previously untouched and untraveled territory, the long shot functions to highlight the wild and natural mise-en-scène of the locales.[6] Responsible for promoting tourism to these areas of the country, these films emphasize the different regions of both the nation and other Latin American locations previously uncovered by the camera eye. The long shot melds the star's presence into the background, identifying Sarli the woman as one with nature. . . . *Y el demonio creó al hombre* captures this fusion between star and nature, prevalent in the duo's early productions. Magda, harassed by men everywhere, escapes on a powerboat, which drifts during a furious storm to Uruguay's Isla de lobos, an island inhabited by hundreds of sea wolves as the name would indicate. Unable to flee her fate as an object of desire, Magda is sought after by the three brothers that dwell on the island. Juxtaposed to the sea wolves, which are violently crushed and killed by the men, Magda becomes but one of the innocent prey. Her tightly fitted black dress and black hair are mistaken for yet another sea wolf on the beach, unleashing the male instinct to possess her. As a continuation of the landscape and an integral part of the land, Sarli's character is always the subject of a possible violation, rape, or struggle that will foreground men who uncontrollably need to possess her and disrupt nature from its surroundings.

As Sarli's stardom grew, so did her detachment from nature. The once accomplished harmony between the key feminine figure and her backdrop began to fade. The shift is clear in later films as Sarli's body attains a central role; the staging and her attire set her apart from the natural world. The ostentatious urban performer of *Furia infernal/Hell Fury* (1972) clearly clashes with the ranch setting where she is taken unwillingly. The extravagant red formfitting dresses that she wears do not coincide with the natural serene landscape of snow-topped mountains and open green spaces of the Patagonia region. This presentation of the movie star contrasts with earlier depictions such as *India/Indian Girl* (1959), whose dress, made from bird's feathers, recycles the natural ambience of the landscape. This marked distinction as a 'star' and shift is further visible in Sarli's onstage performance.

Critics within Argentina have condemned the pinup's lack of talent as an actress. On the other hand, Sarli's performance coincides with the text's constant use of a melodramatic style where gestures reflect emotions, which in turn echo society's moral categories (Dyer, 1981: 137). All of the Sarli-Bó films are framed within moral and social constructions that require additional study.[7] However, in line with the melodramatic plots is Sarli's performance, consisting of signature gestures or body language, which further demonstrates the aforementioned shift towards accentuating the central star. Her performance will consequently mark another shift from submissive victim of the male gaze to more active and desiring subject-object who likewise is fully conscious of her sexuality. Witnessed as early as *La tentación desnuda/Naked Temptation* (1966), Sarli's characters are no longer casualties of circumstance, encumbered by their bodies.[8] The style gesture of constantly looking down, or glancing away coyly before the threatening gaze of the male actor or camera, marks early films, particularly those appearing before the landmark production of *La tentación desnuda.* This expression characterizes Sarli as a passive object, shy about her attributes as a woman unable to exploit these. In many instances her inability to look directly at her onstage partner conveys a sense of shame and dishonor caused by her sexuality, what will quickly be interpreted as naïve. With each ensuing film Sarli surpasses her shame and begins to take control of her sexuality, even though in some cases this sexuality is revealed as exuberant or excessive, beyond the norm. In the latter films, however, this gesture of glancing away disappears, to be replaced by the fully closed eyes of a female enjoying her sexuality. The pleasure of sexual stimulation replaces the shameful look of the early films. This shift identified in Sarli's performance coincides with her growing success internationally and the adaptation of more daring and provocative subject matters in her films.

With the premiere of each new melodramatic story, innocent themes about unrequited love in *Sabaleros/Fishermen* (1958) developed more radical tangents which included controversial issues such as adultery (. . . *Y el demonio creó al hombre*), prostitution (*Intimidades de una cualquiera/Intimacies of a Prostitute,* 1973), lesbianism (*Fuego/Fire,* 1969), violent rape (*Carne/Meat,* 1968), bestiality and drugs (*Fiebre/Fever,* 1970). Each new film exceeded previous works by stressing bold subject matter and shocking audience expectations. Coverage of topics that were challenging society's traditional views of sexuality coincided with increased international acclaim.

Most of Sarli's roles would seem to rather contradict or disallow any possible interpretation as feminist. She often plays a woman who is helpless because of her sensual body, constantly falling victim to men's desires. As a result, she is harassed, kidnapped, or raped (. . . *Y el demonio creó al hombre, La leona/The Lioness* [1964], *Una mariposa en la noche/A Butterfly in the Night* [1975], *Los días calientes/The Hot Days* [1965], *La señora del intendente/The Mayor's Wife* [1966], *La mujer del zapatero/ The Shoe Mender's Wife* [1964]). The other role she commonly interprets is as an unsatiated woman who in the end will be punished for satisfying her needs. In *Insaciable/Insatiable* (1976), she must die; in *Fuego,* she commits suicide; in *Fiebre,* she can never act on her love for the horse; in *Lujuria tropical/Tropical Lust* (1962), she does not achieve happiness with any of her lovers. Uncannily, in only three of the thirty movies Sarli stars in, she has control of her own destiny and use of her body. In *Furia infernal* she punishes her kidnapper by seducing his two sons, and in *Los días calientes* she avenges her brother's death by encouraging exploited workers to overthrow the tyrant boss who is also her brother's killer. The third film where Sarli undertakes an active role is *La dama regresa/The Lady Returns* (Jorge Polaco, 1995), a movie made sixteen years after her last film produced with Bó, and one of three not directed by Bó. She resurfaces in this semibiographical picture that parallels Sarli's own personal experiences. This film tells of an older woman who returns to her hometown, where she was ostracized and exiled by the moralists for her love of a man. Her appearance exposes the highly hypocritical society that judged her while engaged in its own debacle. While we cannot claim that Sarli's films would adhere to a feminist agenda, evidence shows that Sarli's increasingly aggressive roles and performance mark a significant change in her career, one coinciding with her increased international fame and perhaps international standards of women's roles.

This would contradict Rodolfo Kuhn's reading of Sarli as a completely passive object (1984: 17). Nonetheless, he does not deny her "true personality as a woman-object Latina that gives her a unique edge" (Kuhn, 1984: 17). In fact, this unique edge of her performance becomes so excessively involved in her own pleasure where in instances Sarli's onscreen persona adopts a comical even parodic consequence. In both *Fuego* and *Fiebre*, the two most popular, lucrative, and international films that Sarli made, the Latina stereotype is reinforced to a degree that requires additional consideration.[9] As a nymphomaniac in *Fuego*, Sarli's character, Laura, seduces different men in order to satiate her desire. Whenever Laura is on fire, the non-diegetic music "Fire," written and performed by Luis Alberto del Paraná and his trio los Paraguayos, plays in the background as the character seeks an accomplice that would, 'put out her fire.' During a comical scene in the film, Laura is dressed in a fur coat covering her nearly nude body as she approaches her potential mates, opens her coat, and the music signaling her desire starts, as she begins to fondle her breasts (See Figure 13.2). Some fall victim to her actions, while others look at her in surprise and one of her chosen prey even gestures to her insanity. Similarly, in

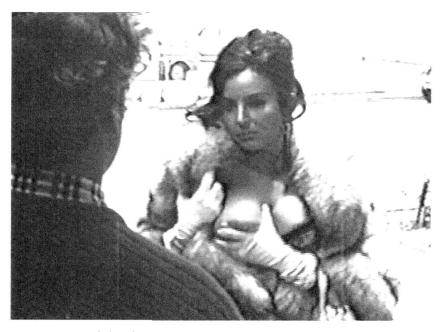

Figure 13.2   Isabel Sarli in *Fuego/Fire* (Armando Bó, 1969).

Fiebre, Sarli's character, Sandra, is obsessed with a horse that she believes to be a reincarnation of José María, her lover who passed away. During the scene when the horse, Fever, penetrates a mare for the first time, Sandra watches anxiously as she celebrates Fever's initiation to love. The camera cuts to Sandra's anticipating face and her extravagant action of suckling her pinkie finger while the horse is engaged in the sexual act. Both these scenes play on the ardent Latina stereotype; the excessive nature of Sarli's performance makes the spectator look twice and laugh.

"HE FORMED A WOMAN OUT OF THE RIB" GENESIS 2:22

To raise the question of Sarli's adeptness as an actress, perhaps the most critiqued aspect of these productions, one must contextualize the films within their methods of filmmaking. Argentine director Rodolfo Kuhn equates her with director Bó's style, what he calls "naive pornography," a special brand of the sexploitation genre *a lo* Argentinean (1984 :12). Sarli and Bó have emphasized the strict guidance of Bó, the creator and director of the star. Testimonies point to Bó's need to steer his star's every move.

> When Isabel started filming, she didn't know anything about neither A, nor B, nor C. She didn't want to know anything. So much so that at the beginning, when we were taking a shot, the camera was on, and she would start walking when all of a sudden she would turn around and ask me: 'Is this right?' (qtd. in Martín, 1981: 16)

Sarli's inexperience during the shooting of her first feature is understandable, since unlike Bó, she was a model and not an actress. To claim that Sarli is a bad actress decontextualizes her from the films she made since the particular way that Bó directed his actors would impact both their credibility and performance in the films' final product. Bó gives evidence to his own approach:

> When I direct my actors I do not let them rehearse, Isabel never rehearsed any scene. I don't want my actors to rehearse. They need to know what they have to say, yes; also they need to know the right movements. But interpretatively, no, because as an actor I would be asked to rehearse and the emotion would be gone in the first take. In the first take one lives the character intensely, but when one is asked to act eight or ten takes the emotion wears out. On the other hand, I do not repeat takes. I prefer changing the angle and continuing to cover the side of an actor that I do not like. (qtd. in Martín, 1981: 59)

Sarli's performance in fact reflects Bó's style of filmmaking more than her abilities in front of the camera. Since none of the actors in the films ever rehearsed, Sarli's fluidity in front of the camera remains relevant to Bó's methods of capturing his star on film. What these stories most disclose is the primary paradox in Sarli's own career: despite her stardom, reports such as these ironically maintain Sarli in the shadows of her director, Bó. Accordingly, media and critical portrayals of the team insist on Bó as discoverer and constructor of Sarli, the archetypal victim that has simply followed the only road paved by her voluptuous body. Under the strict protection of her associate, creator, and Pygmalion, the erotic yet naive image of *la Coca*, her nickname still fondly remembered by fans today, Sarli plays no part in plotting or defining her own career path. Even she herself emphasized in a press article Bó's hand in creating her: "He was smart to have discovered me and professionally I am very grateful to him for it" (qtd. in Balbuena, 1968: 8). Néstor Romano dedicates her biography to Bó for "discovering" the star (Romano, 1995: 7). This tale of discovery takes the onus off Sarli and places it directly on the active male figure, in this case her director in control of her career. This characterization of the star continues to haunt her image as Sarli is hailed as "a local recreation and the sensuality perversely infantile, shaping a feminine naïveté that needs rescuing from barbarous claws by a correct moral and virile figure" (lavaca.org, 2003). Unlike blonde-haired Libertad Leblanc, the "white (Argentine) goddess" who follows Sarli's footsteps, appearing nude in the 1962 *La flor de Irupé/ Love Hunger* (Alberto Dubois), Sarli's image is posited as a feeble female needing guidance from her 'macho' counterpart. In a complicit manner, publicity, promotion, and film criticism deny her any agency in the construction of her own career. Whereas Leblanc, likened to European and U.S. sexploitation actresses, portrays a figure that conscientiously sells her own image as a Sarli alter ego, Sarli herself, the 'other' and quite visibly Latin American performer on the contrary was always a product of and belonged solely to her man, director and creator.

Despite the roles she developed in these melodramatic pictures depicting the poor helpless female victim, Sarli is not as much a victim of circumstance or a creation of Bó as the media and her oeuvre may suggest. Evidence shows that she did have a key role in managing her own career, one envisioned by her well before her association with Bó. To revisit the 1955 interview during her crowning of Miss Argentina, Sarli herself draws attention to her interest in film: "She told us that she really liked film because it would be an extension of her modeling profession and that logically she would enjoy shooting a film, of course she would begin from the bottom, that is to carry out her cinematographic career by taking small roles" (*Mundo radial*, 1955: 5). Even before Bó 'discovered' Sarli she had a contract with Argentina Sono Film (Fernández and Nagy, 1999:129), the closest Argentine equivalent to MGM and one of the most important studios in the country in the age of classical Argentine cinema. This contract did not fully come to fruition because of previous Miss Argentina (1954) Ivana Kislinger's failure to draw audiences to her film premiere. Winning a beauty pageant did not necessarily guarantee instant success as in the case of Kislinger; thus Argentina Sono Film was reluctant to take risks with a newcomer like Sarli. Likewise, Bó himself had similar concerns when first meeting Sarli. He later admits: "Considering that from the beginning she didn't strike me as special. She didn't have any status, she didn't even want to be an actress" (Martín, 1981: 13). If it were not for his Paraguayan producer, Nicolas Bó (unrelated to Armando), who pressured Bó to choose Sarli for the role, perhaps this paper would have no reason for its existence. The explosion and success of the Sarli-Bó films may have never taken place. However, it does seem probable that Sarli would have pursued her dream of becoming an actress since she already was determined in 1955 to do so.

After her bombastic start in *El trueno entre las hojas*, Sarli would acquire a fundamental economic role with regards to her films. In this first film she earned 10 percent of the profits, a figure that would increase with *Sabaleros*, the second film, to 20 percent, and by the third film *India* she was already making 50 percent of the earnings, a figure that would characterize the rest of her cinematic association with Bó (Fernández and Nagy, 1999: 144). As Sarli's stardom was growing, so was her capital. She was tacitly making history not only for her roles in front of the camera but also for her role behind it. Moreover, it was unheard of that an actor, much less an actress, would 'own' his or her films in Argentina or, for that matter, anywhere else in the world. This idea had certainly not been fashionable since the silent period.[10] Bó was encouraging Sarli to maintain control of her trademark films. He advises: "All actors should be associates of their own films because later when tragedy arrives, when successes end, actors at least are owners of something" (qtd. in Fernández and Nagy, 1999: 144). Sarli's 50 percent ownership would no longer limit her to the role of pinup in front of the camera. This partnership agreement, although a verbal contract at first, was later drawn up in writing when Columbia Pictures demanded it as such (Kuhn, 1984: 40). In addition, Sarli's ability to speak English well enough to play a white goddess in the jungles of Africa, in Dirk de Villiers's 1973 production of *The Virgin Goddess*, gave her the added edge she needed to pursue a more active role behind the scenes. Many, including Bó, argue that a large part of the success of SIFA (Bó's production company) had to do with the commercial talent of Sarli (Fernández and Nagy, 1999: 140; Fontán, 1974: 62; Kuhn, 1984: 40). She dedicated herself to negotiating contracts with outside distribution companies, communicated with representatives abroad, and administered the financial side of the productions (Kuhn, 1984: 40). In an early interview, Sarli confirms that she has an interest in the production and creative aspects of filmmaking. She asserts: "The day that I can no longer work as an actress I will be quite happy and content. It doesn't matter to me whether I am in front of the camera or behind it. I guess I could produce. And I could even direct. Armando makes fun of me but sometimes I suggest camera angles. I would love to direct" (qtd. in Gallotti, 1972: 30). Perhaps Bó's early death in 1981 confirmed

Sarli's reliance on her director. While it is clear that his death caused Sarli's grief and consequent early retreat from public life to only resurface sixteen years later in *La dama regresa*, her enterprising role in backstage production contradicts the constructed image of Sarli as a duped female consenting unknowingly to a rape by the camera lens in *El trueno entre las hojas*. Not just the pretty made-up smile on the celluloid screen, Sarli had agency, at least when it came to the direction her career would take.

Sex symbols like Sarli often end on tragic terms, retreating from the public eye to become a long forgotten memory only present in the imagination of some lonely fan. At the height of popularity, these sexual objects usually garner very little respect, and once their power to bewitch no longer entrances millions of spectators the social model reappears yet again in a film that flops. Unfortunately, this trite conclusion is how Sarli's story ends. Sixteen years after her last Sarli-Bó production she reappears in *La dama regresa*. Starring Sarli, this film mimics the roles played by the star at the climax of her career, lastly becoming a caricature of the original star image. Polaco does give Sarli a chance to finally vindicate herself by exposing the pharisaic society that both adored and ostracized her at the same time. Even more tragic in the grand scheme would be a portrait of Sarli that perfectly conformed to class and gender stereotypes generally associated with the star. Her stardom instead is inscribed in problematic myths, as this chapter has attempted to show. Even today she continues to present challenges to what is expected of a sex symbol. Unlike her peers, Sarli has not succumbed to plastic surgeries or heavy aerobics workouts to maintain a picture-perfect figure and appearance. At present, her example could pose a challenge to society's taboos. The verdict is still out.

NOTES

1. All quotes from Martín's (1981) book are direct quotes from Bó. The book is a compilation of interviews conducted with the director between July 1980 and January 1981. I translate all quotes from Spanish language material throughout the chapter unless otherwise noted.
2. Also see the vast work of Mexican cultural critic Carlos Monsiváis on film stars, especially the collection of essays *Mexican Postcards* (1997).
3. As part of Hollywood's Spanish-language experiment, Gardel starred in eight Paramount Picture productions from 1931 until his death in 1935.
4. The Association of Argentine Actors received a letter in the spring of 1974 from the Triple A, the extreme right faction of the Peronist group called the Anti-Communist Argentine Alliance, stating the following: "Because of their ominous influence over the Argentine people and their immoral, obscene, dissolvent and pro-Marxist action, which attacks the Western and Christian base of our society," eleven of the Actors Association members (the list included both Bó and Sarli) were threatened with death "wherever they are found, continuing the necessary purification" of the nation. Despite this intimidation the Sarli-Bó team did not experience the common fate of most artists: exile, silence, or disappearance, but censorship did take its toll on the pair.

5. Paco Jamandreu would design most of Sarli's costumes for her films. He was also the personal designer of Eva Perón (Dujovne Ortiz, 1996: 83).

6. Within Argentina the Sarli-Bó productions explored 'untouched' territories such as the Misiones jungles, Iguazú Falls, Delta del Paraná, General Madariaga, Rio Negro, Neuquén, San Martín de los Andes, San Carlos de Bariloche, Esquel, Junín de los Andes, and Tierra del Fuego. The pair also filmed in other countries such as Uruguay, Paraguay, Venezuela, Mexico, Panama, Brazil, France, and the United States.

7. From the beginning, after working with one of celebrated author Augusto Roa Basto's short stories, 'The Minister's Daughter,' in *El trueno entre las hojas*, the Sarli-Bó productions mostly feature plots about social injustices. Framed within melodramatic structures popular in classical Argentine cinema and *radionovelas*, these story lines underlie the struggles of peasants, indigenous groups, or the working class.

8. As Fernández and Nagy would argue, this shift marks the beginning of the 'Bó myth' whereby Sarli and Bó's roles are inverted. Bó replaces Sarli in her identification with nature and the primitive, while Sarli espouses the role of the active temptress.

9. Until the decade of the 1990s, *Fuego* and *Fiebre* were the two Argentine films screened in more countries than any other film. It is prudent to keep in mind that these movies did not reach world audiences through film festival circuits but rather because of distribution tactics and public demand (Fernández and Nagy, 1999: 237).

10. Since the silent period, once the studio system was well in place, ownership of films by actors had been virtually unheard of. Recently, there are cases in independent productions where actors own a small portion of the film profits, nowhere near the 50 percent that Sarli owned. The textbook case would go far into the silent period with the creation of United Artists. Charlie Chaplin, Mary Pickford, and Douglas Fairbanks Jr. maintained rights to their films. A close look at a similar case to the Sarli-Bó films would prove the progressive nature of Sarli's ownership.

14 Sharksploitation

René Cardona Jr.'s Submarine Gaze

Misha MacLaird

The directorial career of René Cardona Jr. (1939–2003) spanned five decades and almost every genre from horror to comedy to melodrama, including several of the biggest box-office successes in Mexico's film history.[1] While clearly influenced by his father's directorial work in horror and *lucha libre* cinema, Cardona Jr.'s obsession with the ocean and his participation in the first Mexican film to use an underwater camera (*Un mundo nuevo/The New World*, directed by René Cardona Sr., 1956) informs a recurring diptych in his films of the 1960s and 1970s: firstly, the seductive female figure, swimming or emerging from the sea, nude or in bikini; and secondly, the menacing image of the shark, as it prowls the ocean floor for prey. In a number of his films, skin-flick titillation combines with underwater danger to produce differing narrative dynamics through a variety of genres with similar settings, such as espionage-action (*S.O.S. conspiración bikini*, 1966; *Peligro . . . mujeres en acción!/Danger Girls*, 1967), natural-disaster survival dramas (*Ciclón/Cyclone/Terror Storm*, 1978), erotic thrillers (*Tintorera!/Tiger Shark*, 1977), and sci-fi horror (*El triángulo diabólico de las Bermudas/The Bermuda Triangle/The Devil's Triangle of Bermuda,* 1978). In this chapter, I will examine how the traditional vampire/monster trope of the dangers of 'overexposed flesh' is reframed by Cardona's underwater gaze and recycled to meet the genre needs of his stories.[2] In Cardona's movies, female secret agents and sexually liberated *gringas*, often in bikinis, pose a threat to a patriarchal paradigm. What changes with each genre is the relative threat of the feminine figure as juxtaposed with the more bestial predators, showing her as victim or bait, or active initiator of the potential harm.

The period discussed here marks the downfall of Mexico's Golden Age production infrastructure, with the closing of several major studios in the late 1950s and continued decrease in production into the early 1960s. In the 1970s, as Catholic organizations concerned with film content lost some political strength, 'moral' censorship became less prevalent (Ugalde, 2003; Zermeño, 1997: 97), and the transition from Echeverría's state subvention to a primarily commercial industry led to a boom in the sexy *fichera* genre.[3] Alongside Gregorio Wallerstein, Raúl de Anda, and Miguel Zacarías (in-law to the Cardonas), the Cardona family was among the few to continue making films in the era of crisis, pushing forward prolifically with popular genres of the period (De la Vega, 1995: 91). The films discussed in this chapter span fifteen years, a time when the treatment of gender, connected to the filmmaker's aspirations to find an international audience, historically coincides with the changing image and role of women during this era. The earlier films mimic the beginnings of an increased circulation of representations of sexually audacious women in international action cinema. In Mexico, women's liberation and a feminist filmmaking movement sought more authentic depictions of female empowerment at the same time that commercial cinema mass-produced the sexualized *fichera* icon. Consequently, by the late 1970s, as images of the female body lost their exploitative value, Cardona's focus shifted from racy visuals to shocking stories. *Tintorera!*, discussed following, has much in common with other horror from this era, in which women "combine the functions of suffering victim and avenging hero" (Clover, 1992: 17). However, the use of bikinis and nudity to embrace a more liberalized sexuality is eventually revised as another perception of the female body and sexual transgression takes shape. In contrast to the politically charged auteur cinema of this period (by directors such as Felipe Cazals, Arturo Ripstein, and Luis Alcoriza), Cardona's shark films avoid direct political critique and instead use commercial genres to delve into the psychology of human behavior in extreme scenarios. The result is a commentary on social taboos, including female sexuality, cloaked in dramatic suspense and the spectacle of shark attacks.

THE PRODIGAL SON

René Cardona Sr. left his native Cuba at age eighteen to begin a career in Hollywood working on early Spanish sound productions; here he met his future brother-in-law, producer Miguel Zacarías Nogaim (Pelayo, 1993; *El sur*, 2003). The pair later became two of the most successful filmmakers in Mexico's post–Golden Age era. Cardona Jr. grew up assisting his father and uncle with productions, occasionally acting, while observing the changes in the industry. His interest in the technical side of production coalesced with his passion for scuba diving during the making of *Un mundo nuevo*, when he worked with his father to build what he called a *blimp submarino* (underwater blimp), a capsule that would allow the crew to film the first underwater shots in Mexico (Pelayo, 1993).

Cardona's drive to commercially exploit stories into cinematic forms (turning best sellers into screenplays) did not begin as such. His two earliest films, *Los desvergonzados/The Insolent Ones* (1963) and *Un ángel de mal genio/A Bad-Tempered Angel* (1964), were never distributed; the former filmed entirely in point of view (with no shots of the protagonist) and the latter telling the story from the perspective of a newborn baby. During these years, Cardona had difficulty finding work because he was denied access into Mexico's notoriously closed-shop film union (Pelayo, 1993). He directed and coproduced films throughout South America, including the soft-porn film *Vanessa* (1970), which he shot in Ecuador under a pseudonym, hoping to generate "the aura of a European art film" in order to reach international audiences (Alemán, 2004: 106).

In the 1970s, Cardona shot several adventure films in color (*Robinson Crusoe*, 1970; *Viaje fantástico en globo/Fantastic Balloon Voyage*, 1974), while also writing and producing his father's films *La isla de los hombres solos/The Island of Lost Souls* (1974) and *Supervivientes de los Andes/Survive* (1976), adapted from Charles Blair Jr.'s book about the 1972 Uruguayan plane crash. Though some of these include shark footage, *Tintorera!* would be Cardona's personal fusion of passions, aided by collaboration with cinematographer/shark trainer/marine ecologist Ramón Bravo (often referred to as "the Mexican Jacques Cousteau").[4] After exhausting the exploitability of sharks, his career, into the 1980s, continued with a hodgepodge of commercial themes, including action films, dramas, biographies, and sex comedies, until the 1991 release of the first episode of the *La risa en vacaciones/Laughter on Holidays* series. A nonlinear collection of vignettes using comic actors to carry out unscripted humorous antics (imitating the style of *Candid Camera*), the *La risa* films stunned critics and Cardona himself by breaking box-office records with their debased humor, despite simple production standards (Pelayo, 1993).[5] The high return on investment for these low-budget films would allow Cardona the opportunity to make seven more before his death in 2003.

Reflecting on his career in 1993, Cardona regarded himself as a forerunner in commercial cinema, pointing out that *Tintorera!* used live sharks when *Jaws* was only using a mechanical replica (Pelayo, 1993). In the same interview he explains that while in collaboration with a U.S. production company he suggested making a musical biopic about Juan Perón. To the same producers, he had described the "baby" idea behind *Un ángel de mal genio*. After a disagreement, which broke ties with such company, the producers would later make *Evita* and *Look Who's Talking*, crediting him with neither idea (Pelayo, 1993).

THE PROFILMIC OCEAN

Syder and Tierney point out that the insertion of wrestling footage into Mexican *lucha libre* films makes the films "befitting of psychotronic reading protocols" (2005: 51). Following Sconce (1995), they argue that the pleasure in these films lies in the spectator's ironic reading of the film's reality, in which the lesser production value allows one to recognize the set or location as an extradiegetic reality in which the filmmaker struggled to create a cinematic illusion. "Given [the] propensity of psychotronic fans to move between the fictional and the non-fictional, the diegetic and the profilmic, it is perhaps not surprising that mexploitation films have been embraced [by U.S. viewers]" (Syder and Tierney, 2005: 51). In the case of Cardona's films, the submarine fauna functions as a profilmic, extradiegetic reality, which breaks the suture with the dramatic story. For Cardona, this underwater element allowed him to make "fantastic movies" by replacing high-cost adventure-movie sets with the marvels of the sea, an environment in which he and his family of fishermen felt at home (Pelayo, 1993). The visual difference in realities is most clear in *Peligro . . . mujeres en acción!*, in which the filmed sea life appears to be inserted stock footage, poorly integrated with the footage of actors. In the later films with Bravo, director and submarine photographer worked together to develop scenes with enough continuity to be verisimilar.[6] And still the performances of sex-symbol commercial actors such as Andrés García and Hugo Stiglitz in swimwear and the awkwardly dubbed audio contrasts sharply with the sublime serenity of the underwater sequences. As I will discuss following, the films offer both vertical and horizontal divisions between realities: a vertical contrast between the above- and below-the-surface worlds, differentiated by the underwater camera; and a horizontal contrast between the concurrent underwater shots of swimming actors (linked to the diegesis of the above-the-surface drama) and shark footage (linked to the profilmic reality).

The commercially exploitable elements sought by Cardona often coincide with the film's point of entry for psychotronic viewing, as seen in the shark footage and the aforementioned pranks in *La risa en vacaciones*. Yet another technical element that triggered the destabilization of realities in his films was the multiple language tracks. In the 1970s, the drive to reach international audiences pushed Cardona to produce films in multiple languages, most often English. At the same time, as he secured funds from foreign investors (*Tintorera!* was coproduced with Britain, *El triángulo diabólico de las Bermudas* with Italy, *Ciclón* with the United States), he recruited casts of internationally recognized actors, which resulted in a cacophony of performances, sometimes with the actor's real voice, sometimes with a heavily inflected second language, and sometimes dubbed over by another actor. Cardona says of these films that " . . . [t]hey become a little hybrid; they are not real in some ways . . ." (Pelayo, 1993). For example *El triángulo diabólico* was dubbed into English, Spanish, French, and Italian, and was a box-office hit in all markets. The actors were asked to repeat their lines in the various languages in order to synchronize their facial movements with the dubbing. In the English version, John Huston's actual voice clashes with the dubbed voices of García and Stiglitz, calling attention to both the acting and the audio track.[7]

THE BIKINI CONSPIRACY

In 1966, Cardona made *S.O.S conspiración bikini* and *Peligro . . . mujeres en acción!*, two near-identical Ecuadorian coproductions. Shot a few years after the release of *Dr. No* (1962), both casts included Mexican actor Julio Alemán as Alex Dinamo, a James Bond-like agent who, with the help of several bikini-clad, automatic-weapon-toting women, fights against the evildoings of *S.O.S.*, a female-led organization seeking to wreak havoc in Ecuador by taking over its oil refineries. Several female characters in the films are similar to their contemporary post-noir *femmes fatales*: more explicitly sexual and more explicitly dangerous. But if virility and sexual freedom are central in the Bond series and at constant risk through inter-action with an evil seductress or a fellow agent, in Cardona's films these female roles exponentiate and upstage the male hero's centrality, much like in Alfonso Corona Blake's *Santo contra las mujeres vampiro/Santo Versus the Vampire Women* (1962). [8]

A part of *Peligro . . . mujeres en acción!*, shot in costal Ecuador, is a useful point of departure for understanding how Cardona inserts his scuba obsession into action-genre conventions. The scene begins with special agent Barbara (Bárbara Angely) fleeing from *S.O.S* agents who follow her car in a small plane. The pursuit takes her from the road to the beach and into the ocean, where two male agents in a small underwater vehicle fur-ther chase her. In the ocean, Barbara faces the additional danger of various underwater predators, such as sharks, stingrays, and octopuses. During the plane–car chase, Barbara parks on the beach and jumps out of her convert-ible, wearing just a short sundress. She strips down to a bikini and pulls an oxygen tank out of her trunk, ducking behind her car as the plane passes at close range (a visual homage to *North by Northwest*), then drags the tank to the water. Barbara runs back to the trunk for the rest of her equip-ment, eventually putting on a diving mask and fins with the tank harness over her bathing suit. Gunfire just misses her as she dives into the surf. In parallel sequences, the *S.O.S.* agents in a boat are radioed to follow her and, dressed in full scuba gear and wet suits, get into a minisubmarine. The underwater shots that follow cut between Barbara, the agents pursuing her, and the threatening marine life. A speedboat is then added to the mix, showing Alex Dinamo and Agent Maura coming to the rescue.

It is apparent from the montage that the underwater footage comes from different sources. Angely does not actually swim with the shark, and the images of marine life, not threatening in themselves, appear to be stock footage taken from an oceanographic documentary. But the creatures are indeed mysterious in their otherness and natural predatory or self-defense instincts. In this chase scene, the musical track is a slow, suspenseful jazz that suggests a pleasurable level of excitement with emphatic organ chords to provoke tension. Disruptive, high-pitched sound effects are matched to the documentary clips, adding a science-fiction tone, as the odd creatures pulsate in their niches.

Barbara's bikini, worn under her clothes as preparedness for exactly such a situation as an underwater escape, also gives her swimming body a 'natu-ralness' that contrasts with the agents who follow her in the black military wet suits. The swimming female figure is likened to that of the swimming sea life, particularly the shark, simultaneously graceful and seductive, drawing the spectator's gaze. The various sequences of this long scene create a pattern of movement-stasis between the calm Barbara with her fish friends and the pursuing phalli (the speedboat, the male divers, and the submarine capsule), shifting her alliances to the former. Barbara's feminine gentleness lets her hide beneath a reef within striking distance of a number of threatening creatures without being attacked; and it is she who unexpectedly emerges to attack, blowing up the submarine and killing the *S.O.S.* agents.

This scene marks a starting point for Cardona's game of exploiting this combination of sexuality and violence. Here the shark and other marine creatures in one sense are just another action leitmotif, alongside guns and explosives. But like the female figure, they are presented as potential threats that move below the surface of social and cinematic expectations, with both the enigma of otherness and a danger in the visual attraction of their movements. As this chase scene ends, a team of *S.O.S.* commandos (this time mostly male) storms the beach with machine guns, mortally wounding Barbara. Appropriate for its time period, Barbara's treacherous femininity is contained by male force, but not without a generous display of her body.

TINTORERA!: ROMANCING THE SHARK

In an early sequence of *Tintorera!*, the carcass of a hammerhead shark, half eaten by an aggressive tiger shark (*una tintorera*), bleeds at the bottom of a small skiff. One character addresses the local shark fisherman to express his concerns, while menacing music builds and a tiger shark swims under the boat. "Killing these creatures makes me sad, even though they are sharks." The music fades. "I prefer to soak up the sun watching the 'tiger sharks' on the beach in bikinis." The two friends laugh and the sequence ends abruptly with a cut to a binocular view of bikinied female torsos walking on the beach as jazzy, upbeat music begins.

Online commentaries on this erotic thriller—based on a novel by Bravo—tend to arrive at the same conclusion, that it is soft-core pornography loosely disguised (or marketed) as a shark movie.[9] Contemporary viewers, interested in *Jaws*-like action and suspense, are disappointed by the slow pace and the emphasis on sexual relations rather that blood and fear. In a two-hour film, the anticipated shark-attack scenes only materialize a handful of times. These scenes prove doubly disappointing to viewers who expect a monstrous mechanical shark large enough to destroy a fishing vessel but are given an underwater montage: shots of real average-sized tiger sharks swimming and lurking to shots of the same sharks attacking a human dummy to shots of the same swimming away with bloodied clothing clenched in its jaws. The roughly 100 minutes of footage in between is a rather flat narrative about the sexual adventures of both vacationers and locals in a small Caribbean resort town.

Tintorera! begins by introducing three separate character plots that will come together later in the film. The opening scenes introduce Esteban/ Steven (Stiglitz), a tightly wound Mexican businessman close to a nervous breakdown who takes a few months off to live on a yacht in Isla Mujeres; Miguel (García), the playboy-in-residence who spends his free time scuba diving and shark hunting; and two sexually uninhibited young *gringa* sisters, Cynthia and Kelly, who hitchhike into town with a pair of truck drivers and have sex with these *native* chauffeurs atop a truck bed filled with oranges. The film develops the unlikely friendship between Esteban and Miguel, their competitions to pick up women at bars, their interest in shark hunting, and their sexual relations with the sisters. The two men eventually meet Gabriella (Susan George), and their contest to win her love leads to an amorous triangle, with the three living together on the yacht. When a shark kills Miguel, the love affair dissolves and the traumatized Gabriella leaves Esteban to return to her country. Near the end of the film, Esteban finds solace at a party and ends up in another romantic romp with the two sisters. During an underwater orgy, the same tiger shark that killed Miguel kills Cynthia. An ambiguous ending shows Esteban going out late at night to hunt down the tiger shark. He is attacked as he spears the creature, and both shark and diving flashlight sink to the ocean floor, with no view of the diver.

Criticism of *Tintorera!* centers on the lack of cohesion between shark attacks and the story line, the latter a languid melodrama about the transcendence of sexual norms. Yet although the hybrid genre undoubtedly lacks the pacing to maintain the suspense of a horror film, there is a clear thematic connection between the sexual and marine stories. Three main characters' motivations, based on acts of sexual taboo, are directly connected to sharks, both as analogies of savage behavior and punishment for said deviance—a typical horror-film characteristic. Esteban's first conquest, Patricia (Fiona Lewis), is a married woman on vacation alone and seeking uncomplicated sexual encounters. Esteban meets Patricia immediately following his comment about "the tiger sharks on the beach in bikinis," and they begin an affair that lasts a few days, ending with Patricia fleeing when Esteban confesses that he *might* be falling in love with her. She feigns rage at his word choice, but uses it as an excuse to seek a less complicated relationship. As Patricia exits in a fury, the scene cuts to footage of a shark devouring a small fish; the following sequence begins with Patricia on the beach flirting with Miguel. The shark footage inserts a flag of danger, that Patricia's unexpected change of temperament indicates an animalistic quality and a threat to Esteban's blissful love fantasy. We learn more about Patricia when she later tells Miguel that she is married and does not want to fall in love. Patricia's threat, blatantly equated with the shark, is to marriage and male-centered family units, encompassed in her betrayal of her husband and of Esteban, as well as in her fling with Miguel. Waking from a passionate night with Miguel, she walks naked into the ocean. Just seconds into her swim, Patricia is devoured by a tiger shark, leaving behind no trace of blood or clothing.

The subsequent major story is of Esteban and Miguel, who bond over their mutual interest in Patricia. Miguel comments that "she didn't make love with me. She made love with you. I mean, thinking about you," a foreshadowing of the women that the two men will share throughout the film and their eventual unspoken erotic attraction to each other. They bond over their pursuit of single women and an interest in speargun shark hunting, both being a display of aggressive masculine behavior and the latter a violence that begins their feud with Mother Nature. Esteban and Miguel move into the realm of the taboo with the two sisters, who trade off having sex with each of the men while sharks swim by under the yacht. After further showing their affinity for risky behavior in the shark-hunting scenes, they begin the affair with Gabriella. At the emotional apex of this nontraditional "marriage" (explicitly discussed as counter to traditional Mexican *machismo*), a dialogue between Miguel and Esteban reveals that they are experiencing something that they fear, something beyond hedonistic pleasure or heterosexual love. A traditionally paced dialogue about their relationship with Gabriella intensifies verbally and visually as Esteban reveals to Miguel that he likes "what Gabriella does when she is with you" and "[this] frightens me." The camera moves into extreme close-ups of each actor's face and accelerates the pace of the montage, ending with a rapid fire of shot/reverse shots that highlight at once the enamored gaze and the deep fear of both men. This development is truncated by Miguel's death in the following shark-hunting sequence.

The last of the three plots centers on Cynthia and Kelly, beginning with their promiscuous behavior with the truck drivers, followed by their "swapping" with Miguel and Esteban, their move to the local drug orgy scene, and finally Cynthia's death in the bloody skinny-dipping party. The conclusion of these three character developments with shark attacks adds a tension based on the spectator's inability to pinpoint the menacing element. In a film in which the characters' reckless sexual behavior is as high-risk as the sharks that will devour them, the constant fluctuation of the threat destabilizes identification and sympathy. This is most clear with Patricia, who is first the prey of Esteban's advances, then a deceitful woman whose sexuality is analogous to a shark eating a small fish, and finally, unexpectedly, eaten alive.

PROFILMIC MEETS *UNHEIMLICH*

Essential in understanding the role of the shark in horror films in general, and even more so in a sexually charged film such as *Tintorera!*, is first its status as a primitive, even prehistoric being, and second, that its weapon of choice is its piercing teeth. In her analysis of gender dynamics in contemporary horror film, Carol J. Clover points out that " . . . the emotional terrain of the slasher film is pre-technological. The preferred weapons of the killer are knives, hammers, axes, ice picks, hypodermic needles, red hot pokers, pitchforks, and the like" (1992: 31). She follows that films with animal predators, such as *Jaws* and *The Birds*, can be seen as a link between the slasher film and more traditional vampire and werewolf films. "Knives and needles, like teeth, beaks, fangs, and claws, are extensions of the body that bring attacker and attacked into primitive, animalistic embrace" (Clover, 1992: 32). The horror genre is based more on reproducing age-old images and tales of fear and death than it is on auteur distinctions or artistic innovation. "What makes horror 'crucial enough to pass along' is . . . its engagement of repressed fears and desires and its reenactment of the residual conflict surrounding those feelings," creating archetypical monstrous incarnations of these fears (Clover, 1992: 11).

In traditional horror cinema, the fanged monster, ice-pick-wielding psychopath, or avenging hero is generally coded as *male*, with the victim and conquered terrain as female. Beginning with Russian formalist Jurij Lotman's binary myth structure, containing "a mobile, heroic being who crosses boundaries and 'penetrates' closed spaces, and an immobile being who personifies that damp, dark space and constitutes that which is to be overcome" (1992: 13), Clover proposes that horror since Hitchcock's *Psycho* (1960) jumbles this gender binary by giving heroic qualities to female (though often androgynous) characters. [10] Following a psychoanalytic view of gender difference and sexual complexes, she uses Freud's comment that "neurotic men [often] declare that they feel there is something uncanny about the female genital organs" to code the "dark spaces" of horror films as "*unheimlich*" and therefore "intrauterine" (Clover, 1992: 48). According to this argument, the female figure in contemporary horror is ambivalent in its relationship to "repressed fears."

In this light, *Tintorera!* qualifies as contemporary horror: while Miguel and Esteban certainly take up the heroic role of *penetrating*—diving into the "dark, damp" ocean in wet suits, shooting sharks with spearguns, and engaging in sexual intercourse with women—their masculine role is undermined by two foreign beings: the *gringa* women, whose sexual audacity overshadows their own, and the tiger shark, with its ability to *penetrate back* with its bite. The instability of traditional gender roles is visible in the culminating fear in both men as they exchange Mexican *machismo* for North American sexual liberation, which is sequentially linked to Miguel's death in the jaws of the very creature he hunted. In other words, feminists and sharks are both ominous in their potential to emasculate.

For Miguel, both the ocean and the female body are spaces of confidence and masculinity, *heimlich* in their familiarity; Cardona's film shows us the moment in which the *heimlich* turns *unheimlich* on Isla Mujeres, that is, when progressive gender politics begin to invade a traditional fishing island, upsetting the status quo of both culture and nature, unleashing the bestial qualities of the prehistoric guardians of this space. The deep ocean, as the shark's habitat, takes on the uncanny qualities of the animal (see Figure 14.1). The vacationers on Isla Mujeres live out their fantasies in the shallow waters of the beach, in the dangerous limbo between civilization and taboo. Moral values are muddled here, as characters, who see themselves as *evolved* for their ability to free themselves from the social restraints of clothing or monogamy, are presented as primitive and barbaric for being driven by animalistic desire.

Cardona's underwater blimp is the tool that makes visible this border zone between *heimlich* and *unheimlich*, bringing the spectator into a privileged viewing space beyond the power of the human eye, while also drawing out the parallels between sexuality and predatory instincts. In the underwater orgy in which Cynthia is killed, the couples begin undressing on the beach and continue removing articles of clothing in the water. Most of the men are wearing their pants, while the women are topless in bikini bottoms or panties. As the bodies enter the water, there are several quick insertions of a lurking tiger shark, establishing

Figure 14.1   A couple fondling each other in *Tintorera!/Tiger Shark* (René Cardona Jr., 1977). Cardona Jr.'s camera frames the divide between the *heimlich* (above-surface and masculine) and *unheimlich* (underwater and feminine) worlds.

the human figures as potential victims. The camera switches between aerials of all the couples, to medium shots above the surface, to underwater close-ups of the couples fondling each other, primarily male hands on female bodies and often with the women swimming away playfully and being pulled back. The perspective continues to rotate between these shots and the approaching shark, contrasting between the above- and below-surface atmospheres. As the sequence intensifies sexually, the camera chooses solely voyeuristic angles, including the below-surface shots with the camera stealthily moving in close to the bodies (see Figure 14.2), and above-surface shots taken from behind the pylons of the pier, as if spying. The privileged perspective of the spectator is aligned to identify firstly with the shark's predatory hunger; secondly with the carnal desire of the characters in sexual foreplay, emphasized by the camera's fetishizing fragmentation of the bodies; and thirdly with the pleasure of a snorkeling voyeur who, like the moviegoer, is undetected yet well positioned as a witness. The collapsing of these views, both violent and sexual on multiple levels (see Figure 14.3), is the most commercially exploitable aspect of the film and is its ideological conclusion.

Figure 14.2   Underwater shot in *Tintorera!/Tiger Shark* (Cardona Jr., 1977).

Figure 14.3   Shark attack in *Tintorera!/Tiger Shark* (Cardona Jr., 1977).

EL TRIÁNGULO DIABÓLICO DE LAS BERMUDAS AND CICLÓN: LOST AT SEA

Following *Tintorera!*, Cardona continued to include sharks in his stories while gradually deemphasizing gender and sexuality. His next two directorial projects (again including García and Stiglitz) were *El triángulo diabólico de las Bermudas* and *Ciclón,* both man-against-nature tales and both ending in tragedy, although the former presents itself as a historical horror film while the latter is a survivalist suspense drama. Both films take place primarily at sea and were filmed off the coast of Cozumel, Mexico.

Adapted from the book by Charles Berlitz, *El triángulo's* script is a contemporary story based on historical accounts of ships lost in this mysterious geographical zone, yet infused with a horror-film plot about a diabolical doll. The captain and crew of a large yacht take archaeological photographer Edward (John Huston) and his family of expert divers into the Atlantic with the objective of diving and finding the ruins of Atlantis. Early on, Edward's youngest daughter Diane sights a strange doll floating in the water, a visual prologue having told us that the doll fell from another ship in the same area a century earlier. The family and crew members soon discover that the doll can move on its own, has a thirst for fresh blood, communicates telepathically with Diane, and causes the fatal accidents of several characters. It tells Diane the order in which the family and crew meet their demise, that they will not really die but simply "join the others, down there," referring to hundreds of casualties from this zone resting on the ocean floor. At the end of the film, those who have not fallen overboard or been killed in freak accidents are eternally lost at sea in a time–space vortex.

El triángulo's underwater scenes begin midway through the film when Edward's family locates the Atlantis site after a few members dive down to photograph the ruins. Underwater, sharks pursue the divers, who retaliate with spear guns. In a continuation of this sequence, following a conversation among those still aboard the yacht, the divers are swimming between several large stone pillars when a seaquake occurs, destroying the ruins and creating an underwater action spectacle of bodies, which barely escape being crushed to death. Finally, one pillar falls on the leg of Edward's oldest daughter Michelle (Gloria Guida, Italian actress and 1974 Miss Teenage Italy), who before the dive was established as the romantic interest of the yacht's owner, Alan (Andrés García). Young, blonde, and flawless in physique, she is the only female character who appears in a bikini in the film, while her mother and aunt wear jeans or muumuus. In the third and final underwater sequence, Michelle is carried to the surface, her wounded legs bleeding, and her fellow divers must kill yet another hungry shark to protect her.

Above the surface, Michelle's sunbathing scenes and flirtations with Alan lighten the mood of this dark film, while at once setting up the viewer for Michelle's final accident. The spectacle of her body is neutralized when all the characters dive in identical wet suits and become indistinguishable once submerged—the inverse of the gender distinction made in *Peligro . . . mujeres en acción!* The focus of the first underwater sequence is the threat of the sharks, effortlessly slaughtered by the divers. The second sequence, when the seaquake begins, seems to suggest that killing those sharks has created a disturbance in this mystical/supernatural place, reaffirming it as the submarine Hades announced by the doll. After the quake, when several divers swim to the surface, we understand that the trapped diver is Michelle. In the last underwater sequence, when pursued by a shark, the spectator can identify (albeit not visually) this wounded diver. The theme of vampiric creatures preying on the most sexualized character is again solidified, though more subdued than in *Tintorera!*, and without threatening gender dynamics.

These authorial tendencies are even more visible in *Ciclón*. Following a freak storm, the members of a tour boat are lost at sea, later to be joined by the survivors of a downed plane and a sunken fishing boat. With no fuel or radio communication, no food, and a small amount of water, the film shows a *Lord of the Flies*–type clash of personalities under the same extreme survival conditions of *Supervivientes de los Andes*. The desperate characters begin eating raw fish, but are challenged when a dog dies and its dried flesh is offered as food. They finally must decide the limits of their will to survive when humans begin to die. The boat eventually sinks, leaving the remaining characters clinging to driftwood, with the underwater footage focusing on undistinguishable half-submerged bodies. Just before being rescued, several characters are unexpectedly pulled underwater and devoured by sharks. As in *El triángulo, Ciclón's* wardrobe shifts the focus away from gender difference. As the well-dressed characters lose their composure, the clothing, before marking their status as civilized, becomes increasingly tattered and stained. The sharks' symbolic role as vampiric or diabolical is now primitive and savage, a threat to the victims and a baseline to which they can fall as they resist cannibalism in the name of evolution.

As Cardona moved into his phase of disaster and human-tragedy stories (continuing with *Guyana: Crime of the Century* [1979], about the Jim Jones cult murders), his films become increasingly violent, and somewhat less sexualized. Skin, nudity, and sharks repeat throughout his career, but as female sexuality loses its exploitability, Cardona explores the terrain of human psychology in search of shock value. The significance of wardrobe choices seems to change as well: bikinis, bare skin, and wet suits first contrast gender power relations between humans and "carnal" appeal between both humans and animals. With the transition from *Tintorera!* through *Ciclón*, clothes seem to take on a new importance, a visual symbol of civility, a thin and easily penetrated barrier between shark teeth and human flesh, but also a symbolic and literal layer of distinction between man and beast.

NOTES

1. *La risa en vacaciones/Laughter on Holidays 1, 2,* and *3* were among the top-grossing films in Mexico in 1990, 1991, and 1992, respectively.
2. Throughout the chapter, I will refer to the subject of this chapter as "Cardona" and to his father as "Cardona Sr." unless further specification is needed.
3. De la Mora (2006) points out that the *fichera* movies follow a period of government instability after the events of 1968, and the concurrent feminist movement.
4. Bravo attained cult status in international horror cinema when, working as the shark trainer for Lucio Fulci's *Zombi 2* (1979), he played the zombie in the underwater shark fight, biting the shark as it passed above him.
5. "Practical jokes" were scripted and planned, but actors were contracted to participate without knowing the details, thus creating improvisational performances (author interview with René Cardona III, June 2007).
6. Cardona and Bravo would subdue the shark by removing it from the water and transporting it to shallow waters. When it was more docile, they would attach a fishing line to the shark's mouth and release it, and then be able to follow its movements with the camera. This process was repeated several times with different sharks for one sequence.

7. According to Cardona, Spanish-market distributors often preferred English audio with Spanish subtitles, as this "international" status could better compete with Hollywood and European imports (Pelayo, 1993).

8. Sarah Street sees the Bond films as the fantasy flipside of the British New Wave's social-realist depiction of the "masculine nightmare of being trapped in the provinces with a wife and family" (in Chapman 2000: 69).

9. http://www.imdb.com/title/tt0076825/usercomments; http://www.qwipster. net/tintorera.htm; http://www.1000misspenthours.com/reviews/reviewsn-z/ tintorera.htm (accessed May 4, 2008).

10. Clover credits Teresa de Laurentis's *Alice Doesn't: Feminism, Semiotics, Cinema* (Bloomington: Indiana Univ. Press, 1985) for this connection to Lotman.

15 Sex and the Generals

Reading Brazilian *Pornochanchada* as Sexploitation

Stephanie Dennison

> . . . scholars have been drawn to adult movies because they engage
> a larger field of contextual issues: religion and morality, social rela-
> tions, law, biology, psychology, and issues of identity—not to men-
> tion 'the three ps': politics, power and pleasure. As simplistic as the
> films often seem, they are in fact among the most interesting texts
> for scholars to work with because they are at the center of so many
> complex discourses and are charged throughout with powerful, and
> often contradictory, emotions. (Schaefer, 2005: 89)

David Andrews (2007: 51) has observed that within the blossoming field of
porn studies soft-core is understudied, undertheorized, and routinely belittled. Given that the academic study of porn, despite the wealth of material
available and the 'complex discourses' thrown up by domestically produced
porn films, is yet to take off in Brazil, it should come as no surprise that the
country's home-grown soft-core sex films, the so-called *pornochanchadas*,
were and continue to be summarily dismissed (although never completely
ignored) by critics and most cultural commentators.

Pornochanchadas were Brazilian soft-core sex comedies with popular
appeal that dominated local box offices in the 1970s. Their name derives
from the *chanchadas*, comedy films inspired by the Brazilian music-hall tradition which enjoyed unrivaled commercial success from the 1930s to the
end of the 1950s.[1] Taking advantage of a gradual liberalization of sexual
codes, filmmakers churned out 'spicier' versions of the same music-hall-style
film, while opting for a 'trashy' aesthetic: both were self-conscious choices
on the part of producers purely for commercial reasons.[2] *Pornochanchadas*, like many sexploitation films from around the world, provoked moral
outrage on their release, but they are now enjoyed within "the quotation
marks of ironic appropriation or the political amnesia of nostalgia" (Hunt,
1998: 127).

As is the case with many other examples of popular Brazilian cinema
in the 1960s and 1970s, the *pornochanchada* is granted a mention in academic film discussion when it serves to contrast unfavorably with the *cinema
novo*.[3] For a start, the *pornochanchada* appeared in 1969, with Reginaldo

Farias's *Os paqueras*/The Flirts, the year the death of *cinema novo* was finally declared by one of its chief exponents. The year also marked the bedding in of the so-called coup-within-the-coup, the tightening of the military dictatorship, and in particular, the greater use of censorship in the cinema. As a result, *pornochanchadas* (and their bastard offspring, the hard-core feature) are still to this day charged with sounding the death knell of 'quality' and 'politically committed' cinema in Brazil, and they are inescapably associated with the heady days of the dictatorship.

Eric Schaefer (2005: 96) has observed that adult films are often given a variety of definitions and designations (sexploitation, exploitation, pornography, sex films, and so on). Likewise in Brazil, sexploitations films, both at the time of their release and still nowadays, are described as romantic comedies, melodramas, and erotic films, among other terms.[4] According to Nuno Cesar Abreu, the term *pornochanchada* began to be used in the press around 1973, referring at first to what was deemed to be cheap and 'poor-quality' production aimed at popular segments of the population (2006: 140). The label was and continues to be frequently applied to any film from the era with erotic appeal, and thus its application has, quite confusingly, not always been limited to popular comedies. Given that the bulk of what we now term *pornochanchadas* were produced in the red-light district of downtown São Paulo, the *pornochanchada* is also often confused with cinematic production of the so-called Boca do Lixo.[5] The area's most active period, in terms of production, was in the 1980s with the advent of hard core, hence the blurring of the boundaries between soft and hard core in Brazil, a subject to which we will return later. The Boca is also remembered for producing a brief but highly creative and influential series of alternative films referred to as *cinema marginal*, which represented a radicalization of the original purpose of *cinema novo*, in light of a perceived 'selling out' towards the end of the 1960s. While *cinema novo* created a mythical universe made up of the impoverished interior, urban slums, and so on (Salles Gomes, 1995: 251), 'marginal' cineastes dealt with drug abuse; promiscuity; lack of respect for traditional values such as the family, property, professional development; an antiwork ethic, and celebration of laziness; a celebration of an alternative lifestyle; and an empathy with traditionally marginalized groups such as blacks, homosexuals, indigenous populations, and women (Ramos, 1987: 40). Thus, while there were clear overlaps in aesthetic terms between *cinema marginal* and the *pornochanchada*, the former differentiated itself from the latter by its deliberate political inflection and its refusal to bow to demands of the marketplace. As Tanya Krzywinska reminds us, " . . . films that set out with the aim of engaging viewers erotically are often considered to be valueless. It is often the case that great value is placed on those films that focus on the psychological complexities of sex in serious and non-symbolic ways" (2006: 230). Thus, it is the sexy but so-called intelligent marginal films, such as Rogério Sganzerla's *A mulher de todos*/Everybody's Woman (1970), João Callegaro's *O pornógrafo*/

The Pornographer (1970), and Carlos Reichenbach's *Lilian M: relatório confidencial*/Lilian M: Confidential Report (1975) that tended to attract the attention of critics who deigned to comment on the boom in erotic film in Brazil in the 1970s.[6] Likewise, when British documentary filmmaker Simon Hartog made his controversial film on the *pornochanchada*, *Brazil: Cinema, Sex and the Generals*, he notably concentrated on three psychologically complex and/or alternative erotic films; everything, in fact, except *pornochanchada*.[7]

A new definition, or at least a new approach to reading the *pornochanchada*, is long overdue. The purpose of this chapter, then, is to situate the *pornochanchada* within the traditions of international sexploitation as it is broadly understood, in an attempt to break it free from the restrictive and at times ambiguous definitions afforded it up until now in Brazilian film studies. It will argue that, in the 'best' traditions of exploitation cinema, the *pornochanchada* can be said to have offered an alternative worldview to the official line espoused by the then Brazilian military government and an alternative, of sorts, in terms of filmmaking strategies and topics of interest displayed on screen.

PORNOCHANCHADA AND SEXPLOITATION

The *pornochanchada* arose in popularity in the 1970s as a consequence of the introduction of compulsory screen quotas, which resulted in exhibition groups producing their own films, the outcome being cheap, mass-produced soft-core porn films (Brazil's own quota-quickies). Thus, like their counterparts in the United States, Italy, Spain, and so on, 'sexploiters' took commercial advantage of a loosening in censorship and produced made-to-order films in which "everything [took] a back seat to the display of nudity and the mobilization of sexual situations" (Schaefer, 2003: 43). Films were frequently sold to distributors on their highly suggestive titles and taglines alone, and they rarely delivered on their promise of sex.

Like much sexploitation from around the world, the Brazilian *pornochanchada* is characterized by its complex relationship with the censor. For a start, other erotically charged films that dealt with sexual subjects were more heavily censored than the *pornochanchada*, for example, Arnaldo Jabor's late *cinema novo* features *Toda nudez será castigada*/All Nudity Shall Be Punished (1973) and *O casamento*/The Marriage (1976), as well as more politically inflected films such as Jorge Bodanzky and Orlando Senna's *Iracema, uma transa amazônica*/Iracema (1976).[8] Thus, if anything, it was the relative ease with which the *pornochanchada* passed through the hands of the censors that raised the suspicions of cultural commentators, with focus being drawn to the apparent self-censorship of the films instead, in the form of the failure to deliver on the promise of sex and nudity, and the 'strategic reactionary elements' such as the conservative morality seemingly expressed by the plot resolutions (many *pornochanchadas*, after plenty of debauchery, ended in marriage). As Tanya Krzywinska reminds us, cinema often serves up sexual transgression only to censure it (2006: 56). And while critics took umbrage with the conservatism of the films, conservative Brazilians literally took to the streets to complain about the films' seemingly liberal take on the issues of sex and sexuality.[9]

Pornochanchada producers made use of a number of staple exploitation techniques in order to sell their films, such as the use of sexy and innuendo-laden taglines and titillating posters. Many *pornochanchadas*, like the U.S. exploitation 'nudie cutie' films of the 1950s, can be described as movie versions of girlie magazines. Perhaps the most obvious example of this phenomenon is one of the best-known and most successful *pornochanchadas*, Aníbal Massaini Neto's *A superfêmea*/Superwoman, released in 1973 and starring former Miss Brasil Vera Fischer. In the film, a marketing Svengali is given a seemingly impossible task: to sell the male contraceptive pill to a deeply suspicious male Brazilian public. He dreams up the idea of offering in a promotional prize draw a date with a so-called superwoman (the *superfêmea* of the title), in order to challenge the belief that such a pill would adversely affect men's libido. The search then begins to find the perfect woman, with a veritable parade of beauties being screen-tested and thus passing in front of the camera for the marketing executive's/the audience's inspection (see Figures 15.1 and 15.2). Such literal articulation

Figure 15.1 A superfêmea/Superwoman (Aníbal Massaini Neto, 1973). The Svengali of *Supêrfemea* finds his perfect woman. But is she real? And does it matter?

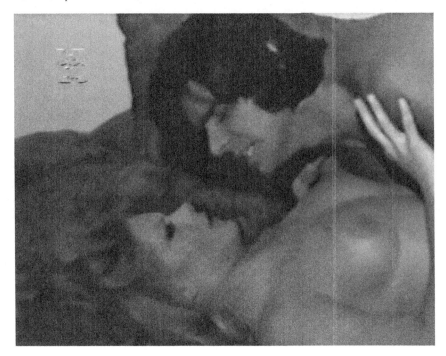

*Figure 15.2   A superfêmea/*Superwoman (Aníbal Massaini Neto, 1973).

of voyeurism was a staple of the *pornochanchada*, and in particular, the furtive voyeurism of peering through telescopes, spy holes, over walls, and around corners. Snatched glances are typical of the furtive kind of behavior displayed by male characters in these films.

Some of the most successful *pornochanchadas* were loose reworkings of blockbusters and popular genres from Hollywood and beyond. Perhaps the best-known and most widely discussed parodic *pornochanchada* is Adriano Stuart's *Bacalhau*/Codfish (1975), a comedy reworking of the smash hit *Jaws* (Steven Spielberg, 1975) in which a large codfish terrorizes the Brazilian coastline. The local police request the help of a Portuguese oceanographer, who is posted to Brazil in a tea chest, and proceeds to bait the cod with broken pieces of old Portuguese *fado* records.[10]

Abreu describes the use of 'parody' in *pornochanchada* films as purely a marketing strategy, suggesting that references to international blockbusters and genres enabled the films to piggyback on the success of the original (2006: 149). Abreu follows the line taken by João Luiz Vieira and Robert Stam in an influential essay, in which such parodies are ultimately dismissed as poor copies which served merely to reinforce the notion of Brazilian cinema's inherent inferiority when compared to big-budget Hollywood productions, for example:

Bacalhau highlights the discrepancies between parody and original in a self-destructive manner, not as a weapon against domination. In a vicious circle, both author and public share and stimulate an attitude of self-contempt based on the alleged Brazilian incompetence in imitation. (1985: 35)[11]

However, as I have argued elsewhere, the self-contempt referred to by Vieira and Stam could arguably be seen as a form of resistance in itself, given the values of progress, order, and technical advance being espoused at the time by the dictatorship.

Schaefer is less dismissive of the use of the device in sexploitation:

Borrowing from, or sending up, familiar genres was a common strategy in sexploitation . . . Not only was generic pilfering a shortcut to a serviceable narrative, but it could also play into common sexual fantasies or fetishes. . . . (2003: 42)

Perhaps the most interesting expression of this 'generic pilfering' can be found in the large number of soft-core films that seem to send up the *pornochanchada* genre itself. For example, one of the episodes of *A noite das taras II*/Night of Perversion II (various, 1982) revolves around a female gang of thieves who unwittingly break into the home of the real-life self-proclaimed king of *pornochanchada* David Cardoso, only to be seduced in turn by the man himself. Cardoso was not the only filmmaker linked to the genre who was happy to send up himself and his work: one of the most prolific *pornochanchada* and later hard-core producers/directors, Fauzi Mansur, produced in 1980 *O inseto do amor*/The Insect of Love, a parody of the *pornochanchada*. And Cláudio MacDowell's popular *Luz, cama, ação*/Lights, Bed, Action (1976) is a *pornochanchada* film about the making of a *pornochanchada* film. There are references to the filmmaking process itself in a large number of *pornochanchadas*: those found in *Bacalhau*, for example, serve to remind the audience just how nonsensical, despite its high entertainment factor, the whole notion of the film *Jaws* really is.

Indeed, a remarkably large number of *pornochanchadas* contain elements that can be described as self-reflexive, which serve, as witnessed in the previous example, to draw attention to the overblown pretensions of the original, in the case of parodies, and which can also serve to draw attention to themselves as porn, or as constructed representations of sex.[12] Richard Dyer suggests, in the context of hard core, that "[t]he self-reflexive mode would not be so consistently returned to, did it not sell—and it would not sell if it did not turn people on" (2004: 105). The assumption held by those cultural commentators who summarily dismiss the *pornochanchada* is that *pornochanchadas* were not sexy and could not conceivably have turned audiences on: perhaps such an assumption needs to be challenged.

Another key aspect of the *pornochanchada* which finds clear resonance elsewhere in international sexploitation is the sustained depiction of excess, and in particular gluttony. By way of example, in *A viúva virgem*/The Virgin Widow (Pedro Carlos Rovai, 1974) the large and decidedly overweight Carlos Imperial plays a dead husband who comes back to haunt the virgin widow of the title: when he catches up with his widow he raids the fridge before attacking her. *Essa gostosa brincadeira a dois*/This Tasty Game for Two (Victor di Mello, 1974) includes not only the stock pre-sex fridge-raiding scene, but another where a fight breaks out as randy guests at a high-society party charge the buffet table en masse. The link established between the world represented by the *pornochanchada* and gluttony/excess is an important one: if, as Krzywinska suggests, the concept of civilization is often defined as the management of appetite (2006: 162), then on this level at least the *pornochanchada* celebrates a state of barbarity that functions as a challenge to the ethos of the dictatorship.

While it is true to say that most *pornochanchadas* were conservative, like many of their counterparts elsewhere in the world they often included surprisingly frank discussions of a number of liberal themes, such as the importance of freedom, of both the individual and society, as well as the potentially corruptive power of the media in Brazil.[13] A number of *pornochanchadas*, for example, simultaneously buy into (for the purposes of entertainment and titillation) and debunk media myths. Take J. Marreco's *Emmanuelle tropical*/Tropical Emmanuelle (1977), Brazil's first leg up onto the *Emmanuelle* bandwagon (the European 'original' was screened in its soft-core version in Brazil, and was a popular success). [14] *Emmanuelle tropical* is another example of a *pornochanchada* that seems to set out to mock itself. First of all, the film criticizes the place of the media in contemporary society, of TV marketing and of consumerism, but in good exploitation tradition, it shamelessly uses these to its own advantage. The tropical Emmanuelle of the title is a model and advertising actress. On the set of an advert an actor tells her that her name is an imitation of the European model, leading to the knowing, self-referential ,and playful comment "pare de imitar a cultura dos outros" (stop imitating other cultures).

Emmanuelle is depicted as a modern woman who always felt the need to work for a living, and thus to have a sense of personal freedom and independence. As it happens, she has a glamorous job that brings her in contact with a world of speedboats, horse racing, art galleries, high fashion, and private jets.[15] Leaving the elements of titillation to one side, then, the film undoubtedly contains a protodiscussion of woman's changing position in society (middle-class women's right to choose to work for a living and have their own income, the power of advertising to make the public conform to certain aesthetic notions, the existence of open relationships and 'free love,' the advantage to losing sexual inhibitions, and so on). Like the character played by Silvia Crystal, the Brazilian Emmanuelle is understood as being in control of, or at least seeking to be in control of, her life and sexual choices.

Thus, in the *pornochanchada* it is not just subaltern groups, such as black and mixed-race women, who are portrayed as being randy. In what can be considered a kind of democratization of female sexuality, in a clear break from the stereotypical image of the sexually voracious *mulata*, for example, as representing female desire in Brazil, the world of the *pornochanchada* is also filled with white, middle-class female characters who actively search for sexual fulfillment. These characters range from the young 'bicho grilo' (hippie) types, inspired by hippie culture and the cult of free love,[16] to middle-class housewives.[17] In José Miziara's *Bem-dotado, o homem de Itu*/Well Endowed, the Man from Itu (1979), Nuno Leal Maia's character is a country bumpkin with undiscovered sexual talents, reminiscent, in fact, of Dennis Busch's character (the Vegetable) in Russ Meyer's *Faster Pussycat, Kill, Kill* (1965). In a scene (one that captures magnificently the 'bad taste' aesthetic of many *pornochanchadas*), a group of wealthy socialites are seen walking with great difficulty after a sexual liaison with the well-endowed young man.

Just as sexploitation in the United States, United Kingdom, and elsewhere can be said to have clearly influenced mainstream film production (so much so, in the U.S. case, that it was ultimately subsumed into the mainstream by the late 1970s) (Schaefer: 1999: 339), so too did the *pornochanchada* influence the Brazilian mainstream (and by mainstream, I am here referring to big-budget films that were widely distributed and starred popular TV actors). By the mid-1970s, occasionally directors and actors associated with mainstream cinema and television would wander into the territory of erotic comedy, usually in an attempt to tap into the huge commercial success that the *pornochanchada* was enjoying at the time. With their big budgets, famous actresses and catwalk models, and high production values, films such as Bruno Barreto's *Dona Flor e seus dois maridos*/Dona Flor and Her Two Husbands (1976) and Neville D'Almeida's *Dama do lotação*/Lady on the Bus (1978) created *pornochic*, or a 'cleaned-up' version of the *pornochanchada*, as Jean-Claude Bernardet has put it (1978).[18] Such was the impact of the *pornochanchada* by 1976 that popular wholesome comedian Amácio Mazzaropi, one of the most successful comedy film actors and producers at the time and noted for his political conservatism, drew influence from the narrative formulas of the *pornochanchada* in *A banda das velhas virgens*/The Gang of Old Virgins (1979). According to the soft- and later hard-core porn actor and producer Cardoso, the *pornochanchada*, despite the almost unanimous suspicion it generated in both cultural and political circles at the time, was responsible for forming the audience that put *Dona Flor* in the record books for the most viewed Brazilian film of all time.[19]

There are thus a number of clear convergences between *pornochanchadas* and soft-core sex comedies produced in the 1960s and 1970s elsewhere. There are, however, a series of potential problems related to labeling the *pornochanchada* as sexploitation as we have come to understand it.[20] The most significant of these, perhaps, are the twin issues of consumption and distribution, and how these produced a different relationship between the *pornochanchada* and the mainstream to the one we associate with 'classic' (s)exploitation elsewhere.

HOW TASTY WAS OUR CINEMA

Nowadays, *pornochanchadas* can be easily accessed via the increasingly widespread cable television networks in Brazil, and in particular via a series entitled "Como era gostoso o nosso cinema" (How tasty was our cinema). The "Como era gostoso" series is afforded a 1:30 a.m. slot on Canal Brasil, a channel owned by Globo Sat, the cable and satellite arm of the all-powerful Globo network. Canal Brasil broadcasts material (films, documentaries, 'making ofs') relating to the national film industry.[21] "Como era gostoso" screens almost exclusively films that fall into the category of what Krzywinska refers to as "sex-positive forms of soft-core" (2006: 56). Thus, the infamous Brazilian WIP (Women in Prison) films, currently popular with paracinematic audiences both in Brazil and abroad, as well as those featuring violence, are not screened. The loosely parodic ones are favored, such as *Pintando o sexo*/Painting the Sex (Jairo Carlos and Egídio Eceio, 1977) and *Seu Florindo e suas duas mulheres*/Florindo and his Two Wives (Mozael Silveira, 1978) (both reworkings of two popular Brazilian films).[22] One of the most frequently screened *pornochanchadas* in the "Como era gostoso" strand is *Histórias que nossas babás não contavam*/Stories our Nannies Never Told Us (Oswaldo de Oliveira, 1979). The film comprises a smutty reworking of the tale of Snow White (and in particular, the Disney animated film version), reinvented here as the story of a sex-mad black woman (ironically named Clara das Neves [Pale as Snow]). The film notably stars Costinha, an old-fashioned comedian of the 'unreconstructed' type whose representations of and jokes about gay men were a staple in many a mainstream TV show in the 1970s, 1980s, and 1990s.

The "Como era gostoso o nosso cinema" strand arguably strips the *pornochanchada* of its transgressive qualities. For a start, much 'raunchier' material is available for viewing on cable television in Brazil in even earlier time slots. The title is a play on words on Nelson Pereira dos Santos's critically acclaimed late *cinema novo* feature *Como era gostoso o meu francês/ How Tasty Was My Little Frenchman* (1971). The new title (How Tasty Was Our Cinema) effortlessly gets across the idea of a cozy, complicit, enjoyable but relatively harmless cinematic past.

By placing the films in the context of nostalgia and screening them late at night, an element of naughty enjoyment is consciously maintained, but this naughtiness now has more to do with indulging in politically incorrect humor than in titillation.[23] That said, without the intervention and 'mainstreaming' on the part of Globosat, most of the twenty or so *pornochanchadas* that are recycled in the "Como era gostoso" strand would join the ranks of the thousands of other 'orphan films' (Schaefer, 2005: 80), bereft of curation by the state and condemned to be forgotten.

Also in relation to the issue of consumption, while it is true to say that the 'hyperbolic cartoonlike' qualities associated with the sexploitation films of the likes of Meyer (Schaefer, 2005: 83) can also be identified in many *pornochanchadas*, they are perhaps more strikingly present in commercially successful mainstream films of the late 1960s and early 1970s, and in particular in films associated with the (critically acclaimed) late *cinema novo* style referred to as *Tropicalismo*.[24] The irony, then, is that when the *pornochanchada* appeared, a number of what might be referred to as "alternative" films with a "neo-camp aesthetic"(Sconce, 1995: 372–3) now associated with exploitation/paracinema were dominating the mainstream. Furthermore, a 'trashy' aesthetic has been one of the mainstays of Brazilian popular culture since at least the nineteenth century, and its presence can be felt in popular cinema from the 1940s and the days of the *chanchada* to the present. Thus it would be erroneous to think of such an aesthetic, which feels familiar to viewers of international sexploitation, as a form of "calculated negation and refusal of 'elite' culture" to which Jeffrey Sconce refers in relation to (principally U.S.) exploitation (1995: 372), given the distinct relationship between popular and elite culture in the Brazilian context.

As we have already established, *pornochanchada* is a very loosely defined term. The kind of "soft-core-hard-core distinction in the American consciousness" to which Andrews refers (2007: 56) does not translate directly into the Brazilian experience. However, like the sexploitation tradition in the United States, the *pornochanchada* was instrumental in the development of hard core in Brazil. Many of these early hard-core films followed the formulas of *pornochanchada*. Take, for example, *A B . . . profunda/Deep A . . . .* The film's title and loose plotline take their inspiration from *Deep Throat* (Gerard Damiano, 1972). In this Brazilian version, the sexually frustrated female lead visits a sex therapist who locates her clitoris in her anus. With her libido recharged, she sets to work recharging the libidos of a variety of frustrated men. With its emphasis on comedy interspersed with strenuous bouts of sexual activity, which are often speeded up and accompanied by a whacky soundtrack,[25] *A B . . . profunda* is more reminiscent of the UK soft-core *Confessions* sexploitation series, and of the *pornochanchada*, than of hard core proper (see Figure 15.3).[26]

It is also worth noting that further evidence of the link between soft and hard core in Brazil can be located in the fact that Rafaele Rossi's *Coisas eróticas*/Erotic Things (1982), the first hard-core film to receive a certificate of exhibition, was originally made as a soft-core film. Hard-core scenes were later inserted in what appears to be a testing of the legal waters once Nagima Oshima's explicit *Ai no corrida/In The Realm of the Senses* (1976) was released in Brazil.[27]

With a veritable red-light district on their doorsteps, and with a filmmaking tradition driven shamelessly by market forces, it was particularly

Figure 15.3   Jayme Cardoso is surprised to discover the location of Teka Lanza's clitoris in *A B . . . Profunda*. (Geraldo Dominó, 1984).

within the Boca do Lixo that erstwhile soft-core porn directors and producers turned without much ado to hard core: Cardoso, Antônio Polo Galante, Tony Vieira, José Mojica Marins, Fauzi Mansur, and Juan Bajon being the leading figures in the move. Given the fact that at first these filmmakers continued to make soft-core films, the audience for hard core, at least initially, was similar to the *pornochanchada* audience.

In terms of distribution, it was only in the second half of the 1970s, as the government made them its target, that *pornochanchadas* began to be sidelined into an alternative viewing circuit of sorts, making them fit more classically within exploitation paradigms. At least in the first half of the 1970s many *pornochanchadas* went on general release, and although São Paulo's Boca do Lixo produced and distributed the bulk of these films, a significant number were distributed by Embrafilme, the state production and distribution agency. Furthermore, unlike their 'sexploiter' counterparts in the United States and the United Kingdom, even those directors and producers who came into filmmaking via unconventional channels cannot be said to have been forging careers exclusively beyond the mainstream. Adriano Stuart, the director of *Bacalhau*, one of the few national films to be included in psychotronic retrospectives in Brazil, also made popular children's films and successful spin-off films from TV series.

And the production company Cinedistri made a large number of *porno-chanchadas*, but it also produced the government-approved epic drama *Independência ou Morte*/Independence or Death (1972).

As I hope to have demonstrated, an analysis of the *pornochanchada* in the context of international sexploitation helps to unearth a number of features which have remained hidden beneath the prejudices of Brazilian film studies. In his seminal defense of the study of exploitation films, Schaefer, *apud* the Bahktinian critics Stallybrass and White, argues that " . . . what is socially peripheral is so frequently symbolically central" (1999: 13). It is this freedom to perceive the *pornochanchada* as socially relevant that viewing the films in the context of (s)exploitation can most importantly offer.

Seemingly a lone voice on Brazil's critical landscape, José Carlos Avellar as early as 1979 offered an alternative reading strategy for the *pornochanchada*, recognizing a carnivalesque defiance of the *pornochanchada* audience in the light of the dictatorship. His arguments are worth reproducing here, given the extent to which they capture the spirit of the contemporary study of exploitation film. Avellar argued that:

> The spectator [of *pornochanchada*] . . . would go to the cinema to take part in a kind of plot, to conspire against the established order, to conspire against conversations in broad daylight, made up of irrelevant subjects or using words that he could not even understand (1979: 84–5).

In the darkness of the cinema, the established order, as depicted by the government propaganda films that regularly preceded feature films at the time, could be freely derided. These advertisements for the dictatorship were shot frequently in soft focus, with smooth, paternalistic voice-overs, echoing messages such as "Meu Brasil, eu amo voce" (My Brazil, I love you), and they dealt with themes like hygiene, health, and work with the objective of improving living conditions and galvanizing the workforce. Also, they served to strengthen "the national character with regard to love of work and patriotism, and to maintain the support and patience of the masses" (Avellar, 1979: 75). *Pornochanchadas* were, by contrast, bad mannered, sluttish, utterly stupid, and they promoted individualism and a rejection of the work ethic. Avellar thus concludes that it is possible that audiences started going to see these films because they knew they were bad—when you cannot deal rationally with your own reality, you (in good Bakhtinian fashion) turn to the absurd. Avellar cites as an example of this Mozael Silveira's 1975 film *Secas e molhadas*/Dried Up and Moist. The critic explains that the film is shoddily produced and plays on its poor quality to attract the public. Perhaps, he argues, it is an unconscious act of revenge on the official publicity that depicted Brazil as a supernation with, among other jewels in the crown, the Trans-Amazonian Highway, Maracanã, the largest football stadium in the world, "and other such things, equally gigantic, but far removed from the experience of the spectator of *pornochanchada*. The film is badly made: if this has been done deliberately or if it is as a result of lack of money and the creative incapacity of the director is of no consequence. What is for certain is that the *pornochanchada* plays with this idea" (Avellar, 1979: 81).

In the context of exploitation/paracinema, Sconce argues:

> While the academy prizes conscious transgression of conventions by a filmmaker looking to critique the medium aesthetically and/ or politically, paracinematic viewers value a stylistic and thematic deviance born, more often than not, from the systematic failure of a film aspiring to *obey* dominant codes of cinematic representation. (1995: 385)

Similarly, in Brazil the assumption has always been that transgression of conventions is only carried out by 'quality' cinema. Sconce leaves out of his equation the possibility of a subconscious or even unconscious transgression of conventions, which is arguably what we find in the *pornochanchada*. Rather than aspiring and failing to *obey* dominant codes of cinematic representation, the value of Brazilian sexploitation films lies in their refusal to conform: to accepted production values, to moral codes, and to the ideologies of both Right and Left.

NOTES

1. Journalists and film critics coined the pejorative term in the 1930s for the highly derivative musical comedies that were often modeled on Hollywood movies of the same era. For more information on the *chanchada*, see Shaw and Dennison (2007: 70–77).
2. It is worth bearing in mind that *chanchadas* in the late 1950s and 1960s gradually became 'saucier,' with the inclusion, for example, of striptease scenes. As elsewhere, Brazil could also boast a number of notionally 'educational' exploitation features in the early 1960s with sexual overtones: see, for example, Konstantin Tkaczenko's *Nudismo não é pecado*/Nudism is Not a Sin (1960) and *Isto é strip-tease*/This is Strip-tease (1962): these films were not unlike the U.S. 'nudie-cuties' of the 1950s and 1960s as described by Schaefer (2002: 5).
3. For an interesting discussion of such unfavorable contrasts in relation to popular performers Mazzaropi and Zé do Caixão (Coffin Joe), respectively, see Bueno (1999) and Tierney (2004).
4. It is interesting to observe that in *pornochanchada* producer Alfredo Sternheim's dictionary of the Boca do Lixo (2005), the term does not appear even once, suggesting that the stigma surrounding its use continues to affect those involved in the films' production.
5. The Boca do Lixo (Mouth of Garbage) is a district in downtown São Paulo that gained its name due to the large number of prostitutes and pickpockets who frequented its streets. Foreign film distributors were attracted to the Boca from the 1920s, due to it its cheap rent and proximity to major coach and railway stations. By the end of the 1950s a number of Brazilian producers were established in the district.

6. Cultural commentators in the 1970s also approved of the intensely erotic psychological dramas of filmmaker Walter Hugo Khoury.

7. Hartog's film was banned twice by the British Independent Broadcasting Authority (IBA): first because of the program's sexual content, and second, when the program makers included a commentary stating that it had been censored by the IBA.

8. The Memória da censura no cinema Web site, which documents the censoring of Brazilian film from 1964 to 1988, reveals the extent to which a wide variety of filmic styles and genres suffered from seemingly random censorship: available at http://www. memoriacinebr.com.br (accessed 1.9.07).

9. Take, for example, the march held in the Brazilian city of Curitiba against the *pornochanchada* (Abreu, 2006: 149).

10. For a more detailed discussion of this film, see Vieira and Stam (1985: 28); Dennison and Shaw (2004: 167–8).

11. Abreu fails to mention that parody, mimicry, and referencing were all well-established traditions in Brazilian popular culture.

12. The *pornochanchada* also gave rise to a number of self-reflexive films that documented its own history: see, for example, *Assim era a pornochanchada/That Was Pornochanchada* (1978), *Os melhores momentos da pornochanchada/The Best of Pornochanchada* (1977), and *Os bons tempos voltaram: vamos gozar outra vez/Good Times Have 'Come' Again* (1985).

13. It is worth noting in this context that telecommunications expanded exponentially during the dictatorship. Since 1962 the national government had been planning to link up Brazil via telephones, telex, and televisual systems. Such a project of national integration was dear to the heart of the dictatorship, on the grounds that it would improve national security (Johnson and Stam, 1995: 390).

14. Other Brazilian examples of films that cashed in on the success of *Emmanuelle* include *A filha de Emmanuelle/The Daughter of Emmanuelle* (Oswaldo de Oliveira, 1980) and *Giselle* (Victor di Mello, 1980).

15. Likewise, the female lead in *Essa gostosa brincadeira a dois* expresses a need to feel useful (while the closest the male lead gets to employment is being Vera Fischer's gigolo). The job she secures is showgirl on a popular TV variety program.

16. See, for example, *Essa gostosa brincadeira a dois*, and the (white, blonde, clearly marked as middle-class) hippie who lives on the beach and sleeps with the male lead.

17. By way of comparison, it is useful to consider the impact of British softcore porn films, and in particular those dealing with naughty suburban housewives, in terms of such a democratization of female sexual desire; see, for example, Derek Ford's *The Wife Swappers* (1969) and *Suburban Wives* (1971).

18. It is worth noting here that, as in the UK case, the term *pornochic* was borrowed from the United States, where it referred to films of the ilk of *Deep Throat* and *Behind the Green Door*, and its meaning was changed somewhat, as a result of such films being banned (McNair, 2002: 62). For further information on the links between *pornochic* and the *pornochanchada*, see Dennison and Shaw (2004: 171–9).

19. Quoted in 'Luz, cama, ação!' (1998). It is particularly revealing to observe that the plotlines of three of the biggest box-office hits of the 1970s, *Dona Flor*, *Xica da Silva/Xica* (1976) and *Dama do lotação*, revolved around female sexual self-discovery, one of the lynchpins of the *pornochanchada*.

20. To date the most extensive work on defining sexploitation has been carried out by U.S. exploitation expert Eric Schaefer: see, for example, 1999: 337–9;

2003: 42–3. See also Luckett, 2003: 142–56. On Spanish and British sexploitation, respectively, see Kowalsky, 2004: 188–208 and Sheridan, 2005.

21. The film production arm of the Globo network, Globo Filmes, is currently dominating national cinema box offices.

22. *Pintando o sete*/Painting the Town Red (1959) and *Dona Flor e seus dois maridos*, respectively.

23. In the UK context, a rough equivalent might be the current screening of politically incorrect 'nostalgia' series on cable TV such as *On the Buses*.

24. The best example of this phenomenon is Joaquim Pedro de Andrade's *Macunaíma* (1969), a film partly financed by the Instituto Nacional do Cinema (National Cinema Institute), the precursor to Embrafilme. See also *Toda nudez será castigada*, with its outrageously kitsch and melodramatic elements, financed by Embrafilme.

25. See Hunt, 1998: 124.

26. For further examples see the hard-core comedies of Mário Vaz Filho, including the parodic *Toda a nudez é perdoada*/All Nudity is Forgiven (1985). See also Mojica Marins's hard-core films, including *24 horas de sexo explícito*/24 Hours of Explicit Sex (1985).

27. Sternheim, 2005: 37. See also Alessandro Gamo and Luís Rocha Melo's documentary on film producer Antônio Polo Galante, *O Galante rei da Boca* (2004).

16 "Tus pinches leyes yo me las paso por los huevos"

Isela Vega and Mexican Dirty Movies

Sergio de la Mora

Isela Vega's dynamic near five-decade career is defined by scandal. Vega herself interprets these 'scandals' as acts of rebellion that shake people up and push them to think critically (Díaz, 2007: 12). As Mexico's most notorious sex symbol, Vega has had, since the early 1960s, a very diverse career, appearing in close to one hundred films ranging from sexploitation (*S.O.S. conspiración bikini*/The Bikini Conspiracy [René Cardona Jr., 1966] and *La pulquería*/The Pulque Bar [Victor Manuel Castro, 1980]) to art cinema (*Las apariencias engañan*/Appearances Can Be Deceiving [Jaime Humberto Hermosillo, 1983]), as well as more difficult to categorize hybrid films that combine both low- and highbrow filmic conventions (*Puños rosas*/Pink Punch [Beto Gómez, 2004]). Her films exhibit the rebellious and anti–status quo attitude of the sexual revolution and the women's liberation movement. As such, her films challenge social taboos, prejudices, sexist double standards, and oppressive Catholic morals regarding women, the body, sexual expression, and freedom of speech. She is also one of the few women to direct a feature film, *Los amantes del señor de la noche*/Lovers of the Lord of the Night (1984), *before* the full-fledged entrance of women into feature length directing in the late 1980s. A transnational figure, she has worked with noted film auteurs, including Sam Peckinpah (*Bring Me the Head of Alfredo García*, 1974), and has crossed national boundaries and national cinemas, moving mostly between Mexico City and Los Angeles. In the 1970s and 1980s, at the height of her career, she acted in three other U.S. productions, two made-for-TV films, and appeared in the miniseries "The Rhinemen Exchange" (Burt Kennedy, 1977) and TV shows ("The Greatest American Hero" [Robert Culp, 1983], "The Yellow Rose" [John Wilder, 1984], "Rituals" [Arlene Sanford et. al, 1984], "Stingray" [Charlie Picerni, 1986]). She works across high and low cultural categories and across media and the performing arts, alternating between film, television, classic, and countercultural avant-garde theater (*Zaratustra*, Alejandro Jodorowsky, 1970) as well as feminist postmodern performance and cabaret theater (*Pedro Paramount*, Jesusa Rodríguez, 2003). In the 1970s and 1980s many of her films broke box-office records in Mexico and in the U.S. Spanish-language cinema circuit. Her histrionic talents have been recognized with three Arieles (the Mexican film industry's equivalent to the Oscar), including one for her comeback performance in *La ley de Heródes/Herod's Law* (Luis Estrada, 1999) after a fifteen-year absence from any significant big-screen production.

Vega's mere name incites heated passions and strong opinions across the emotional spectrum, from "a woman destroyed by all vices" (Monsiváis, 1990: 346) to "the woman who created a revolution in the history of Mexican erotic cinema" (Macías, 1997). Yet despite her position in Mexican cinema and her considerable impact on Mexican and greater Mexican popular culture, she has to date not been the subject of scholarly research.[1] Her cultural impact is only now being accessed by the academy, although public intellectuals such as Carlos Monsiváis and Elena Poniatowska wrote about her in the 1970s. A primary reason for this glaring omission among academics may be attributed to her participation in both trash cinema, such as *fichera* (brothel) comedies *and* internationally acclaimed auteur cinema, which makes it difficult to categorize her body of work within conventional cinematic hierarchies and topologies.[2] While her films occupy an uncertain status, her oeuvre has unique historical and aesthetic importance. This chapter attempts to fill the gap in Mexican film scholarship regarding Vega by performing a star study of her self- presentation in the press, interviews, films, and the marketing and critical reception of her work. It focuses on films that exploit the representation of sexuality but that also purport to be 'artistic,' exploring how elements of sexploitation share the risqué qualities of art films. It takes into consideration how sexploitation promises a commodity through "four primary sexual appeals: excitement, adventure, curiosity, and experimentation" and how excitement, in the form of "shock," dangles the possibility of "shocking viewers or to shake their sensibilities" (Schaefer, 2007: 29). It also explores how sexploitation and exploitation cinemas in general share much with high art "the same images, tropes, and themes" and "often handle explosive material that mainstream cinema is reluctant to touch" (Hawkins, 2000a: 3, 7). This chapter thus explores Vega's cross-genre leaps between art and (s)exploitation to argue that her star persona exceeds her films, suggesting that she has consciously constructed her own persona in the press as a 'bad' girl who rebels against tradition and that this offscreen persona influences the characters she plays in her movies. It also suggests that the same characteristics appear throughout her oeuvre, irregardless of whether she is acting in a high-art auteur film or a low-budget sexploitation flick.

The skewed focus in Mexican film scholarship on either Golden Age cinema (1935–1957) or the new cinemas of the 1970s and 1990s has, with few exceptions, overlooked other periods, film trends, and stars deemed not worthy of scholarly attention. Latin American film scholars such as Victoria Ruétalo (2004), Dolores Tierney (2004) and John King (2003) have noted how the considerable academic interest in these and other areas (i.e., New Latin American Cinema) has meant that the continent's commercially popular lowbrow cinemas have been overlooked. Meanwhile, Mexican film star studies scholarship is still in its infancy. Monsiváis is the major pioneer of this new area of study, with his chronicles focusing primarily on the major figures from the Mexican Golden Age (1940–1957). Following his lead, English-language star studies have also focused on the stars of the Golden Age, including the work of Ana M. López (1998), Joanne Hershfield (2000), and Paulo Antonio Paranaguá (1999), spotlighting primarily the transnational careers of the leading divas of the classic period, Dolores del Río and María Félix. Rosa Linda Fregoso (2003) and William Anthony Nericcio (2007) examine Lupe Vélez's scandal-filled career in Hollywood while I take up the career of Pedro Infante (2006) from a queer perspective. Most of these star studies are indebted to the pioneering work of Richard Dyer (1981), who has taught us to understand the ideological operations which create the star as text.

Exploitation is a relatively new concept in Mexican cinema scholarship. No Mexican critic or historian has used the term thus far to refer to any aspect of the national cinema, although Anglo scholars like Doyle Greene (2005), Andrew Syder and Tierney (2005) have. Films which could be said to fall within the exploitation category (including many of Vega's) are highly stigmatized in Mexican film scholarship but in a way that is different from the stigmatizing of U.S. exploitation indicated by Schaefer (1999), Sconce (1995), and others. Mexican exploitation films are often referred to as *churros*—the filmic equivalent of a deep-fried, inexpensive pastry, a category that identifies low-budget movies made in short shooting schedules and primarily for profit. The bulk of feature film productions made after the Golden Age period (1960s–1980s), with the exception of the new cinemas of the 1960s and 1970s, were popular commercial movies known as *churros,* which could also be labeled exploitation cinema. Indeed, it is likely that more *churros* than 'quality' films were made during this period. Vega, like other actors who work in these kinds of films, would have easily been able to participate in other production categories; in fact, there would be a need for such high-low category hopping in an industry as volatile as Mexico's. This mobility across production categories and taste draws our attention to the blurring of lines between exploitation films and art films (*cine de calidad*) in the Mexican film industry. Vega is intimately associated with low-budget films, especially soft-core *fichera* movies, often singled out as one of the major causes of the decline of Mexican cinema. Because of these disreputable films, the 1980s is seen as one of the darkest periods in the history of Mexican cinema, although Vega has in the past defended these films, citing their huge commercial success and appeal to popular audiences.[3]

In U.S. exploitation scholarship, star studies are rare because exploitation itself is precisely defined by lower budgets that necessarily preclude access to star players (Schaefer, 1999). Nevertheless, in a very different industrial and economic context, Latin American exploitation produces its own stars, including Santo (the Mexican masked wrestler), Mário Almada (Mexican border/drug film), Isabel Sarli (Argentinean sexploitation star), and José Mojica Marins (Brazilian horror director/star Zé do Caixão). In Latin America and particularly in Mexico, a recurring pattern of cinematic boom and bust as well as film industry union quarrels have pushed many mainstream stars to work across genre and taste boundaries in order to secure employment. Furthermore, genre boundaries between exploitation, mainstream and art cinema are porous in Mexico, with some films simultaneously residing in more than one of these categories.

Vega was extremely influential in the sexual education of Mexicans and Chicana/os who came of age in the 1970s and 1980s. Like others, I first discovered what I interpreted as raw sexuality watching Vega at the movies. She got to bed all the beefy hunks, all of them my forbidden objects of desire. She signified an absence of inhibitions and the embrace of outlaw desires and pleasures, as well as a degree of freedom of expression previously unimaginable in the national cinema but permissible during the so-called democratic opening of the 1970–1976 presidential period. While heterosexual males appear to be the target audience of Vega's films, they also offer pleasure to women and queers (areas that require further study). This essay comments on the affirmation of the female look, female sexual desire, and the eroticization of nude male bodies by characters played by Vega in *El llanto de la tortuga/The Turtle's Scream* (Francisco del Villar, 1975). Unlike other Mexican female actors before her, sex scenes with Vega show her enjoying sexual intercourse, taking pleasure in orgasms, and being an active sexual partner (i.e., she is not confined to the missionary position). In *Las apariencias engañan*, where she plays a hermaphrodite, she is shown penetrating her virile fiancée. This essay suggests that through Vega audiences can vicariously experience taboo sexuality. However, at the same time, the characters she plays rarely have an interior life; costumes, camera work, and lighting render her a sexual object.

A STRAIGHT-TALKING STAR WITHIN
CLASS AND GENDER STEREOTYPES

Since the beginning of her acting career, Vega has cultivated the image of a tough and fierce woman, the complete opposite of the traditional submissive Mexican woman. Her characters have consistently challenged gender norms. She has displayed masculine qualities; strong on all fronts, assertive, bold, outspoken, articulate, and sexually promiscuous. Vega cemented this image in *Las pirañas aman en cuaresma/Piranhas Make Love During Lent* (Francisco del Villar, 1971) where she plays a man-eater, a modern version of María Félix as Doña Bárbara, who, as in the classic 1943 film, rejects all local men but then falls in love with the same man as her daughter. While she is independent, she is also a sexual object as much as she wields sexual agency. This contradiction is evident throughout her career. For Monsiváis, the use of improper language popularized in Vega's movies (e.g., her cursing 'like a man' in *La ley de Heródes*) and the new, antiestablishment "status" of bad words in the 1970s is the product of two movements: *La Onda* (the new wave) urban youth literary movement and the 1968 student movement (1990: 343). Her use of bad words links her to the tradition of the *albur* (wordplay), the *pelado* (urban underdog), and thus to the popular classes. Playing the haggard and bristly brothel owner in *La ley de Heródes*, doña Lupe usurps language coded as male (for example, "tus pinches leyes yo me las paso por los huevos"/Your fucking laws can suck my balls), and with it male privilege, but she inhabits it with such authority that it does not seem forced or out of place. Doña Lupe runs her third-rate brothel with an iron fist and exploits the sex workers. Yet masculine qualities do not make her androgynous or erase her sexuality, perhaps because her legacy as a sex icon codes her body as insistently female. If anything, male elements open up a space for reading her as a butch dyke, although this is a role that is not prominent in her filmography and extrafilmic materials. However 'lesbian' seductions and relationships are not uncommon in her work, notably in *El festín de la loba/The She Wolf's Orgy* (Francisco del Villar, 1972). Her on-screen propensity for straight talk, spouting obscenities, and stripping naked earned her the nickname of "Chichela," an obvious reference to her frequent exposure of her breasts (*chichis* in Mexican slang) during her youth. An online Web site dedicated to the subject of censorship in Mexican film notes, "If Isela doesn't get naked in her films she is not being herself."[4] In the general public's view, Vega is characterized as a vedette (little better than a whore), rather than a serious actress. Part of the problem with this (mis)perception is that Vega is viewed as always performing herself on-screen; her film roles are conflated with the real person rather than seen as the fictions they are. Vega is constantly coded as lower-class and a sexual object by the press and fans alike.

ISELA'S SEXUALITY IN THE LIMELIGHT

Vega is conflated with her on-screen characters precisely because she has played an active role in shaping her image, both on-screen and off. In an early interview with Poniatowska she emphasizes how she tries to be as true to her beliefs as possible; this entails modifying the characters she plays, most notably the script. Well known for being a highly intelligent woman, she is aware of how she is partly responsible for her own sexual commodification in roles where she is both sexual object and subject. In another interview she doesn't hesitate to articulate how, although she *wanted* to play "free spirits," the polar opposite of what a good Mexican woman should be, by playing these kinds of roles she ultimately set herself up to be typecast in the same kinds of roles (Reyes, 1999: 36).

While Vega's sex-symbol image clearly follows the cinematic tradition of her previous compatriots who also made it big in Hollywood, she is more of a liminal figure, somewhere between the feistiness of Vélez and the powerful independence of Katy Jurado. Although Vega had two different husbands, her star text never portrays her as being shackled to men. Fiercely independent off and on-screen, Vega agrees that her films' shocking themes were not there merely to shock but were in fact a politically strategic response to the conservative and repressive social context (Moreno, 2000): designed to break with the masochistic archetype of the submissive, chaste, suffering woman all too common in Mexican national cinema. If women characters ever broke with the established gender norms (as in the *cabaretera*/cabaret or dance-hall films that were popular in the late 1940s and early 1950s), they would be punished for their transgression by death or abandonment (Cuban bombshell Ninón Sevilla's characters, especially Elena in *Aventurera*/*Adventuress* [Alberto Gout, 1951] are a notable exception).

In *El festín de la loba*, the sexual curiosity of Teresa (Vega), an utterly proper daughter, interested in becoming a painter, is contained by the intolerance of her embittered, paralytic, and hypocritically religious mother (played by Golden Age icon Gloria Marín). Upon the death of the matriarch, Teresa proceeds to seduce everyone in her path, from a young priest to her half brother, to the nuns at the convent she enters at the film's conclusion. The film is ambiguous in its message, celebrating Teresa's sexual debauchery but also marking it as a threat and a source of corruption—it leads her sexual partners to tragic ends. *El festín de la loba* registers the necessity of breaking from stifling religious oppression. The lesson to be learned, however, is uncertain since, on the one hand, Teresa's escapades encourage the audience to indulge sexual fantasies regarding the rebellious lead actress while, on the other, both ethics and sexual education are implicitly posited as measures to balance excess and religious hypocrisy. These ideological tensions index how *El festín de la loba* struggles to break with bourgeois morality while simultaneously reinforcing it, a pattern that Salvador Elizondo (2001 [1961]) argues characterizes Mexican cinema's approach to the representation of sexuality.

As part of the promotion for her leading role in *Bring Me the Head of Alfredo Garcia*, Vega famously posed for *Playboy* in 1974 in a multiple-page nude spread with the headline "Viva Vega!" The photos were taken during one of her long-term relocations to Los Angeles, a period when, in addition to her performance in Peckinpah's film, she appeared in several U.S. exploitation films, including *The Torture Chamber* (Jack Hill and Juan Ibañez, 1972). Part of the *Playboy* headline reads: "Brace Yourself, America; Mexico's High-Combustion Isela Vega . . . is Heading your Way." The nude pictorial plays on her Mexicanness in one photo in particular, shot at a slight angle, where she poses as a revolutionary, sitting in a wicker chair in front of a fireplace. Clad only with a cartridge belt crossed over her exposed breasts and snaked around her waist, an imposing rifle rests near the fireplace at her feet; whilst her right leg is seductively crossed over the other leg (potentially to prevent a crass beaver shot). She looks straight out at the camera/spectator. The sensuous pose invites while the phallic rifle hints at danger. Both the *Playboy* spread and Pekinpah's film enhanced her international profile and reconfirmed Vega as Mexico's leading sex icon. The photographs trade on the stereotype of exoticism, violence, bandits, and excess associated in the U.S. popular media with the 1910 Mexican Revolution. The *Playboy* photos themselves and their sexy 'Revolution' theme considerably advanced her notoriety as a 'bad girl' and pinup and are evidence of the concrete ways in which she rebelled against the past and tradition.

In the 1960s and 1970s, for a traditionally Catholic society, nudity was read as a rebellion against social conventions. Nudity in the cinema significantly contributed to carving greater freedom, albeit restricted primarily to women in the cinema, visual media, and performing arts.[5] To strip naked was a marker of freedom of expression. For Vega, nudity was a step forward in fighting religious prohibitions against sexuality, a way to reclaim the body as something not sinful and not a source of shame and a vehement rejection of sexually repressed female characters in the national cinema. Furthermore, nudity on screen challenged censorship. Beyond her films, in interviews she repeatedly expresses a healthy relationship to the body and sexuality and is also aware that sexuality is a politically charged field. In an interview from 2004 she reconfirms that nudity was a necessary step for the liberation of Mexican men and women (Vértiz, 2004).

Only the legendary Golden Age actress María Félix rivaled Vega for her arresting transgressions of gender conventions. Like Félix, Vega's on-screen persona is that of the Devoradora, a man-eater. However, unlike the Golden Age diva, Vega never cultivated a haughty, upper-class arrogance. In fact, the bulk of her work in cinema is directed toward the popular classes. In a chronicle by Monsiváis she refers to her *carpa* (popular tent theater) audience as "*la raza*" (1990: 341), the well-known populist term used to refer to the common people, racialized as *mestizo* (mixed race). To reach this mass audience of common folks she uses colloquial language when addressing them, for example, as "[my] dirty, *rascuache* [low-class] public . . . You are my audience, like my brothers and family, we are children of *la chingada*" (Monsiváis 1990: 341).[6]

THE EXPLOITATION INDUSTRY IN MEXICO

The sexual revolution and the countercultural movement contributed to the proliferation of erotic films from 1968 onwards. Out of 103 films produced in 1968, over 50 percent were classified either as "only for adults" or for those "21 and over" (García Riera, 1998: 263). According to Emilio García Riera, the eroticization of commercial Mexican cinema was a box-office strategy for producers more interested in catering to middle-class desires for picaresque vulgarity rather than in maintaining family values (1996b: 8). That more and more films were classified as adults only was because of increasing amounts of female nudity (usually not full frontal), risqué themes, and 'adult language.' García Riera notes that these filmic conventions were indicative of the supposed modernity of the national cinema that sought to imitate an increasingly more daring foreign cinema (1996b: 8). This period of eroticization in Mexican cinema was continued and further radicalized by the liberal regime of Luis Echeverría that followed in 1970. The bottom line was that Mexican spectators lined up at the box office for almost any combination of sex and comedy as proven by the two-decade reign of *fichera* movies, sexy comedies, and *albur* comedies.[7] Images of strong self-empowered women proliferated from this period onwards as a result of women's liberation. Also key in these images of strong women was the participation of film-school-trained women directors in the film industry (Marcela Fernández Violante) and the films of 'out' gay filmmaker Jaime Humberto Hermosillo.

Exploitation cinema occupies a contested position in relation to Mexican national cinema. However, despite its low status, the sheer volume of exploitation-type films made and their enormous commercial success makes their inclusion in any account of Mexican national cinema almost inevitable, if only as examples of naïve popular culture. Low genres (masked wrestler movies, sexy comedies, *albur* comedies, narco traffic action films) consistently earned the most money at the box office from the 1960s through the 1980s. In fact, if we take consumption (i.e., what audiences are watching) as a marker of what constitutes a national cinema, as Higson suggests (1989: 38), it can be argued that exploitation effectively *became* Mexican national cinema from the 1960s onwards when in the midst of an ongoing crisis due to the advent of television and loss of foreign markets the majority of Mexican film production (and the biggest audience draws) became cheap, often low-quality serial/compilation genre films. Jorge Ayala Blanco, an institution in Mexican film criticism, is one of the few Mexican critics to champion this 'trash' cinema. The attention he gives to films that could be classified as exploitation validates trash cinema as legitimate popular cinematic expression (Ayala Blanco, 1974, 1986, 1991).

Many of Vega's films draw on conventions of exploitation and its related fields of trash and 'badfilm,' including those 'art films' made by famous Mexican auteurs (Arturo Ripstein and Paul Leduc). In keeping with Hawkins's argument cited earlier, these films, often transgressive in a Mexican context, generated huge amounts of publicity and were highly censored, particularly because of their sexual content: male and female homosexuality (*Las apariencias engañan*) and pedophilia (*La primavera de los escorpiones*); prostitution, substance abuse, and lesbianism (*Las reglas del juego/ The Rules of the Game*, Mauricio Walerstein, 1970); incest (*El festín de la loba*); graphic displays of women taking pleasure in sex acts (*La india/The*

Indian Woman, Rogelio A. González, 1976); audacious depictions of taboo subjects, such as the combination of sex and religion (*La viuda negra/The Black Widow,* Arturo Ripstein, 1977); and black-white racial miscegenation (*Drum,* (Steve Carver, 1976) the sequel to the cult film *Mandingo,* Richard Fleischer, 1975). Other more politically transgressive films she worked on also include critiques of Mexico's historically corrupt political system (*La ley de Heródes*) and a recent exposé of the links between terrorism and the exploitation of 'Third World' human labor and resources, *Cobrador, In God We Trust* (Paul Leduc, 2007). The titles of most of these films reveal how Vega is enshrined as a figure connected with the daring, the liberated, and the sexual in the popular imaginary and in Mexican film history. The films' daring subject matter, representation of taboo subjects, explicit sexuality, and excessive violence are all elements that mainstream cinema tends to shy away from but are the mainstay of exploitation cinema (and also, according to Hawkins, of European art cinema and avant-garde films).

Despite depicting Vega as a rebel and 'liberated' woman, many of her films can also be seen as conservative and sexist in their objectification of her body, catering to male heterosexual voyeuristic pleasures. However, although edgy content is easily contained by these heterosexual, mainstream tendencies in the films, their subversive quality lingers. A case in point is the daring Oedipal drama *La india,* where Vega appears nude 90 percent of the time figuring seemingly as *only* a body that functions as visual spectacle and object of sexual desire (she has no more than ten lines of dialogue in the entire film). Vega's performance in *La india,* however, contests this conservative interpretation, because her sheer excessiveness suggests an ironic undermining of her as body/object (this is the case in many of the films she made with Francisco del Villar). In most of del Villar's films she portrays independent women with agency who speak their mind and are unafraid of social norms or the potential threat of male sexual aggression. Even when she is a survivor of sexual violence she is never a passive victim. In *La viuda negra,* for instance, a seemingly proper small-town doctor attempts to rape her but, to his surprise, she fights him off with fists and screams. A similar rape scene is repeated in the film *El llanto de la tortuga,* which, in its treatment of daring, outrageous, and shocking subject matter is very typical of Vega's films, but shows some of the problems with seeing her work as purely progressive.

WHO HAS BIGGER PECS, ISELA OR JORGE?

Rather than focusing exclusively on Vega's star image in *El llanto de la tortuga,* this next section explores how she became a notorious figure by looking at the film's marketing and international reception. Although her fourth and most commercially successful collaboration with zoophilic del

Villar includes an all-star cast of regulars in (s)exploitation-type movies, Vega gets top billing. The film is set in an opulent ocean-side mansion in Acapulco and was advertised as a raw exposé and social denunciation of the decadent excesses of four young and wealthy individuals from Mexico City. What starts out as a weekend birthday bash in honor of Héctor (Hugo Stiglitz) escalates into an aggressive orgy, culminating in murder. The party is attended by Héctor's virginal sister Isabel (Cecilia Pezet), with whom Héctor has an incestuous relationship; Carlos (Jorge Rivero), his childhood friend and rival; and Diana (Vega), Carlos's partner. At the film's conclusion, their social status makes them immune to punishment; the detectives assigned to investigate the (butler's) murder choose to look the other way as the group leaves for a party that evening. In the stalwart tradition of Mexican melodrama, class conflicts are contained by simply affirming that the wealthy middle classes are an unhappy crowd.

The camp elements in this film make it a highlight of Vega's career. As the first evening progresses, hosts and guests, drunk on champagne, are portrayed as utterly cynical, arrogant, perverse, cruel, and decadent, as they (particularly Diana and Carlos) continually hurl insults at each other (e.g., "you're full of debts and stupidity" and "shut your latrine, you bitch!"). Their actions continually reinforce their callousness and dehumanity. The ultramuscular Carlos, a playboy architect and unsuccessful gambler, who is supported by Diana, has an inferiority complex, especially in relation to his childhood friend Héctor, a successful millionaire architect from a prominent family of unscrupulous politicians. To feel better, Carlos continually invokes Héctor's lack of sexual experience while Héctor and Diana, in turn, take every opportunity to humiliate Carlos for being an economic failure and a coward. Diana's use of crude language is contrasted to the proper expressions used by Isabel. The film maximizes Vega's image of a woman with a dirty mouth. Out of all the relationships, described as "sickly" and "tortured" in publicity materials, the ultimate symbol of decadence and deviance is the incest between the rich siblings.

El llanto de la tortuga aims to fulfill the conventions of sexploitation as outlined by Schaefer previously cited. Lurid teasers in newspaper advertising promise difference and transgression. The 'adults only' content is suggested through use of key words such as "orgy," "intimate," "raw," "violate," "degradation," and "violent." These adjectives emphasize how the film is also unusual and courageous, 'boldly' revealing secrets about the jet set's social transgressions with one tagline reading: "An audacious chronicle that bravely reveals the intimate life of a privileged class." In sexploitation fashion the latter tagline makes explicit the film's claim to a critical content of denunciation (in the style of yellow press). Promotional materials also highlight the film's timid staging of lesbianism, one of the film's many allegedly racy sexual variations. The ad's text that highlights lesbianism reads, "behind every act an offense, after every word degradation": a close-up two shot of Vega and Pezet standing very close and face-to-face while looking into each other's eyes is the corresponding visual image. Vega holds one of Pezet's hands while with the other she touches the younger woman's lips. Only a glass of liquor in Pezet's hand stands between them, hinting of what is to come once the liquor is consumed. Another ad focuses on wealth, leisure, and promiscuity. A woman's full nude figure stands center frame with her back to the camera and her arms akimbo; she is standing in front of a huge pool, with the ocean in the immediate background. The woman seems to follow the figure of a muscular man in tight swimsuit who's on the other side of the pool in the background. These teasers appeal to viewer curiosity, promising privileged access to intimacies never before caught on film and enticing audiences to witness the novelty of previously invisible orgies: "We invite you to attend one of these intimate gatherings about which so much has been said but that no one has witnessed" and "narrated with a raw cinematic language." The ads underscore how the film treats controversial topics using realistic language and explicit sexuality.

What is most interesting about this film is its overt sexualization of men (which makes it apt for queer appropriation). Male bodies are displayed in skimpy swim trunks and skin-tight clothing like jumpsuits. They also appear shirtless a great deal of the time, with the ex-bodybuilder Rivero displaying his formidable six-pack at every possible opportunity. Both Rivero and Gregorio Casal (the Butler, Sergio) are objects of the camera's desire while Casal, fetishized as the only working-class character in the film, is also the object of desire for the female characters. Not coincidentally, Sergio occupies the conspicuous narrative function of being the most sexually desirable and available since both women make advances on him and he becomes a rival for Héctor and Carlos. After spending a good deal of time trying to seduce Sergio, Diana spurns his come-on and he retaliates by raping her. Earlier in the film, Sergio has sex with Isabel. Throughout *El llanto de la tortuga* Vega emphasizes her own subjectivity, swearing and being positioned as the subject of erotic pleasure. However, at one point in the film she is gang raped by four fishermen (which causes her to spontaneously miscarry). Hence, although Vega never loses her edge, her character is punished for being aggressive and rebellious.

Critics almost unanimously discredit Vega's collaborations with del Villar. The screening of *El llanto de la tortuga* at the Cartagena International Film Festival received virulently negative reviews in the Colombian press when it screened in the mid-1970s. Reactions included general indignation and accusations that it was a basic imitation of "pornographic films from New York" (Cineteca Nacional). In another critic's opinion, the film was excessive in its risible insults but held back on the graphic nudity it had promised. The critic also noted the sexism of displaying female full frontal nudity during sex scenes in which men keep their pants on. The film, however, did upset critics. One critic, commenting on the film's title and offensive content, states, "the one crying here is the spectator who screams for an end to so much infamy, mediocrity and trash accumulated in an hour and a half" (Cineteca Nacional). Another critic claims the film is repugnant and induces nausea. The film is successful in shocking audiences. Yet, as these critics note, it is also involuntarily comical in its accumulation of profanities and acts of degradation.

El llanto de la tortuga is excessive and artificial in many respects. The acting is hyperbolic with characters shouting the cruelest and most hurtful

Figure 16.1   Isela Vega in *Las reglas del juego/The Rules of the Game* (Mauricio Walerstein, 1970). Courtesy Cineteca Nacional.

things possible at each other. *El llanto de la tortuga* effectively shows that sex is power and that sexuality is a mechanism for economic well-being as well as an instrument for exploitation. The cryptic title, which refers to the displacement of tortoises from their oceanic realm, underscores the film's recurrent theme of loss of innocence, while also drawing a parallel between animals and the primitive behavior of the characters.

As Vega matured in years, her career took a turn in the late 1990s toward greater prestige, symbolized by award-winning performances in roles that departed from her sexual icon image but continued her signature blunt talk. No longer shackled by obligatory nudity and sexuality, her career revival in her 'old age' confirmed Vega as a serious character actor, especially in campy comedies such as the queer, postexploitation border *narcofronteriza* (border/drug trafficking) prison film, *Puños rosas*. In this highly stylized homage to 'bad' cinema, she plays La Güera, a ferocious matriarchal figure involved in the trafficking of cars whose daughter's husband is romantically involved with an amateur boxer and ex-con. Vega continues championing edgy films that blur the boundary between art and mainstream cinema.

NOTES

1. Aside from numerous journalistic pieces, the most significant popular press account is a chapter-length homage by Reséndiz and Villareal (1995).
2. Fichera films are Mexico's major contribution to Latin American sexploitation and a contemporary counterpart of Brazilian pornochanchadas.
3. "We need optimism and these films that intellectuals do not concede any value to, are optimistic. They are entertaining and thus fulfill a very valuable function." A. Talavera Serdán, (1980), "Isela dentro y fuera," *Cine*, 24 April, 55.
4. http://www.cinemexicanosincensura.org/cine/viewtopic.php?p=1859&sid=021219e100b43e5818501072bb611e4 (accessed 18 February 2008).
5. José M. Ponce (2004) makes a similar argument for post-Franco dictatorship in Spain.
6. La chingada madre refers to the historical figure of La Malinche, Hernán Córtez's translator, symbolic mother of the Mexican mestizo, mythologized as being a product of rape.
7. These comedies are among the few examples of contemporary Mexican cinema available for rent at chains like Blockbuster both in Mexico and in U.S. Spanish-language markets.

Epilogue

17 At the Margin of the Margins
Contemporary Ecuadorian Exploitation Cinema and the Local Pirate Market

Gabriela Alemán

A simple maxim would state that anything that circulates through illegal channels carries subversion at its core. If, as is my intention in this chapter, I am to concentrate on the subject of pirate copies, a distinction should be made from the start. I will marginally touch upon the subject of the reproducer of these pirate works but concentrate on the circulation and the consumption of these works in a market where legal copies are restricted, due to high costs or inaccessibility to them. It is in this context that I will 'think' about piracy and how it is largely the result of the global diffusion of consumerism under an unequal distribution of world wealth as well as the result of an affable climate towards the free entrepreneur and commercial traffic (Pang, 2004a: 102). The case of Ecuador is singular in that the pirate market is not only flooded with international blockbusters but also with low-fare national productions which have not entered commercial film circuits. This chapter concentrates on three specific areas of these low-fare national productions, the hit men from Manabí series, the documentary/gore film, and the *Kichwa* melodrama, to explore the ways in which these movies were made. It then looks at how these DVD-released films fit into the category of exploitation cinema as it is understood internationally.

THE NEW DISTRIBUTORS: PIRATES

Ecuador did not escape the worldwide decline of movie theaters in the mid-1990s; most of the old buildings were turned into evangelical temples or Bingo Halls. The large multinational video rentals had not yet made it to Ecuador, and whatever circulated in VHS format was Hollywood fare. By the time the declining interest of audiences began to show, distributors had long stopped bringing Chinese, Indian, or European features. PelMex (the Mexican company that distributed throughout Latin America) had shut its offices in Ecuador, and the only way to see Latin American movies was at the occasional film festival. At this point the multiplex, with its simultaneous world premieres, as well as art-house movie theaters arrived in Ecuador. Ticket prices sky rocketed with the dollarization of the economy at the end of the twentieth century. Ecuador, almost overnight, entered the global community with its acquired tastes, needs, and desires. At this point, the VCD[1] appeared in the market. This popular low-end technology, with its poor audio and visual quality, offered a foot inside the glittering world of Hollywood *and* another foot outside, in the practice of people's everyday life in a socially constructed political economy (Pang, 2004b: 21). Watching VCDs was/is an adventure in and of itself: the TV screen pixilates; the image is frozen innumerable times. If the movie was filmed during a screening, you not only dimly hear the dialogues of the plot line but people munching on popcorn, couples kissing, teenagers laughing, the occasional child crying, and ever so rarely a parent getting up from his/her seat and blocking the screen to take their children to the bathroom. On the other hand, if the VCD came out before the national screening, in an undubbed version, the unofficial subtitles told a completely different story from what was happening on-screen. As technology advanced, the VCD was replaced by the DVD (although the VCD never actually disappeared) with its multiple options and features; the *Criterion Collection* slowly trickled into the stores with its making of documentaries, interviews with screenwriters, directors, photography directors, and storyboard options. Along with these features, virtual film schools were established through the stop-rewind "how did they do that?" play options. At the same time, digital cameras and camcorders started to arrive in stores as well as Korean Dae Woo DVD multizone reproducers, which could also read VCDs. Simultaneously, pirated software programs for editing became available. It is only in this context that the transfer of Ecuadorian cinema direct to DVD, bypassing commercial distribution, profits for the producers, and nationwide sales, could come about and become a new product with a different cultural status. The precedent to these productions would lie in the exploitation films shot in the 1960s and 1970s. No less than eleven movies were shot in Ecuador by Mexican, Argentinean, and Spanish production companies alongside their Ecuadorian counterparts. All of them were exploitation flicks: teenage bikini films, spy thrillers, and soft porn (Alemán, 2004). These movies were distributed throughout the continent by PelMex and had great commercial success in Ecuador. It is important to remember that in the 1960s and 1970s Ecuador had 150 movie theaters nationwide; and therefore, one could watch movies on the big screen not only in the larger cities of Ecuador but also in its small towns, something which in 2008 is now no longer possible. [2]

THE COLONIALITY OF KNOWLEDGE AND COPYRIGHTS

The discussion of pirated goods inevitably leads us into the quicksand of illegality. Before talking about contemporary exploitation in Ecuador, I would like to ponder some of the arguments concerning the moral and economic dilemmas of copyright as they are intertwined with the circulation of knowledge and access to it in Ecuador. As Rocío Silva Santisteban (2007) points out, knowledge has been organized in the major centers of power and it is the elites who have direct access to it; in order to overcome the obstacles shared by those without economic resources, knowledge has to be accessed by different means. In the case of academics or students in Latin America, the photocopying of texts has become the major way of surmounting the coloniality of knowledge (Silva Santisteban, 2007: 250). Although Silva Santisteban's argument follows the route of the photocopy and not pirated goods, whose logic is different, I would argue that computer software and the different DVDs available of specialized films can also form part of that knowledge not easily accessible to those interested in film from low-income levels, living in countries in the periphery. Although the circulation of pirated DVDs is a worldwide phenomenon, it is linked in the media with mafias or the laundering of money; and it has most recently resurfaced as a negotiating factor in trade agreements with the United States,[3] used to pressure governments through the World Trade Organization to accept the universality of intellectual property rights (IPR) (http://www.variety.com/VR1117984389.html). I would like to contend that the discussion concerning pirated cultural products cannot only take place at an economic level. The moral/economic dilemmas of copyright, as defended by the WTO, are only part of a larger discussion that surrounds the significance of the circulation of cultural goods in Asia, Africa, and Latin America. This discussion also has to do with the 'place' these three continents occupy in the divide between modernity and colonialism. Walter Mignolo asserts that capitalism is of the essence for both the conception of modernity and its darker side, coloniality (2005: 6). Modernity is the name for the historical process in which Europe (later the United States) began to progress toward world hegemony, its flip side being coloniality (Mignolo, 2005: xiii). Coloniality unveils an embedded logic that enforces control, domination, and exploitation disguised in the language of salvation, progress, and modernization. The perspective of modernity is also geopolitically grounded, although it is disguised as the natural course of universal history. The logic of coloniality can be understood as working through four domains of human experience: the economic; the political; the civic; the epistemic and the subjective/personal control of knowledge and subjectivity. As power and capital concentrate in fewer and fewer hands and poverty increases all over the world, the logic of coloniality only becomes more oppressive (Mignolo, 2005: 6–11). It is Joost Smiers's argument that the real beneficiaries of copyrights around the globe are not authors but rather large cultural conglomerates which have the property rights on nearly all artistic creations of the past and present and TRIPs, the intellectual property treaty of the WTO, makes it possible for this 'intellectual landgrab' of buying copyrights to take place all over the world, without restrictions or borders. The once sympathetic concept of copyright (invented during the Romantic period in the West, but alien to many cultures) is turning into a means of control over intellectual and creative commons by a very limited number of cultural industries which also own the means of production, as well as the distribution channels of cultural products. Once conglomerates 'own' the rights, it is they who set the prices for the reproduction of the material they hold through their oligopolies; it is also they, and not the artists, who are the chief beneficiaries of profits when reproducing these materials. As Smiers points out:

> One of the reasons that mass-scale piracy is so easy is the increase in excess production capacity of CDs, DVDs and so on. There is currently more than double the manufacturing capacity available worldwide than is needed for legitimate production. The cost of new and second-hand machinery is falling . . . The major rights holders are actually causing this excess capacity themselves. They operate in very tense and nervous markets that 'oblige' them to have instantly sufficient production capacity . . . There is no reason to imagine that the 'struggle' against this mass-scale piracy can be won, not even by the invention of very sophisticated safety measures against copying and by the introduction of police brigades[4] against piracy, which, by the way, will cost Third World Countries more than they can afford (2002: 122).

Although the situation differs from country to country, in Ecuador piracy can be considered a business but not an industry. In the majority of cases the 'matrix' of the different films come from Peru; what the local sellers do is burn copies.[5] This is mostly the case of the 'commercial films,' that is, Hollywood films; an interesting offshoot of this is the specialized 'arthouse' pirate *cinéphile* stores that cater to an otherwise untapped public. In these taxpaying stores[6] you can find anything ranging from Andrei Tarkovsky to Wes Anderson to Luis Buñuel, John Huston, Pedro Almodóvar, Francisco Lombardi, Wong Kar Wai, François Truffaut, Ingmar Bergman, or Michelangelo Antonioni[7] for two dollars; all these DVDs come with the extra materials found in the original copies. These DVDs eventually trickle down to the 'other' stores, as they themselves are pirated. This, in itself, causes a new and very interesting phenomenon: the novel categories these films enter into and their new routes of circulation. Not unlike Borges's Chinese Encyclopedia, the miscegenation of the high and the low ends of culture brings about new ways of imagining things (Foucault, 2001: xv–xvii). The untrained/unspecialized vendors recommend Lucrecia Martel's *La niña santa/The Holy Girl* (2004) as the latest horror movie or Buñuel's *Gran casino/Big Casino* (1946) as a simple Mexican musical. Buñuel's high-art status is displaced in favor of Jorge Negrete's popular appeal. On the shelves of these DVD stores *Ringu* (Hideo Nakata, 1998) is placed next to *The Blair Witch Project* (Daniel Myrick and Eduardo Sánchez, 1999), which sits next to *Cannibal Holocaust* (Ruggerio Deodato, 1980), *Bride of Chucky* (Ronny Yu, 1998), *Night of the Living Dead* (George A. Romero, 1969), *Freddy vs. Jason* (Ronny Yu, 2003), and *Tesis/Thesis* (Alejandro Amenábar, 1996): exploding/exposing the categories we tend to accept as fixed. In a country without a film culture,[8] where cinema tickets cost $4 and cinema-going is mostly a middle-class activity, people pick up whatever they can at their nearest DVD shop and later circulate it amongst friends, family, and neighbors. Pierre Bourdieu's (1984) notion of taste somehow goes awry; something new seems to be at play. Also, as we will later see, the little access the directors featured in this chapter have had to a cinematic education is through the DVDs that have fallen into their hands.

LOW-FARE NATIONAL PRODUCTIONS

When speaking of exploitation movies we think of forbidden spectacles and thrills, of movies with an extra edge. Eric Schaefer has recognized three distinctive features of the classical exploitation flicks: forbidden topics, low production values, and independent distribution (1999: 6). The films focused on in this chapter—the action, terror and melodrama films that make up the bulk of Ecuador's pirate market—fit part of Schaefer's exploitation typology in that they have low production values and are independently produced but may not necessarily cover forbidden topics. In fact, melodrama is one of the most distinctive genres of Latin America's classical and contemporary media industries, from silent films through the Golden Age of Mexican cinema to present day *telenovelas* (soap operas). Similarly, action films are part of the everyday fare of global cinema, and gore is no longer a taboo genre, as can be seen in the displays of DVD shops all over Ecuador.

HIT MEN FROM MANABÍ

Under the heading of 'action,' a new exploitation subgenre has emerged in recent years in Ecuador: films about hit men. What is important in these movies is the on-screen visualization of gunshots, kidnappings, shady business, and killings, no matter what the origin of the films or the cultural capital that backs them. In the same DVD we may find the award-winning Venezuelan film *Sicario/Hit Man* (José Ramón Novoa, 1994); winner of the Cartagena Film Festival, the Colombian film *Soñar no cuesta nada/A Ton of Luck* (Jorge Ali Triana, 2006); the low-budget 2003 Mexican production *La cruz de marihuana* (2003);[9] and *Sicarios manabitas 1* (Fernando Cedeño), 2 (*Avaricia*, Fernando Cedeño 2000), and 3 (*Me convertí en asesino*).[10] Presently, this hit-men collection, titled *Sicarios manabitas/ Hit Men from Manabí*, which compresses these six films, on MPEG-4, for

1 dollar) is the hottest-selling item in the popular sectors of the large cities or small provincial towns.[11] *Sicarios manabitas* has reached national circulation within the pirate market. The way it was produced distances it from the 'legitimate' centers of audiovisual production in Ecuador (first produced on VHS and then converted to DVD). The traditional centers of production have been, since the 1920s, Guayaquil and Quito (the most populated and economically robust cities of Ecuador). Guayaquil and Quito are also where Ecuador's only film schools are located and to where those who have studied filmmaking abroad come back to make their own films.

Fernando Cedeño, who has not studied filmmaking at all (much less in Ecuador or abroad) and who makes films in neither of these filmmaking centers (but in Chone, a town in coastal Manabí province), writes, directs, produces, and acts in the films he makes in his spare time. He has made four feature films since 1995: *En busca del tesoro perdido*/In Search of the Lost Treasure (1995), *Avaricia*/Greed (2000), *Barahúnda en la montaña*/Rumble in the Mountain (a2004), and *Sicarios manabitas*/Hit Men from Manabí (2005). In order to make a living, he sells wood and is an itinerant merchant. His hobbies are martial arts and motorcycles. His first film was made with friends: "We weren't looking for money, all we wanted was for people to see us . . . The obvious question was: What will the movie be about? . . . Well, we thought, about the only things that we know how to do, fighting and motorcycles" (Andrade, 2007: 112). Nixon Chalacama, a professional electrician, began working with Cedeño, but later went on to direct and produce two feature films of his own: *El cráneo de oro*/The Golden Skull (2001) and *El destructor invisible*/The Invisible Destroyer (2002). In the 1990s, these filmmakers filmed with a camera that was borrowed from a friend and they edited on an S-VHS machine that belonged to that same friend, who had brought them from a trip to the United States, looking to set up a business that never quite worked out. According to Fernando, "The sound track [of *En busca del tesoro perdido*] was recorded live, with a small electronic piano that moved along next to the camera, accentuating the moments of tension" (Andrade, 2007: 116). This first film, starring Cedeño and Chalacama (without the use of doubles in action scenes), was exhibited for four days, with two daily shows in the now defunct Oriflama Cinema and had an audience of five thousand; with the money received, they were able to pay the salaries of all the participants. With *Avaricia*, they sold more than three hundred copies in VHS format and the film was shown on local television. For this film, which Cedeño describes as "The story of a rich man that recruits a band of heartless thugs to buy out farmlands any way possible," 80 percent of the ammunition used was real. Blank cartridges were too expensive and they were looking to cut costs (Andrade, 2007: 118). In one of the scenes from the film, we witness a chase through the central market of Chone, aboard a motorcycle, and the actors shoot real bullets; no one took the precaution of warning the merchants, and much less the buyers, that a movie was being filmed (a fact attested to by the very real terror evident in their faces). *El cráneo de oro* had a cost of $800. It was shown for five days in the assembly hall of the city of Chone and made $6,000 at the box office.

By 2005, *Sicarios manabitas* received the unexpected support from a dentist (Rangel García) born in Manabí living in the United States, who decided to invest in the movie, while at the same time playing the leading role and creating the main musical theme. García invested $35,000, which was used to cover the cost of professional equipment, hire a Mexican editor who worked for two weeks in Ecuador, and the cost of image correction in New York. Subsequently the film had a premier in Queens (which has a large Ecuadorian diaspora) before a public of four hundred spectators; it was later screened in the Long Island Boulton Center and then in Manabí at the Chone Mechanics Syndicate. At the present time, these films, with the exception of *En busca del tesoro perdido* and *Barahúnda en la montaña*, are circulating throughout Ecuador in two compilations: *Secuestros, drogas y muerte: Sicarios manabitas en colección*/Kidnappings, Drugs and Death: Hit Men from Manabí in Collection and *Colección producción nacional: películas ecuatorianas de acción*/National Production Collection: Ecuadorian Action Films. The first collection includes parts 1, 2, and 3 from *Sicarios manabitas*; in reality, Volume 1 is *Sicarios manabitas*, Volume 2 is *Avaricia*, and Volume 3 is a short film (twenty-five minutes) from Riobamba[12] titled *Me convertí en asesino*/I Turned into a Killer. The story of how this short film, *Me convertí en asesino*, came into being serves to illustrate how popular and successful the Ecuadorian 'action' movies being distributed through the pirate market network have become. Henry Guano, of the Draks-Corpios Martial Arts Academy, contacted a small production company in Riobamba to make a TV spot for his institute; after the producers witnessed the skills of the instructor and noticed his 'resemblance' to Bruce Lee, they decided to join efforts to produce a film that would be popular while also publicizing the academy. The end result is a film faithful to the spirit of Lee's films: unexplainable situations, bands of truants who terrorize innocent victims, and fights galore. The film begins with a gang of bad guys dressed as martial artists who, according to the voice-over, "terrorize the city of Riobamba." What we see on the screen is a group of boys hitting an ice-cream vendor and then kidnapping a girl who chats with her boyfriend (the instructor). In the next scene, we hear the voice-over of the boyfriend, saying that he will learn martial arts in order to rescue his girl. Appropriately, the next scene starts with the Lee clone reading a photocopy of a karate manual. We then hear some 1980s music and see the boy clumsily practicing exercises while some letters appear on the screen, "After a month . . ." The boy is now an expert in kung-fu (knowledge acquired through photocopies) and, with the background music of *Mission Impossible*, he goes off to rescue his girlfriend, who is being detained by the karate-practicing bad guys, who, after raping the girl, listen to bar music and drink beer along with their boss. The Ecuadorian Lee arrives, kicks, punches, and, without much of a fight, defeats the bad guys and frees his girlfriend. The producers of these tapes for the local market didn't hesitate in giving it the title of *Sicarios manabitas 3*, even though there is no connection with the Cedeño and Chalacama productions, save the common theme of martial arts and kidnappings.

What is particularly interesting about the hit-men series is the transnational elements of these films. They are considerably indebted to the action films of the Van Damme-Stallone-Segal trinity; as well as to the Mexican *narcofronteriza* (border/drug) film. *Sicarios manabitas 1* begins with a Mexican/Manabita corrido (song) composed by the producer of the film that 'narrates' the story of the film. There is also a great debt to the fight-scene-focused Lee films, and to the sensual discretion of the Bó-Sarli productions of the mid-1970s, where sex is insinuated but never shown. In all the films of the series, whenever there is a sexual encounter, it is portrayed at the foot of a waterfall; when the couples begin to kiss, the camera discretely pulls back from the falling water. On occasion, these films pay homage to the widely read (and heard on the radio) Mexican comic book hero Kaliman, whom Cedeño cites among his favorite action heroes.

GORE AS DOCUMENTARY

The VCD *El caso Cabrera*/The Cabrera Case (2005) is an unseeming audio-visual piece. It fits into as many categories as exist in the shelves of pirate businesses: documentary, gore, comedy, reality TV. Because of its closeness in topic and material with the subject of death, in the exploitation circuit, it would be classed as a mondo film. As Andrew Syder points out:

> Far from avoiding death, mondo has become a genre of documentary practice that is founded precisely on its *display* and on the transgression of the social taboos that keep it hidden. Furthermore, the mondo film invariably refuses to comply with the demand for an ethical space. Rather, it flaunts a position of questionable taste and morality, offering images of the deaths of others for shock and/or entertainment value. (2000: 2)

At its worst, this offering questionable images of death for shock and/or entertainment is what *El caso Cabrera* does. In October 2005 the 'Cabrera Case' made the headlines of Ecuadorian newspapers; José Cabrera Román, the seventy-one-year-old notary public of Machala, died in bed in Quito next to his eighteen-year-old mistress. More than fifty thousand people from all over the country came to Machala, to recover the investments they had made with him. Unlike banks, which paid a 2 to 4 percent yearly interest rate, Cabrera paid a monthly 10 percent; his investments ran in the millions but, soon after he died, the money vanished. Many of the investors of the illegal operation had been prominent politicians, retired and active military, and police officers. His children fled the country and his offices were looted by desperate investors who wanted to recover some of their money; shortly after, his tomb was desecrated. Those who had lost their life savings wanted to make sure that he had actually died (some skeptically stuck sticks in his corpse to make sure it was real). The TV stations sent in reporters, and the news programs showed some of the desperate scenes of what was going on in Machala; certain images, though, were believed to be too strong for public viewing and edited out. A bold reporter took this rejected material, made an 'uncut' version, and disseminated it on VCD that sold like hotcakes in the streets of Machala. The images were spectacular: close-ups of policemen with bags full of dollar bills, others with bills coming out of their antibullet vests, all the while professing that they were there to protect the 'public' interest; people doubting the authenticity of Cabrera inside the casket, "He's plastic, his skin isn't real." The VCD did not have a narrative structure: the grainy hyperreal TV image lacked a *story*. What we saw in *El caso Cabrera* was something closer to the spectacle of the early "cinema of attractions" (Gunning, 1989). The interest in this 'documentary' lay in the recognition factor, its interactivity with its local audience, "Look, it's the chief of police with one of the sacks of money!"; "It's Doña Rosa trying to get ahead in line; she lost three hundred thousand and all the money her children sent over, even the land she inherited from her deceased mother." We could imagine the people from Machala pointing at the TV screen and recognizing the characters of their own drama. It was *that*, plus reality TV and "candid camera" at its worst. The TV stations would not touch the VCD, not only because of its 'disturbing' images, but because *local* authorities were easily recognizable, committing illegal acts. Another interesting fact about this 'documentary,' or strewn-images-with-no-commentary-of-different-events-during-the-days-following-Cabrera's-death, was that a copy made its way to Quito and was screened in a special session during the prestigious EDOC Documentary Film Festival (2006). What was singular about that event was the discussion that ensued; it did not deal with the structure of the 'document,' and the 'text' itself hardly entered the discussion, or what category it could fit into. A discussion of the strategies of representation of mondo and documentary, their bond with the real, was not of interest; the debate centered mostly on the dilemma of the organizers about including it in the festival because it wasn't an 'authored' text. The argument went that because it didn't carry an authorized voice, lacked credits, *and* circulated in an unofficial pirate circuit it didn't 'exist,' and yet, it is the only audiovisual document still in circulation of that major event in Ecuadorian public life. In the discussion, other factors were measured: that it was in bad taste and that it was perturbing; the public was also reprimanded for its nervous laughter by the chair of the discussion. The hyperreality (tied in the public eye to the TV image) in 'that' space seemed a montage, plus the pixilated screen of the VCD made obvious its low production values. What became apparent was the lack of dialogue between the different audiovisual sectors of Ecuador. In a double move, the ethics of the illegal pirate community (and its consumers) were put in doubt while the legal and authorized 'texts' circulating in the festival were redefined as the intellectual and socially authorized voice.

KICHWA MELODRAMA

The air waves have been 'contaminated' with satellite signals, white noise, Wi-Fi; electricity has reached even the remotest villages in the mountain-side or jungle and through user-friendly technology people communicate through Skype, Hi5, or Messenger. Digital videos with home movies or spoken letters are sent through courier services or over the Internet if broadband is available and Internet cafés are everywhere to be found. DVDs and VCDs are not a luxury but a very accessible form of entertain-ment and the only way, for the vast majority of the Ecuadorian popula-tion, to watch movies. Of the vast pool of films in DVD format, more than 90 percent are still Hollywood fare with its tropes and transparent realistic editing style, racial stereotypes and narrative structures, individ-ual protagonist, and its ever endless strive towards happiness and (mate-rial) progress. Have Ecuadorian direct-to-DVD productions escaped this logic? Has the viewing public accepted that representation as universal? In some ways recent *Kichwa* productions are an experiment within the boundaries of those representations. A group of evangelical *Kichwa* youth, originally from the surrounding areas of Riobamba, but all living at present in Quito, has come together in the collective Sinchi Samay to make audiovisual productions. According to William León, one of the founders of the group,

> in . . . 2004, a group of friends and I participated in an acting workshop with the TECC (Experimental Theater of the *Casa de la Cultura*), and in order to continue with our preparation we made an experimental video, with myself at the forefront of the project, since I had acquired certain empirical knowledge while working at several acting gigs. That is how I got my start in the production of videos dealing with the social theme of cultural indigenous vindication. (León, 2008)

What is singular about León's productions *Pollito* (2006) and *Pollito II* (2007) is that they are extremely popular, not only in Ecuador but also with the larger migrant community of Ecuadorians; he has received a number of e-mails from such faraway places as Turkey, Germany, Eng-land, Spain, and the United States, commending his work. Both *Pollito I* and *II* [13] are spoken in *Kichwa*, with Spanish subtitles, and deal with the issues of peasant migration not only from countryside to city but from the countryside directly to Spain. It is curious that these productions, which the director vindicates as having a social and cultural stance, characterize the indigenous as infantile and tragic and choose a soap-opera structure to convey their 'message.' Pollito, an eight-year-old who works shining shoes, has a drunk father who hits him, his mother dies, his father migrates, he misplaces the ball of his only friend, he looses his friend, his grandmother gets sick and eventually dies, he's kidnapped by crooks who use him to rob houses, his father gets beaten up and robbed, and this goes on and on until his regretful father returns to the country-side, realizing that that is his only place in life, thus restoring harmony and peace to his and his son's lives. The soap-opera structure does not allow for anything other than stereotypical characterization and we get plenty of it. According to León,

> Like most people, while growing up, I think I've been influenced by Hollywood films, but I have also viewed others, especially European and other Latin American productions, with a more profound content and at the present time I'm interested in Hindi films because of the in-teresting mixture between the traditional and the contemporary, with-out compromising their cultural essence. The productions of Sanjay Leela Bhansali are the most interesting ones, and within these I should mention *Devdas and Hum Dil De Chuke Sanam*, also the Korean soap opera, *Stairway to Heaven* by Pak Mook Hwan. (León, 2008)

León has also recognized *Pollito*'s debt to the Iranian director Majid Majidi and his film *Bacheha-Ye aseman /The Children of Heave*n (1997). León is now working on a new project, a fantasy/horror film based on an indigenous mythological creature that eats wayward children; he told me he was thinking of using the structure of *The Blair Witch Project* because "it makes such a good use of suspense" (Léon, 2008). Léon's adherence to dominant aesthetic modes directly influences the story he tells. The Bolivian filmmaker Jorge Sanjinés made films (*Yawar malku/Blood of the Condor*, 1969; *Llocsi Caimanta, fuera de aquí/Get out of Here*, 1977) that attempted to directly reflect the Aymara and Kichwa understanding of time and respect their traditional narrative strategies, that is, using a narrator to anticipate the action, and the community rather than a single protagonist. With León we have to rethink the way 'time' is considered, taking into consideration how it has lost its traditional sense in the indig-enous world, or at least in his representation of it. The connection with Sanjinés is pertinent, inasmuch as León's discourse constantly returns to his predecessor, and in light of Sinchi Samay's reclaiming of indigenous roots and recurrent defense of this work as the faithful representation of the tragic reality of the Ecuadorian indigenous communities. That León chooses a melodramatic structure to *tell* that reality, though, does not seem a problem to him.

EPILOGUE

What has become apparent in this chapter is that an enormous divide exists between viewing publics in Ecuador and that a single cultural geography cannot be superimposed across the country. For the public that can pay a ticket to the cinema, for journalists, cultural critics, authorities, academics, and international audiences, Ecuadorian films are those that enter the film festival circuit or are shown in multiplex theaters: *Cuando me toque a mí/My Time will Come* (Victor Arregui, 2008); *¿Qué tan lejos?/How Much Further?* (Tania Hermida, 2007); *Esas no son penas/Anytime Soon* (Anahí Hoeneisen/Daniel Andrade, 2007); *1809–1810 mientras llega el día/1809–1810, Awaiting the Day* (Camilo Luzuriaga, 2004); and *Problemas personales/Personal Problems* (Lisandra Rivera/Manolo Sarmiento, 2002). For street vendors and a large number of people who buy, swap, or watch VCDs and DVDs, Ecuadorian movies are those found in the three collections mentioned in this essay. This, as we have briefly seen, has to do with precise social and economic locations, inequalities that are spatially constituted, access to new technologies, marketing and exhibition strategies, which, all put together, generate meanings in the transnational space of the new Ecuadorian territory (that is, inside and outside its geographical boundaries)., which is not divorced from the liminal space where globalization equals economic inequity.

Having discussed the miscegenation of categories in these different movies, with all experiencing the same zero degree of cultural capital, one would have to question the very idea of the existence of classically defined 'exploitation' cinema in Ecuador. If we go by what Ephraim Katz has defined as exploitation, "Films made with little or no attention to quality or artistic merit but with an eye to a quick profit, usually via high-pressure sales and promotion techniques emphasizing some sensational aspect of the product," then the low-budget national productions that circulate internally in the pirate market are something else altogether. Although these national productions can be made to fit into that category, they are—after all—divorced from institutional support, based on topical events, have no recognizable stars, and have low production values—I would have to argue, along with Roberto Schwarz, that, in so doing, I would be perpetuating the Latin American "necessity" to imitate the cultural categories of the metropolis and the logic of coloniality instead of problematizing "the share of the foreign in the nationally specific, of the imitative in the original and of the original in the imitative" (1995: 280). These movies are not made with a quick profit in mind; their low production values have less to do with quickness of output or little regard to recognition and more to do with a lack of technology and know-how. If they circulate nationwide it is not because of specific distribution-advertising-exhibition strategies but because the reproducers from the pirate market can make a profit from them. With the demise of PelMex, 'exploitation' ceased to exist as an industrial category in Latin America. Without distribution channels, producers do not make profits. What is, nevertheless, interesting about these later-day 'Ecua-exploitation' films is that they question long established categories and put in doubt dominant values. One of these would be the category of the 'national.' The MPG-4 *National Productions* where *Pollito* is included contains five movies: three were shot in Ecuador, one is from the north of Argentina, and the other is a Peruvian production. All of them touch upon the *Kichwa/Kechwa*-speaking communities of these three countries. These share Julio Ramón Ribeyro's vision in his 1964 short story "Los moribundos" (*The Dying*), which ridicules the 1941 war between Ecuador and Peru where the wounded soldiers, regardless of their nationalities, understand each other in Kichwa/Kechwa, while the *mestizo* Spanish-speaking authorities remain in the background, unable to understand them. Ribeyro's story would be the prelude to the Pan Andeanism present in the 2008 collection. Furthermore, these videos are more in accord with Maalouf's idea of planetary tribes (2002) that have less to do with territorial units or national communities and more with the search of alliances amongst shared identities; in this case, the shifting migrant Andean *Kichwa/Kechwa* communities of Argentina, Peru, and Ecuador. As Schaefer states, it is inadvisable to either valorize or demonize 'exploitation' movies; like the culture that produced them, they are complex and filled with contradiction (1999: 14). The productions studied here, be they exploitation or not, deal with attitudes, desires, and pleasures and undeniably form part of the cultural landscape of Ecuador in the twenty-first century.

NOTES

1. For a very interesting discussion concerning the ethics of technology vis-à-vis VCD and DVDs, see Pang in *Culture, Theory, and Critique.*
2. In 2008 only six cities have movie theaters or, rather, multiplexes: Quito, Guayaquil, Cuenca, Manta, Salinas, and Loja. We can hardly talk about national distribution of a movie when only six cities possess the facilities to view movies on the big screen.
3. In 2006, the Palacio government in Ecuador, whilst negotiating a pre-trade Agreement with the United States, was told that the pirate DVD and CD shops across the country would have to "disappear" if the talks between governments were to continue.
4. According to data, Ecuador, with its own funds and those of the Inter-American Development Bank, and with the aid of the Ecuadorian Institute of Intellectual Property (IEPI), invested $350,000 during a two-year period to train public prosecutors, policemen, and judges to stop the pirate industry (Andrade, 2006: 109).
5. Some movies are downloaded from the Web for free through the Web site www.movieflix.com. The price of a hundred blank DVDs is $45; a DVD burner that makes seven copies in eight minutes, without the need of a computer, can be bought at the local market for $820. The profits of the merchants range from $30 (during weekdays) to $100 (during weekends).

6. They, of course, do not 'declare' selling illegal merchandise and have their business in order with the IRS.
7. You can 'order' movies in these stores. The owner usually buys through the Internet or asks people in either Europe or the United States to send him legally bought copies which he later burns. He also trades. If his customers bring him a rare copy of something interesting, he lets them choose from any of the movies of his catalog, in this way expanding *his* catalog.
8. The national "Cinemateca" was founded in 1981; the first art-house film theater "Ocho y 1/2" opened in 2001 in Quito. There exist no specialized/long-running film magazines or journals in Ecuador.
9. Available for downloading from a porno film site (http://www.sumotorrent.com/searchResult.php?search=La%20Cruz%20De%20Marihuana).
10. Due to the noninstitutional nature of pirated reproduction and the informal independent circulation of many of these films, it can at times be difficult to determine who directed these films and the dates that they were produced or released. In these cases this information is not provided.
11. For this investigation I followed the pirate market in Quito (downtown and north of the capital), Guayaquil, Cuenca, and different towns in the provinces of Bolívar, Cotopaxi, Chimborazo, Imbabura, Loja (Andean Region), Manabí (Coastal Region), and Sucumbíos (Amazon Region).
12. A small Andean city.
13. *Pollito 1* and *2* circulate in a different collection; this one is simply called *Producción nacional*/National Productions. Of the five movies in the MPEG-4 DVD, three were shot in Ecuador, both *Pollitos* and a short called *El pastorcito*; the other two deal with themes related with the countryside, poverty, and indigenous roots but are Argentinean and Peruvian productions, although the Argentinean movie offers a very different viewpoint and proceeds from an altogether different cultural background. *El cielito* won five international awards in different categories in the Havana and the San Sebastián film festivals. *Huerfanito,* by Flaviano Quispe Chaiña, leans more towards the melodramatic structure of *Pollito.* All are considered NATIONAL productions. The tongue-in-cheek commentary by Barnet and Cavanagh seems appropriate with all the current talk of a Latin American Union (ALBA, Mercosur, Abya-Yala or whatnot), "While intellectuals and politicians in poor countries denounced the 'cultural imperialism' of the global media giants, underground entrepreneurs do something about it."

Contributors

Gabriela Alemán is a writer, university lecturer, and researcher. She received her PhD from Tulane University and is a Guggenheim Fellow who has been contributing to the *International Film Guide* since 2005. She is finishing a History of Ecuadorian Fiction Film and is currently working as a screenwriter for ALER on a Kichwa TV miniseries for the Andean region.

Adán Avalos is a PhD candidate at the University of Southern California's School of Cinematic Arts. His dissertation focuses on Latino migrant communities and media consumption and production. Avalos presented chapters of his dissertation nationally and internationally and believes in exploring both theory and practice of art, and directing his own documentaries and installations.

Catherine L. Benamou is Associate Professor of Film and Media Studies at the University of California–Irvine. She is the author of *It's All True: Orson Welles's Pan-American Odyssey* (University of California Press) and is currently at work on a book about transnational television flows and diasporic Latina/o audiences.

Josetxo Cerdán is Associate Professor at the URV in Tarragona, Spain. He has edited *Mirada, memoria y fascinación* (2001); *Documental y vanguardia* (2005); *Al otro lado de la ficción* (2007); and *Suevia Films-Cesáreo González* (2005). He is author of *Ricardo Urgoiti. Los trabajos y los días* (2007).

Gerard Dapena is a Visiting Assistant Professor of Film Studies at Bard College. He received his PhD in Art History at the Graduate Center, CUNY, with a dissertation on cinema in post–Civil War Spain. He has lectured and published on the cinema and visual arts of Spain and Latin America.

Sergio de la Mora is Associate Professor of Chicana/o Studies at the University of California, Davis. He is the author of *Cinemachismo: Masculinities and Sexuality in Mexican Film* (University of Texas Press, 2006).

Stephanie Dennison is Reader in Brazilian Studies at the University of Leeds, England. She has coauthored two books on Brazilian cinema: *Popular Cinema in Brazil* (Manchester UP, 2004) and *Brazilian National Cinema* (Routledge, 2007). She coedited *Remapping World Cinema: Identity, Politics and Culture on Film* (Wallflower, 2005) and coedits *New Cinemas* film journal.

Miguel Fernández Labayen is Assistant Professor at the Universidad Autónoma de Barcelona. His research focuses on experimental filmmaking and contemporary Spanish cinema and is codirector of "Xperimenta: Contemporary Looks on Experimental Filmmaking," a biannual event held at the Centro de Cultura Contemporánea de Barcelona.

Antonio Lázaro-Reboll is a Lecturer in Hispanic Studies at the University of Kent. He is the author of *Spanish Horror Film* (Edinburgh UP, forthcoming) and the coeditor (with Mark Jancovich et al.) of *Defining Cult Movies: The Cultural Politics of Oppositional Taste* (Manchester University Press, 2003) and (with Andrew Willis) of *Spanish Popular Cinema* (Manchester University Press, 2004).

Ana M. López is Associate Provost for Faculty Affairs and Director of the Cuban Studies Institute at Tulane University. She teaches film and cultural studies in the Department of Communication. Her research is focused on Latin American and Latino film and cultural studies. In addition to several coedited works and translating key texts in the field, she has more than twenty-five book chapters in anthologies and collections, contributions to the main reference books in her field, and twenty-six articles in scholarly journals. She is currently working on early sound cinema in Latin America and the radiophonic imagination.

Misha MacLaird is an independent film scholar and a PhD candidate at Tulane University. She received a Fulbright-Hays award for her doctoral research on the political, economic, and aesthetic changes in Mexico's film industry since 1994. She resides in Oakland, California.

Jeffrey Middents is an Assistant Professor of Literature at American University in Washington, DC, where he teaches film and world literature. He is the author of *Writing National Cinema: Film Journals and Film Culture in Peru* (University Press of New England, 2009).

Victoria Ruétalo is Associate Professor of Spanish and Latin American Studies at the University of Alberta. Her essays on Latin American film and culture have been published in *Studies in Latin American Popular Culture, Quarterly Review of Film and Video, Journal of Latin American*

Cultural Studies, and *Cultural Critique*. She is currently working on a manuscript about the work of Argentine sexploitation duo Armando Bó and Isabel Sarli.

Eric Schaefer chairs the Department of Visual and Media Arts at Emerson College in Boston and is the author of *"Bold! Daring! Shocking! True!": A History of Exploitation Films, 1919–1959*. He is working on a history of sexploitation movies of the 1960s and 1970s.

Andrew Syder is an Assistant Professor in the College of Motion Picture, Television and Recording Arts at Florida State University. His research ranges from obscure cult movies of the past to ubiquitous digital cultures of the present, and he is currently directing a documentary about a hippie commune in Northern California.

Dolores Tierney is Lecturer in Film at Sussex University. Her recent book on Emilio Fernández (2007) was published by Manchester University Press. She has published widely on Mexican classical Cinema, Mexican and Brazilian exploitation cinema, Spanish horror and digital filmmaking in *Screen*, *Quarterly Review of Film and Video*, *Journal of Latin American Cultural Studies*, *Cuadernos Americanos*, and *Revista Iberoamericana* and is currently working on a monograph about Mexico's contemporary traveling filmmakers.

Glenn Ward is pursuing a PhD on the films of Jess Franco, in the Department of Media and Film, University of Sussex, UK. He teaches Visual Culture at the University of Brighton and is the author of *Teach Yourself Postmodernism* (Hodder and Stoughton, 2003, revised edition, forthcoming).

Andy Willis is a Reader in Film Studies at the University of Salford, UK. He is the coauthor, with Peter Buse and Núria Triana Toribio, of *The Cinema of Álex de la Iglesia* (Manchester University Press, 2007), editor of *Film Stars: Hollywood and Beyond* (Manchester University Press, 2004), coeditor, with Antonio Lázaro Reboll, of *Spanish Popular Cinema* (Manchester University Press, 2004), and, with Mark Jancovich, Antonio Lázaro Reboll, and Julian Stringer, of *Defining Cult Movies: The Cultural Politics of Oppositional Taste* (Manchester University Press, 2003).

David Wilt wrote *The Mexican Filmography 1916–2001* and *Hardboiled in Hollywood*, cowrote *Doing Their Bit: Wartime American Animated Films*, and *Hollywood War Films*, and contributed to *Mondo Macabro*, *The Columbia Companion to American History on Film*, and *Film and Comics*. He is a librarian at the University of Maryland.

Bibliography

Abreu, N. C. (2006) *Boca do Lixo: Cinema e classes populares*, Campinas: Unicamp.

———. (2000) "Boca do Lixo," *Enciclopédia do cinema brasileiro*, F. Ramos and L. F. Miranda (eds), São Paulo: Editora Senac, 59.

Acevedo, M. (1982) *El 10 de Mayo*, Mexico City: Cultura SEP/Martín Casillas.

Agramonte, A. and L. Castillo (2003) *Ramón Peón: El hombre de los glóbulos negros*, Havana: Editorial de Ciencias Sociales.

Aguilar, G. (2004) "La generación del 60. La gran transformación del modelo," *Cine argentino: modernidad y vanguardias 1957/1983*, Claudio España (ed.), Buenos Aires: Fondo Nacional de las Artes, 82–97.

Agustín, J. (1990) *Tragicomedia mexicana: La vida en México de 1940 a 1970*, Mexico City: Planeta.

Alba, F. (1989) "The Mexican Demographic Situation," *Mexican and Central American Population and U.S. Immigration Policy*, F. D. Bean, J. Schmandt, and S. Weintraub (eds.), Austin: University of Texas.

Alemán, G. (2004) "An International Conspiracy: Ecuadorian Cinema of the Sixties and Seventies," *Journal of Latin American Cultural Studies*, 13(1): 97–113.

Alfaro Salazar, H. and A. Ochoa Vega (1997) *Espacios distantes aún vivos: Las salas cinematográficas de la Ciudad de Mexico*. Mexico City; Universidad Autónoma Metropolitana.

Alvaray, L. (2008) "National, Regional and Global: New Waves of Latin American Cinema," *Cinema Journal* 47(3): 48–65.

Álvarez, C. (2002) 'Abezatadario geográfico psicotrónico y juguetón. Caribe Mix' in *2000 maniacos*, Winter, 20–27.

Anchou, G. (2004a) "El sueño indusrial en emergencia," *Cine argentino: modernidad y vanguardias 1957–1983*, C. España (ed.), Buenos Aires: Fondo Nacional de las Artes, 452–54.

———. (2004b) "Emilio Vieyra y sus películas con Sandro," *Cine argentino: modernidad y vanguardias 1957/1983*, C. España (ed.), Buenos Aires: Fondo Nacional de las Artes, 426–27.

Andrade, I. (2002) 'Picadillo picante' in *2000 maniacos*, Winter, 64–67.

Andrade, J. F. (2007) "Los Cineastas de Chone," *Soho* 44: 112–19.

———. (2006) "Pirata," *Soho* 90: 108–13.

Andrews, D. (2007) "What Soft-Core Can Do for Porn Studies," *The Velvet Light Trap* 59: 51–61.

Appadurai, A. (1996) *Modernity at Large: Cultural Dimensions of Globalization*, Minneapolis: University of Minnesota Press.

Armes, R. (1987) *Third World Filmmaking and the West*, Berkeley: University of California Press.

Avalos, A. (2007–2008) Unpublished focus group interviews, Madera, California.

Avedaño Trujillo, O. (n.d.) "Entrevista con Alejandro Jodorowsky y Leonora Carrington. Dos surrealistas en México," available at: www.tuobra.unam.mx/publicadas/070627192333 (accessed 23 June 2008).

Avellar, J. C. (1979) "Teoria da Relatividade," *Anos 70: cinema*, Rio de Janeiro: Europa.

Ayala Blanco, J. (1993) *La aventura del cine mexicano: En la epoca de oro y después*, Mexico: Grijalbo.

——. (1991) *La disolvencia del cine mexicano: Entre lo popular y lo esquisito.* Mexico City: Grijalbo.

——. (1986) *La condición del cine mexicano*, Mexico City: Posada.

——. (1974) *La búsqueda del cine mexicano*, Mexico City: Posada.

Balbuena, A. (1968) 'Bomba argentina Isabel Sarli llegó a Lima y estremeció a admiradores,' *La crónica*, 26 July, 8.

Barcinski, A. and I. Finotti (1998) *Maldito: A vida e o cinema de José Mojica Marins, o Zé do Caixão*, São Paulo: Editora 34.

Barnet, R. and J. Cavanagh (1994) *Global Dreams: Imperial Corporations and the New World Order*, New York: Simon & Schuster.

Bedoya, R. (1998) *Un cine reencontrado: Diccionario ilustrado de las películas peruanas*, Lima: Universidad de Lima/Fondo de Desrrollo Editorial.

——. (1995) *100 años de cine en el Perú: Una historia crítica*, Lima: Universidad de Lima/Fondo de Desrrollo Editorial.

Benshoff, H. (2000) "Blaxploitation Horror Films: Reappropriation or Reinscription?" *Cinema Journal* 39 (2): 31–50.

Berenstein, R. (1996) *Attack of the Leading Ladies: Gender, Sexuality and Spectatorship in Classic Horror Cinema*, New York: Columbia University Press.

Bernardet, J. (1978) "Uma pornô grã-fina para a classe média," *Última hora*, 29 April.

Betz, M. (2003) "Art, exploitation, underground," *Defining Cult Movies: The Cultural Politics of Oppositional Taste*, M. Jancovich, A. Lázaro-Reboll, J. Stringer, and A. Willis (eds.), Manchester: Manchester University Press, 202–22.

Bhabha, H. K. (1994) *Nation and Narration*, New York: Routledge.

Birri, F. (1997) "Cinema and Underdevelopment," *New Latin American Cinema: Theory, Practices and Transcontinental Articulations*, M. T. Martin (ed.), Detroit: Wayne State University Press, 86–94.

Bohr, J. (1987) *Desde el balcón de mi vida*, Buenos Aires: Sudamericana.

Bondanella, P. (1983) *Italian Cinema: From Neorealism to the Present*, New York: Frederick Unger.

Brophy, P. (1983) "Horrality—the Textuality of Contemporary Horror Films," *Screen* 27(1): 2–13.

Brottman, M. (2005) *Offensive Films*, Nashville, TN: Vanderbilt University Press.

Bueno, E. (1999) "The Adventures of Jeca-Tatu: Class, Culture and Nation in Mazaropi's Films," *Studies in Latin American Popular Culture* 18: 33–54.

Calistro, M. (1984) "Aspectos del Nuevo Cine 1957–1968," *Historia del cine argentino*, Buenos Aires: Centro Editor de América Latina, 109–38.

Calleja, P. (2002) 'Carne sobre carne' in *2000 maniacos*, Winter, 44–47.

Caretas (1986a) "El cordon de Eric," 28 April, 45.

——(1986b) "Muerte a la hora señalada," 28 April, 44–46.

Chapman, J. (2000) *Licence to Thrill: A Cultural History of the James Bond Films.* New York: Columbia University Press.

Caughie, J. (1981) *Theories of Authorship*, London: British Film Institute.

Churnin, N. (2002) "He's Proud When His Stars Act Like Animals." *Dallas Morning News*, 23 July, 4C, available through: RosaGloriaChagoyán.NewsBank.rtfd (accessed 2 July 2007).

Cine-Aztlán (1992) "Ya Basta con Yankee Imperialist Documentaries!" *Chicanos and Film: Representation and Resistance*, C. A. Noriega (ed.), Minneapolis: University of Minnesota Press. 307–315.

Cineteca Nacional, Centro de Documentación e Investigación, File *El llanto de la tortuga*, item number A-1120, Mexico City.

Clover, C. J. (1992) *Men, Women, and Chain Saws: Gender in the Modern Horror Film*, Princeton, NJ: Princeton University Press.

Corman, R. with J. Jerome (1998) *How I Made a Hundred Movies in Hollywood and Never Lost a Dime*, Cambridge, MA: Da Capo Press.

Corradi, J. E., P. Weiss Fagen and M. A. Garretón (eds.) (1992) *Fear at the Edge: State Terror and Resistance in Latin America*, Berkeley: University of California Press.

Couselo, J. M. (1988) "Argentine Cinema from Sound to the Sixties," *The Garden of the Forking Paths: Argentine Cinema*, J. King and N. Torrents (eds.), London: British Film Institute. 27–36.

Couselo, J. M. et al. (eds.) (1984) *Historia del cine argentino*, Buenos Aires: Centro Editor de América Latina.

Creed, B. (1993) *The Monstrous-Feminine: Film, Feminism, Psychoanalysis*, New York: Routledge.

Crespo, B. (2006) "Manuel Valencia: 'Internet universaliza el frikismo,' " available at: www.elcorreodigital.com/evasion/cine, 29 June (accessed 12 July, 2007).

Crofts, S. (1998) "Concepts of National Cinema," *The Oxford Guide to Film Studies*, J. Hill and P. Church Gibson (eds.), Oxford: Oxford University Press, 385–94.

Curubeto, D. (1998) "'Meat on Meat!' Argentina," *Mondo Macabro: Weird and Wonderful Cinema from Around the World*, P. Tombs (ed.), New York: St. Martin's Griffin, 128–35.

———. (1996) *Cine bizarro. 100 años de películas de terror, sexo y violencia*, Buenos Aires: Editorial Sudamericana.

———. (1993) *Babilonia Gaucha: Hollywood en la Argentina, La Argentina en Hollywood*, Buenos Aires: Planeta.

Dávalos Orozco, F. (1996) *Albores del cine mexicano*, Mexico City: Clío.

De Andrade, O. (1928) *Manifesto Antropófago*, available at: www.lumiarte.com/luardeoutono/oswald/manifantropof.html (accessed 27 May 2007).

De la Mora, S. (2006) *Cinemachismo: Masculinites and Sexuality in Mexican Film*, Austin: University of Texas Press.

De la Vega Alfaro, E. (1999) "The Decline of the Golden Age and the Making of the Crisis," *Mexico's Cinema: A Century of Film and Filmmakers*, J. Hershfield and D. R. Maciel (eds.), Wilmington, DE: Scholarly Resources Books.

———. (1995) "Origins, Development and Crisis of the Sound Cinema (1929–64)," *Mexican Cinema*, P. A. Paranaguá (ed.), A. López (trans.), London: British Film Institute.

———. (1992) *José Bohr: Pioneros del cine sonoro* Guadalajara: Centro de Investigaciones y Enseñanzas Cinematográficas.

———. (1987) *Juan Orol*, Guadalajara: Centro de Investigaciones y Enseñanzas Cinematográficas.

De los Reyes, A. (1987) *Medio siglo de cine mexicano (1986–1947)*, Mexico City: Editorial Trillas.

De Montaigne, M. (1580) *Of Cannibals*, available at: www.victorianweb.org/courses/nonfiction/montaigne/cannibals.html (accessed 30 May 2007).

de Orellana, M. (2003) *Filming Pancho Villa: How Hollywood Shaped the Mexican Revolution*, London: Verso.

De Usabel, G. (1982) *The High Noon of American Films in Latin America*, Ann Arbor, MI: UMI Research Press.

282 Bibliography

Del Boca, A. (2003) "The Myths, Suppressions, Denials, and Defaults of Italian Colonialism," *A Place in the Sun: Africa in Italian Colonial Culture from Post-Unification to the Present*, P. Palumbo (ed.), Berkeley: University of California Press.

Del Diestro, L. A. (1994) *"Juana la Cubana." Dicine* (Mexico City) 59 (November-December): 38.

del Toro, G. (1999) 'Mi muy personal inventario del psicotrónico mexicano' in *2000 maniacos*, December, 5–11.

Dennison, S. and L. Shaw (2004) *Popular Cinema in Brazil*, Manchester, UK: Manchester University Press.

Diario El/La Prensa (1967), 3 September.

Di Nubila, D. (1998) *La época de oro: Historia del cine argentino I*, Buenos Aires: Ediciones del Jilguero.

Díaz, O. (2007) *Milenio*, 25 March, 12.

D'Lugo, M. (2003) *"Amores perros," The Cinema of Latin America*, A. Elena and M. Díaz López (eds), London: Wallflower Press, 221–29.

Dujovne Ortiz, A. (1996) *Eva Perón*, S. Fields (trans.), New York: St. Martin's Press.

Durgnat, R. (2000) "The Subconscious: From Pleasure Castle to Libido Motel," *The Horror Film Reader*, A. Silver and J. Ursini (eds.), New York: Limelight, 39–50.

Dyer, R. (2004) "Idol Thoughts: Orgasm and Self-reflexivity in Gay Pornography," *More Dirty Looks: Gender Pornography and Power* (2nd ed.), P. Church Gibson, (ed.) London: British Film Institute, 102–09.

———. (1981) *Stars*, London: British Film Institute.

Elena, A. (2003) "El cine latinoamericano en España: Materiales para una historia de la recepción," available at: www.elojoquepiensa.udg.mx,1 August (accessed 26 October 2005).

———. (1999) "Avatares del cine latinoamericano en España," *Archivos de la Filmoteca*, 31 February, 228–41.

———. (1998) "La difusión del cine latinoamericano en España: Una aproximación cuantitativa," *Cuadernos de la Academia*, 2 January, 221–30.

Elizondo, S. (2001) "Moral sexual y moraleja en el cine mexicano," *El cine mexicano a través de la crítica*, G. García and D. R. Maciel (eds.), Mexico: UNAM/Instituto Mexicano de Cinematografía/Universidad Autónoma de Juárez, 221–34.

España, C. (ed.) (2004) "Censura, vanguardia y digression, 1966–1973," *Cine argentino: Modernidad y vanguardias 1957–1983*, Buenos Aires: Fondo Nacional de las Artes, 336–37.

Estrada, M. (2007) "La censura en el cine mexicano," *lengua lengua*, available at: http://lengualengua.blogspot.com/2007/11/corte-corte-y-ms-cortela-censura-en-el.html (accessed 7 July 2008).

———. (2003) "Historia de película . . . ," *Revista mexicana de comunicación*, available at: www.mexicanadecomunicacion.com.mx/Tables/fmb/foromex/pelicula.htm (accessed 7 July 2008).

Estrada E. and D. Seay (1997) *Erik Estrada: My Road from Harlem to Hollywood*, New York: William Morrow.

Fagen, P. W. (1992) "Repression and State Security," *Fear at the Edge: State Terror and Resistance in Latin America*, J. E. Corradi, P. Weiss Fagen and M. A. Garretón (eds.), Berkeley: University of California Press, 39–71.

Falicov, T. L. (2007) *The Cinematic Tango: Contemporary Argentine Film*, London: Wallflower Press.

———. (2004) "U.S.-Argentine Co-productions, 1982–1990: Roger Corman, Aires Production, 'Schlockbuster' Movies, and the International Market," *Film and History* 34(1): 31–38.

Feitlowitz, M. (1998) *A Lexicon of Terror: Argentina and the Legacies of Torture*, Oxford: Oxford University Press.

Fernández, R. and D. Nagy (1999) *La gran aventura de Armando Bó: Biografía total*, Buenos Aires: Perfil Libros.

Fontán, D. (1974) 'El pensamiento vivo de Armando Bó,' *Siete días*, 29 September, 58–62.

Foster, G. A. (1999) *Captive Bodies: Postcolonial Subjectivity in Cinema*, New York: State University of New York Press.

Foucault, M. (2001) *The Order of Things: Archaeology of the Human Sciences*, New York: Routledge Classics.

Fregoso, R. L. (2003) '"Fantasy Heritage": Tracking Latina Bloodlines,' *MeXicana Encounters: The Making of Social Identity on the Borderlands*, Berkeley: University of California Press, 103–25.

Freire, P. (1971) *Pedagogy of the Oppressed*, New York: Herder & Herder.

Gallotti, A. (1972) 'Isabel Sarli: Las dos grandes razones de su carrera,' *Satiricón*, 27–30.

García Canclini, N., A. Rosas Mantecón, and E. Sánchez Ruiz (eds.) (2006) *Situación actual y perspectives de la industria cinematográfica en México y en el extranjero*, Guadalajara: Universidad de Guadalajara; México, DF: Instituto Méxcano de Cinematografía.

García Espinosa, J. (1997b [1983]) "Mediations on Imperfect Cinema," *New Latin American Cinema: Theory, Practices and Transcontinental Articulations*, M. T. Martin (ed.), Detroit: Wayne State University Press, 83–86.

———. (1997a [1969]) "For an Imperfect Cinema," *New Latin American Cinema: Theory, Practices and Transcontinental Articulations*, M. T. Martin (ed.), Detroit: Wayne State University Press, 71–82.

García Riera, E. (1998) *Breve historia del cine mexicano. Primer siglo, 1897–1997*, Mexico DF: Ediciones Mapa/IMCINE.

———. (1996a) *Historia documental del cine mexicano, Vol. 13, 1966–1967*, Guadalajara: Universidad de Guadalajara, Consejo Nacional para la Cultura y las Artes, Gobierno de Jalisco, Instituto Mexicano de Cinematografía.

———. (1996b) *Historia documental del cine mexicano, Vol. 14, 1968–1969*, Guadalajara: Universidad de Guadalajara, Consejo Nacional para la Cultura y las Artes, Gobierno de Jalisco, Instituto Mexicano de Cinematografía.

———. (1993a) *Historia documental del cine mexicano, Vol. 1, 1929–1937*, Guadalajara: Universidad de Guadalajara, Consejo Nacional para la Cultura y las Artes, Gobierno de Jalisco, Instituto Mexicano de Cinematografía.

———. (1993b) *Historia documental del cine mexicano*, Vol. 5, Guadalajara: Universidad de Guadalajara, consejo Nacional para la Cultura y las Artes, Gohierno de Jalisco, Instituto mexicano de cinematografia.

Gasca, L. (1972) "Mojica Marins: donde el instinto supera a la razón," *Terror Fantastic* 5: 40–47.

———. (1971) "Tropicalismo sangriento: El extraño mundo del brasileño Zé do Caixão," *Nuevo Fotogramas*, 1173, April, 10–11.

Getino, O. (2005) *Cine Argentino: entre lo possible y lo deseable*, Buenos Aires: Ediciones CICCUS.

Gilbert, J., A. Rubenstein and E. Zolov (eds.) (2001) *Fragments of a Golden Age: The Politics of Culture in Mexico Since 1940*, Durham, NC: Duke University Press.

Giunta, A. (2007) *Avant-Garde, Internationalism, and Politics: Argentine Art in the Sixties*, P. Kahn (trans.), Durham, NC: Duke University Press.

González Dueñas, D. (2006) 'Nota del editor,' *Fábulas pánicas*, A. Jodorowsky, México DF: Grijalbo.

González, R. and J. Lerner (1998) *Cine mexperimental: 60 años de medios de vanguardia en México/Mexperimental Cinema: 60 years of Avant-garde Media Arts from Mexico*, Santa Monica, CA: Smart Art Press.

González Martínez, J. L. (2002) 'Samba, horror y picante' in *2000 maniacos*, Winter, 70–71.

Grant, B. K. (2000) "Second Thoughts on Double Features: Revisiting the Cult Film," *Unruly Pleasures: Cult Film and Its Critics*, X. Mendik and G. Harper (eds.), London: FAB Press, 15–27.

———. (ed.) (1996) "Introduction," *The Dread of Difference: Gender and Horror Film*, Austin: University of Texas Press, 1–14.

Gray, B. (2000) *Roger Corman: The Unauthorized Biography of the Godfather of Indie Filmmaking*, Los Angeles: Renaissance Books.

Greene, D. (2005) *Mexploitation Cinema: A Critical History of Mexican Vampire, Wrestler, Ape-man and Similar Films, 1957–1977*, Jefferson, NC: McFarland.

Guardian, G2, The (2006) "The legacy of Jane Longhurst," Friday 1 September, 18.

Gunning, T. (1989) "The Cinema of Attractions: Early Film, Its Spectator and the Avant-Garde," *Early Cinema: Space, Frame, Narrative*, T. Elsaesser and A. Barker (eds.), London: British Film Institute.

Hallin, D. (2000) " 'La nota roja': Popular Journalism and the Transition to Democracy in Mexico," *Tabloid Tales*, C. Sparks and J. Tulloch (eds.), Lanham, MD: Rowman & Littlefield.

Hansen, C., C. Needham and B. Nichols (1991) "Pornography, Ethnography and the Discourses of Power," *Representing Reality: Issues and Concepts in Documentary*, B. Nichols, Bloomington: Indiana University Press, 201–28.

Hardy, P. (1993) *Aurum Film Encyclopedia*, London: Aurum Press.

Hawkins, J. (2000a) *Cutting Edge: Art Horror and the Horrific Avant-Garde*, Minneapolis: Minnesota University Press.

———. (2000b) "Sleaze Mania, Euro-Trash and High Art: The Place of European Art Films in American Low Culture," *Film Quarterly* 53(2): 14–29.

Hayes, J. E. (2000) *Radio Nation: Communication, Popular Culture, and Nationalism in Mexico, 1920–1950*, Tucson: University of Arizona Press.

Hebditch, D. and N. Anning (1988) *Porn Gold: Inside the Pornography Business*, London: Faber & Faber.

Henenlotter, F. (2003) *The Curious Dr Humpp* (Dir. Emilio Vieyra), DVD Liner Notes, Something Weird Video.

Herranz, P. (2002) 'Delicias mexicanas' in *2000 maniacos*, Winter, 72–75.

Herrera-Sobek, M. (1979) "The Theme of Drug Smuggling in the Mexican Corrido," *Revista Chicano-Riqueña*, 7(4): 49–61.

Hershfield, J. (2000) *The Invention of Dolores del Rio*, Minneapolis: University of Minnesota Press.

———. (1999) "Race and Ethnicity in the Classical Cinema," *Mexico's Cinema: A Century of Film and Filmmakers*, J. Hershfield and D. R. Maciel (eds.), Wilmington, DE: Scholarly Resources Books.

Higson, A. (1989) "The Concept of National Cinema," *Screen*, 30(4): 36–46.

Hillier, J. and A. Lipstadt (1980) *Roger Corman's New World Pictures*, London: British Film Institute.

Hills, M. (2002) *Fan Cultures*, London: Routledge.

Historia del plagio, available at: http://www.elplagio.com (accessed 20 March, 2008).

Hoberman, J. (2006) "You Had to Be There . . . ," *Village Voice*, 12 December, available at: www.villagevoice.com/film/0650,hoberman,75276,20.html (accessed 20 August 2007).

Hoberman, J. and J. Rosenbaum (1991) "El Topo: Through the Wasteland of Counterculture," *Midnight Movies*, New York: Da Capo Press, 77–109.

Hollows, J. (2003) "The Masculinity of Cult," *Defining Cult Movies: The Cultural Politics of Oppositional Taste*, M. Jancovich, A. Lazaro Reboll, J. Stringer, and A. Willis (eds.), Manchester, UK: Manchester University Press, 35–53.

Holmlund, C. (2005) "Wham! Bam! Pam! Pam Grier as Hot Action Babe and Cool Action Mama," *Quarterly Review of Film and Video* 22(2): 97–112.

Hunt, L. (1998) *British Low Culture: From Safari Suits to Sexploitation*, London: Routledge.

Iglesias Prieto, N. (2003) "Border Representations: Border Cinema and Independent Video," *Postborder City: Cultural Spaces of Bajalta California*, M. Dear and G. Leclerc (eds.), New York: Routledge.

———. (1991) *Entre yerba, polvo y plomo: Lo fronterizo visto por el cine mexicano, Volumen I y II*, Tijuana: El Colegio de la Frontera Norte.

———. (1989) "La producción del cine fronterizo: Una industria de sueño." *Frontera Norte*: 97–130.

Inclán, R. (2004) "Defensoras del Folklore," *La opinión* (Los Angeles), 10 November, available through: RosaGloriaChagoyán.NewsBank.rtfd (accessed 2 July 2007).

———. (2002) "Ondas Espectaculares," *La opinión* (Los Angeles), 24 April, available through: RosaGloriaChagoyán.NewsBank.rtfd (accessed 2 July 2007).

———. (2000) "Ondas Espectaculares," *La opinión* (Los Angeles), 23 May, available through: RosaGloriaChagoyán.NewsBank.rtfd (accessed 2 July 2007).

Jacquet, J. (1997) "Cornering Creativity," *The Nation*, 17 March.

James, D. E. (2005) The Most Typical Avant-Garde: History and Geography of Minor Cinemas in Los Angeles, Berkeley: University of California Press.

Jameson, F. (1981) *The Political Unconscious: Narrative as a Socially Symbolic Act*, Ithaca, NY: Cornell University Press.

Jancovich, M. (2002) "Cult Fictions: Cult Movies, Subcultural Capital and the Production of Cultural Distinctions," *Cultural Studies* 16(2): 306–22.

Jancovich, M., A. Lázaro Reboll, J. Stringer and A. Willis (eds.) (2003) *Defining Cult Movies: The Cultural Politics of Oppositional Taste*, Manchester, UK: Manchester University Press.

Jodorowsky, A. (2007) *Teatro sin fin (tragedias, comedias y mimodramas)*, Madrid: Siruela.

———. (2006) "Cómo hacer cine," available at: www.clubcultura.com/clubliteratura/clubescritores/jodorowsky/diablo01 (accessed 24 August 2007).

———. (2003) "Óperas Pánicas," available at: www.clubcultura.com/clubliteratura/clubescritores/jodorowsky/operas (accessed 4 July 2008).

———. (1973) "Alexandro Jodorowsky—A Biography," press book for *The Holy Mountain* (Dir. Alejandro Jodorowsky).

———. (1971) *El Topo: A Book of the Film*, New York: Douglas Books, available at: www.subcin.com/bookfilm00 (accessed 31 August 2007).

Jodorowsky Project, The, (n.d.) available at: www.iua.upf.es/~fvasques/flash/jodo (accessed 31 August 2007).

Johnson, E. and E. Schaefer (1993) "Soft Core/Hard Gore: Snuff as a Crisis in Meaning," *Journal of Film and Video* 45(2–3): Summer–Fall, 40–59.

Johnson, R. (1987) *The Film Industry in Brazil: Culture and the State*, Pittsburgh: University of Pittsburgh Press.

———. (1984) "Popular Cinema in Brazil," *Studies in Latin American Popular Culture*, 3.

Johnson, R., and R. Stam (1995) *Brazilian Cinema* (expanded ed.), New York: Columbia University Press.

Kael, P. (1975) "El Poto-Head Comics," *Deeper into Movies*, London: Calder & Boyars, 334–40.

Katz, E. (1979) *The Film Encyclopedia*, New York: Perigee Books.

286 Bibliography

Kerekes, D. and D. Slater (1993) *Killing for Culture: An Illustrated History of the Death Film from Mondo to Snuff*, London: Creation Books.

King, J. (2003) "Stars: Mapping the Firmament," *Contemporary Latin American Cultural Studies*, S. Hart and R. Young (eds.), 140–50.

———. (2000) *Magical Reels: A History of Cinema in Latin America* (2nd ed.), London: Verso.

———. (1990) *Magical Reels: A History of Cinema in Latin America*, New York: Verso.

———. (1988) "The Social and Cultural Context," *The Garden of the Forking Paths: Argentine Cinema*, J. King and N. Torrents (eds.), London: British Film Institute, 1–14.

King, J. and N. Torrents (eds.) (1988) *The Garden of the Forking Paths: Argentine Cinema*, London: British Film Institute.

Knight, A. (1994) "The Cardenismo: Juggernaut or Jalopy?" *Journal of Latin American Studies* 26: 73–107.

Kowalsky, D. (2004) "Rated S: Softcore Pornography and the Spanish Transition to Democracy, 1977–1982," *Spanish Popular Cinema*, A. Lazaro Reboll and A. Willis (eds.), Manchester, UK: Manchester University Press.

Kraszewski, J. (2002) "Recontextualizing the Historical Reception of Blaxploitation: Articulations of Class, Black Nationalism, and Anxiety in the Genre's Advertisements," *Velvet Light Trap*, Fall, 50: 48–61.

Krzywinska, T. (2006) *Sex and the Cinema*, London: Wallflower.

Kuhn, R. (1984) *Armando Bó, el cine, la pornografía ingenua y otras reflexiones*, Buenos Aires: Ediciones Corregidor.

LaBelle, B. (1980) "*Snuff*—The Ultimate in Woman-Hating," *Take Back the Night: Women on Pornography*, L. Lederer (ed.), New York: William Morrow & Company, 272–78.

Lalo, "*Muñecas de medianoche*," available at: www.cinemexicanosincensura. org/cine/viewtopic.php?p=1859&sid=021219e100b43e5818501072bb611e4 (accessed 18 February 2008).

Lasseca, F. (2005) "Por favor . . . farli no, ¡Sarli!" *2000 maniacos* 34: 52–55.

lavaca.org (2003) "La verdadera historia de la morocha," available at: www.lavaca. org/notas/nota022.sthml (accessed 13 March 2008).

Lavia, D. (2002) 'Sexo, vampiras, robots y chatarra' in *2000 maniacos*, Winter, 34–35.

Lechner, N. (1992) "Some People Die of Fear: Fear as a Political Problem," *Fear at the Edge: State Terror and Resistance in Latin America*, J. E. Corradi, P. Weiss Fagen and M. A. Garretón (eds.), Berkeley: University of California Press, 26–38.

Lederer, L. (ed.) (1980) *Take Back the Night: Women on Pornography*, New York: William Morrow & Company.

León, W. Personal interview, January 2008.

León Frías, I. (1987) "Ojo al cine: *Misión en los Andes*," *Caretas*, 7 September, 60.

Lerner, J. (ed.) (1999) "Superocheros," *Wide Angle*, 21(3): 2–35.

Lethem, J. (2008) "Acerca del plagio," *Etiqueta negra*, Año 7–Número 62, Perú, 68–84.

Lieja, Dr. P.K. (1999a) 'Primer Mundial Caspa 1999' in *2000 maniacos*, November, 20–27.

———. (1996b) '10 razones para ser abducido por el cine fantástico mexicano' in *2000 maniacos*, December, 22–23.

Limón, J. E. (1994) *Dancing with the Devil: Society and Cultural Poetics in Mexican-American South Texas*, Madison: University of Wisconsin Press.

Llosa, L. (2007) Personal communication, 26 October.

Lola la trailera (2008) Video clip "Rosa Gloria Chagoyán Performing at the Festival de Mesquite in Las Vegas, Nevada. Posted by casanuevoleon on YouTube, 20 April," available at: www.youtube.com/watch?v=huSxYDMvWmk (accessed 20 August 2008).

Lomnitz, C. (2001) *Deep Mexico, Silent Mexico: An Anthropology of Nationalism*, Minneapolis: University of Minnesota Press.

López, A. M. (2000) "Early Cinema and Modernity in Latin America," *Cinema Journal* 40(1): 48–78.

———. (1998) "From Hollywood and Back: Dolores Del Rio, a Trans(National) Star," *Studies in Latin American Popular Culture* 17: 5–32.

———.(1994) "A Cinema for the Continent," *The Mexican Cinema Project*, C. Noriega and S. Ricci (eds.), Los Angeles: UCLA Film and Television Archive, 12–35.

———. (1993a) "Are All Latins from Manhattan? Hollywood, Ethnography and Cultural Colonialism," *Mediating Two Worlds: Cinematic Encounters in the Americas*, J. King, A. M. López and M. Alvarado (eds.), London: British Film Institute, 67–80.

———. (1993b) "Tears and Desire: Melodrama in the 'Old' Mexican Cinema,'" *Mediating Two Worlds: Cinematic Encounters in the Americas*, J. King, A. M. López and M. Alvarado (eds.), London: British Film Institute, 147–63.

———. (1988) "Argentina, 1955–1976: The Film Industry and Its Margins," *The Garden of the Forking Paths: Argentine Cinema*, J. King and N. Torrents (eds.), London: British Film Institute, 49–80.

López, D. (2004) "El cine que da ganancia," *Cine argentino: Modernidad y vanguardias 1957–1983*, C. España (ed.), Buenos Aires: Fondo Nacional de las Artes, 250–52.

Lowenstein, A. (2005) *Shocking Representation: Historical Trauma, National Cinema and the Modern Horror Film*, New York: Columbia University Press.

Luckett, M. (2003) "Sexploitation as Feminine Territory: The Films of Doris Wishman," *Defining Cult Movies: The Cultural Politics of Oppositional Taste*, M. Jancovich, A. Lazaro Reboll, J. Stringer and A. Willis (eds.), Manchester, UK: Manchester University Press.

Maalouf, A. (2002) *Identidades asesinas*, Madrid: Alianza Editorial.

Macías, R. (1997) "Isela Vega, imagen de rebeldía y ejemplo de mujer independiente," *Crónica*, 14, August, E-05.

Maciel, D. R. (1990) *El Norte: The U.S.-Mexican Border in Contemporary Cinema*, San Diego: San Diego State University.

Maranghello, C. (2005) *Breve historia del cine argentino*, Buenos Aires: Laertes.

———. (2004) "El discurso represivo. La censura entre 1961 y 1966," *Cine argentino: modernidad y vanguardias 1957–1983*, C. España (ed.), Buenos Aires: Fondo Nacional de las Artes, 268–78.

Marks, L. (2001) "Live Video," *The End of Cinema as We Know It: American Film in the Nineties*, J. Lewis (ed.), New York: New York University, 305–15.

Martín, J. A. (1981) *Los films de Armando Bó con Isabel Sarli*, Buenos Aires: Ediciones Corregidor.

McLean, A. L. (2004) *Being Rita Hayworth: Labor, Identity, and Hollywood Stardom*, New Brunswick, NJ: Rutgers University Press.

McNair, B. (2002) *Striptease Culture: Sex, Media and the Democratisation of Desire*, London: Routledge.

———. (1996) *Mediated Sex: Pornography and Postmodern Culture*, London: Arnold.

Melville, H. (1968[1846]) *Typee: A Peep at Polynesian Life*, Chicago: Northwestern University Press.

Mendik, X. and G. Harper (2000) *Unruly Pleasures: The Cult Film and Its Critics*, Guilford UK: FAB Press.

Middents, J. J. R. (2001) *Hablemos de Cine: Locating the Film Journal in the Development of Peruvian National Cinema*, Ph.D. thesis, University of Michigan.

Mignolo W. (2005) *The Idea of Latin America*, Malden, MA: Blackwell Publishing.

Mondo, available at: http://en.wikipedia.org/wiki/Mondo_film (accessed 7 August 2008).

Monsiváis, C. (1997) *Mexican Postcards*, J. Kraniauskas (ed. and trans.), London: Verso.

——. (1990) "Isela Vega. ¡Viva México hijos de la decencia! (Del nuevo status de las 'malas palabras')," *Amor perdido* (10th ed.), Mexico: Era, 319–46.

Montalvo, S. (2004) *Cine de Leonidas Zegarra*, available at: www.pucp.edu.pe/revista/periodismo_digital/trab2004-1/Susan/listauniverso (accessed 28 June 2008).

Mora, C. J. (1989) *Mexican Cinema: Reflections of a Society*, Berkeley: University of California Press.

——. (1982) *Mexican Cinema: Reflections of a Society, 1896–1980*, Berkeley: University of California Press.

Moreno, A. (2000) "La ley de Isela," *Reforma*, 19 March, Magacine Section: 35.

MPEG4, available at: http://en.wikipedia.org/wiki/MPEG-4 (accessed 29 March 2008).

Mraz, J. (1984) "Mexican Cinema of Churros and Charros," *Jump Cut* 29: 23–24.

Muller, E. and D. Faris (1997) *That's Sexploitation! The Forbidden World of 'Adults Only' Cinema*, London: Titan.

Mundo Radial (1955) "Miss Capital no es belleza sofisticada: Una conversación con Isabel Sarli," 7: 3, 16 June, 4–5.

Nericcio, W. A. (2007) "Lupe Vélez Regurgitated: Or, Jesus's Kleenex. Cautionary, Indigestion-Inspiring Ruminations on 'Mexicans' in 'American' Toilets," *Tex[t]-Mex: Seductive Hallucinations of the 'Mexican' in America*, Austin: University of Texas Press, 153–225.

Nesbet, A. (2003) *Savage Junctures: Sergei Eisenstein and the Shape of Thinking*, London: I.B. Tauris.

Nichols, B. (1991) *Representing Reality: Issues and Concepts in Documentary*, Bloomington: Indiana University Press.

Noble, A. (2005) *Mexican National Cinema*, New York: Routledge.

Novo, S. (1951) *Este y otros viajes*, Mexico City: Stylo.

Opinión, La (2000) "¿Qué se ve en TV?" (Los Angeles), 13 November, available through: RosaGloriaChagoyán.NewsBank.rtfd (accessed 2 July 2007).

Orso, F. (2001) "La farándula," *La Opinión* (Los Angeles) 7 December, available through: RosaGloriaChagoyán.NewsBank.rtfd (accessed 2 July 2007).

Ortiz, C. K. (1995) *The Representation of Sexuality in Contemporary Mexican Cinema 1970–1990*, Los Angeles: UCLA.

Palacios, J. (n.d.) "Entrevista a Alejandro Jodorowsky," *Generación XXI. Semanario Interactivo Universitario*, available at: www.generacionxxi.com/jodo.htm (accessed 30 August 2007).

——. (2002) 'De charla con el judio errante' in *2000 maniacos*, Winter 36–41.

Palumbo, P. (ed.) (2003) "Italian Colonial Cultures," *A Place in the Sun: Africa in Italian Colonial Culture from Post-Unification to the Present*, Berkeley: University of California Press.

Pang, L. (2004a) "Piracy/Privacy: The Despair of Cinema and Collectivity in China," *Boundary* 2(31)3, Fall, 101–24.

——. (2004b) "Mediating the Ethics of Technology: Hollywood and Movie Piracy," *Culture, Theory & Critique* 45(1): 19–32.

Pankhurst, R. (2004) *The "Financial Times" and the Aksum Obelisk*, available at: www.addistribune.com/Archives/2004/07/16–07–04/The.htm (accessed 1 June 2007).

Paranaguá, P. A. (1999) "María Félix: imagen, mito y enigma," *Archivos de la Filmoteca* 31 (February), 76–87.

——. (1995) *Mexican Cinema*, London: British Film Institute.

Payne, S. (1984) *Spanish Catholicism: An Historical Overview*, Madison: University of Wisconsin Press.

Peary, G. (1978) "Woman in Porn: How Young Roberta Findlay Grew Up and Made 'Snuff,' " *Take One*, September, 28–32.

Pelayo, A. (1993) *Memoria del cine mexicano: René Cardona, Jr.* (DVD), Mexico City: CONACULTA/IMCINE.

Peterson, J. (1994) *Dreams of Chaos, Visions of Order: Understanding the American Avant-Garde Cinema*, Detroit: Wayne State University Press.

Petley, J. (2000) "'Snuffed Out': Nightmares in a Trading Standards Officer's Brain," *Unruly Pleasures: The Cult Film and Its Critics*, X. Mendik and G. Harper (eds.), Guilford: FAB Press, 205–19.

Pierrot (1972) "Elucubraciones, desmayos y gritos sobre el Teatro-Pánico de Alejandro Jodorowsky," *Terror Fantastic* 4: 58–60.

Pilcher, J. M. (2001) *Cantinflas and the Chaos of Mexican Modernity*, Wilmington, DE: Scholarly Resources.

Ponce, J. M. (2004) *El destape nacional*, Barcelona: Ediciones Glénat España.

Poniatowska, E. (2007) "Soy la libertad en el sexo: Isela Vega," available at : www.jornada.unam.mx/2006/12/10/index.php?section=opinion (accessed 3 May 2008).

Prensa, La. (1971) "Review of 'La venganza del sexo,'" 21 March.

——. (1967) "Review of 'Placer sangriento,'" 23 November.

Primera plana (1967) "Alucinógenos. Viaje al centro de la historia," 3 January.

——(1967) "Hacia la generación de la marijuana," 7 November.

——(1966) "Adolescentes. La bohemia de los fines de semana," 16 August.

——(1966) "Happenings. El gabinete de la doctora Minujín," 18 October, 199: 77.

——(1966) "Happenings . . . y llegó el gran día," 19 November, 201: 20.

——(1966) "Unisexo. Chicas como muchachos que parecen chicas," 22 March.

Pujol, S. (2002) *La década rebelde. Los años sesenta en Argentina*, Buenos Aires: Emecé Editores.

Quarles, M. (1993) *Down and Dirty: Hollywood's Exploitation Filmmakers and Their Movies*, Jefferson, NC: McFarland.

Quezada, M. A. (2005) *Diccionario del cine mexicano*, Mexico City: Universidad Autónoma de México.

Ramírez Berg, C. (2002) *Latino Images in Film: Stereotypes, Subversion and Resistance*, Austin: University of Texas Press.

——. (1992) *Cinema of Solitude: A Critical Study of Mexican Film, 1967–1983*, Austin: University of Texas Press.

Ramos, F. (1987) *Cinema marginal 1968–1973: A representação em seu limite*, São Paulo: Brasiliense.

Read, J. (2003) "The Cult of Masculinity: From Fan-Boys to Academic Bad-Boys," *Defining Cult Movies: The Cultural Politics of Oppositional Taste*, M. Jancovich, A. Lazaro Reboll, J. Stringer and A. Willis (eds.), Manchester, UK: Manchester University Press, 54–70.

Reséndiz, E. and R. Villareal (1995) "Una perversión llamada Isela," *Esas extrañas mexicanas del celuloide*, Monterrey, Nuevo León, Mexico: Ediciones Castillo, 27–52.

Revista domingo do Jornal do Brasil (1998) "Luz, cama, ação!" 3 May.

Reyes de la Maza, L. (1973) *El cine sonoro en Mexico*, Mexico City: UNAM.

Reyes, R. (1999) "Isela Vega y la necesidad del mito," *El Financiero*, 2 January, Espectador 36.

Ribeyro, J. R. (1992) "Los moribundos," *La palabra del Mudo, Tomo I*. Lima: Jaime Campodónico Editores.

Ricalde, M. C. (2004) "Popular Mexican Cinema and Undocumented Immigrants," *Discourse*, 26(1–2): 194–213.

Rivas, J. R. (1999a) "Danny Rivera cantará el la ACE." *El Diario/La Prensa* (New York), 3 March 24, available through ProQuest (accessed 3 July 2007).

——. (1999b) "Lola la trailera conducirá por NY," *El Diario/La Prensa*, New York, 13 January, 25, available through ProQuest (accessed 3 July 2007).

Robben, A. (2005) *Political Violence and Trauma in Argentina*, Philadelphia: University of Pennsylvania Press.

Rock, D. (2002) "Racking Argentina," *New Left Review* 17, September–October, 1–19.

Rogoff, I. (1996) " 'Other's Others': Spectatorship and Difference," *Vision in Context: Historical and Contemporary Perspectives on Sight*, T. Brennan and J. Martin (eds.), New York: Routledge, 187–202.

Romano, N. (1995) *Isabel Sarli al desnudo*, Buenos Aires: Ediciones de la Urraca SA.

Romero, L. (2002) *A History of Argentina in the Twentieth Century*, J. Brennan (trans.), University Park: Pennsylvania State University Press.

"Rosa Gloria Chagoyán," *Web page from IMDb Internet Movie Database*, available at: www.imdb.com/name/nm0149611/ (accessed 19 August 2008).

"Rosa Gloria Chagoyan [sic]," *Página no Oficial* (Unofficial Web site), available at: www.geocities.com/rosagloriach/ (accessed 17 August 2008).

——. famosas mexicanas.com Web site, available at: www.famosasmexicanas.com/rosagloria-chagoyan.htm (accessed 20 August 2008).

——. Desnuda, famosas mexicanas desnudas.com Web site, available at: www.famosasmexicanasdesnudas.com/fotos/rosagloria-chagoyan/rosagloria-chagoyan.htm (accessed 20 August 2008).

"Rosa Gloria Chagoyán diva del cine mexicano," archivo hose blog site, 18 June, 2008, available at: archivohose.blogspot.com/search/label/Rosa%20Gloria%20Chagoyan (accessed 20 August 2008).

Rowe, W. and V. Schelling (1991) "Breaks & Continuities," *Memory and Modernity: Popular Culture in Latin America*, New York: Verso Books.

Ruétalo, V. (2004) "Temptations: Isabel Sarli Exposed," *Journal of Latin American Cultural Studies* 13(1): 79–95.

Ruiz, O. (1998) "Visiting the Mother Country: Border-Crossing as a Cultural Practice," *The U.S.-Mexico Border: Transcending Divisions, Contrasting Identities*, D. Spener and K. Staudt (eds.), Boulder, CO: Lynne Reinner, 105–120.

Salles Gomes, P. E. (1995) "Cinema: A Trajectory within Underdevelopment," *Brazilian Cinema* (expanded ed.), R. Johnson and R. Stam (eds.), New York: Columbia University Press.

Schaefer, E. (2007) "Pandering to the 'Goon Trade' Framing the Sexploitation Audience through Advertising," *Sleaze Artists: Cinema at the Margins of Taste, Style, and Politics*, J. Sconce (ed.), Durham, NC: Duke University Press.

——. (2005) "Dirty Little Secrets: Scholars, Archivists and Dirty Movies," *The Moving Image* 2(2): 79–105.

——. (2003) "Showgirls and the Limits of Sexploitation," *Film Quarterly* 56(3): 42–43.

——. (2002) "Gauging a Revolution: 16mm Film and the Rise of the Pornographic Feature," *Cinema Journal* 41: 3.

———. (1999) *Bold! Daring! Shocking! True! A History of Exploitation Films, 1919–1959*, Durham, NC: Duke University Press.

———. (1997) "The Obscene Seen: Spectacle and Transgression in Postwar Burlesque Films," *Cinema Journal* 36(2): 41–66.

Schneider, S. J. and T. Williams (eds.) (2005) "Introduction," *Horror International*, Detroit: Wayne State University Press, 1–12.

Schwarz, R. (1995) "National by Imitation," *The Postmodernism Debate in Latin America*, A Boundary 2 Book, J. Beverly, M. Arrona and J. Oviedo (eds.), Durham, NC: Duke University Press, 264–81.

Sconce, J. (2003) "I Have Grown Weary of Your Tiresome Cinema," *Film Quarterly*, 56(3): 44–46.

———. (1995) "'Trashing' the Academy: Taste, Excess, and an Emerging Politics of Cinematic Style," *Screen* 36(4): 371–93.

Sconce J. (ed.) (2007) *Sleaze Artists: Cinema at the Margins of Taste, Style and Politics*, Durham, NC: Duke University Press.

Sergei (2002) 'El vampiro de los Andes' in *2000 maniacos*, Winter, 68–69.

Servat, A. (2008) "¿Cuál es tu película favorita?" *La Soga*, available at: http://blogs.elcomercio.com.pe/lasoga/2008/03/cual-es-tu-pelicula-peruana-fa (accessed 28 June 2008).

Silva-Santisteban, R. (2007) "Fotocopias: por una política cultural latinoamericana," *Industrias culturales. Máquina de deseos en el mundo contemporáneo*, Lima: Red para el desarrollo de las Ciencias Sociales en el Perú.

Sims, Y. D. (2006) *Women of Blaxploitation: How the Black Action Film Heroine Changed American Popular Culture*, Jefferson, NC: McFarland & Company.

Skal, D. J. (1993) *The Monster Show: A Cultural History of Horror*, London: Plexus.

Shaw, L. and S. Dennison (2007) *Brazilian National Cinema*, London: Routledge.

Sheridan, S. (2005) *Keeping the British End Up: Four Decades of Saucy Cinema*, London: Reynolds & Hearn.

Smiers, J. (2002) "The Abolition of Copyrights: Better for Artists, Third World Countries and the Public Domain," *Copyright in the Cultural Industries*, R. Towse (ed.), Cheltenham, UK: Edward Elgar, 119–39.

Smith, P. J. (2000) *Desire Unlimited: The Cinema of Pedro Almódovar*, London: Verso.

Sorlin, P. (1996) *Italian National Cinema 1886–1986*, New York: Routledge.

Soto, M. (2005) "El rey del bizarro," Radar, Pagina/12.com, 30 April, available at: www.pagina12.com.ar/diario/suplementos/radar/9–2198–2005–04–30 (accessed 28 September 2007).

Staden, H. (1557) *The Captivity of Hans Staden of Hesse. In A.D. 1547–1555. Among the Wild Tribes of Eastern Brazil*, London: The Hakluyt Society.

Stam, R. (2000) "Tropical Detritus: *Terra em transe*, Tropicália and the esthetics of Garbage," *Studies in Latin American Popular Culture* 19: 83–92.

———. (1995) "On the Margins: Brazilian Avant Garde Cinema," in R. Johnson and R. Stam (eds.) *Brazilian Cinema* (expanded ed.), New York: Columbia University Press.

Stam, R. and T. Miller (eds.) (2000) *Film and Theory: An Anthology*, Oxford, UK: Blackwell Publishers.

Sternheim, A. (2005) *Cinema da Boca: Diccionário de diretores*, São Paulo: Imprensa Oficial.

Sugimoto, L. (2002) "Boca dos sonhos," *Jornal da Unicamp*, 202.

Sunkel, G. (ed.) (1999) *El consumo cultural en América Latina*, Bogotá: Convenio Andrés Bello.

Sur (2003) "Depositan las cenizas del cineasta René Cardona Jr. en el lecho submarino del Puerto," available at: www.suracapulco.com.mx/anterior/2003/mayo/13/pag4.htm (accessed 30 August 2007).

Syder, A. (2000) "Death and Mondo: Toward a Phenomenology of Fraudulent Documentary," unpublished manuscript.

Syder, A. and D. Tierney (2005) "Importation/Mexploitation: Or, How a Crime-Fighting, Vampire-Slaying Mexican Wrestler Almost Found Himself in an Italian Sword-and-Sandals Epic," *Horror International*, S. Schneider and T. Williams (eds.), Detroit: Wayne State University Press.

Taddia, I. (2005) "Italian Memories/African Memories of Colonialism," *Italian Colonialism*, R. Ben-Ghiat and M. Fuller (eds.), New York: Palgrave Macmillan.

Talavera Serdán, A. (1980) 'Isela dentro y fuera.' *Cine*, 24 April, 55.

Telotte, J. P. (1991) *The Cult Film Experience: Beyond All Reason*, Austin: University of Texas Press.

Tierney, D. (2007) *Emilio Fernández: Pictures in the Margins*, Manchester, UK: Manchester University Press.

———. (2004) "José Mojica Marins and the Cultural Politics of Marginality in Third World Film Criticism," *Journal of Latin American Cultural Studies* 13(1), March, 63–78.

Tombs, P. (1997) "The Strange World of Mr Marins," *Mondo Macabro: Weird and Wonderful Cinema around the World*, New York: St. Martin's Griffin, 117–27.

Torres San Martín, P. (1993) *Crónicas tapatías del cine mexicano*, Guadalajara: Universidad de Guadalajara.

Treviño, J. (1979) "The New Mexican Cinema," *Film Quarterly* 32: 26–37.

Triana Toribio, N. (2003) *Spanish National Cinema*, London: Routledge.

Ugalde, V. (2003) "Censura cinematográfica: La punta del iceberg," *Palabra malditas*, available at: www.palabrasmalditas.net/portada/ (accessed 30 August 2007).

Vale, V. and A. Juno (eds.) (1986) *Incredibly Strange Films*, San Francisco: Re/Search Publications.

Valencia, M. (2002) *Bizarre Latino*, 26.

———. (1999a) "Primer Mundial Caspa 1999," *2000 maniacos* 21: 20–27.

———. (1999b) *2000 maniacos, Mexico loco superespecial. Chili Terror*, 22.

Vallejo, J. (2006) "Aquí, un mostrenco," available at: www.freekmagazine.com, 1 March (accessed 12 July 2006).

Vargas, M (2008) "Los hijos del destierro. Migración, consumo y fragmentación en los mojarras," *Revista casa de citas*, Perú, abril, 28–33.

Vargas Llosa, M. (2001) *The Storyteller*, New York: Picador Books.

Vasconcelos, J. (1925) *La raza cósmica: Misión de la raza iberoamericana*, Barcelona: Agencia Mundial de Librería.

Vaughan, M. K. and S. E. Lewis (eds.) (2006) "Introduction," *The Eagle and the Virgin: Nation and Cultural Revolution in Mexico, 1920–40*, Durham, NC: Duke University Press, 1–20.

Vértiz, C. (2004) "Isela Vega. Sin censura," *Proceso*, 28 March, 74.

Vieira, J. L. and R. Stam (1985) "Parody and Marginality: The Case of Brazilian Cinema," *Framework*, 28.

Viruete, J. (2005) "Entrevista a Manuel Valencia," available at: www.viruete.com, 9 September (accessed 12 July 2007).

Vivanco, M. (2006) *El Pregonero*, Washington, DC, 26 June, 29:26, 12 (accessed through ProQuest, 3 July 2007).

Vivas Sabroso, F. (2001) *En vivo y en directo: Una historia de la televisión peruana*, Lima: Universidad de Lima/Fondo de Desarrollo Editorial.

'Viva Vega!' *Playboy* (1974) July, 80–83.

Weber, R. (2004) "Un reto paralas cinematografías nacionales: Globalización, excepción cultural y diversidad cultural," *Butaca sanmarquina* 20: 33–43.

Weldon, M. (1996) *The Psychotronic Encyclopaedia of Video*, London: Titan.

———. (1983) *The Psychotronic Encyclopaedia of Film*, New York: Ballantine.

Wiener, C. (2003) "Ed Wood no tiene la culpa: Leonidas Zegarra al desnudo," *Butaca sanmarquina* 19: 19.

Williams, L. (1999) *Hardcore: Power, Pleasure and the 'Frenzy of the Visible'* (expanded ed.), Berkeley: University of California Press.

———. (1996) "When the Woman Looks," *The Dread of Difference: Gender and Horror Film*, B. Grant (ed.), Austin: University of Texas Press, 15–34.

———. (1990) *Hardcore: Power, Pleasure and the Frenzy of the Visible*, London: Pandora Press.

Willemen, P. (2004) "For a Pornoscape," *More Dirty Looks: Gender, Pornography and Power*, P. Church Gibson (ed.) (2nd ed.), London: British Film Institute, 9–26.

———. (1994) *Looks and Frictions: Essays in Cultural Studies and Film Theory*, Bloomington: Indiana University Press.

Wood, R. (1986) *Hollywood from Vietnam to Reagan*, New York: Columbia University Press.

Zermeño Padilla, G. (1997) "Cine, censura y moralidad en México. En torno al nacionalismo cultural católico, 1929–1960" in *Historia y Grafia*, n. 8, 77–102.

Zinéfilo, A. (2002) 'Os delirios de un genio diabólico' in *2000 maniacos*, Winter, 30–33.

———. (1999) "Horror y uñas largas," *2000 maniacos* 21: 48–51.

Filmography

24 horas de sexo explícito (24 Hours of Explicit Sex). Dir. José Mojica Marins. With Vânia Bonier and Albano Catozzi. Fotocena Filmes, 1985.

300 millas en busca de mamá (300 Miles in Search of Mama). Dir. Leonidas Zegarras. With Mariana Liquitaya and El Mero Loco. Cine 2000, 2007.

800 Leagues Down the Amazon. Dir. Luis Llosa. With Daphne Zuniga and Tom Verica. Iguana Producciones, 1993.

1809–1810 mientras llega el día (1809–1810, Awaiting the Day). Dir. Camilo Luzuriaga. With José Alvear and Alfredo Espinosa. No Production Company, 2004.

1990: I guerrieri del Bronx (1990: The Bronx Warriors). Dir. Enzo G. Castellari. With Mark Gregory and Vic Morrow. Deaf Internacional Film, 1982.

2019: Dopo la caduta di New York (2019: After the Fall of New York). Dir. Sergio Martino. With Michael Sopkiv and Valentine Monnier. Les Films du Griffon/Medusa Produzione/Nuova Dania Cinematografica, 1983.

A B. . . . profunda (Deep A . . .) Dir. Geraldo Dominó. With Jayme Cardoso and Teka Lansa. Empresa Cinematográfica Haway, 1984.

À bout de souffle (Breathless). Dir. Jean-Luc Godard. With Jean Paul Belmondo and Jean Seberg. Les Productions de George Beauregard, 1960.

À meia noite levarei sua alma (At Midnight I'll Take Your Soul). Dir. José Mojica Marins. With José Mojica Marins and Magda Mei. Indústria Cinematográfica Apolo, 1964.

Act of Seeing with One's Own Eyes, The. Dir. Stan Brakhage. Canyon Cinema, 1972.

Ad ogni costo (Grand Slam). Dir. Giuliano Montaldo. With Janet Leigh and Klaus Kinski. Constantin Film Produktion/Coral Producciones/Jolly Film, 1967.

Africa addio (Africa: Blood and Guts). Dir. Gualtiero Jacopetti and Franco Prosperi. With Sergio Rossi. Cineriz, 1966.

Aguas blancas, pueblo sacrificado (Aguas Blancas, Sacrificed Town). Dir. Ángel Rodríguez. With Roberto "Flaco" Guzmán and Toño Infante. Productora Cinematográfica Aner, 1997.

Ahí está el detalle (Here is the Point). Dir. Juan Bustillo Oro. With Mario Moreno "Cantinflas" and Sara García. Grovas-Oro Films, 1940.

Ai no corrida (In The Realm of the Senses). Dir. Nagima Oshima. With Tatsuya Fuji and Eiko Matsuda. Argos Films, 1976.

Allá en el rancho grande (Over There on the Big Ranch). Dir. Fernando de Fuentes. With Tito Guizar and Esther Fernández. Alfonso Rivas Bustamante, 1936.

Alucarda (Sisters of Satan [Innocents from Hell]). Dir. Juan López Moctezuma. With Claudio Brook and Tina Romero. Films 75-Yuma Films, 1975.

Amantes del señor de la noche, Los (Lovers of the Lord of the Night). Dir. Isela Vega. With Isela Vega and Emilo Fernández. Audiovideo Producciones de América and Producciones Fénix, 1986.

Amores perros (*Love's a Bitch*). Dir. Alejandro González Iñárritu. With Gael García Bernal and Emilio Echevarría. Altavista Films, 2000.

Anaconda. Dir. Luis Llosa. With Jennifer Lopez and Ice Cube. Cinema Line Film Corporation/Columbia Pictures/Iguana Producciones/Middle Fork Productions/Skylight Cinema Fiti Art/St. Tropez Films, 1997.

Ángel de mal genio, Un (*A Bad Tempered Angel*). Dir. René Cardona Jr. With Pancho Córdova and Pompín Iglesias, 1964.

Ángel exterminador, El (*The Exterminating Angel*). Dir. Luis Buñuel. With Silvia Pinal and Enrique Rambla. Producciones Gustavo Alatriste, 1962.

Angelitos negros (Little Black Angels). Dir. Joselito Rodríguez. With Pedro Infante and Rita Montaner. Producciones Rodríguez Hermanos, 1948.

Apariencias engañan, Las (*Appearances Can Be Deceiving*). Dir. Jaime Humberto Hermosillo. With Isela Vega and Gonzálo Vega. Hermosillo y Asociados and Héctor López, 1983.

Aquella joven de blanco (*A Little Maiden in White*). Dir. León Klimovsky. With Cristina Galbó and Luisa Sala. Estela Films, 1965.

Asalto en Tijuana (Armed Robbery in Tijuana). Dir. Alfredo Gurrola. With Mário Almada and Noé Murayama. Filmadora Mor-Ben–Metropolitan's Million Dollar Prods., 1983.

Assim era a pornochanchada (That Was *Pornochanchada*). Dir. Víctor di Mello and Cláudio MacDowell. With Jorge Dória and Paulo César Pereio. Di Mello Produções Cinematográficas, 1978.

Automóvil gris, El (*The Grey Automobile*). Dir. Enrique Rosas, Joaquín Coss, and Juan Canals de Homs. With Joaquín Coss and Juan Canals de Homs. Rosas y Compañía, 1919.

Avaricia (Greed). Dir Fernando Cedeño. No players available. No production company, 2000.

Aventuras prohibidas (*Prohibited Adventures*). Dir. Augusto Tamayo San Román, José Carlos Huayhuaca, and Luis Llosa. Cinevisión/Cinematográfica Horizonte, 1980.

Aventurera (*Adventuress*). Dir. Alberto Gout. With Ninón Sevilla and Andrea Palma. Cinematográfica Calderón S.A., 1950.

Babel. Dir. Alejandro González Iñárritu. With Brad Pitt and Cate Blanchett. Paramount Pictures, 2006.

Bacalhau (Codfish). Dir. Adriano Stuart. With Helena Ramos and Hélio Souto. Omega Filmes, 1975.

Bacheha-Ye aseman (*The Children of Heaven*). Dir. Majid Majidi. With Mohammad Amir Naji and Amir Farrokh Hashemian. The Institute for the Protection of Children and Young Adults, 1997.

Bad Taste. Dir. Peter Jackson. With Terry Potter and Pete O'Heme. Australian Film Commission and WingNut Films, 1987.

Banda da velhas virgens, A (The Gang of Old Virgins). Dir. Amácio Mazzaropi and Pio Zamuner. With Amácio Mazzaropi and Geny Prado. PAM Filmes, 1979.

Banda del carro rojo, La (The Red Car Gang). Dir. Rubén Galindo. With Mário Almada and Pedro Infante Jr. Filmadora Chapultepec, 1976.

Bandido da luz vermelha, O (*Red Light Bandit*). Dir. Rogério Sganzerla. With Paulo Villaça and Helena Ignez. Urano Films, 1968.

Barahúnda en la montaña (*Rumble in the Mountain*). Dir. Fernando Cedeño. No players available. No production company, 2004.

Barón del terror, El (*The Brainiac*). Dir. Chano Urueta. Cinematográfica ABSA, 1962.

Barravento. Dir. Glauber Rocha. With Antonio Pitanga and Luiza Maranhão. Iglu Films, 1962.

Behind the Green Door. Dir. Jim Mitchell. With Marilyn Chambers and Johnny Keys. Mitchell Film Production, 1972.

Bem-dotado, o homem de Itu (Well Endowed, the Man from Itu). Dir. José Miziara. With Nuno Leal Maia and Helena Ramos. Cinedistri, 1978.

Bestia desnuda, La/El monstruo asesino (The Naked Beast). Dir. Emilio Vieyra. With Aldo Barbero and Gloria Prat. Orestes A. Trucco, 1966.

Bien esquivo, El (The Elusive Good). Dir. Augusto Tamayo San Román. With Diego Bertie and Jimena Lindo. Argos Interactiva/CONACINE, 2001.

Bienvenida al clan (Welcome to the Clan). Dir. Carlos Franco. With Manuel Ojeda and Isaura Espinosa. Tintorera-Cinema Inc., 2000.

Big Sleep, The. Dir. Howard Hawks. With Humphrey Bogart and Lauren Bacall. Warner Bros., 1946.

Birds, The. Dir. Alfred Hitchcock. With Tippi Hedren and Rod Taylor. Universal Studios, 1963.

Blair Witch Project, The. Dir. Daniel Myrick and Eduardo Sánchez. With Heather Donahue and Joshua Leonard. Haxan Films, 1999.

Blood Feast. Dir. Herschell Gordon Lewis. With William Kerwin, Mal Arnold, and Connie Mason. Friedman Lewis Productions Inc., 1963.

Blue Velvet. Dir. David Lynch. With Isabella Rossellini and Kyle MacLachlan. De Laurentiis Entertainment Group, 1986.

Boca del lobo, La (The Lion's Den). Dir. Francisco Lombardi. With Gustavo Bueno and Toño Vega. Inca Film/New People's Cinema/Tornasol Films S.A., 1988.

Bonnie and Clyde. Dir. Arthut Penn. With Warren Beatty and Faye Dunaway. Tatira-Hiller Productions/Warner Brothers/Seven Arts, 1967.

Bons tempos voltaram: vamos gozar outra vez, Os (Good Times Have 'Come' Again). Dir. Ivan Cardoso and John Herbert. With Carla Camurati and Vanessa Alves. Cinearte Produções Cinematográficas/Cinedistri/Embrafilme, 1984.

Braindead. Dir. Peter Jackson. With Timothy Balme and Diana Peñalver. WingNut Films, Australian Film Commission, Avalon/NFU Studios, 1992.

Brazil: Cinema, Sex and the Generals. Dir. Simon Hartog. Large Door Productions, 1985.

Bride of Chucky. Dir. Ronny Yu. With Jennifer Tilly and Brad Dourif. Midwinter Productions, 1998.

Bring Me the Head of Alfredo Garcia. Dir. Sam Peckinpah. With Warren Oates and Isela Vega. Estudios Churubusco Azteca and Optimus Films, 1974.

Cabalgata del circo, La (The Circus Cavalcade). Dir. Eduardo Boneo and Mario Soffici. With Libertad Lamarque and Hugo del Carril. Estudios San Miguel, 1945.

Cafajestes, Os (The Scoundrels). Dir. Rui Guerra. With Jece Valadão and Norma Bengell. Magnus Films, 1962.

Caged Heat. Dir. Jonathan Demme. With Juanita Brown and Roberta Collins. New World Pictures, 1974.

Caída de un dictador, La (The Fall of a Dictator). Dir. Jorge Alberto Cano Jr. With Armando Silvestre and Eric del Castillo. ONAC Productions, 1999.

Camioneta gris, La (The Grey Pickup). Dir. José Luis Urquieta. With Mário Almada and Los Tigres del Norte. Cinematográfica Tamaulipas–Los Tigres del Norte Inc.–Técnicos y Manuales del STPC, 1989.

Cannibal ferox (Make Them Die Slowly). Dir. Umberto Lenzi. With Giovanni Lombardo Radice and Lorraine De Selle. Dania Film/Medusa Produzione/National Cinematografica, 1981.

Cannibal Holocaust. Dir. Ruggero Deodato. With Robert Kerman and Francesca Ciardi. F.D. Cinematografica, 1980.

Canoa, memoria de un hecho vergonzoso (Canoa, Memoir of a Shameful Act). Dir. Felipe Cazals. With Enrique Lucero and Salvador Sánchez. CONACINE-STPC, 1975.

Canto a mi tierra (Song to My Land). Dir. José Bohr. With Pedro Armendariz and Carmelita Bohr. Virgilio Calderon/Mexico Films, 1938.

Captive Wild Woman. Dir. Edward Dmytryk. With John Carradine and Milburn Stone. Universal Pictures, 1943.

Cargo de conciencia (Guilty Conscience). Dir. Emilio Vieyra. With Rodolfo Ranni and Pepe Soriano. EJV Producciones Cinematográficas, 2005.

Carnaval des barbouzes, Le (Killer's Carnival). Dir. Alberto Cardone, Robert Lynn, Sheldon Reynolds, and Louis Soulanès. With Stewart Granger and Lex Barker. Intercontinental Filmproduktion/Metheus Film/Paris Interproductions, 1966.

Carne (Meat). Dir. Armando Bó. With Isabel Sarli and Victor Bó. Sociedad Independiente Filmadora Argentina, 1968.

Casa del ángel, La (The House of the Angel). Dir. Leopoldo Torre Nilsson. With Elsa Daniel and Lautaro Murúa. Argentina Sono Film S.A.C.I., 1957.

Casamento, O (The Marriage). Dir. Arnaldo Jabor. With Paulo Porto and Adriana Prieto. RF Farias Produções Cinematográficas/Sagitário/Ventania Filmes, 1976.

Caso Cabrera, El (The Cabrera Case). No director. No production company, 2005.

Caso Huayanay: Testimonio de parte, El (The Huayanay Case: A Partial Testimony). Dir. Federico García. With Hugo Alvarez and Jaime Prada. Producciones Cinematográficas Kausachum S.A, 1981.

Caso María Soledad, La (The Maria Soledad Case). Dir. Héctor Olivera. With Valentina Bassi and Alfonso de Grazia. Aries Cinematográfica Argentina, 1993.

Castillo de la pureza, El (The Castle of Purity). Dir. Arturo Ripstein. With Claudio Brook and Rita Macedo. Estudios Churubusco Azteca, 1972.

Ciclón (Cyclone). Dir. René Cardona Jr. With Andrés Garcia, Hugo Stiglitz, and Mário Almada. Conacine, 1977.

Ciudad de ciegos (City of the Blind). Dir. Alberto Cortés. With Gabriela Roel and Blanca Guerra. IMCINE-Cinematográfica Bataclán, 1990.

Ciudad y los perros, La (The City and the Dogs). Dir. Francisco Lombardi. With Pablo Serra and Gustavo Bueno. Inca Films, 1985.

Cobrador, In God We Trust. Dir. Paul Leduc. With Peter Fonda and Lázaro Ramos. Arca Difusión, Buena Onda, CNC, El Deseo S. A., Fidecine, Fonds Sur, Grioloco, Ibermedia, Instituto Mexicano de Cinematografía, Morena Films, New Art Digital, Salamandra Producciones, Televisión Española, Tequila Gang, 2007.

Coisas eróticas (Erotic Things). Dir. Rafaele Rossi. With Zaira Bueno and Regina Celia. Empresa Cinematográfica Rossi, 1982.

Como era gostoso o meu francês (How Tasty Was My Little Frenchman). Dir. Nelson Pereira dos Santos. With Arduíno Colassanti and Ana Maria Magalhães. Condor Filmes/LCB Produções Cinematográficas, 1971.

Conan the Barbarian. Dir. John Milius. With Arnold Schwarzenegger and Max von Sydow. Dino De Laurentiis Company/Universal Pictures, 1982.

Conde de Montecristo, El (The Count of Monte Cristo). Dir. León Klimovsky. With Jorge Mistral and Elina Colomer. Argentina Sono Film and Cinematográfica Calderón, 1953.

Contacto chicano (The Chicano Connection) Dir. Federico Curiel. With Rosa Gloria Chagoyán and Gerardo Reyes. Producciones de Rey (Mexico), 1979.

Corrupción (Corruption). Dir. Ismael Rodríguez. With Carmen Salinas and Alberto Rojas. Películas Rodríguez-IRVSA, 1983.

Coyote emplumado, El (The Plumed Coyote). Dir. María Elena Velasco. With María Elena Velasco and Miguel Ángel Rodríguez. Producciones Matouk, 1983.

Cráneo de oro, El (The Golden Skull). Dir. Nixon Chalacama. No players available. No production company, 2001.

Cravate, La (The Severed Heads). Dir. Alejandro Jodorowsky. With Micheline Beauchemin and Raymond Devos. Anchor Bay Entertainment/Allen & Betty Klein and Company (ABKCO), 1957.

Crime Zone (Calles peligrosas). Dir. Luis Llosa. With Sherilyn Fenn and David Carradine. New Horizons Pictures/Iguana Films, 1988.

Cronos. Dir. Guillermo del Toro. With Claudio Brook and Federico Luppi. CNCAIMC, 1993.

Cruz de marihuana, La. (The Marihuana Cross). No director. With Eleazar García Jr and Iñaki Goci. No production company, 2003.

Cuando los hijos se van (When the Children Leave). Dir. Julián Soler. With Fernando Soler and Alberto Vásquez. Filmadora Chapultepec, 1969.

Cuando me toque a mí (My Time Will Come). Dir. Victor Arregui. No players available. No production company, 2008.

Dama do lotação, A (Lady on the Bus). Dir. Neville D'Almeida. With Sônia Braga and Nuno Leal Maia. Embrafilme/Regina Filmes/Tecla, 1978.

Dama regresa, La (The Lady Returns). Dir. Jorge Polaco. With Isabel Sarli and Edgardo Nieva. Aleph Producciones S.A., 1995.

Day of the Jackal, The. Dir. Fred Zinneman. With Edward Fox and Terence Alexander. Warwick Film Production, 1973.

Dawn of the Dead. Dir. George A. Romero. With Gaylen Ross and Ken Foree. Laurel Group, 1978.

Deep Throat. Dir. Gerard Damiano. With Linda Lovelace and Ted Street. Vanguard Productions, 1972.

Deer Hunter, The. Dir. Michael Cimino. With Robert De Niro and Chrstopher Walken. Universal Pictures, 1978.

Delírios de um anormal (Hallucinations of a Deranged Mind). Dir. José Mojica Marins. With José Mojica Marins and Jorge Peres. Produçöes Cinematográficas Zé do Caixão, 1977.

Derecho y el deber, El (The Right and the Duty). Dir. Juan Orol. With Consuelo Moreno and Juan Orol. Aspa Films, 1937.

Derrumbe (Collapse). Dir. Eduardo Carrasco Zanini. With Eduardo Palomo and Yirah Aparicio. Canario Rojo-Víctor Films, 1985.

Despertar da besta, O/Ritual dos sádicos (Awakening of the Beast). Dir. José Mojica Marins. With José Mojica Marins and Angelo Assunção. Fotocena Filmes, 1969.

Destructor invisible, El (The Invisible Destroyer). Dir. Nixon Chalacama. No players available. No production company, 2002.

Desvergonzados, Los (The Insolent Ones). Dir. René Cardona Jr. Filmadora Panamericana, 1963.

Detrás de la mentira (Behind the Truth). Dir. Emilio Vieyra. With Alfonso de Grazia and Julia Sandoval, 1962.

Deus e o diabo na terra do sol (Black God, White Devil). Dir. Glauber Rocha. With Geraldo Del Rey and Yoná Magalhães. Banco Nacional de Minas Gerais, 1963.

Día de los albañiles 3, El (Day of the Bricklayers Part III). Dir. Gilberto Martínez Solares. With Alfonso Zayas and Angélica Chaín. Frontera Films, 1987.

Días calientes, Los (The Hot Days). Dir. Armando Bó. With Isabel Sarli and Argentino Alleres. Sociedad Independiente Filmadora Argentina, 1965.

Dirty Dozen, The. Dir. Robert Aldrich. With Lee Marvin and Charles Bronson. MGM and Seven Arts, 1967.

Dirty Harry. Dir. Don Siegel. With Clint Eastwood and Andrew Robinson. Warner Bros., 1971.

Dona Flor e seus dois maridos (Dona Flor and Her Two Husbands). Dir. Bruno Barreto. With Sônia Braga and José Wilker. Carnaval Unifilm/Cocine/Companhia Cinematográfica Serrador/LCB Produções Cinematográficas, 1976.

Donna nel mondo, La (Women of the World). Dir. Paolo Cavara, Gualtiero Jacopetti, and Franco Prosperi. With Peter Ustinov. Cinematografica RI.RE/Cineriz/Tempo Film, 1963.

Dracula. Dir. Tod Browning. With Bela Lugosi and Helen Chandler. Universal Pictures, 1931.

Dragão da maldade contra o santo guerreiro, O (Antonio das Mortes). Dir. Glauber Rocha. With Mauricio del Valle and Odete Lara. Antoine Films, 1969.

Drum. Dir. Steve Carver. With Warren Oates and Ken Norton. Dino de Laurentiis Company, 1976.

Duello nel mondo (Ring Around the World). Dir. Georges Combret and Luigi Scattini. With Richard Harrison and Hélène Chanel. Leone Film/Radius Productions/Zenith Cinematografica, 1966.

Durazo la verdadera historia (Durazo, the True Story). Dir. Gilberto de Anda. With Sergio Bustamante and Hugo Stiglitz. Churubusco S.A., 1998.

Dynamite Women. Dir. Michael Pressman. With Claudia Jennings and Tara Stroheimer. New World Pictures, 1976.

E tu vivrai nel terrore—L'aldilà (The Beyond). Dir. Lucio Fulci. With Catriona MacColl and David Warbeck. Fulvia Film, 1981.

Earthquake. Dir. Mark Robson. With Charlton Heston and Ava Gardner. Universal, 1974.

Easy Rider. Dir. Dennis Hopper. With Peter Fonda and Dennis Hopper. Columbia Pictures, 1969.

Eat. Dir. Andy Warhol. With Robert Indiana. Andy Warhol, 1963.

Emanuelle e gli ultimi cannibali (Emanuelle and the Last Cannibals). Dir. Joe D'Amato. With Laura Gemser and Gabriele Tinti. Flora Film/Fulvia Film/Gico Cinematografica, 1977.

Emanuelle in America. Dir. Joe D'Amato. With Laura Gemser and Gabriele Tinti. New Film Production, 1977.

Emanuelle nera (Black Emanuelle). Dir. Bitto Albertini. With Laura Gemser and Karin Schubert. Emaus Films/Flaminia Produzioni Cinematografiche/San Nicola Produzione Cinematografica, 1975.

Emanuelle nera: Orient reportage (Emanuelle in Bangkok). Dir. Joe D'Amato. With Laura Gemser and Gabriele Tinti. Flaminia Produzioni Cinematografiche/Kristal Film/San Nicola Produzione Cinematografica, 1976.

Emanuelle: perché violenza alle donne? (Emanuelle Around the World). Dir. Joe D'Amato. With Laura Gemser and Ivan Rassimov. Embassy Productions, 1977.

Emmanuelle tropical (Tropical Emmanuelle). Dir. J. Marreco. With Monique Lafond and Matilde Mastrangi. Empresa Cinematográfica Haway, 1977.

Eraserhead. Dir. David Lynch. With Jack Nance and Charlotte Stewart. American Film Institute, Libra Films, 1977.

Esas no son penas (Those Aren't Sorrows). Dir. Anahí Hoeneisen/Daniel Andrade. With Anahí Hoeneisen and Amaya Merino. No production company, 2007.

Escorpião escarlate O (The Scarlet Scorpion). Dir. Ivan Cardoso. With Andréa Beltrão and Herson Capri. Topázio Films, 1998.

Esqueleto de la Sra. Morales, El (Skeleton of Mrs. Morales). Dir. Rogelio A. González. With Arturo de Córdova and Amparo Rivelles. Alfa Films, 1959.

Essa gostosa brincadeira a dois (This Tasty Game for Two). Dir. Víctor di Mello. With Dilma Lóes and Vera Fischer. Bernardo Goldzal Produções Cinematográficas/Condor Filmes/Di Mello Produções Cinematográficas/E.A. Cury Administração e Participação/Kiko Filmes/Vydia Produções Cinematográficas, 1974.

Esta noite encarnarei no teu cadáver (At Midnight I Will Possess Your Corpse). Dir. José Mojica Marins. With José Mojica Marins and Tina Wohlers. Ibérica Filmes, 1966.

Estranho mundo de Zé do Caixão, O (The Strange World of Coffin Joe). Dir. José Mojica Marins. With José Mojica Marins and Vany Miller. Ibéria Filmes, 1966.

Evita. Dir. Alan Parker. With Madonna and Jonathan Pryce. Cinergi Pictures, 1996.

Extraña invasión (Stay Tuned for Terror). Dir. Emilio Vieyra. With Richard Conte and Ann Mizrahi. Producciones Trucco, 1965.

Extraño del pelo largo, El (The Stranger with Long Hair). Dir. Julio Porter. With Liliana Caldini and Letto Nebbia, 1969.

Falling Down. Dir. Joel Schumacher. With Michael Douglas and Robert Duvall. Alcor Films, 1993.

Familia hippie, La (The Hippy Family). Dir. Enrique Carreras. With Palito Ortega and Ángel Magaña, 1971.

Fando y Lis. (Fando and Lis). Dir. Alejandro Jodorowsky. With Sergio Kleiner and Diana Mariscal. Producciones Pánicas, 1967.

Faster Pussycat, Kill, Kill! Dir. Russ Meyer. With Tura Satana and Haji. Eve Productions, 1965.

Fea más bella, La (The Prettiest Ugly Girl) (television series). Dir. Sergio Jiménez. With Angélica Vale and Jaime Camil. Televisa (Mexico), 2006–2007.

Festín de la loba, El (The She Wolf's Orgy). Dir. Francisco del Villar. With Isela Vega and Gloria Marín. Producciones del Villar and Columbia, 1972.

Fiebre (Fever). Dir. Armando Bó. With Isabel Sarli and Armando Bó. Sociedad Independiente Filmadora Argentina, 1970.

Fiesta del chivo, La (The Feast of the Goat). Dir. Luis Llosa. With Isabella Rossellini and Tomás Milian. Future Films/Lolafilms. 2005.

Filha de Emmanuelle, A (The Daughter of Emmanuelle). Dir. Oswaldo de Oliveira. With Vanessa Alves and Sérgio Hingst. Produções Cinematográficas Galante, 1980.

Fire on the Amazon. Dir. Luis Llosa. With Craig Sheffer and Sandra Bullock. Concorde-New Horizons, 1993.

Flor de Irupé, La (Love Hunger). Dir. Alberto Dubois. With Libertad Leblanc and Héctor Pellegrini. Gloria Films, 1962.

Flor silvestre/Wildflower Dir. Emilio Fernández. With Dolores Del Rio and Pedro Armendáriz. Films Mundiales, 1943.

Fórmula secreta, La (The Secret Formula). Dir. Rubén Gámez. With Jaime Sabines and Pilar Islas. Salvador López, 1965.

Freaks. Dir. Tod Browning. With Wallace Ford and Leila Hyams. Metro-Goldwyn-Mayer, 1932.

Freddy vs. Jason. Dir. Ronny Yu. With Robert Englund and Ken Kitzinger. New Line Cinema, 2003.

French Connection, The. Dir. William Friedkin. With Gene Hackman and Roy Scheider. 20th Century-Fox, 1971.

Fuego (Fire). Dir. Armando Bó. With Isabel Sarli and Armando Bó. Sociedad Independiente Filmadora Argentina, 1969.

Fuga del chacal, La (The Flight of the Jackal). Dir. Augusto Tamayo San Román. With Jorge García Bustamante and Toño Vega. Inca Films S.A./Sideral Films, 1987.

Full Fathom Five. Dir. Carl Franklin. With Michael Moriarty and Todd Field. Concorde-New Horizons, 1990.

Furia infernal (Hell Fury). Dir. Armando Bó. With Isabel Sarli and Victor Bó. Sociedad Independiente Filmadora Argentina, 1972.

Galante rei da Boca, O (Galante, King of the Boca). Dir. Alessandro Gamo and Luis Rocha Melo. CPC-UMES, Inventarte e Maloca Filmes, 2004.

Giselle. Dir. Víctor di Mello. With Alba Valéria and Carlo Mossy. Vydia Produções Cinematográficas, 1980.

Gitano (Gypsy). Dir. Emilio Vieyra. With Sandro and Soledad Silveyra. Arroyo, 1970.

Glen or Glenda. Dir. Edward D. Wood Jr. With Edward D. Wood Jr. and Bela Lugosi. Screen Classics Inc., 1953.

Gloria, víctima de la fama (*Gloria, Victim of Fame*). Dir. Enrique Murillo. With Miguel Ángel Rodríguez and Vicky Palacios. Provisa, 2000.

Gran casino (*Big Casino*). Dir. Luis Buñuel. With Jorge Negrete and Libertad Lamarque. Películas Anahuac S.A., 1946.

Gregorio. Dir. Grupo Chaski. With Marino León de la Torre and Vetzy Pérez Palma. Producciones Grupo Chaski, 1985.

Guerrillero de Chiapas, El (*The Guerrilla of Chiapas*). Dir. Juan José Pérez Padilla. With Sergio Goyri and Pamela Pizarro. J.J. Pérez Padilla, 1999.

Guyana, el crimen del siglo (*Guyana, Cult of the Damned*). Dir. René Cardona Jr. With Stuart Whitman and Gene Barry. CONACINE-Izaro Films-Care Productions-Real Productions, 1979.

Heroes Stand Alone. Dir. Mark Griffiths. With Chad Everett and Bradford Dillman. Concorde-New Horizons, 1989.

Histórias que nossas babás não contavam (Stories our Nannies Never Told Us). Dir. Oswaldo de Oliveira. With Adele Fátima and Costinha. Cinedistri, 1979.

Holocausto porno (*Porno Holocaust*). Dir. Joe D'Amato. With George Eastman and Dirce Funari. Kristal Film, 1981.

Hombre vino a matar, Un (*Rattler Kid*). Dir. León Klimovsky. With Brad Harris and Richard Wyler. Copercines and Nike Cinematográfica, 1968.

Hombre violento, Un (A Violent Man). Dir. Valentín Trujillo. With Valentín Trujillo and Mário Almada. Cinematográfica Sol, 1983.

Hora de los hornos, La (*The Hour of the Furnaces*). Dir. Octavio Getino and Fernando Solanas. Grupo Cine Liberación, 1968.

Horripilante bestia humana, La (*Night of the Bloody Apes*). Dir. René Cardona Sr. With José Elías Moreno and Armando Silvestre. Cinematográfica Calderón, 1968.

Hour of the Assassin (*Misión en los Andes*). Dir. Luis Llosa. With Erik Estrada and Robert Vaughn. Iguana Films/Concorde-New Horizons, 1987.

I Am Curious Yellow. Dir. Vilgot Sjöman. With Lena Nyman and Vilgot Sjöman. Sandrews, 1967.

Independência ou morte (Independence or Death). Dir. Carlos Coimbra. With Tarcísio Meira and Glória Menezes. Cinedistri, 1972.

India (*Indian Girl*). Dir. Armando Bó. With Isabel Sarli and Guillermo Murray. Sociedad Independiente Filmadora Argentina, 1959.

India, La (*The Indian Woman*). Dir. Rogelio A. González. With Isela Vega and Jaime Moreno. Conacine, 1976.

Indiana Jones and the Temple of Doom. Dir. Steven Spielberg. With Harrison Ford and Kate Capshaw. Paramount, 1984.

Inferno in diretta (*Cut and Run*). Dir. Ruggero Deodato. With Lisa Blount and Richard Lynch. Racing Pictures, 1985.

Informer, The. Dir. John Ford. With Victor McLaglen and Heather Angel. RKO, 1935.

Insaciable (*Insatiable*). Dir. Armando Bó. With Isabel Sarli and Jorge Barreiro. Sociedad Independiente Filmadora Argentina, 1976.

Inseto do amor, O (The Insect of Love). Dir. Fauzi Mansur. With Rossana Ghessa and Helena Ramos. J. Dávila Produções Cinematográficas, 1980.

Intimidades de una cualquiera (*Intimacies of a Prostitute*). Dir. Armando Bó. With Isabel Sarli and Jorge Barreiro. Sociedad Independiente Filmadora Argentina, 1973.

Invisible Man, The. Dir. James Whale. With Claude Rains and Gloria Stuart. Universal, 1933.

Iracema, uma transa amazônica (*Iracema*). Dir. Jorge Bodanzky and Orlando Senna. With Edna de Cássia and Paulo César Pereio. Stop Film/Zweites Deutsches Fernsehen, 1976.

Isla de los hombres solos, La (Island of the Lost Souls). Dir. René Cardona. With Mário Almada and Eric del Castillo. Productora Fílmica Real,1974.

Isto é strip-tease (This is Strip-tease). Dir. Konstantin Tkaczenko. With Irene de Luca and Françoise. Realista Filmes, 1962.

Janitzio. Dir. Carlos Navarro. With Emilio Fernández and María Teresa Orozco. Crisoforo Peralta Jr., 1935.

Jaula de oro, La (The Golden Cage). Dir. Sergio Véjar. With Mário Almada and Los Tigres del Norte. Cin. Tamaulipas–Técnicos y Manuales–Los Tigres del Norte Inc.–Antonio Hernández Campuzano, 1987.

Jaws. Dir. Steven Spielberg. With Roy Scheider and Richard Dreyfuss. Universal Pictures, 1975.

Juana la cubana. Dir. Raúl Fernández, With Rosa Gloria Chagoyán and Erik Estrada. Televicine/Cinematográfica Fernández (Mexico), 1994.

Jugador, El (The Player). Dir. León Klimovsky. With Alberto Bello and Angel Boffa. Pampa, 1948.

Juliana. Dir. Grupo Chaski. With Rosa Isabel Mortino and Julio Vega. Producciones Grupo Chaski/ZDF, 1989.

Kalimán. Dir. Alberto Mariscal. With Jeff Cooper and Susana Dosamantes. Kalifilms, 1970.

King Kong. Dir. Peter Jackson. With Naomi Watts and Jack Black. Universal, 2005.

Kuntur Wachana (Where Condors Go to Die). Dir. Federico García. With Delfina Paredes and Luis Alvarez. Producciones Cinematográfica Huarán S.A., 1977.

Lady in Red, The. Dir. Lewis Teague. With Pamela Sue Martin and Robert Conrad. New World Pictures, 1979.

Last House on the Left. Dir. Wes Craven. With David Hess and and Sandra Cassel. Lobster Enterprises/Sean S. Cunningham Films/The Night Co., 1972.

Laulico. Dir. Federico García. With Honorato Ascue and Aurora Bravo. Producciones Cinematográficas Kausachum Perú S.A., 1980.

Leona, La (The Lioness). Dir. Armando Bó. With Isabel Sarli and Armando Bó. Sociedad Independiente Filmadora Argentina,1964.

Ley de Heródes, La (Herod's Law). Dir. Luis Estrada. With Damián Alcázar and Isela Vega. Alta Vista Films, 1999.

Lilian M: relatório confidencial (Lilian M: Confidential Report). Dir. Carlos Reichenbach. With Célia Olga and Sérgio Hingst. Brasecran/Jota Filmes, 1975.

Little Red Riding Hood and the Monsters (Caperucita y Pulgarcito contra los monstrous). Dir. K Gordon Murray [Roberto Rodríguez]. AIP [Películas Rodríguez], 1962.

Llanto de la tortuga, El (The Turtle's Scream). Dir. Francisco del Villar. With Isela Vega and Jorge Rivero. Conacine, 1975.

Llocsi Caimanta, fuera de aquí (Get out of Here). Dir. Jorge Sanjinés. No production company. 1977.

Llorona, La (The Weeping Woman). Dir. Ramón Peón. With Ramón Pereda and Virginia Zurí. Eco Films, 1934.

Lo negro del Negro (The Dark Side of Blackie). Dir. Ángel Rodríguez Vázquez and Benjamín Escamilla Espinosa. With Ricardo de Loera and Rodolfo de Anda. Cinematográfica Esgón, 1984.

Lola la Trailera. Dir. Raúl Fernández. With Rosa Gloria Chagoyán and Rolando Fernández. Cinematográfica Fernández (Mexico), 1983.

Lola la Trailera III. Dir. Raúl Fernández. With Rosa Gloria Chagoyán and Guillermo "El Borras" Rivas. Cinematográfica Fernández (Mexico), 1991.

Look Who's Talking. Dir. Amy Heckerling. With John Travolta and Kirstie Alley. TriStar Pictures, 1989.

Lord of the Rings, The: The Fellowship of the Ring. Dir. Peter Jackson. With Elijah Wood and Vigo Mortensen. New Line, 2001.

Lord of the Rings, The: The Return of the King. Dir. Peter Jackson. With Elijah Wood and Vigo Mortensen. New Line, 2003.

Lord of the Rings, The: The Two Towers. Dir. Peter Jackson. With Elijah Wood and Vigo Mortensen. New Line, 2002.

Luca il contrabbandiere (Contraband). Dir. Lucio Fulci. With Fabio Testi and Ivana Monti. Surf Films, 1980.

Lujuria tropical (Tropical Lust). Dir. Armando Bó. With Isabel Sarli and Armando Bó. Sociedad Independiente Filmadora Argentina and Tropical Films, 1962.

Luponini, el terror de Chicago (Luponini, the Terror of Chicago). Dir. José Bohr. With José Bohr and Anita Blanch. Duquesa Olga y José Bohr, 1935.

Luz, cama, ação (Lights, Bed, Action). Dir. Cláudio MacDowell. With Tania Scher and Cláudio MacDowell. Sincro Filmes, 1976.

Macunaíma. Dir. Joaquim Pedro de Andrade. With Grande Otelo and Paulo José. Condor Filmes/INC/Filmes do Serro/Grupo Filmes, 1969.

Madre querida (Dear Mother). Dir. Juan Orol. With Luisa María Morales and Alberto Martí. Aspa Films, 1936.

Madrina del diablo, La (The Godmother of the Devil). Dir. Ramón Peón. With Jorge Negrete and María Fernández Ibañez. Gonzalo Varela, 1937.

Mafia de la frontera, La (Border Mafia). Dir. Jaime Fernández. With Mário Almada and Alicia Juárez. Cin. Grovas–Pels. Mexicanas, 1979.

Magnificent Seven, The. Dir. John Sturges. With Yul Bryner, Steve McQueen, and James Coburn. Mirisch Corporation and Alpha Productions, 1960.

Maldita miseria (Damn Misery). Dir. Júlio Aldama. With Mercedes Castro and Juan Valentín. Perumex–Prods. Rodas,1980.

Maldito, o estranho mundo de Zé do Caixão (Damned, the Strange World of Coffin Joe). Dir. André Barcinski and Ivan Finotti. Praticamente Films, 2001.

Mangiati vivi! (Eaten Alive!). Dir. Umberto Lenzi. With Robert Kerman and Janet Agren. Dania Film/National Cinematografica/Medusa Distribuzione, 1980.

Manhattan Baby. Dir. Lucio Fulci. With Christopher Connelly and Martha Taylor. Fulvia Film, 1982.

Mano en la trampa, La (The Hand in the Trap). Dir. Leopoldo Torre Nilsson. With Elsa Daniel and Francisco Rabal. Producciones Angel, 1961.

Mansión de la locura, La. (The House of Madness). Dir. Juan López Moctezuma. With Claudio Brook and Arthur Hansel. Producciones Prisma, 1973.

Margem, A (The Margin). Dir. Ozualdo Candeias. With Mario Benvenutti and Valeria Vidal. Ozualdo R. Candeias Produções Cinematográficas, 1967.

María Candelaria. Dir. Emilio Fernández. With Dolores del Rio and Pedro Armendáriz. Films Mundiales, 1943.

Mariachi, El. Dir. Robert Rodriguez. With Carlos Gallardo and Reinol Martinez. Columbia Pictures Corporation, 1992.

Marihuana (Marijuana). Dir. León Klimovsky. With Pedro López Lagar and Fanny Navarro. Argentina Sono Film, 1950.

Marihuana, el monstruo verde (Marijuana, the Green Monster). Dir. José Bohr. With José Bohr and Lupita Tovar. Duquesa Olga y José Bohr, 1936.

Mariposa en la noche, Una (A Butterfly in the Night). Dir. Armando Bó. With Isabel Sarli and Armando Bó. Sociedad Independiente Filmadora Argentina, 1975.

Mariscal del infierno, El (The Devil's Possessed). Dir. León Klimovsky. With Paul Naschy and Norma Sebre. Profilmes and Orbe Producciones, 1974.

Masacre en el Río Tula (Massacre in Río Tula). Dir. Ismael Rodríguez Jr. With Narciso Busquets and Hugo Stiglitz. Películas Rodríguez-Cineproducciones IRVSA, 1985.

Mataviejitas, La (The Silent Lady). Dir. Christian González. With Salvador Pineda and Lina Santos. Laguna Productions, 2006.

Mataviejitas: Asesina serial, La (The Old-Lady Killer). Dir. Miguel Marte. With Eleazar García Jr. and Claudia Calderón. GMC, 2006.

Matou a família e foi ao cinema (Killed the Family and Went to the Movies). Dir. Júlio Bressane. With Marcia Rodrigues and Antero de Oliveira. Belair Filmes, 1970.

Mavri Emmanouella, I (Emanuelle: Queen of Sados). Dir. Ilias Mylonakos. With Laura Gemser and Gabriele Tinti. Andromeda International Films/Othellos Films, 1979.

Max Is Missing. Dir. Mark Griffiths. With Toran Caudell and Victor Rojas. Iguana Producciones/Lantana Productions/Showtime Networks/Trinity Pictures, 1995.

Me convertí en asesino (I Turned into a Killer). No director. With Henry Guano. No production company. No year.

Meet the Feebles. Dir. Peter Jackson. With Donna Akersen and Stuart Devenie. WingNut Films, 1989.

Melgar, poeta insurgente (Melgar: Insurgent Poet). Dir. Federico García. With Oscar Romero and Elvira Travesí. Producciones Cinematográfica Kausachum S.A./Instituto Cubano de Arte e Industria Cinematográfica (ICAIC), 1982.

Melhores momentos da pornochanchada, Os (The Best of Pornochanchada). Dir. Víctor di Mello. With Jorge Dória and Sandra Barsotti. Di Mello Produções Cinematográficas, 1977.

Mondo balordo (A Fool's World). Dir. Roberto Bianchi Montero and Albert T. Viola. With Boris Karloff. Cinematografica Associati/Ivanhoe Productions, 1964.

Mondo Bizarro. Dir. Lee Frost. With Claude Emmand. International Theatrical Amusements, 1966.

Mondo cane. Dir. Paolo Cavara, Gualtiero Jacopetti, and Franco Prosperi. Cineriz, 1962.

Mondo cane 2. Dir. Gualtiero Jacopetti and Franco Prosperi. Cineriz, 1963.

Mondo cannibale (White Cannibal Queen/Cannibals). Dir. Jesus Franco. With Al Cliver and Sabrina Siani. Eurociné/Eurofilms/J.E. Films/Lisa-Film, 1980.

Mondo Freudo. Dir. Lee Frost. With Judy Adler and Baby Bubbles. Olympic International Films, 1966.

Mondo Hollywood. Dir. Robert Carl Cohen. With Margaretta Ramsey and Bobby Beausoleil. Omega-Cyrano Productions, 1967.

Mondo Mod. Dir. Bethel Buckalew. With Harve Humble and Midget Farrelly. Timely Motion Pictures, 1967.

Mondo nudo (Naked World). Dir. Francesco De Feo. Columbus Film/Mida Cinematografica, 1963.

Mondo Topless. Dir. Russ Meyer. With Babette Bardot and Pat Barrington. Eve Productions, 1966.

Montagna del dio cannibale, La (Mountain of the Cannibal God). Dir. Sergio Martino. With Stacy Keach and Ursula Andress. Dania Film/Medusa Produzione, 1978.

Montagna di luce (Jungle Adventurer). Dir. Umberto Lenzi. With Richard Harrison and Luciana Gilli. Filmes, 1965.

Montaña sagrada, La. (The Holy Mountain). Dir. Alejandro Jodorowsky. With Alejandro Jodorowsky and Horacio Salinas. Allen and Betty Klein and Company (ABKCO), Producciones Zohar, 1973.

Motivos de Luz, Los (The Motives of Luz). Dir. Felipe Cazals. With Patricia Reyes Spíndola and Delia Casanova. Chimalistac Producciones, 1985.

Muertas de Juárez, Las (The Dead Women of Juárez). Dir. Enrique Murillo. With Salvador Pineda and Eleazar García Jr. Laguna Productions, 2002.

Muerte de un cardenal, La (The Death of a Cardinal). Dir. Christian González. With Eric del Castillo and Guillermo Quintanilla. CIVIDISA Producciones, 1993.

Muerte del Paco "eSe," La (The Death of Paco S). Dir. unknown. With Jorge Reynoso and Rafael Goyri. Mexcinema, 2000.

Mujer del puerto, La (The Woman of the Port). Dir. Arturo Ripstein. With Damián Alzácar and Evangelina Sosa. Dos Producciones, 1991.

Mujer del puerto, La (The Woman of the Port). Dir. Arcady Boytler. With Andrea Palma and Domingo Soler. Eurindia Films, 1934.

Mujer del zapatero, La (The Shoe Mender's Wife). Dir. Armando Bó. With Isabel Sarli and Pepe Arias. Sociedad Independiente Filmadora Argentina, 1964.

Mujeres engañadas (Women Who Have Been Cheated) (television series). Dir. Sergio Jiménez. With Laura León and Andrés García. Televisa (Mexico), 1999–2000.

Mujeres sin alma (Soulless Women). Dir. Ramón Peón/Juan Orol. With Consuelo Moreno and Alberto Marti. Aspa Films, 1934.

Mulher de todos, A (Everybody's Woman). Dir. Rogério Sganzerla. With Helena Ignez and Jô Soares. Rogério Sganzerla Produções Cinematográficas/Servicine, 1969.

Mundo nuevo, Un (The New World). Dir. René Cardona. With Rafael Alcayde and Arturo Arias. Cinematográfica Latino Americana S.A. (CLASA), 1956.

Narcotic. Dir. Dwain Esper. With Harry Cording and Joan Dix. Dwain Esper, 1934.

Navajeros/Dulces navajas. Dir. Eloy de la Iglesia. With Isela Vega and José Luis Manzano. Acuarius Films S.A., 1980.

New Crime City. Dir. Jonathan Winfrey. With Rick Rossovitch and Sherrie Rose. Iguana Producciones, 1994.

Ni de aqui, ni de allá (Neither from Here nor from There). Dir. María Elena Velasco. With María Elena Velasco and Rafael Banquells. Prods. Vlady, 1987.

Night of the Living Dead. Dir. George A. Romero. Duane Jones and Judith O'Dea. Latent Image, 1969.

Niña santa, La (The Holy Girl). Dir. Lucrecia Martel. With Mercedes Morán and Carlos Belloso. El Deseo S. A., 2004.

Niño y el Papa, El (The Boy and the Pope). Dir. Rodrigo Castaño. With Andrés García and Verónica Castro. Cineproducciones Internacionales-FOCINE-Producciones Casablanca, 1986.

No basta ser madre (It's Not Enough to Be a Mother). Dir. Ramón Peón. With Sara García and Carlos Orellana. Vicente Saiso Piquer, 1937.

No importa morir (The Legion of No Return). Dir. León Klimovsky. With Tab Hunter and Howard Ross. Atlánta Films and Leone-Daiano Films, 1969.

Noche de buitres (Night of Vultures). Dir. Ismael Rodríguez Jr. With Mário Almada and Edgardo Gazcón. Películas Rodríguez-Gazcón Films-Producciones EGA, 1987.

Noche de los lápices, La (Night of the Pencils). Dir. Héctor Olivera. With Alejo García Pintos and Vita Escardó. Aries Cinematográfica Argentina, 1986.

Noche de los mil gatos, La (Night of a Thousand Cats/Blood Feast). Dir. René Cardona Jr. With Hugo Stiglitz and Anjanette Comer. Avant Films, 1970.

Noche de Walpurgis, La (Werewolf Shadow). Dir. León Klimovsky. With Paul Naschy and Gaby Fuchs. Plata Films and HIFI Stereo 70, 1971.

Noite das taras II, A (Night of Perversion II). Dir. Ody Fraga and Cláudio Portioli. With David Cardoso and Matilde Mastrangi. DACAR Produções Cinematográficas, 1982.

North by Northwest. Dir. Alfred Hitchcock. With Cary Grant and Eva Marie Saint. Metro-Goldwyn-Mayer, 1959.

Nosferatu. Dir. F.W. Murnau. With Max Schreck and Gustav von Wangenheim. Jofa-Atelier Berlin-Johannisthal, 1922.

Nosotros los pobres (*We the Poor*). Dir. Ismael Rodríguez. With Pedro Infante and Blanca Estela Pavón. Producciones Rodríguez Hermanos, 1947.

Notti erotiche dei morti viventi, Le (*Erotic Nights of the Living Dead*). Dir. Joe D'Amato. With George Eastman and Dirce Funari. Stefano Film, 1980.

Nudismo não é pecado (Nudism is Not a Sin). Dir. Konstantin Tkaczenko. With Maria Benvenutti and Nuvem Branca. Sinofilmes, 1960.

Nudo e selvaggio (*Massacre in Dinosaur Valley*). Dir. Michele Massimo Tarantini. With Michael Sopkiw and Milton Morris. Doral Film/DMV Distribuzione, 1985.

Obras maestras de terror (*Master of Horror*). Dir. Enrique Carreras. With Narciso Ibáñez Menta and Mercedes Carreras. Argentina Sono Film S.A.C.I, 1960.

Odio mi cuerpo (*I Hate my Body*). Dir. León Klimovsky. With Alexandra Bastedo, Luis Ciges, and Narcisco Ibáñez Menta. Galaxia Films, 1974.

Once Upon a Time in the West. Dir. Sergio Leone. With Charles Bronson and Henry Fonda. Rafran–San Marco and Paramount Pictures, 1968.

Orgasmo nero (*Black Orgasm*). Dir. Joe D'Amato. With Nieves Navarro and Richard Harrison. Santo Domingo Universal, 1980.

Otro crimen, El (*The Other Crime*). Dir. Carlos González Morantes. With Enrique Rocha and Claudio Obregón. DAC-UNAM, 1988.

Paese del sesso selvaggio, Il (*Man From Deep River*). Dir. Umberto Lenzi. With Ivan Rassimov and Me Me Lai. Medusa Produzione/Roas Produzioni, 1972.

Pagó cara su muerte (*Tierra Brava*). Dir. León Klimovsky. With Guglielmo Spoletini and Wayde Preston. Estela Films and Nike Cinematográfica, 1969.

Pantano de los cuervos, El (*The Swamp of the Ravens*). Dir. Manuel Caño. With Gaspar Bacigallipi and Maria Bichette. All American Films, 1973.

Pantera, El (The Panther) (television series). Dir. Raúl Araiza, with Luis Roberto Guzmán and Andrés García. Televisa (Mexico), 2007–2008.

Papaya dei Caraibi (*Papaya: Love Goddess of the Cannibals*). Dir. Joe D'Amato. With Melissa Chimenti and Sirpa Lane. Mercury Cinematografica, 1978.

Paqueras, Os (The Flirts). Dir. Reginaldo Farias. With Reginaldo Farias and Adriana Prieto. RF Farias Produções Cinematográficas, 1969.

Paroxismus (*Venus in Furs*). Dir. Jesus Franco. With James Darren and Maria Rohm. Cinematografica Associati/Terra-Filmkunst/Towers of London Productions, 1969.

Pasaporte a la muerte (*Passport to Death*). Dir. Ismael Rodríguez Jr. With Fernando Almada and Álvaro Zermeño. Películas Rodríguez, 1987.

Patagonia rebelde, La (*Rebellion in Patagonia*). Dir. Héctor Olivera. With Federico Luppi and Héctor Alterio. Aries Cinematográfica Argentina, 1974.

Paura nella città dei morti viventi (*City of the Living Dead*). Dir. Lucio Fulci. With Christopher George and Catriona MacColl. Dania Film/Medusa Distribuzione/National Cinematografica, 1980.

Peligro . . . mujeres en acción! (*Danger Girls*). Dir. René Cardona Jr. With Julio Alemán and Alma Delia Fuentes. Filmadora Panamericana,1967.

Pelo nel mondo, Il (*Go! Go! Go! World*). Dir. Antonio Margheriti and Marco Vicario. With Coccinelle and Stephen Garret. Atlantica Cinematografica Produzione Films, 1964.

Perro callejero (Street Dog). Dir. Gilberto Gazcón. With Valentín Trujillo and Eric del Castillo. Gazcón Films, 1979.

Pintando o sete (Painting the Town Red). Dir. Carlos Manga. With Oscarito and Cyl Farney. Atlântida Cinematográfica, 1959.

Pintando o sexo (Painting the Sex). Dir. Jairo Carlos and Egídio Eccio. With Meiry Vieira and Joshey Leão. Cinedistri/JC Mil Filmes, 1977.

Pirañas aman in cuaresma, Las (*Piranhas Make Love During Lent*). Dir. Francisco del Villar. With Isela Vega and Julio Alemán. Producciones del Villar, 1971.

Pirati della Malesia, I (*The Pirates of Malaysia*). Dir. Umberto Lenzi. With Steve Reeves and Jacqueline Sassard. Filmes-Euro International Films/La Société des Films Sirius/Lacy Internacional Films, 1964.

Placer sangriento (*The Deadly Organ*). Dir. Emilio Vieyra. With Gloria Prat and Ricardo Bauleo. Orestes A. Trucco, 1966.

Plaga zombie: Zona mutante (*Plaga Zombie: Mutant Zombie*). Dir. Pablo Parés and Hernán Sáez. With Alejandro Nagy and Berta Muñiz. Farsa Producciones, 2001.

Plan 9 from Outer Space. Dir. Edward D. Wood Jr. With Gregory Walcott and Mona McKinnon. Reynolds Pictures, 1959.

Play Murder for Me. Dir. Héctor Olivera. With Jack Wagner and Tracy Scoggins. Aries Cinematográfica Argentina/Aries Film International/Concorde-New Horizons, 1990.

Pollito. Dir. William León. No players available. Sinchi Samay, 2006.

Pollito II. Dir. William León. No players available. Sinchi Samay, 2007.

Poquianchis, Las. Dir. Felipe Cazals. With Malena Doria and Leonor Llausás. CONACINE-Alpha Centauri, 1976.

Por mis pistolas (*By my Guns*). Dir. José Bohr. With Sara García and Narciso Busquets. DOSA, 1938.

Pornógrafo, O (*The Pornographer*). Dir. João Callegaro. With Stênio Garcia and Sérgio Hingst. Itu Produções Cinematográficas/Servicine, 1970.

Poseída por el diablo (*en las garras de Lúcifer*) (*Possessed by the Devil (in Lucifer's Grasp)*). With Mariana Liquitaya and Rocky Belmonte. Cine 2000, 2006.

Presídio de mulheres violentadas (Raped Women's Prison). Dir. Antônio Polo Galante and Oswaldo de Oliveira. With Eudoxia Acuña and Esmeralda Barros. Grupo Internacional Cinematográfico, 1976.

Primavera de los escorpiones, La (Spring of the Scorpions). Dir. Francisco del Villar. With Isela Vega and Enrique Álvarez Félix. Del Villar Films, 1971.

Problemas personales (*Personal Problems*). Dir. Lisandra Rivera/Manolo Sarmiento. No players available. Pequena Nube, 2002.

Profanación (Desecration). Dir. Chano Urueta. With Isidro D'Olace and Fernando A. Rivero. Indo America, 1933.

Profanadores de tumbas/Santo contra los profanadores de tumbas (Santo Versus the Grave Robbers). Dir. José Díaz Morales. With Santo and Gina Romand. Fílmica Vergara, 1964.

Profesión: Detective (*Profession: Detective*). Dir. José Carlos Huayhuaca. With Orlando Sacha and Eduaro Yépez. Cinevisión, 1986.

Profesor hippie, El (*The Hippy Professor*). Dir. Fernando Ayala. With Luis Sandrini and Soledad Silveyra. Aries Cinematográfica, 1968.

Profeta Mimí, El (*The Prophet Mimi*). Dir. José Estrada. With Ignacio López Tarso and Carmen Montejo. Estudios Churubusco, 1972.

Psycho. Dir. Alfred Hitchcock. With Anthony Perkins and Janet Leigh. Shamley Productions, 1960.

Pulgarcito (*Tom Thumb*). Dir. René Cardona. With Cesáreo Quezadas and María Elena Marqués. CLASA Films Mundiales, 1957.

Pulquería, La (*The Pulque Bar*). Dir. Victor Manuel Castro. With Isela Vega and Jorge Rivero. Cinematográfica Calderón, 1980.

Puños rosas (*Pink Punch*). Dir. Beto Gómez. With José Yenque and Rodrigo Oviedo. Dejame Disfrutar, Instituto Mexicano de Cinematografía, Plural Entertainment, Televicine, Televisa Cine, Videocine, 2004.

¿Qué tan lejos? (*How Much Further?*). Dir Tania Hermida. With Tania Martinez and Pancho Aguirre. No production company, 2007.

Quella villa accanto al cimitero (*The House by the Cemetery*). Dir. Lucio Fulci. With Catriona MacColl and Paolo Malco. Fulvia Film, 1981.

¿Quién mató a Eva? (Who Killed Eva?). Dir. José Bohr. With José Bohr and Joaquin Busquets. Duquesa Olga y José Bohr, 1934.

Quiero llenarme de tí (I Want to Be Full of You). Dir. Emilio Vieyra. With Sandro and Marcela López Rey. Arroyo, 1969.

Rainbow Thief, The. Dir. Alejandro Jodorowsky. With Peter O'Toole and Omar Sharif. Burrill Productions, Rink Anstalt, 1990.

Rambo: First Blood, Part II. Dir. George P. Cosmatos. With Sylvester Stallone and Richard Crenna. Anabasis N.V, 1985.

Redes (Nets). Dir. Emilio Gómez Muriel and Fred Zinneman. With Silvio Hernández and David Valle González. Azteca Films, 1936.

Reglas del juego, Las (The Rules of the Game). Dir. Mauricio Walerstein. With Isela Vega and José Alonso. Filman International, 1970.

Reverendo Colt (Reverend Colt). Dir. León Klimovsky. With Guy Madison and Richard Harrison. Oceania Produzioni, PIC, RM Films and Talía Films, 1971.

Rey del barrio, El (The King of the Neighborhood). Dir. Gilberto Martínez Solares. With Germán Valdés "Tin Tan" and Silvia Pinal. As Films, 1949.

Ringu. Dir. Hideo Nakata. With Nanako Matsushimi and Miki Nakat. Omega Project, 1998.

Rio 40 graus (Rio 40 Degrees). Dir. Nelson Pereira dos Santos. With Modesto de Souza and Roberto Bataglin. Equipe Moacyr Fenelon, 1955.

Río Escondido (Hidden River). Dir. Emilio Fernández. With María Félix and Carlos López Moctezuma. Producciones Raúl de Anda, 1947.

Rio zona norte (Rio Northern Zone). Dir. Nelson Pereira dos Santos. With Grande Otelo and Jece Valadão. Nelson Pereira dos Santos Produções Cinematográficas, 1957.

Risa en vacaciones 1, La (Laughter on Holidays 1). Dir. René Cardona Jr. Televicine, 1990.

Risa en vacaciones 2, La (Laughter on Holidays 2). Dir. René Cardona Jr. Televicine, 1990.

Risa en vacaciones 3, La (Laughter on Holidays 3). Dir. René Cardona Jr. Televicine, 1992.

Ritual dos sádicos/O despertar da besta (Awakening of the Beast). Dir. José Mojica Marins. With José Mojica Marins and Giorgio Attili. Multifilmes, 1969.

Robinson Crusoe. Dir. René Cardona Jr. With Hugo Stiglitz and Ahui Camacho. Avant Films, 1970.

Romancing the Stone. Dir. Robert Zemeckis. With Michael Douglas and Kathleen Turner. 20th Century-Fox, 1984.

Rosa blanca (White Rose). Dir. Roberto Gavaldón. With Ignacio López Tarso and Rita Macedo. CLASA Films Mundiales, 1961.

Sabaleros (Fishermen). Dir. Armando Bó. With Isabel Sarli and Armando Bó. Araucania Films, 1958.

Sagrario (Sanctuary). Dir. Ramón Peón. With Ramón Pereda and Julio Villareal. Aspa Films, 1933.

Sandok, il Maciste della giungla (Temple of the White Elephant). Dir. Umberto Lenzi. With Sean Flynn and Alessandra Panaro. Filmes/Capitole Films, 1964.

Sandokan, la tigre di Mompracem (Sandokan the Great). Dir. Umberto Lenzi. With Steve Reeves and Geneviève Grad. Comptoir Français du Film Production/Filmes/Ocean Films, 1963.

Sangre de vírgenes (Blood of the Virgins). Dir. Emilio Vieyra. With Susana Beltrán and Walter Kliche. Orestes A. Trucco, 1967.

Sangre manda, La (Blood Rules). Dir. José Bohr. Producciones Cinematográficas Internacionales, 1934.

Santa. Dir. Antonio Moreno. With Lupita Tovar and Carlos Orellana. Compañía Nacional Productora de Películas, 1932.

Santa sangre. (*Holy Blood*). Dir. Alejandro Jodorowsky. With Axel Jodorowsky and Blanca Guerra. Productora Fílmica Real/Produzioni Intersound, 1989.

Santo contra el Dr. Muerte (*Doctor Death/Santa vs. Doctor Death/The Saint vs. Doctor Death*). Dir. Rafael Romero Marchent. With Santo and Helga Liné. Cinematográfica Pelimex, 1973.

Santo contra las mujeres vampiro (*Samson Versus the Vampire Women*). Dir. Alfonso Corona Blake. With Santo and María Duval. Filmadora Panamericana, 1962.

Santo el enmascarado de plata vs. la invasión de los marcianos (*Santo vs. the Martians*). Dir. Alfredo B Crevanna. With Santo and Wolf Ruvinskis. Producciones Cinematográficas, 1967.

Satan's Sadists. Dir. Al Adamson. With Russ Tamblyn and Scott Brady. Independent International Pictures, 1969.

Schiave bianche: Violenza in Amazzonia (*Amazonia: The Catherine Miles Story*). Dir. Mario Gariazzo. With Elvire Audray and Will Gonzales. Cinevega/G.P.I. Grandi Produzioni Italiane, 1985.

Se abre el abismo (*Open the Abyss*). Dir. Pierre Chenal. With Pablo Acciardi and Ana Arneodo. EFA, 1944.

Se tutte le donne del mondo (*Kiss the Girls and Make Them Die*). Dir. Henry Levin and Arduino Maiuri. With Mike Connors and Dorothy Provine. Dino de Laurentiis Cinematografica, 1966.

Secas e molhadas (*Dried Up and Moist*). Dir. Mozael Silveira. With Zezé Macedo and Mozael Silveira. Brasecran/Brasil Internacional Cinematográfica, 1977.

Secta de la muerte, La (*The Sect of Death*). Dir. Román Hernández. With Sebastián Ligarde and Mário Almada. Cineproducciones IRVSA-Mexcinema, 1990.

Secuestro de Camarena, El/El secuestro de un policía (*The Kidnapping of Camarena/The Kidnapping of a Policeman*). Dir. Alfredo B. Crevenna. With Armando Silvestre and Sasha Montenegro. Filmadora DAL, 1987.

Secuestro de Lola, El—Lola la Trailera II. Dir. Raúl Fernández. With Rosa Gloria Chagoyán and Emilio Fernández. Cinematográfica Fernández (Mexico), 1986.

Señora del intendente, La (*The Mayor's Wife*). Dir. Armando Bó. With Isabel Sarli and Pepe Arias. Sociedad Independiente Filmadora Argentina, 1966.

Señoritas (*Young Ladies*). Dir. Fernando Méndez. With Christiane Martel and Ana Bertha Lepe. Radeant Films, 1958.

Sentença de Deus (*God's Sentence*). Dir. José Mojica Marins. With José Mojica Marins. Indústria Cinematográfica Apolo, 1953.

Sette uomini e un cervello (*Seven Men and One Brain*). Dir. Rossano Brazzi. With Ann-Margret and Rossano Brazzi. Chiara Film Internazionali/Lam Pie Film, 1968.

Seu Florindo e suas duas mulheres (*Florindo and His Two Wives*). Dir. Mozael Silveira. With Wilza Carla and Mozael Silveira. Reflexo Filmes, 1978.

Seven Secrets of Sumuru, The (*The Girl From Rio*). Dir. Jesus Franco. With Shirly Eaton and Richard Wyler. Ada Films/Terra-Filmkunst/Udastex Films, 1969.

She-Devils on Wheels. Dir. Herschell Gordon Lewis. With Betty Connell and Nancy Lee Noble. Mayflower Pictures, 1968.

Shivers. Dir. David Cronenberg. With Paul Hampton and Lynn Lowry. Canadian Film Development Corporation, Cinépix, DAL Productions, 1975.

Sicario (*Hit Man*). Dir. José Ramón Novoa. With Laureano Olivares and Herman Gil. Credesca, 1994.

Simón del desierto (*Simon of the Desert*). Dir. Luis Buñuel. With Claudio Brook and Enrique Álvarez Félix. Estudios Churubusco Azteca, 1964.

Sina do aventureiro, A (*The Adventurer's Fate*). Dir. José Mojica Marins. With Shirley Alves and Nádia Belar. Indústria Cinematográfica Apolo, 1959.

Sindicato del crimen, El (*Crime Syndicate*). Dir. Juan Orol. With Victor Alcocer and Israel Camus. España Sono Films, 1954.

Sniper. Dir. Luis Llosa. With Tom Berenger and Billy Zane. Baltimore Pictures/ Iguana Producciones/Sniper Productions, 1993.

Snuff. Dir. Michael Findlay, Roberta Findlay, and Horacio Fredriksson. With Mirtha Massa and Aldo Mayo. August Films, 1976.

Sombra al frente, Una (Crossing a Shadow). Dir. Augusto Tamayo San Román. With Diego Bertie and Vanessa Saba. Argos P.C./Filmosonico/Instituto Cubano del Arte e Industrias Cinematográficas (ICAIC), 2007.

Sombra del caudillo, La (The Shadow of the Leader). Dir. Julio Bracho. With Tito Junco and Ignacio López Tarso. Técnicos y Manuales del STPC, 1960.

Soñar no cuesta nada (A Ton of Luck). Dir. Jorge Ali Triana. With Diego Cadavid and Juan Sebastian Aragón. Barakcine Producciones, 2006.

S.O.S. conspiración bikini (The Bikini Conspiracy). Dir. René Cardona Jr. With Julio Alemán and Sonia Furió. Filmadora Panamericana, 1966.

Specialist, The. Dir. Luis Llosa. With Sylvester Stallone and Sharon Stone. Iguana Producciones/Jerry Weintraub Productions/Warner Brothers, 1994.

Squartatore di New York, Lo (The New York Ripper). Dir. Lucio Fulci. Jack Hedley and Almanta Suska. Fulvia Film, 1982.

Submarine. Dir. Frank Capra. With Jack Holt and Dorothy Revier. Columbia Pictures, 1928.

Suburban Wives. Dir. Derek Ford. With Eva Whishaw and Peter May. Blackwater Film Productions Ltd, 1971.

Suor Emanuelle (Sister Emanuelle). Dir. Giuseppe Vari. With Laura Gemser and Mónica Zanchi. MEN Cinematografica/Rizzoli-Pallavicini, 1977.

Superfêmea, A (Superwoman). Dir. Aníbal Massaini Neto. With Vera Fischer and Perry Salles. Cinedistri, 1973.

Supervivientes de los Andes (Survive). Dir. René Cardona. With Hugo Stiglitz and Norma Lazareno. Productora Filmica Real, 1976.

Tell Your Children. Dir. Louis J. Gosiner. With Dorothy Short and Kenneth Craig. G&H Productions, 1936.

Tentación desnuda, La (Naked Temptation). Dir. Armando Bó. With Isabel Sarli and Armando Bó. Sociedad Independiente Filmadora Argentina, 1966.

Terra em transe (Land in Anguish). Dir. Glauber Rocha. With Jardel Filho and Paulo Autran. Mapa Filmes, 1967.

Terremoto en Guatemala (Earthquake in Guatemala). Dir. Rafael Lanuza. With Norma Lazareno and Leonardo Morán. Producciones Tikal-Producciones Fílmicas Agrasánchez, 1976.

Tesis (Thesis). Dir. Alejandro Amenábar. With Eduardo Noriega and Ana Torrent. Los Producciones del Escorpión S.L., 1996.

Testigo para un crimen (Violated Love). Dir. Emilio Vieyra. With Libertad Leblanc and José María Langlais. Orestes A. Trucco, 1963.

Tía Alejandra, La (Aunt Alejandra). Dir. Arturo Ripstein. With Isabela Corona and Diana Bracho. Estudios Churubusco Azteca, 1978.

Tintorera! (Tiger Shark). Dir. René Cardona Jr. With Andrés García and Hugo Stiglitz. Hemdale-CONACINE, 1976.

Tire dié (Throw Us Ten). Dir. Fernando Birri. Instituto de Cinematografía de la Universidad Nacional del Litoral, 1958.

To Die Standing. Dir. Louis Morneau. With Cliff De Young and Jamie Rose. Concorde-New Horizons, 1990.

Toda a nudez é perdoada (All Nudity Is Forgiven). Dir. Mário Vaz Filho. With Oásis Minitti and Márcia Ferro. No production company, 1985.

Toda nudez será castigada (All Nudity Shall Be Punished). Dir. Arnaldo Jabor. With Paulo Porto and Darlene Glória. Ipanema Filmes/RF Farias Produções Cinematográficas/Ventania Filmes, 1973.

Tonta, tonta pero no tanto (*Dumb, Dumb But Not that Dumb*). Dir. Fernando Cortés. With María Elena Velasco and Sergio Ramos. América Films–Diana Films–Teleprogramas Acapulco, 1971.

Topo, El (*The Mole/The Gopher*). Dir. Alejandro Jodorowsky. With Alejandro Jodorowsky and Brontis Jodorowsky. Producciones Pánicas, 1970.

Torture Chamber, The. Dir. Jack Hill and Juan Ibáñez. With Boris Karloff and Isela Vega. Azteca Films, 1968.

Touch of Her Flesh, The. Dir. Michael Findlay. With Suzanne Marre and Claudia Jennings. Rivamarsh, 1967.

Traficantes de niños (*Traffickers in Children*). Dir. Ismael Rodríguez Jr. With Mário Almada and Sebastián Ligarde. Películas Rodríguez, 1990.

Tragedia en Waco, Texas (*Tragedy in Waco, Texas*). Dir. Fernando Durán. With Jorge Reynoso and Jorge Ortín. R. Ramos. No production company, 1993.

Trágico terremoto en México (*Tragic Earthquake in Mexico*). Dir. Francisco Guerrero. With Mário Almada and Miguel Ángel Rodríguez. Productora Metropolitana, 1987.

Treinta segundos para morir (Thirty Seconds to Die). Dir. Rúben Benavides and Jesús Marín. With Mário Almada and Fernando Almada. Morben, 1978.

Triángulo diabólico de las Bermudas, El (*Devil's Triangle of Bermuda*). Dir. René Cardona Jr. With John Huston, Andrés García, and Hugo Stiglitz. Productora Fílmica Real, 1978.

Trip, The. Dir. Roger Corman. With Peter Fonda and Susan Strasberg. American International Pictures (AIP), 1969.

Trotacalles (*Street Walker*). Dir. Matilde Landeta. With Miroslava Stern and Elda Peralta. TACMA, 1951.

Trueno entre las hojas, El (*Thunder Among the Leaves*). Dir. Armando Bó. With Isabel Sarli and Armando Bó. Film AM, 1957.

Tu hijo (*Your Son*). Dir. José Bohr. With Julio Villarreal and Elena D'Orgaz. Duquesa Olga y José Bohr, 1934.

Túnel, El (*The Tunnel*). Dir. León Klimovsky. With Margarita Burke and Alfredo Distasio. Argentina Sono Film, 1952.

Tupac Amaru. Dir. Federcio García. With Reynaldo Arenas and Zully Azurín. Cinematográfica Kuntur S.A./Instituto Cubano de Arte e Industria Cinematográfica (ICAIC), 1984.

Tusk. Dir. Alejandro Jodorowsky. With Cyrielle Clair and Anton Diffring. Films 21, Yang, 1980.

Two to Tango. Dir. Héctor Olivera. With Don Stroud and Adrienne Sachs. Aries Cinematográfica Argentina/Concorde Pictures, 1988.

Ultimo mondo cannibale (*Jungle Holocaust/Last Cannibal World*). Dir. Ruggero Deodato. With Massimo Fochi and Me Me Lai. Erre Cinematograsica, 1977.

Ultimos días de la víctima (*Last Days of the Victim*). Dir. Adolfo Aristarain. With Federico Luppi and Soledad Silveyra. Aries Cinematográfica Argentina, 1982.

Ultra Warrior. Dir. Augusto Tamayo San Román and Kevin Tent. With Dack Rambo and Clare Beresford. Concorde-New Horizons, 1990.

Ustedes los ricos (*You the Rich*). Dir. Ismael Rodrígez. With Pedro Infante and Evita Muñuz. Producciones Rodríguez Hermanos, 1948.

¡Vámonos con Pancho Villa! (*Let's Go with Pancho Villa!*). Dir. Fernando de Fuentes. With Antonio R. Frausto and Domingo Soler. CLASA, 1936.

Vampiro, El (*The Vampire*). Dir. Fernando Méndez. With Abel Salázar and Ariadna Weller. Cinematográfica ABSA, 1957.

Vampiro negro, El. (The Black Vampire). Dir. Román Viñoly Bareto. With Olga Zubarry and Roberto Escalada. Argentina Sono Film, 1953.

Vanessa. Dir. René Cardona Jr. With Laila Novak and Arthur Hansel. Productora Fílmica Real, 1970.

Vedettes al desnudo (Nude Models). Dir. Leonidas Zegarra. With Susy Díaz and Jackye Castañeda. Del Mazo Producciones, 2003.

Venganza del sexo, La (The Curious Case of Dr Humpp). Dir. Emilio Vieyra. With Aldo Barbero and Ricardo Bauleo. Orestes A. Trucco, 1967.

Via della prostituzione, La (Emanuelle and the White Slave Trade). Dir. Joe D'Amato. With Laura Gemser and Gabriele Tinti. Flora Film/Fulvia Film/Gico Cinematografica, 1978.

Viaje de novios (Honeymoon). Dir. León Klimovsky. With Analía Gadé and Fernando Fernán Gómez. Agata Films, 1956.

Viaje fantástico en globo (Fantastic Balloon Voyage). Dir. René Cardona Jr. With Hugo Stiglitz and Jeff Cooper. Avant Films, 1974.

Víctimas del pecado (Victims of Sin). Dir. Emilio Fernández. With Ninón Sevilla and Tito Junco. Cinematográfica Calderón, 1950.

Vida continúa, La (Life Goes On). Dir. Emilio Vieyra. With Sandro and Cunny Vera. Arroyo, 1969.

Vidas secas (Barren Lives). Dir. Nelson Pereira dos Santos. With Maria Ribeiro and Átila Iório. Luis Carlos Barreto Produções Cinematográficas, 1963.

Videodrome. Dir. David Cronenberg. With James Woods and Deborah Harry. Filmplan International/Canadian Film Development Corporation/Famous Players Limited, 1983.

Virgen de la Caridad, La (Our Lady of Charity). Dir. Ramón Peón. With Diana Marde and Matilde Maun. B.P.P. Pictures, 1930.

Virgin Goddess, The. Dir. Dirk de Villiers. With Isabel Sarli and Armando Bó. Columbia Pictures, 1973.

Viuda negra, La (The Black Widow). Dir. Arturo Ripstein. With Isela Vega and Mário Almada. CONACINE, 1977.

Viúva virgem, A (The Virgin Widow). Dir. Pedro Carlos Rovai. With Adriana Prieto and Carlos Imperial. Sincro Filmes, 1974.

Watchers III. Dir. Jeremy Stanford. With Wings Hauser and Gregory Scott Cummins. Concorde Pictures/Iguana Producciones, 1994.

Wife Swappers, The. Dir. Derek Ford. With James Donnelly and Larry Taylor. Salon Productions, 1970.

Wild Women of Wongo The. Dir. James L. Wolcott. With Jean Hawkshaw and Mary Ann Webb. Jawall Productions, 1958.

Wolf Man, The. Dir. George Waggner. With Claude Rains and Lon Chaney. Universal Pictures, 1941.

Xica da Silva (Xica). Dir. Carlos Diegues. With Zezé Motta and José Wilker. Embrafilme/Terra Filmes, 1976.

... Y el demonio creó al hombre (... And the Devil Created Men). Dir. Armando Bó. With Isabel Sarli and Armando Bó. Sociedad Independiente Filmadora Argentina and Punta del Este Film, 1960.

Y tu mamá también. Alfonso Cuarón. With Gael García Bernal and Diego Luna. Alianza Films International, 2001.

¡Ya tengo a mi hijo! (I Have My Son Now). Dir. Ismael Rodríguez. With Isabel Corona and Fernando Bohigas. Rodríguez Hermanos, 1946.

Yawar malku (Blood of the Condor). Dir. Jorge Sanjinés. Grupo Ukamau, 1969.

Zombi 2 (Zombie). Dir. Lucio Fulci. With Tisa Farrow and Ian McCulloch. Variety Film Production, 1979.

Zombi Holocaust (Zombie Holocaust). Dir. Marino Girolami. With Ian McCulloch and Donald O'Brien. Dania Film/Flora Film/Fulvia Film/National Cinematografica, 1980.

Index

Please note 'n' indicates a footnote on that page.
Please note page numbers in *italics* indicate an illustration

A

Abreu, Nuno Cesar, 231, 234, 243nn9, 11
Adamson, Al, 154
  Satan's Sadists, 154
Agata Films, 134
Agrasánchez Jr. Rogelio, 45, 54n18
Alarma! 160, 164-165
Albertini, Bitto, 84n4
  Emanuelle nera, 84n4
Aldama, Júlio, 186
  Maldita miseria, 186
Alemán, Gabriela, 1, 4, 58, 66, 217, 262
Ali Triana, Jorge, 265
  Soñar no cuesta nada, 265
Allende, Isabel, 41
Almada, Fernando, 186, 192
Almada, Mário, 186, 192, 248
Amadori, Luis César, 130
Amenábar, Alejandro, 265
  Tesis, 265
Andrade, Daniel, 272
  Esas no son penas, (with Anahí Hoeneisen), 272
Anger, Kenneth, 109
Anning, N. (with D. Hebditch), 147, 154
Antín, Manuel, 91
Apold, Raúl Alejandro, 133
Appadurai, Arjun, 2
Argentina Sono Film, 91, 132–133, 211-212
Aristarain, Adolfo, 57

Ultimos días de la víctima, 57
Arrabal, Francisco, 52, 103-104, 106
Arregui, Victor, 272
  Cuando me toque a mí, 272
Artaud, Antonin, 109
Atlantida Films, 138
Auer, John, 16
Avellar, José Carlos, 241–242
Ayala, Fernando 91, 95
  El profesor hippie, 95
Ayala Blanco, Jorge, 12n2, 252

B

Balagueró, Jaime, 38
Ballesteros Studios, 134
Barcinski, André, 115
  Maldito, The Strange World of Coffin Joe, (with Ivan Finotti), 115, 117-118, 121
Barenholtz, Ben, 110–111
Barreto, Bruno, 237
  Dona Flor e seus dois maridos, 237, 243n19, 244n23
Bassols, Narciso, 26
Bava, Mario, 94
Beckett, Samuel, 104
Bedoya, Ricardo, 56, 59, 65
Berlitz, Charles, 226
Bernadet, Jean-Claude, 237
Bhabha, Homi, 71, 83
Bianchi Montero, Roberto, 73
  Mondo balordo, 73
Bindel, Julie, 149
Birri, Fernando, 91, 101n20, 127n4, 127n7
  Tire dié, 127n7
Blasco, Rodolfo, 90
  La madrastra, 90

Quinto año nacional, 90

Bó, Armando, 1, 10, 11, 37, 40, 45–46,
    49, 54n9, 89, 100n2, 127n5,
    201-214, 268
  Carne 40, 45, 208
  El trueno entre las hojas, 1, 201,
    204-206, 212, 213, 214n7
  Fiebre,1, 40, 208-210, 214n9
  Fuego, 40, 208–209, 214nn6, 9
  Furia infernal, 207, 208
  India, 207, 212
  Insaciable, 208
  Intimidades de una cualquiera, 208
  La leona, 208
  La mujer del zapatero, 208
  La señora del intendente, 208
  La tentación desnuda, 207
  Los días calientes, 40, 208
  Lujuria tropical, 208
  Sabaleros, 208, 212
  Una mariposa en la noche, 208
  ...Y el demonio creó al hombre,
    206-208
Boca do Lixo, 121, 231, 240, 242nn4–5
Bodanzky, Jorge, 232
  Iracema, uma transa amazônica,
    (1976, with Orlando Senna), 232
Boneo, Eduardo, 202
  La cabalgata del circo, (1945, with
    Mario Soffici), 202
Bohr, José, 7, 13-33
  La sangre manda, 14, 21, 23–25
  Luponini, (El terror de Chicago) 24,
    26, 28-31
  Marihuana, el monstruo verde, 32
  Mujeres sin alma, 25
  Por mis pistolas, 32
  ¿Quién mató a Eva? 24-25, 28
  Tu hijo, 26
border cinema, 10, 171, 185–187. *See
    cine fronterizo*
Bourdieu, Pierre, 265
Boytler, Arcady, 16, 33n4
  La mujer del puerto, 21, 24
Brakhage, Stan, 114n9, 123
  *The Act of Seeing with One's Own
    Eyes*, 123
Bravo, Ramón, 217–218, 220, 228nn4, 6
Brazzi, Rossano, 81
Bressane, Julio, 121
  Matou a família e foi ao cinema, 121
Browning, Tod, 43, 114n8, 117
  Dracula, 117
  Freaks, 43, 114n8

Brottman, M., 147-149, 151, 154, 155
Buchino, Victor, 92, 98
Buckalew, Bethel, 84n2
  Mondo Mod, 84n2
Buñuel, Luis 53n2, 115, 264. *See
    Buñuelian*
  El ángel exterminador, 53n2
  Gran casino, 264
  Simón del desierto, 53n2
Buñuelian, 110
Bueno, Eva, 116, 242n3

C

cabaretera, 21, 31, 187, 250
Cahiers du Cinéma, 59
Callegaro, João, 231
  O pornógrafo, 231
Calleja, Pedro, 46, 51, 54n9
Calles, Plutarco, 14, 26
Campaign for Decency, 147
Cano Jr., Alberto,168
  La caída de un dictador, 168
Cantinflas, 189
  Ahí está el detalle, 189
Candeias, Ozualdo, 121
  A margem, 121
Cannes Film Festival, 112–113, 114n2,
    131
cannibal films, xi, 8, 70-84, 152, 163,
    228
Caño, Manuel, 40
  El pantano de los cuervos, 40
Cárdenas, Lázaro, 26
Cardona, Jr. René, xiii, 4, 159, 162–
    163, 215-228, 245
  Ciclón, 215, 218, 226–228
  *El triángulo diabólico de las Bermu-
    das*, 215, 218, 226-228
  Guyana, el crimen del siglo, 159,
    163, 228
  La noche de los mil gatos, 162
  La risa en vacaciones, 217-218,
    228n1
  Los desvergonzados, 216
  Peligro...mujeres en acción!, 215,
    218-219
  Robinson Crusoe, 162, 217
  S.O.S. conspiración bikini, 4, 25,
    218, 245
  Tintorera!, 162, 215-218, 220–223,
    224, 225, 226, 226-228
  Un ángel de mal genio, 216–217
  Vanessa, 217
  Viaje fantástico en globo, 217

Cardona, Sr. René, 37, 50, 160,
162–163, 215, 216, 228n2
La horripilante bestia humana, 50,
162
La isla de los hombres solos, 217
Supervivientes de los Andes, 160,
163, 166-167
Un mundo nuevo, 215–216
Cardone, Alberto, 81
Le carnaval des barbouzes, 81
Cardoso, David, 235, 237, 240
Cardoso, Iván 37, 45, 49, 54n13
O escorpião escarlate, 45
Carlos, Jairo, 238
Pintando o sexo (with Egídio Eceio),
238
carnival, 8, 81, 109, 152, 154–156
Carrasco Zanini, Eduardo, 169n3
Castaño, Rodrigo, 169n3
Derrumbe, 169n3
El niño y el Papa, 169n3
Carreras, Enrique, 50, 95
La familia hippie, 95
Carrington, Leonora 51, 104
Cartagena Film Festival 255, 265
Carver, Steve, 253
Drum, 253
Castellari, Enzo, 71, 81
1990: I guerrieri del Bronx, 81
Castro, Victor Manuel, 245
La pulquería, 245
Catalonia Film Festival (Sitges), 53n2,
53n7, 113
Cavara, Paolo, 73
Mondo cane (with Franco Prosperi
and Gualtiero Jacopetti), 73
Cazals, Felipe, 158–159, 161–162, 189,
216
Canoa, 162
Las Poquianchis, 162
Los motivos de Luz, 162
Cedeño, Fernando, 265–266, 268
Avaricia, 265–267
Barahúnda en la montaña, 266–267
En busca del tesoro perdido, 266–267
Sicarios manabitas, 265-268
censorship
in Argentina, 90, 94, 96, 99, 100n14,
213n4
in Brazil, 121–122, 231–232, 243n8
in Ecuador, 269
in Mexico, 31, 104, 161, 164–166,
169, 173, 215, 249, 251
in Spain, 40, 137-138, 140

Cerdá, Nacho, 38
Chalacama, Nixon, 266, 268
El cráneo de oro, 266, 267
El destructor invisible, 266
Chagoyán, Rosa Gloria, 171–183, 186
chanchadas, 230, 242n2
charro(s), 107, 177, 189
Chenal, Pierre, 129
Se abre el abismo, 129
churro(s), 177–8, 182, 189, 247
Chevalier, Maurice, 103
Chicago Underground Film Festival,
113
cines de barrio, 40, 53n6
cine de denuncia,158-159, 162
Cinedistri, 241
cine fronterizo, 171-173, 176–177,
179, 182-183. *See* border cinema
cinema do lixo, 115, 119–123. *See*
garbage cinema; *udigrudi*
cinema marginal, 121, 123, 124, 231
cinema novo, 40, 115–116, 118–124,
126, 127n9, 148, 230, 232,
238–239
Clover, Carol J., 97, 216, 223, 229n10
Clubcultura, 41
Coffin Joe, 41, 115, 117, 242n3. *See* Zé
do Caixão
Como era gostoso o nosso cinema, 238
Cohen, Robert Carl, 84n2
Mondo Hollywood, 84n2
Colina, Enrique, 133
colonialism, xii, 9, 70–80, 83, 120–121,
260, 263
colonial adventure stories, 72–74, 76
Combret, Georges, 81
Duello nel mondo (with Luigi Scattini), 81
comedia ranchera, 15, 32, 161, 176
Conde, Manuel S., 49
Contacto chicano, 178, 180–181
Contreras Torres, Miguel, 16, 33n4
coproductions, xiii, 6, 40, 56–58, 66,
101n22, 148, 218
copyright, 262–264
Corman, Roger, 4, 6, 55–69, 94, 122,
135, 148
Corona Blake, Alfonso, 53n2, 219
Santo contra las mujeres vampiro,
219. (see *Santo vs. las mujeres
vampiro*)
Santo vs. las mujeres vampiro, 43,
53n2, 54n16
corridos, 188, 191

narcocorridos, 188, 191, 195
Cortázar, Julio, 41
Cortés, Alberto, 170n3
　Ciudad de ciegos, 170n3
Cosa, La, 49
Costa, Jordi, 51, 53n6, 67, 69
Couselo, Jorge Miguel, 99n2, 130
Craven, Wes, 74, 117
　The Last House on the Left, 74
Crevenna, Alfredo, B., 3, 165
　Santo el enmascarado de plata vs. la invasión de los marcianos, 3
　El secuestro de Camarena, 165–166
Cristina, 173, 174, 176–177
Criterion Collection, 262
Cronenberg, David, 102
　Shivers, 102
　Videodrome, 102
Cuarón, Alfonso, 183, 186
　Y tu mamá también, 183, 186
cult movies, *See* exploitation: genres
Cummins, Samuel, 12n3
Curiel, Federico, 37, 181
Curubeto, Diego, 88, 94n4, 100nn6, 7, 10, 150

D

Daiano Film, 138
D'Almeida, Neville, 237
　Dama do lotação, 237, 243n19
D'Amato, Joe, 4, 70–71, 84n4, 147
　Emanuelle e gli ultimi cannibali, 70, 73-75, 79–80, 82
　Emanuelle in America, 84n4, 147
　Emanuelle nera: Orient reportage, 84n4
　Emanuelle: Perché violenza alle donne? 84n4
　Holocausto porno, 70
　La via della prostituzione, 84n4
　Le notti erotiche dei morti viventi, 70, 76, 80
　Orgasmo nero, 70
　Papaya dei Caraibi, 70, 76
Damiano, Gerard, 239
　Deep Throat, 239, 243n18
de Anda, Gilberto, 165
　Durazo, la verdadera historia, 165
de Anda, Raúl, 215
de Andrade, Joaquim Pedro, 121, 127, 244n24
　Macunaíma, 121, 244n24
de Andrade, Oswald, 70, 83
　Manifesto antropófago, 70, 83

De Feo, Francesco, 73
　Mondo nudo, 73
de Fuentes, Fernando, 26, 31, 33n4
　Allá en el rancho grande, 31, 188
　¡Vámonos con Pancho Villa!, 26
Delgado, Miguel M., 37
de la Iglesia, Eloy, 40
　Navajeros, 40
Del Boca, Angelo, 77
de Oliveira, Oswaldo, 238, 243n14
　A filha de Emmanuelle 243n14
　Histórias que nossas babás não contavam, 238
del Paraná, Luis Alberto y los Paraguayos, 209
Del Rio, Dolores, 16, 201, 247
del Toro, Guillermo, 43, 45, 186
del Villar, Francisco, 248–249, 253, 255
　El festín de la loba, 249–252
　El llanto de la tortuga, 248, 253–256
　Las pirañas aman en cuaresma, 248
　La primavera de los escorpiones, 252
Demme, Jonathan, 55
　Caged Heat, 135
Deodato, Ruggero, 4, 70-71, 78, 265
　Cannibal Holocaust, 70–71, 73–77, 79–80, 82, 265
　Inferno in diretta, 70
　Ultimo mondo cannibale, 78
de Pascal, Vincent, 133
De Villiers, Dirk, 212
　The Virgin Goddess, 212
Díaz Morales, José, 50
　Profanadores de tumbas, 50
Diegues, Carlos, 127n9
di Mello, Victor, 236, 243n14
　Essa gostosa brincadeira a dois, 236, 243nn15–16
　Giselle, 243n14
Di Nubila, Domingo, 129
Dmytryk, Edward, 155
　Captive Wild Woman, 155
Do Caixão, Zé, 37, 41, 54n10, 115, 117, 122, 124, 127n3, 242n3, 248. *See* José Mojica Marins
Dominó, Geraldo, 240
dos Santos, Nelson Pereira, 116, 120, 127n9, 238
　Como era gostoso o meu francês, 116, 120, 238
　Rio 40 graus, 127n9
　Rio zona norte, 127n9
　Vidas secas, 116
Dostoyevsky, Fyodor, 130

Dubois, Alberto, 211
  La flor de Irupé, 211
Dumas, Alexander, 130
Durán Rojas, Fernando, 167
  Tragedia en Waco, Texas, 167
Durgnat, Raymond, 95
Dyer, Richard, 201, 207, 235, 247

E

Eceio, Egídio, 238
  Pintando o sexo (with Jairo Carlos), 238
Echeverría, Luis, 162, 169, 189, 190, 215, 252
EDOC Documentary Film Festival, 269
efímero, 104, 106, 108
Eisenstein, Sergei, 16, 26
El caso Cabrera, 268–269
Elena, Alberto, 53n5
Elizondo, Salvador, 250
Embrafilme, 240, 244n24
Escamilla Espinosa, Benjamin, 159, 164
  Lo negro del Negro (with Angel Rodríguez Vázquez), 159, 164
Escuela Internacional de Cine y Tele-
    visión, 118
Esper, Dwain, 12n3, 33n9, 131
  Narcotic, 33n9
esthetics of hunger, 121. *See* esthetics of
    violence
esthetics of violence, 120
Estrada, Erik, 55, 60, 61, 63
Estrada, José, 159, 161-162
  El profeta Mimí, 162
Estrada, Luis, 169n2, 246
  La ley de Heródes, 169n2, 246, 249, 253
Exploitation
  Genres
    blaxploitation, 5, 180, 183
    badfilm, xi, 118, 119, 146, 252
    cult, 2–3, 38, 41, 51, 88, 101–2, 112, 129, 137, 228n4 (*see* cult movie(s)/cinema/film); (*see* cult directors/auteurs/filmmakers); (*see* cult film fans/audiences); (*see* cult film criticism)
  cult directors./auteurs/filmmakers, 49, 51, 97;
  cult film fans/audiences, 110–113, 141
  cult film criticism, 135–6

cult movie(s)/cinema/film, xi, 6,42, 50, 51, 54nn13–14, 101-3, 139–40; 114n1, 129, 136, 253
classical exploitation film, 12n3, 54n17, 158, 265
giallo, 50, 72 110, 113
gore, 1, 11, 42–43, 50, 94, 110, 115, 123–124, 146, 148, 261, 265, 268
mondo, 66, 72–76, 78–79, 83n2, 152, 268–269
nudie cutie, 233, 242n2
sexploitation, 1, 5, 75, 90, 95, 146, 155, 178, 210–211, 230–232, 235, 237, 239, 241–242, 243n20, 245–246, 248, 254, 257n2
paracinema, xi, 2, 3, 7, 42, 46, 49, 52, 88, 97, 102–103, 114n1, 115, 119, 123–126, 128n13, 129, 146, 238, 239, 242
psychotronic films, xi, 38, 41–43, 49, 51, 52, 54n14, 97, 100n11, 101n21, 102, 110, 112–113, 114n1, 217–218, 240
trash, xi, 2–3, 9, 37, 49-50, 52, 98, 109, 115, 118–119, 121, 126, 129, 136, 246, 252
women in prison films, 87, 238

F

Falicov, Tamara, 57-58, 99n2, 132–133, 148
fan culture 7, 37–38, 41–43, 46, 49, 50, 52, 53n2, 54nn9, 13–14, 88, 97, 101n21, 102–103, 110, 112–113, 115, 126, 140–141, 146, 174–175, 184n5, 202, 211, 213, 217, 249
Farias, Reginaldo, 231
  Os paqueras, 231
Faris, Daniel (with Eddie Muller), 150
Favio, Leonardo, 91
Félix, María, 247–248, 251
Fernández, Emilio, 3, 5, 16, 33n6, 188
  Flor Silvestre, 3
  María Candelaria, 3, 5, 188,
  Rió Escondido, 3
  Víctimas del pecado, 5
Fernández, Jaime, 185
  La mafia de la frontera, 185
Fernández, Raúl,
  Juana la cubana, 172, 174, 177–178, 182

Lola la trailera, 171, 174, 177–178, 180-181, 184n9
Fernández Violante, Marcela, 252
fichera, 257n2
Filmfax, 42
Film Ideal, 40
Film Threat, 49
Findlay, Michael, 4, 145–157
  Snuff (with Roberta Findlay), 145-157
  The Slaughter (*see Snuff*), 145–151, 153–154
  Touch of Her Flesh, 157n2
Findlay, Roberta, 4, 145–156
  Snuff (with Michael Findlay), 145–157
  The Slaughter (*see Snuff*), 145–151, 153–154
  Touch of Her Flesh, 157n2
Finotti, Ivan, 115, 117–118, 121
  Maldito: The Strange World of Coffin Joe (with André Barcinski), 115
Fisher, Ross, 16
Flash-back, 53n2
Fleischer, Richard, 253
  Mandingo, 253
Ford, Derek, 243n17
  Suburban Wives, 243n17
  The Wife Swappers, 243n17
Fons, Jorge, 161
Fraga, Ody
  A noite das taras II, 235
Franco, Carlos, 170n4
  Bienvenida al clan, 170n4
Franco, Jesús (Jess), 70, 81, 136
  Mondo Cannibale, 70, 75
  Paroxismus, 81
  The Seven Secrets of Sumuru, 81
Franco, Francisco (General) 136–140, 141n2, 257n5
Fregoso, Rosa Linda, 247
French New Wave, The, 91
Frias, Issac León, 63
Friedkin, William, 72
  The French Connection, 72
Friedman, David F., 146
Frost, Lee, 84n2
  Mondo Bizarro, 84n2
  Mondo Freudo, 84n2
Fulci, Lucio, 70–71, 81, 228n4
  E tu vivrai nel terrore – L'aldilà, 84n5
  Lo squartatore di New York, 81, 84n5

Luca il contrabbandiere, 84n5
Manhattan Baby, 81, 84n5
Quella villa accanto al cimitero, 84n5
Zombi 2 70–71, 74, 79, 82, 84n5, 228n4

G

Galindo, Rubén, 185
  La banda del carro rojo, 185, 188, 190–195
Gamboa, 61–62
Gámez, Rubén, 106
  La fórmula secreta, 106
garbage cinema, 115, 119–122. *See* *udigrudi*; *cinema do lixo*
García, Federico, 59, 68nn2–3
  El caso Huayanay, 68n2
  Kuntur Wachana, 68n2
  Laulico, 68n2
  Melgar, poeta insurgente, 68n2
  Tupac Amaru, 68n2
García, Sara, 22, 32
García Espinosa, Julio, 59, 68n3, 118–119, 127nn4, 8
García Márquez, Gabriel, 127nn4, 7
García Riera, Emilio, 19, 104–105, 114n2, 161, 251–252
Gardel, Carlos, 101, 202, 213n3
Gariazzo, Mario, 70
  Schiave bianche: Violenza in Amazonia, 70, 73, 75
Gavaldón, Roberto, 169n1
  Rosa blanca, 169n1
Gazcón, Gilberto, 186
  Perro callejero, 186
genre
  comedy 32, 120, 129, 134, 171, 187, 215, 230, 234, 237, 239, 252, 268
  documentary, 60–61, 65, 73–75, 79–80, 82, 98, 115, 139, 147, 152, 160-162, 166, 261, 268-269
  historical epics, 129
  horror, 1–2, 12n2, 17–18, 32, 38, 41, 43, 45, 51–52, 53nn2–3, 54nn11, 13, 74, 88–98, 100nn11, 19, 101nn20-21, 102, 104–105, 117, 119–120, 123–124, 126, 128n13, 135, 138–139, 146, 150, 162, 187, 215–216, 221–223, 226, 228n4, 248, 264, 271
  melodrama, 3, 15, 21, 25, 27, 32, 129, 133–134, 163, 167, 189, 195–196, 207–208, 211, 214n7,

215, 221, 231, 244n24, 254,
  261, 265, 270–271, 274n13
musical, 22, 25, 27, 31, 87, 87, 93,
  100n8, 171, 189, 217, 242n1,
  264
porno-chic, 164, 237, 243n18
pornography, 40, 145–147, 210, 220,
  231
  hard core, 146, 157n1, 231, 235,
    237, 239, 240, 244n26
  soft core, 97, 146, 153, 155, 220,
    230, 232, 235–240, 247
spaghetti western, 53n6, 72, 107,
  110, 138
thrillers, 72, 87, 129, 174, 176, 215,
  262
war films, 59,129, 134, 135, 138
western, 87, 106, 114n4, 129, 135,
  139, 162, 187 (*see* spaghetti
  western)
Getino, Octavio 98, 130
  La hora de los hornos (with Fer-
    nando Solanas), 98
Girolami, Marino, 78
  Zombi holocaust, 78
globalization, 2, 6, 272
Globo, 238, 244n21
Godard, Jean-Luc, 121
  A bout de souffle, 121
Gómez, Beto, 245
  Puños rosas, 245
Gómez Muriel, Emilio
  Redes, (with Fred Zinneman), 26,
    33n6
González, Christian, 167–168
  La Mataviejitas, 168
  La muerte de un Cardenal, 167
González, Rogelio A., 45, 253
  El esqueleto de la Sra. Morales, 45
  La india, 252, 253
González Iñárritu, Alejandro, 186, 196
  Amores perros, 186
  Babel, 196
Gónzalez Morantes, Carlos, 169n3
  El otro crimen, 169n3
González Paz, Aníbal, 92, 98
Gosiner, Louis,
  Reefer Madness (*see* Tell Your Chil-
    dren)
  Tell Your Children, 130–131
Gout, Alberto, 5, 250
  Aventurera, 5, 250
Grant, Barry K., 6, 95
Gray, Beverly, 55-56, 65

Greene, Doyle, 173, 247
Grinberg, Miguel Angel, 95
Grito, El, 53n2
Grupo Chaski, 60, 65
  Gregorio, 60, 65
  Juliana, 60, 65
Grupo Pánico, 41, 51, 104, 106
Guerra, Rui, 120, 124, 127n9
  Os cafajestes, 124
Guerrero, Francisco, 166
  Trágico terremoto en México,
    166–167
Gurrola, Alfredo, 185
  Asalto en Tijuana, 185
Gutiérrez Alea, Tomás, 127n4

H
Hablemos de Cine, 59
Hammer, 51, 94
Harper, Graeme, (with Xavier Mendik)
  6, 136, 140
Hartog, Simon, 232, 243n7
  *Brazil: Cinema, Sex and the Gener-
    als*, 232
Hawkins, Joan, 2–3, 42, 49, 52, 102,
  109, 114n7, 120, 123–124, 136,
  145, 246, 252-253
Hebditch, D., (with N. Anning), 147,
  154
Heckerling, Amy,
  Look Who's Talking, 217
Henenlotter, Frank, 96, 101n21
Hermida, Tania, 272
  ¿Qué tan lejos?, 272
Hermosillo, Jaime Humberto, 161, 189,
  245, 252
  Las aparencias engañan, 245, 248,
    252
Hernández, Román, 168
  La secta de la muerte, 168
Herrera-Sobek, María, 188
Hershfield, Joanne, 188, 247
Higson, Andrew, 56, 187, 252
Hill, Jack, 250
  The Torture Chamber (with Juan
    Ibañez), 250
Hillier, Jim (with Aaron Lipstadt), 135,
  137
Hoberman, James, 109–111
Hoeneisen, Anahí, 272
  Esas no son penas, (with Daniel
    Andrade), 272
Hollows, Joanne, 141
Hollywood Reporter, The, 133

322   *Index*

Hopper, Dennis, 154
  Easy Rider, 154, 156
Huayhuaca, José Carlos, 59
  Profesión: Detective, 59

I

Ibañez, Juan, 250
  The Torture Chamber (with Jack
    Hill), 250
Ibañez Menta, Narciso, 37, 51,
  140
Ibañez Serrador, Narciso, 51
Iglesias, Norma, 186–187, 195
immigration, 74, 173, 183n4,
  193–195
imperfect cinema, 59, 68n3, 118–119,
  127n8, 148
indigenismo, 26
Infante, Pedro, 189, 192, 247
Infante, Pedro Jr., 192
Instituto di Tella, 93, 95
Instituto Nacional de Cinematografía,
  91
Instituto Cubano de Arte e Industria
  Cinemográficos, 118
Instituto Superior de Arte, 118
Intrator, Jerald, 96–98, 100n17
Ionesco, Eugène, 104
Isaac, Alberto, 161
Italian cinema, 70–84
Italian film industry, 80–83

J

Jabor, Arnaldo, 232
  O casamento, 232
  Toda nudez será castigada, 232,
    244n2
Jackson, Peter, 102
  Braindead, 102
  Bad Taste, 102
  King Kong, 102
  Lord of the Rings I, II and III, 102
  Meet the Feebles, 102
Jacopetti, Gualtiero, 73, 78
  Africa addio, (with Franco Prosperi),
    73, 78–79
  La donna nel mondo, (with Franco
    Prosperi), 73
  Mondo cane, (with Franco Prosperi,
    and Paolo Cavara), 73
  Mondo cane 2, (with Franco Pros-
    peri), 73
Jameson, Frederic, 99
Jancovich, Mark, 2, 4, 88, 102

Jodorowsky, Alejandro, 41, 45–46,
  49–52, 53nn2, 7, 54n11,
  102–114, 245
  La cravate, 113
  El topo, 45, 51, 54n11, 103–104,
    106–113, 114n8
  Fando y Lis, 45, 51, 53nn2, 7,
    54n11, 103–107, 110–111, 113,
    114n2
  La montaña sagrada, 45, 51, 54n11,
    103–104, 107–113
  Melodrama sacramental, 108
  The Rainbow Thief, 103
  Santa sangre, 45, 53n2, 103–104,
    108–110, 113
  Tusk, 103
Johnson, Eithne (with Eric Schaefer),
  145–6, 148, 157n1
Johnson, Randall (with Robert Stam),
  116, 120, 121, 125, 126n1,
  243n13

K

Kael, Pauline, 112
Katz, Ephraim, 272
Kelly Ortiz, Christopher, 108
Kerekes, D. (with D. Slater), 145,
  147–149
Kichwa, 261, 270, 271, 273
King, John, 99n1, 105, 124, 127n9,
  132-133, 148, 246
Kirkland, David, 16
Klein, Allen, 112–113
Klimovsky, León, 6, 37, 40, 129–141
  Aquella joven de blanco, 139
  El conde de Montecristo, 130, 132
  El jugador, 130
  El mariscal del infierno, 137, 138
  El túnel, 130, 132
  La noche de Walpurgis, 135
  Marihuana, ix, 130, 131, 133
  No importa morir, 135, 138
  Pagó cara su muerte, 135
  Reverendo Colt, 139
  Un hombre vino a matar, 138
  Viaje de novios, 134
Kohon, David, 91
Krzywinska, Tanya, 231, 233, 236,
  238
Kuhn, Rodolfo, 91, 209–210, 212

L

Lamarque, Libertad 101n22, 132, 202
Landeta, Matilde, 5

Trotacalles, 5
Lanuza, Rafael, 166
   Terremoto en Guatemala, 166
latsploitation, xi-xii, 2–3, 5–6, 12, 17, 32
Leblanc, Libertad, 37, 90, 99n2, 211
Leduc, Paul, 252–253
   Cobrador, In God We Trust, 253
Legrand, Mirta, 202
Lennon, John, 111, 112
León, William, 270–271
   Pollito, 270–273, 274n13
   Pollito II, 270, 274n13
Leone Film, 138
Leone, Sergio, 110
   Once Upon a Time in the West, 139
Lenzi, Umberto, 70–73, 78
   Cannibal ferox, 70–72, 74, 75, 77, 79–80, 82
   Il paese del sesso selvaggio, 73
   I pirati della Malesia, 73
   Mangiati vivi!, 78
   Montagna di luce, 73
   Sandokan, la tigre de Mompracem, 73
   Sandok, il Maciste della giungla, 73
Levin, Henry, 81
   Se tutte le donne del mondo, (with Arduino Maiuri), 81
Lewis, Herschell Gordon, 42, 123–124, 154
   2,000 Maniacs, 42
   Blood Feast, 123
   She-Devils on Wheels, 154
Lieja, Dr. P.K., 37, 43, 45
Limiñana, Eva, 21
Lipstadt, Aaron (with Jim Hillier), 135, 137
Llosa, Luis, 55–69
   800 Leagues Down the Amazon, 65, 68n1
   Anaconda, 56, 66
   Aventuras prohibidas, 61
   Crime Zone/Calles peligrosas, 55, 64–66
   Fire on the Amazon, 65, 68n1
   Hour of the Assassin/Misión en los Andes, 55, 57, 60–61, 63–65, 67–68
   La fiesta del chivo, 67
   Sniper, 65
   The Specialist, 56, 65
Lombardi, Franciso, 59, 65–67, 264
   La boca del lobo, 59, 65
   La ciudad y los perros, 65

London Film Festival, 104, 112–113
López, Ana M., 13–14, 21, 32, 132, 201–202, 247
López Moctezuma, Juan, 50–51, 53n2, 105
   Alucarda, 51, 53n2
   La mansión de la locura, 53n2
López Portillo, José, 162, 164, 165, 190
Lords, Traci, 43
Lowenstein, Adam, 94
lucha libre (wrestling) films, xiii, 2, 180, 215, 217
Luzuriaga, Camilo, 272
   1809-1810 mientras llega el día, 272
Lynch, David, 102
   Eraserhead, 102
   Blue Velvet, 102

M

Maalouf, A., 273
Maciel, David, 186–187
Maiuri, Arduino, 81
   Se tutte le donne del mondo, (with Henry Levin), 81
Majidi, Majid, 271
   Bachecha-Ye aseman, 271
Manson, Charles, 145-147, 149, 151, 154
Mansur, Fuzi, 235, 240
   O inseto do amor, 235
Maranghello, César 100n14, 131, 132
Marceau, Marcel, 103, 104, 106
Margheriti, Antonio, 71, 73
   Il pelo nel mondo (with Marco Vicario), 73, 76
Mariscal, Alberto, 43
   Kalimán, 43
Marreco, José, 236
   Emmanuelle tropical, 236
Marshall, Nini, 202
Martel, Lucrecia, 264
   La niña santa, 264
Martino, Sergio, 71, 78, 81
   Dopo la caduta di New York, 81
   La montagna del dio cannibale, 78
Marte, Miguel, 168
   La Mataviejitas: Asesina serial, 168
Marvel comics, 119, 124
Martínez Solares, Gilberto, 169n3
   El día de los albañiles, 169n3
Massaini Neto, Aníbal, 233–234
   A superfêmea, 233, 234
Massimo, Michele, 70
   Nudo e selvaggio, 70

Matute, Ana Maria, 41
Mazzaropi, Amácio, 116, 237, 242n3
    A banda das velhas virgens, 237
McDowell, Cláudio, 235
    Luz, cama, ação, 235, 243n19
McLean, Adrienne, 179
McNair, B., 147, 243n18
Me convertí en asesino, 265, 267
Melville, Herman, 73, 76, 79
    Typee: A Peep at Polynesian Life, 73,
        76, 79
Méndez, Fernando, 45, 53n2, 94, 166
    El vampiro, 53n2
    Ladrón de cadáveres, 94
    Señoritas, 166
Mendik, Xavier (with Graeme Harper),
    6, 136, 140
Mendoza, Eduardo, 41
Merello, Tita, 202
mexicanidad, 172
Meyer, Russ, 84n2, 97, 105, 237, 239
    Faster Pussycat, Kill, Kill, 237
    Mondo Topless, 84n2
midnight movie, 2, 11, 38, 102–104,
    111–113, 114n8. *See* Alejandro
    Jodorowsky
Mignolo, Walter, 263
military dictatorship
    in Brazil, 231, 235–236, 241, 243n13
    in Spain, 40, 137, 138, 257n5
Miller, Toby (with Robert Stam), 118
Miranda, Carmen, 178, 201
Miziara, José, 237
    Bem-dotado, o homem de Itu, 237
Mojica Marins, José, xiii, 2, 37, 40–41,
    45–46, 49–52, 53n2, 54nn10,
    13, 15, 115–128, 136, 240,
    244n26, 248
    24 horas de sexo explícito, 244n26
    À meia noite levarei sua alma, 45, 51,
        94, 115, 117, 123–124
    A sina do aventureiro, 117
    Delírios de um anormal, 127n3
    Esta noite encarnarei na sua cadáver,
        45, 51–52, 115, 124
    *O despertar da besta/Ritual dos sádi-
        cos*, 45, 51–52, 115, 120–123,
        127n3
    O estranho mundo de Zé do Caixão,
        115
    Sentença de Deus, 117
    Mondo Macabro, 42, 88
Monsiváis, Carlos, 105, 160, 213n2,
    246, 247, 249, 251

Montaigne, Michel de, 79
Montaldo, Giuliano, 81
    Ad ogni costo, 81–82
Morrisey, Paul, 52, 103
Mraz, John, 189
Mugica, Francisco, 130
Muller, Eddie (with Daniel Faris), 150
Murillo, Enrique, 159, 170n4
    Gloria, víctima de la fama, 170n4
    Las muertas de Juárez, 159
Murnau, F. W.,117
    Nosferatu, 117, 125
Murray, K. Gordon, xi, 2. *See* Roberto
    Rodríguez
Mylonakos, Ilias, 84n4
    I mavri Emmanouella, 84n4
Myrick, Daniel, 264
    The Blair Witch Project (with Edu-
        ardo Sánchez), 264, 271

N

naco, 9, 10, 175, 185–197
NAFTA, 172, 175, 183, 195
narcofronteriza. *See cine fronterizo*;
    fronterizo (border) Films; border
    films; *La banda del carro rojo*
national cinema, 1, 5, 6, 8, 13, 15, 26,
    55–69, 71–72, 92, 94, 116, 119,
    148, 173, 186–188, 244n21,
    245, 247–248, 250–252
Navarro, Carlos, 33n6
    Janitzio, 33n6
Nazi 133, 140, 154
Nericcio, William Anthony, 247
New Latin American Cinema, 5, 40,
    60, 68n3, 91, 118, 123, 125–
    126, 127nn4,7, 153, 246
New World, 135, 137
nota roja, 10, 160
Novarro, Ramón, 16
Novoa, José Ramón, 265
    Sicario, 265–268
Nuestro Cine, 40
Nuevo cine argentino, 91, 100n10
Nuevo cine español, 40
Nuevo cine mexicano, 189
Nuevo Fotogramas, 41

O

Obras maestras de terror, 51
Olguín, Jorge, 49
Olivera, Héctor, 57
    El caso María Soledad, 57
    La noche de los lápices, 57

La Patagonia rebelde, 57
Play Murder for Me, 57
Two to Tango, 57
Onganía, Juan Carlos, 94–95
Ono, Yoko, 111
Orestes, Trucco, 8, 89–90, 92, 99n2, 100n9
Orol, Juan, 1, 7, 13, 17, 21, 25–28, 32, 33n5
El derecho y el deber, 32
El sindicato del crimen, 1
Madre querida, 26-28, 31
Mujeres sin alma, 25
Orwell, George, 64
Oshima, Nagima, 239
Ai no corrida, 239

P

Pantera, El, 177
Paranaguá, Paulo Antonio, 186, 247
Parés, Pablo, 45
Plaga zombie: Zona mutante (with Hernán Saéz), 45
Peckinpah, Sam, 110, 245, 250
Bring me the Head of Alfredo García, 245, 250
PelMex, 261–262, 273
Penn, Arthur, 64
Bonnie and Clyde, 64
Peón, Ramón, 7, 13, 17–21, 25, 32, 43
La Llorona, 13, 17–21, 43
La virgen de la Caridad, 13
Sagrario, 13, 21
Pereira dos Santos, Nelson, 116, 120, 127n9, 238
Como era gostoso o meu francês, 116, 120, 238
Pérez Padilla, Juan José, 167
El guerrillero de Chiapas, 167
Perón, Eva, 132, 202, 214n5
Perón, Juan Domingo, 94, 132–133, 202–204, 213n4, 217
Petley, Julian, 145, 147, 149
Phillips, Alex, 16, 21, 24, 25
pirate copy, 2, 5, 261–274
Playboy, 250–251
Plaza, Paco, 38
Polaco, Jorge, 208, 213
La dama regresa, 208, 213
Poniatowska, Elena, 246, 249
pornochanchada, 4, 10, 11, 230–244, 257n2
Porter, Julio, 95
El extraño del pelo largo, 95

Pressman, Michael
Dynamite Women, 135
Primera Plana, 95, 100n12
Production Code (Administration) (PCA), 4, 12n3, 28, 30
Prosperi, Franco, 73, 78
Africa addio (with Gualtiero Jacopetti), 73, 78–79
La donna nel mondo (with Gualtiero Jacopetti), 73
Mondo cane (with Gualtiero Jacopetti, and Paolo Cavara), 73
Mondo cane 2 (with Gualtiero Jacopetti), 73
Psychotronic Video, 42, 114n1
Psychotronic Video Watchdog, 49
Pujol, Sergio, 95

R

Radio Belgrano, 129
radionovelas, 15, 21, 27–28, 214n7
Rambo, 60
Ramírez Berg, Charles, 3, 108, 172, 173, 176, 189, 190, 194
Read, Jacinda, 141
Reality based exploitation (rbe), 10, 158–170
Reel Wild Cinema, The, 97
Reichenbach, Carlos, 232
Lilian M: Relatório confidencial, 232
Reyes de la Maza, Luis, 15
Ricalde, Maricruz Castro, 186–187, 197n5
Ripstein, Arturo, 53n2,108, 158, 161–162, 169n2, 189, 192, 216, 252–253
La mujer del puerto, 108
La tía Alejandra, 53n2
Rivera, Lisandra, 272
Problemas personales (with Manolo Sarmiento), 272
Roa Bastos, Augusto, 201
Robson, Mark, 167
Earthquake, 167
Rocha, Glauber, 118–119, 120, 121, 122, 124, 127–128n9
Barravento, 124
Deus e o diabo na terra do sol, 120, 122
O dragão da maldade contra o santo guerreino, 122
Terra em transe, 122, 128n9
Rodríguez, Ismael, 168, 189
Corrupción, 168

Noche de buitres, 169
Nosotros los pobres, 189
Pasaporte a la muerte, 169
Traficantes de niños, 169
Ustedes los ricos, 189
Rodríguez, Ismael Jr., 161, 165, 168
  Masacre en el Río Tula, 165,
    168–169
  ¡Ya tengo a mi hijo!, 161
Rodríguez, Joselito, 5
  Angelitos negros, 5
Rodríguez, Robert, 101n20, 195
  El mariachi, 195
Rodríguez, Roberto, xi
Rodríguez Vázquez, Angel, 159, 167
  Aguas Blancas, pueblo sacrificado, 167,
  Lo negro del Negro (with Escamilla
    Espinosa), 159, 164
Rogoff, Irit, 156
Roland, Gilbert, 16
Romano, Néstor, 203, 211
Romero, George, 74, 265
  Dawn of the Dead, 74
  Night of the Living Dead, 265
Romero Marchent, Rafael, 40
  Santo contra el Dr. Muerte, 40
Rosas, Enrique, 160
  El automóvil gris, 160–161
Rosenberg, Moisés, 105
Rosenberg, Sam, 105
Rossi, Rafaele, 239
  Coisas eróticas, 239
Rovai, Pedro Carlos, 236
  A viúva virgem, 236
Rubinskis, Wolf (aka Neutron), 37
Rubio Ortiz, Pascual, 15
Ruétalo, Victoria, 101n22, 246
Ruta 66, 53n2

S

Sábato, Ernesto, 130
Saez, Hernán, 45, 49
  Plaga zombie: Zona mutante (with
    Pablo Parés), 45
Salinas de Gortari, Carlos, 172
San Sebastián Horror and Fantasy Film
  Festival, 7, 38, 39, 43, 45, 48,
  52, 53n2, 54n11
Sánchez, Eduardo, 264
  The Blair Witch Project (with Daniel
    Myrick), 264, 271
Sandrini, Luis, 202
Sandro, 87, 99n3. *See* Emilio Vieyra
Sanjinés, Jorge, 271

Santo, 3, 37, 40, 43, 50, 53nn2, 6,
  54n16, 108, 189, 219, 248
Santo Street, 45
Sarli, Isabel, 1, 5, 37, 40–41, 45–46,
  49, 54n9, n15, 101n22, 201–
  215, 248, 268
Sarmiento, Manolo, 272
  Problemas personales (with Lisandra
    Rivera), 272
Saslavsky, Luis,132
Satiricón, 203
Scattini, Luigi, 81
  Duello nel mondo (with Georges
    Combret), 81
Semana de cine fantástico y terror de
  San Sebastián. *See* San Sebastián
  Horror and Fantasy Film Fes-
  tival
Schaefer, Eric, xv, 2, 3, 4, 12 n3,
  13, 54n17, 60, 67, 71, 95,
  98,100n18, 110, 119, 120, 145,
  158, 159, 173, 175, 183n3, 230,
  231, 232, 235, 237, 239, 241,
  242n2, 243n20, 246, 247, 254,
  265, 273
  (with Eithne Johnson), 145–146,
    148, 157n1
Schneider, Stephen Jay (with Tony Wil-
  liams), 126
Schnitzler, Authur, 104
Schumacher, Joel, 149
  Falling Down, 149
Schwarz, Roberto, 272
Sconce, Jeffrey, 42
Senna, Orlando, 232
  Iracema, uma transa amazônica (with
    Bodanzky, Jorge), 232
Sequeyro, Adela, 25
Sevilla, Raphael J., 16
Sganzerla, Rogério, 115, 121, 231
  A mulher de todos, 231
  O bandido da luz vermelha, 115,
    121
Siegel, Don, 72
  Dirty Harry, 72
Silveira, Mozael, 238
  Secas e molhadas, 241
Sinister Cinema, 42
Sjöman, Vilgot
  I am Curious Yellow, 96
Skal, David, 150
Slater, D. (with D. Kerekes), 145, 147–149
Smiers, Joost, 263-264
Soffici, Mario, 130, 202

La cabalgata del circo (with Eduardo Boneo), 202
Solanas, Fernando, 98, 101n20
   La hora de los hornos (with Octavio Getino), 98
Soler, Julián, 3
   Cuando los hijos se van, 3
   soldadera, 172
Something Weird Video, 88, 115, 131
Spielberg, Steven, 73, 234
   Indiana Jones and the Temple of Doom, 73
   Jaws, 162, 217, 220, 223, 234, 235
Staden, Hans, 70, 73, 75
   The Captivity of Hans Staden, 73
Stam, Robert, 119, 122, 125
   (with Randall Johnson), 116, 120, 121, 125, 126n1, 243n13
   (with Toby Miller), 118
   (with João Luiz Vieira), 234–235, 243n10
Stiglitz, Hugo, 163, 218, 221, 226, 254
Strand, Paul, 26
Strindberg, August, 104
Stuart, Adriano, 234, 240
   Bacalhau, 234-235, 240
Syder, Andrew, 268
   (with Dolores Tierney) 1, 54n14, 217–218, 247

T
Taddia, Irma, 78
Tales from the Crypt, 119, 124
Tamayo, Augusto, 59, 66, 68n1
   El bien esquivo, 66
   La fuga del chacal, 59, 63
   Ultra Warrior, 66, 68n1
   Una sombra al frente, 66
Tarantino, Quentin, 101n20, 124, 127n5
Teague, Lewis
   The Lady in Red, 135
Telemundo, 177
telenovelas, 175, 177, 191, 265
Terror Fantastic, 41
Third Cinema, 148
Tierney, Dolores, 17, 87, 136, 156, 189, 242n3, 246
   (with Andrew Syder), 1, 54n14, 217–218, 247
Tigres del norte, Los, 171, 188, 191
Tin Tan, 189
   El rey del barrio, 189
Tlatelolco massacre, 107
Topor, Roland,103, 104, 106

Torre de Babel, La, 61
Torre Nilsson, Leopoldo, 89, 91, 101
   La casa del ángel, 3
   La mano en la trampa, 3
Tourneur, Jacques, 74
   I Walked with a Zombie, 74
Tovar, Lupita, 16
Tropicália. See Tropicalism
Tropicalism, 41, 122, 239
Trucco, Orestes, 8, 89–90, 92
Trujillo, Valentín, 186, 191
   Treinta segundos para morir, 191
   Un hombre violento, 191
Tupinamba, 70–75
2000 maniacos, 7, 37–38, 41–47, 49–50, 52, 53nn1–2, 54n9

U
udigrudi, 120–121, 126n1. *See* trash cinema, and *cinema do lixo*
underground cinema, 9, 24–25, 52, 102–104, 108, 111–113, 120. *See* Alejandro Jodorowsky
Universal, 98, 117, 119–120, 124, 163
Univisión, 173, 177
Urquieta, José Luis, 191
   La camioneta gris, 191
Urueta, Chano, xiii, 16, 43
   Profanación (1933), 43
   The Braniac/El barón de terror, xii
U.S. Hispanic market, 2, 4, 89, 90, 101n2

V
Vallejo, Ángel, 51
Vargas Llosa, Mario, 61, 65, 67–68
Vari, Guiseppe, 84n4
   Suor Emanuelle, 84n4
Vasconcelos, José, 14
VCD, 262, 268–270, 272, 273n1
Vega, Isela, 245–257
Véjar, Sergio, 191
   La jaula de oro, 191
Velasco, María Elena, 187, 196n2
Velázquez, Murciélago, 37
Vélez, Lupe, 16, 178, 201, 247, 250
Vicario, Marco, 73
   Il pelo nel mondo (with Antonio Margheriti), 73, 76
videohome, 158, 167–168, 169, 170
Video Watchdog, 42
Vieira, João Luiz (with Robert Stam), 234–235, 243n10
Vieyra, Emilio, 4, 8, 37, 49, 50, 87–101

Cargo de conciencia, 87
Extraña invasión, 90, 100n7
Gitano, 87
La bestia desnuda/The Naked Beast,
    50, 90, 92, 93, 95, 98, 101nn9, 13
*La venganza del sexo/The Curious
    Dr. Humpp*, 50, 88, 90, 92,
    95-98, 100n9
La vida continúa, 87
Placer sangriento/The Deadly Organ,
    88, 90–93, 95, 100nn5, 17,
    101n21
Quiero llenarme de tí, 87
*Sangre de vírgenes/Blood of the Vir-
    gins*, 50, 88, 90, 93, 95, 100nn9,
    13
Testigo para un crimen, 90
Viskin, Roberto, 105
Vraney, Mike, 115

W

Waggner, George, 150
    The Wolf Man, 150
Walerstein, Mauricio, 252, 256
    Las reglas del juego, 252
Wallerstein, Gregorio, 215
Warhol, Andy, 103, 105, 109
    Eat, 105
Waters, John, 52
Weldon, Michael, 42, 49, 114n1
Whale, James, 110

Willer, Tex, 74
Williams, Linda, 97, 147
Williams, Tony (with Stephen Jay Sch-
    neider), 126
Wishman, Doris, 127n5
Wood, Robin, 74
Wolcott, James L., 155
    Wild Women of Wongo, 155
Wood Jr., Edward D., 3, 97
    Glen or Glenda, 3
    Plan 9 From Outer Space, 3
World Trade Organization, 263

Y

Yu, Ronny, 265
    Freddy vs. Jason, 265

Z

Zacarías, Miguel, 16, 215, 216
Zegarra, Leonidas, 66–67
    300 millas en busca de mamá, 66
    Poseída por el diablo, 66
    Vedetes al desnudo, 66
Zemeckis, Robert, 73
    Romancing the Stone, 73
Zinéfilo, A, 43, 49–52
Zinneman, Fred, 60
    Redes, (with Emilio Gómez Muriel),
    26, 33n6
zombie films, 8, 70–74,76, 78–83,
    228n4

Printed in Great Britain
by Amazon